Deviance in Everyday Life

Deviance in Everyday Life

Personal Accounts of
Unconventional Lives

Erich Goode

University of Maryland

WAVELAND
PRESS, INC.
Prospect Heights, Illinois

For information about this book, write or call:
    Waveland Press, Inc.
    P.O. Box 400
    Prospect Heights, Illinois 60070
    (847) 634-0081
    www.waveland.com

Cover art by William J. Goode

Printed in the United States of America

7 6 5 4 3 2 1

This book is dedicated
to Danny

Contents

Preface and Acknowledgments

At an investigation into police mishandling of homicide cases, a father whose son was murdered shouts, "I don't want my son to become a statistic!" Banging on a table for emphasis, he insists that his son's case, story—and life—not get swallowed up in a bureaucratic abyss. All too often, the results of sociological research resemble that feared bureaucratic abyss. The human beings whose lives they purport to describe are lost in bloodless, abstract patterns, generalizations, and statistical analyses so arcane and convoluted that even most sociologists can't understand them.

Jack Katz suggests that in pursuing their notion of the natural science method, sociologists have produced "only scattered evidence of what it means, feels, sounds, tastes, or looks like to commit a particular crime" (1988, p. 3).

> Readers of research on homicide and assault do not hear the slaps and curses, see the pushes and shoves, or feel the humiliation and rage that may build toward the attack. . . . How adolescents manage to make the shoplifting or vandalism of cheap and commonplace things a thrilling experience has not been intriguing to many students of delinquency. Researchers of adolescent gangs have never grasped why their subjects so stubbornly refuse to accept the outsider's insistence that they wear the "gang" label. The description of "cold-blooded, senseless murders" has been left to writers outside the social sciences. . . . Sociological and psychological studies of robbery rarely focus on the *distinctive* attractions of robbery. . . . In sum, only rarely have sociologists taken up the challenge of explaining the qualities of deviant experience. (p. 3)

This book does not present the lives of the contributors in the form of statistics but as personal accounts. I quote their words, though the reader encounters my selection of their words as well as my interpretation of what they told me (or a friend, or a student of mine). For the most part, these are the contributors' accounts of their lives in their words.

I decided to write *Deviance in Everyday Life* for two reasons. One, to present a counterweight to the all-too-frequently misinformed commentary promulgated in the social sciences, the media, and the public at large about the phenomenon of deviance; and two, to give a voice to the human beings who lead unconventional lives and experience stigma as a result. I am interested in how people who live those lives *experience* and *discuss* them with others.

What is there to say about said misinformed commentary about deviance? It often comes, inexplicably, from observers who are otherwise intelligent and informed. Supposedly, the sociological study of deviance is on its death bed, in need of an "obituary" (Sumner, 1994); collaborates with the rich and the powerful in oppressing the poor and the weak (Smith, 1973); is "biased" because it focuses on behavior that is in fact condemned but perhaps shouldn't be, rather than behavior that isn't much condemned but should be (Liazos, 1972); is hung up on the trivial, the inconsequential, "the world of hip, drug addicts, jazz musicians, cab drivers, prostitutes, night people, drifters, grifters, and skidders" instead of the "defiant" deviant and the world of the "overdogs" (Gouldner, 1968, p. 104); has "gone by the wayside," has "outlived its usefulness," is "stuck in the 1970s" (to quote several anonymous former instructors of the course). And this doesn't begin to address the issue of the claim that the use of the concept, and the term, "deviance" stigmatizes and colludes in the oppression of the people encompassed by them. I still shake my head in bafflement over that claim. This book represents an effort to demonstrate the silliness and erroneousness of those opinions.

All but three of the accounts in these pages were gathered by me. "Jerry," a former graduate student of mine, tape-recorded an interview with "Lenny," the S&M devotee, and made it available to me. Rick Troiden, also a former graduate student and now deceased, tape-recorded an interview with "Jeff," a retired male madam, and urged me to publish the transcript. And "Diane," a friend, tape-recorded her statement as well as an interview with "Sally." Hence, I owe a debt of gratitude to my three collaborators, two of whom prefer to remain anonymous, and to Rick Troiden, tragically struck down in what should have been the full bloom of his life.

As his father, I wrote Danny's account. For several weeks, I took verbatim notes of my interaction with Danny. The account rendered here is a fairly representative slice of a two or three-week period in our lives. If he is prepared to receive it, I give thanks to Danny for his forbearance and for simply being himself. I tape-recorded my interviews with "Dwight," "Harry," and "Leslie" and "Helen." I conducted two interviews with "Sam" as an assignment for a journalism course; one was tape-recorded, and for the other, I took copious notes. "Annette" wrote a paper for me about her experiences; it is that paper, slightly edited, that appears in these pages. "Fred," a convict, wrote a dozen or so letters to me describing his life of crime. I wove those letters into a coherent narrative, editing their prose a bit for continuity, readability, and relevant referents. All the names in this book are of course pseudonyms except for mine, Danny's, and most of those of the persons who appear in Danny's account.

I am profoundly indebted to my informants for their candor, time, and generosity, the last of which permitted me to produce their accounts in the pages of this book. Anonymous or not, it takes a rare and precious species of courage to expose details of one's life about which even many intimates are unaware. And I would like to express my gratitude to Carol and Neil Rowe of Waveland Press for taking a chance on publishing the results of yet another quirky, offbeat project. I would also like to thank Barbara Weinstein and Temma Kaplan for insightful comments on a portion of the manuscript of this book. I am also grateful to Carol Rowe for a first-rate job of editing.

Quirky or not, I profoundly hope that this book will make a contribution to the recognition that an understanding of deviance is essential to understanding everyday life. Deviance is both an analytic sociological concept and a lived experience, both a label that is applied and an emotional reality that is sustained. As such, it is fundamental to the human condition—timeless and without boundaries. It is one of the central facts of our existence on this planet. As such, it deserves far more systematic attention than it has received. It is my sincerest wish that this book manages to focus a ray of enlightenment on what is one of the more fascinating and primal phenomena of social life.

Foreword

I love autobiographies and I read a lot of them. I don't like self-serving autobiography, in which the author presents a kind of defensive legal brief on behalf of his or her life and its accomplishments. I don't like autobiographies that settle scores with the author's enemies and adversaries. I detest "feel good" or survivor autobiographies that detail the author's triumph over adversity. These examples of the genre are too simplistic for me. In fact, I believe good autobiography should be brutally honest; it should make the reader feel disconcerted, uncomfortable, not quite right about our place in the universe. I prefer nuance to simplicity; irony to sincerity; clay feet to sainthood; and people who decide to live with adversity to those who heroically overcome it. Not only do I disagree with John Keats' Grecian urn ("'Beauty is truth, truth beauty'—that is all/Ye know on earth, and all ye need to know"), I believe the exact opposite is true: Beauty is by its very nature factually false, and factual truth is very often ugly.

What I love most about good autobiography is that it permits the reader to inhabit a life, enter a world previously unknown, smell the flowers in the vase, hear the chirp of the cricket on the hearth, taste the slurpy peach when the author bites into it, feel the shock of recognition as an old friend walks through the door. An actual person lived this life, I think, and now it's being shared with me. When I'm seized by an awareness like this, my throat tightens up and the hairs on the back of my neck stand on end.

I have been using personal accounts to understand deviance for 30 years (1972, pp. 138, 167 ff.). An account follows nearly every chapter of two of my books—*Deviant Behavior* (2001) and *Drugs in American Society* (1999). The purpose of each account is to illustrate, enliven, and personalize the principles and ideas contained in the chapter that precedes it.

Readers identify much more strongly and actively with a principle or idea when it is illustrated by life stories told or written by real people who live real lives—people whom they could meet, who might be in their classes, live next door, or be walking down the street.

Accounts written by informants at the request of social researchers are not exactly the same thing as autobiographies, of course. In some ways, they differ more than they are similar. Both are social and cultural products. Autobiographers are not free to reconstruct their lives any way they choose. For instance, they are constrained by the cultural climate (that is, what the society considers an acceptable rendering of a life) and the marketplace (what is likely to sell), not to mention the culture and social and economic structure of the publishing industry. The constraints on persons who are asked to write or talk about certain details of their lives for a particular purpose by a sociologist are considerable, but they are different from those facing the prospective author of a book-length autobiography. Since the process of initiating these accounts is undertaken by the researcher, not the informant, they are likely to display the researcher's interests and concerns. (Of course, informants can always turn accounts to their own interests, in a sense—as Certeau [1984] argues for everyday life in general—*subverting* the researcher's interests and concerns.) As I'll explain in more detail in a bit, the social context in which accounts are generated or gathered influences their content. This principle should be kept in mind when reading the accounts in this book.

A great deal has been written on the use of personal accounts to understand social life. In fact, the literature examining life stories or narrative is immense. Since 1993, Amia Lieblich and Ruthellen Josselson have edited a yearly publication entitled *The Narrative Study of Lives*, and the works the essays in those volumes cite would fill the shelves of a small library. In the past generation, the field of narratology (largely inhabited by philosophers and students of literature) has sprung forth, leaving an immense profusion of books and articles in its wake. A substantial number of journals, including *Narrative Inquiry* and *Journal of Narrative and Life History*, have been established to house research, debate, theory, and analysis on the subject. From time to time, professional journals, customarily devoted to a broad coverage of an entire field, publish an entire issue on the study of lives. For instance, volume 43, nos. 2/3 of *Current Sociology* is entitled "Biographical Research"; volume 27, no. 1 of *Sociology* is on "Auto/ Biography in Sociology."

Lieblich, Tuval-Mashiach, and Zilber (1998) divide the research literature on the narrative account of lives into three main "domains" or areas of focus.

First, there are studies in which the narrative is used to investigate or reveal a particular area of social life (pp. 3–5). For instance, narrative provides a more "in-depth understanding" of a group than a questionnaire or interview survey is capable of doing (p. 3); it can "represent the character or the lifestyle of specific subgroups in society" (p. 4). Here, the narrative is employed as a reflection—refracted to be sure—of the behavior, the thinking, and the beliefs of a segment of the population.

Second, there are studies in which the structure of the narrative itself is an object of study. In this area of study, linguistic features of the narrative, or its plot, communication devices, metaphors, and so on, may be examined. Such studies prevail in the fields of literature, communications, and linguistics (pp. 5–6).

And third, narrative is studied as a platform for philosophizing about science, nature, epistemology (how reality may be studied), ontology (the ultimate or essential nature of reality), the postmodern condition, the self, identity—in short, for the light it sheds on important theoretical concerns (pp. 6–7).

Inhabiting the spaces between these three endeavors we find the many studies that attempt to understand how narrative accounts are constructed, what the selection and distortion processes that put them together tell us about history (Stille, 2001), literature (Adams, 1990), culture (Tonkin, 1992), gender (Callaway, 1992), the society in which account-givers live (Glassner and Hertz, 1999), and intra-psychic processes that produced accounts of one or another sort (de Rivera and Sarbin, 1998; Kotre, 1995).

This book falls more into the first of these concerns, as well as in the spaces between all three. Here, I gather together accounts by persons whose lives, in one way or another, are, would be, or are likely to be deemed unconventional or sociologically "deviant." Can these personal accounts offer insight into what it means to engage in behavior, hold beliefs, or possess a physical characteristic that is stigmatizing—that many of the members of the society consider unacceptable, cause for condemnation, or social rejection? Can we use these accounts as a means of unlocking doors leading to an understanding of deviance and conventionality? Do they give us an idea of how it feels to face societal rejection? What the deviant experience is like? What do we know about deviance after reading these accounts? What are the forces that impel someone whose identity is likely to be saturated with public scorn to construct a narrative of his or her life that permits a sense of dignity and self-worth? And what do personal accounts tell us about how social relations work, how society is put together?

Erich Goode

CHAPTER 1

Introduction

For myself I believe that human social life is ours to study naturalistically. . . . From the perspective of the physical and biological sciences, human social life is only a small irregular scab on the face of nature, not particularly amenable to deep systematic analysis. And so it is. But it's ours. With a few exceptions, only students in our [the 20th] century have managed to hold it steadily in view in this way, without piety or the necessity to treat traditional issues. Only in modern times have university students been systematically trained to examine all levels of social life meticulously. I'm not one to think that so far our claims can be based on magnificent accomplishment. Indeed I've heard it said that we should be glad to trade what we've produced so far for a few really good conceptual distinctions and a cold beer. But there's nothing in the world to trade for what we do have: the bent to sustain in regard to all elements of social life a spirit of unfettered, unsponsored inquiry, and the wisdom not to look elsewhere but ourselves and our discipline for this mandate. That is our inheritance and that so far is what we need to bequeath.

Erving Goffman (1983)

The decision to appreciate is fateful in an . . . important way. It delivers the analyst into the arms of the subject who renders the phenomenon, and commits him [or her], although not without regrets or qualifications, to the subject's definition of the situation. This does not mean the analyst always concurs with the subject's definition of the situation; rather that his [or her] aim is to comprehend and to illuminate the subject's view and to interpret the world *as it appears to him [or her]*.

David Matza (1969)

1

Are deviants different from or very much like the rest of us—the conventional, law-abiding, mainstream members of the society? Two images have dominated sociological discussions of deviance and crime. They may be referred to as the "Deviants Are Different" and the "Deviants Are Us" images.

The "Deviants Are Different" image tends to predominate in the field of criminology, that is, in the study of "hard" deviance. "Why do some people engage in crime?" criminologists ask. A major sector of the field replies: "Because they are different from the rest of us."

The birth of modern criminology is often pinpointed to the nineteenth-century perspective that is referred to as "the positive school." Associated with the name of Cesare Lombroso, it argued that crime is caused by biological defects (or "atavisms") that characterize a certain proportion of the society. A major theoretical thrust in contemporary criminology—and the descendant of nineteenth-century positivism, *trait* theory—argues that some people "have" certain biological or psychological traits or characteristics that force or *impel* them to commit criminal acts. "They have to do it," the trait theorist argues, "because they are born or formed that way" (Siegel, 2000, Chapter 6). Another major school of criminology that bills itself "a general theory of crime" agrees, and argues that people whose parents did not monitor or sanction their naughty behavior while they were growing up develop poor self-control. As a result, they engage in impulsive, destructive, exploitative, risky, self-indulgent, and dangerous—that is to say, criminal (and even more generally, *deviant*)—behavior (Gottfredson and Hirschi, 1990).

While some schools of criminology do underplay the differences between the criminal and the law-abiding citizen, most emphasize them. As a general rule, the more serious the crime, the greater the contrast between the law violator and the rest of us. In a sense, the criminal—the most serious deviant—is the "other." The deviant is in a world apart yet, at the same time, in some versions, he is poised to swoop down on innocent folk, threatening us, disrupting our lives, attempting to exploit the rest of us, *preying* on us. This is in fact precisely why we are interested in explaining why criminals do it: to put a stop to their predatory behavior.

On the structural level, the *social disorganization* or "Chicago" school of thinking caters to the "Deviants are Different" image. The predominant perspective in the sociology of crime and deviance between the 1920s and the 1940s, social disorganization theory, made a comeback sometime between the late 1980s and early 1990s (Bursik and Grasmick, 1993; Skogan, 1990; Stark, 1987). It is based on the view that violent (murder, rape, and robbery), property (burglary and larceny-theft), and "vice" crimes (prostitution and drug addiction), as well as mental disorder (schizophrenia, alcoholism, and depression), tended to be concentrated in the poorer neighborhoods in the inner cities because their residents were most likely to experience the consequences of community disintegration, decay, and disorder—in a phrase, social disorganization. In contrast, the perspective argued, cohesive, middle-class communities experienced vastly lower rates of crime and other serious deviance. In the communities in which *we* live, practitioners of this approach seemed to be saying, "folks like us" (that is, researchers, professors, and students at the University of Chicago, where this theory first emerged) neither engaged in nor were likely to encounter the kinds of crime and deviance we had to go into the inner city to study.

To their credit, the social disorganization theorists did invite empathy with the deviant, and in two ways. One, they were generous in gathering first-hand accounts and narratives from the unconventional denizens they studied. (But did they also gather accounts from middle-class enactors of deviance? As far as I know, they did not.) And two, they argued that *if* the rest of us lived in socially disorganized communities, we *would be* vastly more likely to commit (and be a victim of) untoward behavior (Pfohl, 1994, p. 209). But the fact is, they also argued that "folks like us" *don't* live in those communities and, hence, don't engage in such untoward behavior. Social disorganization theorists concluded that deviants act differently because they live in locations that are, in a sense, deviant "reservations" physically removed from where polite, middle-class, conventional folk live. Quite literally, deviance is "a world apart."

Anomie theory, likewise, argues in favor of the "Deviants are Different" hypothesis. Anomie theory had its heyday in the 1950s, declined in importance during the second half of the 1960s, but made a comeback sometime between the late 1980s and early 1990s. It is true that anomie theory adopts the view that, in contemporary industrial society, we are all subject to forces that lead us into the temptation of deviance and crime. Those forces include the message that every member of the society should and can become materially successful. *Combined with* the social and economic reality that not all of us can *in fact* achieve the economic goals we have grown up to expect, the inability to achieve those goals leads to strain. In turn, the strain leads to various deviant "adaptations," such as money-making crime, prostitution, depression, alcoholism, and drug addiction (Merton, 1938; Messner and Rosenfeld, 1997). Even though the forces that create this strain are society-wide in that everyone in contemporary industrial society is subject to them, the people who end up being least capable of achieving material success are members of the lower and working classes; consequently, it is they, not us, who are most likely to end up committing deviant acts (Merton, 1957, p. 144–146). Again, deviants are different from the rest of us in that they failed to achieve their life-goals. They have to develop "adaptations" to that failure, and, as a result, they engage in deviant and criminal behavior. Once again, deviants are distinctly *not* "folks like us."

Perhaps the clearest expression of the "Deviants Are Different" school of thought may be found in the perspective that is referred to as the *culture transmission* theory. Associated with the name of Walter Miller (1958), culture transmission argues that the conventional norms of lower-class culture actually *encourage* violations of the law. Lower-class boys are exposed to a number of "focal concerns," such as trouble, toughness, fate, and excitement that almost guarantee that they will engage in criminal and deviant behavior—for example, fighting, gambling, sexual promiscuity, bar-hopping, and substance abuse. In other words, being conformist members of lower-class culture almost inevitably entails violating the law and engaging in behaviors that, from the perspective of the middle class, are distinctly nonnormative. Like social disorganization and anomie theory, culture transmission theory argues that members of the lower class are vastly more likely to engage in illegal and deviant behavior than is true of members of the middle classes. Hence, once again, the deviant is depicted as "the other," "different," living in "a world apart," most distinctly "not like us."

In contrast, the "Deviants Are Us" image is more likely to be expressed in the study of "soft" deviance as opposed to crime (Ben-Yehuda, 1985, pp. 3–4). In this image, the deviant is not radically different from the world of conventionality and tradition, the boy and girl next door. In fact, the line between "vice and virtue" is fuzzy, indistinct, wayward, often difficult to draw (Matza, 1969). The same forces that produce conventional, law-abiding behavior may also result in serious violations of the norms; the same cultural values that brought us religion, mainstream politics, and the economy also produced prostitution, organized crime, and rape; the same processes that solidify an identification with being a physician, a student, a sexually faithful spouse, and a dedicated parent also draw us into drug dealing, homosexuality, and nude lap dancing. Deviance is not a world apart; instead, it is around us, with us, in us, *of* us. The "Deviants Are Us" image reminds us, "There but for the grace of God, go I." To be more precise about it, this image insists, "There go I," because it is based on the assumption that, on some dimensions, *all* of us stand outside acceptable definitions of normalcy and conventionality. Deviance, this image suggests, is common to all social life. It is, in other words, an essential ingredient in everyday life (Adler and Adler, 2000; Rubington and Weinberg, 1999).

The differential association perspective of Edwin Sutherland is one early statement of the "Deviants Are Us" approach to the subject: Criminal behavior is learned by associating with significant others who define violating the law in positive terms. And these "significant others" could be anyone, including friends, lovers, relatives, neighbors, coworkers. They need not even be criminals. All that is necessary for us to end up engaging in a life of crime is that they be close to us and they define criminal behavior as good. The theory of differential association is applicable to persons who occupy positions up and down the class system, including white-collar criminals (Sutherland, 1949). This perspective most emphatically reminds the middle-class denizen of society that deviants are not only very much *like* us—in point of fact, they *are* us.

To the labeling perspective of Howard S. Becker and his colleagues, another variety of the "Deviants Are Us" approach, what counts in becoming a deviant is society's condemnation. The labeling perspective shifted the focus of attention away from what generated the condemnation (for instance, the nature of the behavior) and away from the objective characteristics of the persons who attracted that condemnation (for instance, characteristics of the actor that "caused" the behavior) to the societal and interpersonal processes that produced the condemnation. The phenomenological school, which emphasizes how people construct reality and experience their everyday world, likewise affirms the parallels between deviance and conventionality. Here, meaning and interpretation are central; they are continually made and remade in all social worlds. Indeed, it is through such processes that deviance and conventionality are called into being.

BUT, DEVIANTS *REALLY ARE* DIFFERENT FROM THE REST OF US—AREN'T THEY?

Sociologists who work within the positivist or natural science model try to explain deviant behavior by means of "factors" or "variables" such as social disorganization, anomie, and early childhood experiences. They insist that the behavior we refer to as deviant is an intrinsically real phenomenon in the world—and recognizably different from conventional, conformist behavior—and that the person who enacts it is a recognizably different sort of person from the rest of us. All theories in the positivistic or natural science tradition are instances of the "Deviants Are Different" thinking. Travis Hirschi argues:

> The person may not have committed a "deviant" act, but he [or she] did (in many cases) do *something*. And it is just possible that what he [or she] did was a result of things that had happened to him [or her] in the past; it is also possible that the past in some inscrutable way remains with him [or her] and that if he [or she] were left alone he [or she] would *do it again*. (1973, p. 169)

Gwynn Nettler puts the matter even more emphatically: "Some people *are* more crazy than others; we can tell the difference; and calling lunacy a name does not *cause* it" (1974, p. 894).

These statements are true, but they are truisms—cliches that don't tell us very much. Sociologists who minimize the differences between deviance and conventionality, between norm violators and conformists, do not argue that there's no difference at all between these two categories of people and these two categories of behavior. Nor do they deny that past experiences may have something to do with current behavior. They are making several quite different—and absolutely crucial—points.

First (a point Hirschi slides over, by putting the word *deviant* in quotation marks and acknowledging that the behavior in question may not even be "deviant" in the first place): The behavior that is supposedly enacted by "the person" is *judged* to be deviant by the society, by audiences witnessing it, perhaps even by the actor. How do certain behaviors come to be regarded as deviant by the members of the society? And how does a person who enacts them come to be labeled a deviant? Is this a simple outgrowth of the nature of the behavior itself? The designation of behavior and people *as* deviant is an interesting and important process in itself, one that is very much worth investigating.

Second (another point Hirschi slides over, by acknowledging that "the person" engaged in a certain act "in many cases"): The focus on the cause of the behavior ignores the existence of *false accusations*. True, most people who are called "crazy" *are* "crazier" than the rest of us; in all likelihood, most people who are arrested actually *did* engage in criminal behavior; persons accused of juvenile delinquency *were* more likely to have engaged in illegal behavior than youths not so accused. But false accusations of wrongdoing are extremely common, and at certain times, in certain places, a false accusation can be as powerful in its impact as a true one. Consider witches in Renaissance Europe (Ben-Yehuda, 1985, pp. 23–73) and the satanic ritual abuse in the 1980s (Richardson, Best, and Bromley, 1991; Victor, 1993). Both were "scares"—false accusations with no actual behavioral basis. Such cases as these *cannot* be investigated by the sociologist searching only for the causes of deviant behavior.

Third, the exclusive focus on the causes of deviant behavior—and the consequent assumption that "deviants are different"—forces us to ignore deviant *conditions*. What is the cause of blindness, extreme ugliness, dwarfism, albinism, physical disability? The sociological positivist runs into a dead end here because the factors that cause these conditions are not social in origin; they are caused by genes or by accident. But the sociologists who seeks to understand the everyday *experience* of the person who suffers from society's judgments of them as inferior have their hands on a crucial and centrally important issue: How do persons who are *disvalued* by mainstream society reflect on their lives in a society that does not respect them? Such an investigation forces us to be *empathetic*—to see the world through the eyes of the person whose experiences we wish to understand. And our investigation of *all* sources of disvaluation permits us to seek out the experiences of the physically stigmatized *as well as* enactors of behavior that violates the norm.

The fourth reason why a single-minded focus on the causes of deviant behavior is too narrow and perhaps misguided is that *deviance is a matter of degree*. Some acts, conditions, and beliefs are mildly condemned while others are strongly—even savagely—condemned. And the more mildly condemned something is, the more common it is; the stronger the condemnation, the rarer it is. This means that most of what is referred to as "deviant" is made up of behavior, beliefs, and conditions that only *slightly* violate a rule; hence, in sheer numbers, persons designated as "deviant" are likely to be a great deal more like the rest of us than the stereotype would admit. In other words, there are a lot more shoplifters than murderers and a lot more marijuana smokers than crack addicts. And the fact is, shoplifters and marijuana smokers are a great deal more similar to the societal mainstream than murderers and crack addicts are. In short, the "Deviants Are Different" image is seriously flawed, and the "Deviants Are Us" image makes a great deal of sense.

In a strictly scientific sense, neither image is right, neither one is wrong. They are models, visions, perspectives, figures of speech. In the words of the early twentieth-century German sociologist Max Weber, these images are "ideal types"—not scientific hypotheses. Strictly speaking, the two images are not so much contradictory as they are complementary. In some ways, people who violate society's most strongly-held norms *are* different from those who don't. The simple fact that many of them "did it"— that is, engaged in a deviant act—makes them different, in a way. Likewise, in some important and significant ways, norm violators *are* like the rest of us. In fact, in some sense, *all* of us are norm violators. The key to the enigma that these two images pose lies in what we, as observers of the social world, find interesting. And it is here that our story begins.

IS THE TERM "DEVIANT" PEJORATIVE?

Sociological definitions of things often differ quite a bit from those that are used by the man and woman on the street. Sociologists usually try to avoid stereotypes while, all too often, much of the public embraces them. To the general public, the term "deviant" typically means *perverted* or *abnormal*. If we say "He's a deviant" or "She's a deviant," we generally don't want to have anything to do with him or her. The popular connotations of the term "deviant" are condemnatory, pejorative, and distinctly negative.

In contrast, perversion and abnormality have *nothing to do* with the sociological understanding of deviance. In fact, the sociological definition of deviance is *descriptive,* not condemnatory. It points *not* to what something or someone *is* but what something or someone is *thought to be.* Sociologically, deviance simply refers to behavior, beliefs, or conditions that *violate social norms* and become the basis for *social rejection, condemnation,* and *punishment.* The sociological definition of deviance contains no implication of perversion or abnormality whatsoever. Sociologists of deviance *take note of* these social evaluations of and reactions to certain forms of behavior, beliefs, traits, and people—they do not *endorse* those evaluations or reactions. Will some people reject, condemn, or punish you if you engage in certain behavior, espouse certain beliefs, or possess certain characteristics? If the answer is yes, then the sociologist regards them as examples of deviance.

To repeat: To the sociologist, the term "deviant" is *not* pejorative or downputting. It is not an insult or a sign of disrespect, and it does not mean perverted, pathological, "bent," twisted, or mentally ill or disordered. Plain and simple, it means behavior, beliefs, conditions that, and persons who, violate a norm and are likely to be condemned. There is no negative connotation implied in the term. When sociologists use the term, they are not referring to anyone or anything as "really" or "truly" deviant. They are saying that *others*—the public, the general population, the members of a society or a social group or category—regard that behavior, those beliefs or conditions, and those persons unacceptable and unconventional. When anthropologists describe a religious ceremony in another society, they say, "This is how it's done in Bora-Bora." When sociologists use the term "deviant," they say, "This is what a majority of the residents of Hillandale consider worthy of condemnation." The term means that and nothing more.

Some critics claim that the term "deviant" is inherently pejorative (Liazos, 1972). They argue that the popular or psychiatric meaning of the word will "rub off on" the sociological meaning, that persons, acts, beliefs, or conditions will be contaminated whenever the sociologist writes or utters the magic word, "deviant." Philosophers refer to this as *the fallacy of reification*, transforming a concept or an idea into a concrete thing.

Certain critics seem to think the sociologist's use of the term "deviance" *reinforces* the disordered condition of unpopular persons, ideas, traits, or behavior. But in fact, exactly the opposite is the case. It is the *critic* of the term "deviant" who reinforces the term's pathological, pejorative connotations. In contrast, it is the *sociologist* who says, let's put aside the negative connotations of the term. *In a sociological context*, the term means "condemned by members of some social category as nonnormative." If you can't wrap your mind around shifts in contextual meaning, perhaps you are incapable of engaging in the enterprises of reading, thinking, and writing about deviance. My guess is, the reader is intellectually flexible enough to grasp this point. "Deviant" is what—or who—is likely to be condemned or socially shunned *by a specific audience*—regardless of who makes up that audience.

In the final analysis, this issue boils down to what word or term is best to use to refer to the phenomenon sociologists call *deviance*. If critics don't like the term, what one do they prefer? None has suggested a better term.

Does "different" describe the territory of deviance? Not really, since many forms of deviance are not different from what most of us do. Most of us lie at some time or another, but lying is still deviant. Many behaviors, beliefs, and physical characteristics are "different" but do not elicit condemnation or social isolation. Someone who is more attractive than average is "different" from the rest of us but is unlikely to attract rejection; an outstanding athlete, likewise, is "different" but not deviant. What about "extraordinary" as a substitute for the term deviant (Peck and Dolch, 2001)? Unfortunately, "extraordinary" has the same drawbacks as the word "different." The remarkable feature about most forms of deviance is how *ordinary* they are. Does "unconventional" convey the same meaning as "deviant"? What about "nonconforming"? Both of these terms are very close to what sociologists mean by deviance, but they only imply a violation of social norms without indicating that the violator is likely to be punished. Only deviance conveys *both* a normative violation *and* certain likelihood of a consequent social rejection. No other term is as richly or concretely descriptive of what sociologists mean when they use the term "deviance." Unless a better word comes along, it seems we are stuck with the one we have.

Deviance as a Social Construction

What's the most interesting way of looking at the subject sociologists refer to as *deviance*? What would you like to know about it? How should it be approached, studied, examined, thought about? What about the people designated by members of society as deviants? Wouldn't you like to hear their side of the story?

In this book, we'll meet an autistic boy, a recovering alcoholic, a former anorexic, a man who frequents prostitutes and makes extensive use of pornography, two obese women, a homeless man, a former male madam of a homosexual "house" of prostitution, a devotee of sado-masochistic sexual practices, a lesbian couple, and a convict. If you met them, what questions would you ask? If you conducted research on their behavior, their beliefs, or the way society treats them, how would you go about it? What do you want to know about their deviance?

When confronted with deviance and its perpetrators, most of us—and traditionally, most sociologists of deviance as well—would immediately ask: *Why*? Why do they do it? What's different about rule violators that entices them to stray from the straight and narrow? Why drug use, why political radicalism, murder, suicide, sexual infidelity, drug use, and alcoholism? We assume that there must be something that's different, special, and unique about the nonconformist that impels him or her to violate society's rules when the rest of us obey them. Or, on a more sophisticated and sociological level, what societal *conditions*—such as poverty, socioeconomic or racial inequality, urban life, society-wide chaos, upheaval, normlessness, or war—produce variations in rates of deviance and crime?

The "Why?" question is legitimate. Indeed, most sociologists of deviance pursue this line of inquiry. To my mind, however, an even more interesting way of thinking about the phenomenon of deviance is to adopt the perspective of rule violators themselves. How do rule violators look upon their own behavior, beliefs, conditions, their lives in mainstream society, and the way they are treated by the more conventional members of that society?

When we examine deviance, we are looking not merely at rule violations and their social causes and consequences but also at two even more interesting social phenomena: One, differing *interpretations* of an act, a belief, a physical characteristic, and/or the persons who convey them; and two, the lived *experience* of someone who engages in a certain act, holds a certain belief, or possesses a certain trait that most of the members of a society find repellent. The twin issues of varying systems of meaning or *interpretations* of behavior, beliefs, and characteristics and the subjective *experience* of engaging in, holding, or possessing them provide the foundation of this book.

A focus on subjective interpretations and experiences is based on an approach to reality that is referred to as *social constructionism*. Constructionism argues that the most interesting features of the world we confront are *internal* rather than external, *subjective* rather than objective, relative to time and place, variable according to the observer, rather than true, absolute, essentially real, and changeless for all time. Constructionists argue that deviance is a social product. What counts is how behavior, beliefs, and conditions are conceptualized, viewed, evaluated, thought about, judged. *And* how their conveyors—enactors of behavior, holders of beliefs, possessors of characteristics—are treated by others. In other words, what's important is how audiences *react* to a phenomenon, not the essential nature of the phenomenon itself. Constructionism asks: What do things *mean* to participants and actors? And how do they bring that subjective meaning into their interactive relations with others? And how do they act on their subjective meanings? The constructionist says the most important characteristic of an act, a belief, or a physical trait is how the members of a society view it and react to it. Behavior, beliefs, and traits are not deviant in themselves; they become deviant when they are evaluated and reacted to in a society, a particular social circle, or a situational context. Nothing is deviant in and of itself; something becomes deviant only when it is evaluated and dealt with.

In other words, what's deviant is not an objective reality—a hard, concrete thing we can lay our hands on, an essential reality that is pretty much the same the world over. Instead, as we've seen, it is a *social construction*, a product of seeing and judging things or people in a certain way. It shifts around according to a society's, a group's, or a social circle's rules, norms, or standards, and how those rules, norms, or standards translate into behavior—that is, how people who believe in those rules *treat, deal with,* or *act toward* persons who violate them. In short, in order to be deviant, an action, a belief, or a person has to be *judged* to be deviant—by one or more audiences—and *treated* as such.

Scientists with a scientific, positivistic, or explanatory approach ask: Why do people become homosexuals? They assume that there's some common core or "essence" within homosexuality that is the same the world over. Homosexuality is a preexisting, objectively real entity that is pretty much the same everywhere, much like diamonds and rubies, apples and oranges (Trioden, 1988, p. 101).

In contrast, the social constructionist asks: What's the meaning of homosexuality in societies around the world? How is homosexuality defined?

Does a category, "homosexuality," exist in a given society? Are homosexuals condemned or accepted? Is homosexual (that is same-sex genital) behavior condemned, accepted, encouraged—or demanded? What sort of lives do homosexuals lead? What's their identity? How do they view their own behavior? The "Why homosexuality?" question is an *objectivistic* or *explanatory* approach. The "What's the *meaning* of homosexuality?" is a constructionist approach.

All phenomena can be looked at through the lens of these two approaches—the positivistic, objectivistic, or explanatory, and the subjectivistic, constructionist, or meaning-oriented. Is the most interesting aspect of mental illness its essential reality and the causes of its condition? (the objectivistic approach). Or is the most interesting aspect how mental illness is defined and how persons regarded as mentally ill are looked upon and treated? (the constructionist approach). Again, these two approaches are not so much contradictory as complementary. They look at different aspects or features of things in the world. They ask different questions and arrive at different conclusions. They are two sides of the same coin. Certain behaviors, beliefs, and conditions *may very well have* certain features in common the world over. And some may be caused pretty much everywhere by the same factors or conditions. (I suspect this is true, for example, of autism, schizophrenia, mental retardation, dwarfism, and albinism.) In other words, the positivists may be right, but their answers are incomplete. These behaviors, beliefs, and traits are also *defined* differently in societies around the world, and their enactors, holders, and possessors are also *treated* differently the world over. This differential treatment has *consequences* for the person so treated. In other words, *regardless* of the causes of certain behaviors, beliefs, or traits, what counts is the social reaction *to* the person who enacts the behavior, holds the belief, or possesses the trait (Lemert, 1951). It is the social constructionist approach that will inform the accounts and the discussions in this book.

WHAT'S DEVIANT? *WHO* IS THE DEVIANT?

What—or who—comes to mind when you encounter the word "deviant"? What sort of person or behavior is conjured up in your mental image?

Karen is an atheist; she does not believe in the existence of God. Harry is a fundamentalist Christian; he believes that every word in the Bible literally issued from the mind of God. Hence, those words are incapable of being wrong—they are eternal, unchangeable, true for all time. Are Karen and Harry deviants? Are their *beliefs* deviant?

Rob belongs to Unarius, a UFO cult; Jane is devoted to what she sees as the communist cause; Jack is a white supremacist; Bill smokes four packs of cigarettes a day; in the past two years, Ron has accumulated eight speeding tickets and has smashed up four cars; Tod is four feet tall; Andrea is an albino; Roberta is clinically depressed and can't leave the house or talk to anyone without bursting into tears; Fred cheats on his wife; James cheats on his income taxes; Claudia cheats on her exams. Are Rob, Jane, Jack, Bill, Ron, Tod, Andrea, Roberta, Fred, James, and Claudia *deviants*? Are what they *are, do,* or *believe* deviant?

Does atheism violate a norm? Sure it does. More than nine out of ten people in the United States believe in God. Many feel that godlessness is unacceptable, sinful, and wrong—indeed, immoral. They don't trust an atheist and wouldn't feel comfortable voting for one for president, being friends with one, having their children taught by one, or having their family physician be one. In other words, most Americans regard atheism as deviant and atheists as deviants.

Likewise, in many social circles in the United States, fundamentalist Christianity is nonnormative—a violation of social convention. Beliefs based on such a position are often the basis for social rejection, condemnation, and punishment. Most Americans have a weak, tepid form of religious expression and belief; they feel uncomfortable about others who take their religion too seriously. On Wall Street or in Silicon Valley, employees will be told to keep their views on biblical infallibility to themselves; in most college classrooms, charismatic religious expression will be thought silly and out of place; in most mainstream media, expressions of creationism or the necessity for a more Christian approach to the news will be met by disbelief and derision; strong religious conviction rarely finds a place in the majority of television dramas or comedies—or, if it does, it is the butt of jokes; in most social circles in the United States, drinking alcohol is expected and shunning it—a requirement of fundamentalist Christianity— distinctly unacceptable, nonnormative, unconventional. Hence, in these— extremely wide—social contexts, Bible Christianity is a form of deviance.

Can two different groups or categories define *one another* as deviant? Of course they can! This may be referred to as "mutual deviantization." Bible Christians regard atheists as even more deviant than does mainstream society; likewise, atheists see fundamentalist Christians as more deviant than the so-called average American does. Members of the survivalist, white supremacist, militia groups in the United States (who refer to themselves as "patriots") define the federal government as evil—in a word, deviant. Contrarily, members of the government define members of these militias as deviant and take steps to make sure they do not harm, bring down, or destroy the government. Here, two social groups or categories "deviantize" (or "demonize") one another. To each, the other is the embodiment of evil (Aho, 1994).

Deviance inevitably turns on power. That is, in every society that has ever existed, notions of right and wrong vary from one member to another, from one category or subgroup to another. So, the question becomes, *whose* notion of right and wrong prevails? When certain behavior, beliefs, or characteristics are considered acceptable by the members of a small, powerless category of people but unacceptable by the members of a large, powerful category, it is usually the latter's definition that is successful. Members of the smaller, weaker category usually find themselves running afoul of the dominant definition more often than is true the other way around. An atheist in Europe in the Middle Ages was more likely to get into trouble for proclaiming his or her beliefs than a believer in God, not because atheism was or is "wrong" in some abstract sense, but because at that time, believers wielded more power than atheists did.

The term "hegemony" refers to the domination of one social category over another. In the original Marxist formulation, developed by Antonio Gramsci, it was specifically the domination of the subordinate, relatively powerless class (the proletariat) by the superordinate class (the bourgeoisie). Hegemony is achieved through a combination of force or *coercion*, and *consent*. Consent is achieved, many theorists believe, because the dominant categories or classes control the content of the major institutions—education, religion, the media, politics, art, the criminal justice system—that convey society's culture and hence, can socialize (or, according to a more biased term, "brainwash") members of the subordinate categories or classes to believe what they want them to believe.

Among intellectuals and academics, the Marxist paradigm no longer holds the allure it once had, and so they no longer conceive of hegemony as turning specifically or exclusively around notions of class. Indeed, any and all differences between and among social categories can become the basis of struggles for dominance and subordination—most notably, differences in race, sex, sexual preference or orientation, age, religion, even lifestyle. Hegemony is always incomplete. In fact, in any large, complex society, a number of *competing* interpretations of right and wrong exist simultaneously. Intellectuals of a leftish persuasion use the term "counter-hegemony" to refer to notions that challenge the status quo. However, it is clear that most behavior, beliefs, or physical characteristics that are widely regarded as unacceptable are *not* "counter-hegemonic" in that they directly undermine, subvert, or challenge prevailing notions of what's right or wrong. A very low proportion of persons who are regarded as "deviants" have much interest in overturning the prevailing moral or ideological order. (Some do; most don't.) Most deviants are distinctly apolitical; they usually want to avoid the condemnation or punishment that often accompanies violating mainstream norms.

At the same time, definitions of right and wrong, as well as the way that people who embody them are treated, are not static; they are fought over in political and ideological struggles. In fact, a major sector of the political and ideological arena is devoted to definitions of right and wrong—in effect, devoted to *defining what's deviant*. Is the fetus a human being? Is performing an abortion a deviant act? Should abortion be against the law? Is it murder? Is killing an abortion doctor a righteous act? How should the handicapped be treated? Should all public facilities be wheelchair accessible? Should all movie theaters and commercial airplanes be required to have seats that accommodate extra-large patrons? Should laws that ban discriminating against minorities include the physically handicapped? What about the obese? What about homosexuals? Is violence against homosexuals a "hate crime," very much like violence against members of racial minorities? Why the recent hysteria over drug use? What's behind the huge increase during the past two or three decades in the incarceration of drug offenders? Is turning mental patients out onto the street with little more than a prescription for their condition the most humane and effective treatment for them? Is banning smoking in public locations the right thing to do? What about the drinking age?

The point is, all of these are *political* questions; the struggle to answer them is determined in part by which segments of the society wield the most power. All segments define specific behavior as right or wrong—all, in other words, spell out what's conventional and what's deviant. In short, deviance is, by its very nature, a *political* phenomenon.

The role of power in definitions of deviance and conventionality is revealed in ways that are both *directly* and *indirectly* political. Domination of the political process results in legislation that favors one's outlook, reflects the ideology of the social categories to which one belongs. For instance, the legalization of abortion and certain kinds of gambling and sexually explicit materials represents a defeat for the religious right and a success for the more secular and libertarian sectors of the society. But legislation is only one among a wide range of fronts on which the issue of legitimacy is fought. Certain categories, classes, and segments of the population wield considerable influence in the major social institutions; their definitions of deviance and conventionality tend to prevail in the media, in education, religion, science, and the arts. In other words, *representations* of morality—what's disseminated and promulgated concerning what should be considered right and wrong, what's acceptable and unacceptable—also have political *implications* even though they are not *directly* political.

For instance, when television dramas represent homosexual characters as sympathetic and normal and homosexuality as an acceptable lifestyle, that reflects and affirms the legitimacy of being gay—in effect, announcing that it should not be regarded as deviant. When the latest research indicates that obesity is largely a genetic, hormonal, neurological product, this affirms the illegitimacy of condemning fat people. When evolution is taught in the public classroom and creationism is not, this affirms not only the truth and acceptability of the former but also the dominance of its believers, as well the falsity and unacceptability of the latter and the marginal, subordinate status of those who hold that position. When drug arrestees receive prominent media attention, this underscores that they are criminals, beyond the pale, not like the rest of us—in a word, deviants. In short, *images count*. The way behavior, beliefs, characteristics, or a category of human beings are depicted in the media, educational curricula, religious teaching, entertainment, scientific reports, and the fine arts *reflects* and *affirms* definitions of deviance; *results from* the power of the social segments, classes, or categories who endorse such images; and *changes* over time as a result of struggles between and among these segments with different views of right and wrong. In other words, deviance is both a directly and an indirectly political phenomenon.

Audiences: Situational versus Societal Deviance

What's an audience? *Who* makes up an audience? An audience is any actual or potential group or category of people who does or would evaluate someone's act, belief, or traits. Friends can be such an audience. So could parents and other relatives, neighbors, members of a community, bystanders and witnesses, the police, judges, juries, social workers, psychiatrists, teachers—in fact, *anyone and everyone* who watches or hears about someone's doings, beliefs, and characteristics.

Does this mean that absolutely *any* behavior, belief, characteristic, or person can be regarded as deviant? Are all audiences equally influential in defining the nature of deviance? In other words, are we *all* deviants? Not quite. There are two ways of thinking about the role of audiences in defining what's deviant. One is *situationally* and the other is *societally* (Plummer, 1979, pp. 97–99).

"Situational" (or contextual) deviance is the violation of a norm *within a specific situation or context*. Here, someone is subject to the negative evaluations of a specific audience whose judgments are strictly local. That is, the judgment is formed by a specific group, social circle, or setting. For instance, in a delinquent gang, a boy's unwillingness to rob a store or join in a fight with a rival gang would be regarded as an act of cowardice. Such a refusal would result in that boy being condemned, rejected, socially shunned, and physically punished by the other members of his gang—in other words, he would be branded as a deviant. This is a case of *situational* deviance because such an evaluation—being condemned for refusing to commit a crime—is limited to circumstances or contexts such as delinquent gangs. Radicals and other persons on the left of the political spectrum condemn corporate crime and other immoral actions of the rich and powerful. To the extent that such acts do not attract widespread public condemnation, they remain strictly situational or contextual deviance—applying to a limited set of circumstances prescribed by radicals and other such utopians.

"Societal" deviance is the violation of a norm that has society-wide relevance. Robbing a store is an example of an illegal criminal act that can result in arrest and imprisonment, forms of punishment, or *formal* condemnation. The norm "thou shalt not rob" is not limited to a particular situation or context. As a formal law, it applies to all of us, all the time. In addition, it is socially, informally, and interpersonally deviant as well. As an *informal* norm, it applies to nearly all of us, nearly all the time. Hence, robbery is *societal* deviance. That is, the rule against it is not limited to particular members of the society; it applies society-wide. In a like fashion, being a homosexual or engaging in homosexual behavior is widely regarded as deviant. Homosexuality is condemned by many—indeed, most—audiences in this society. In a particular locale, neighborhood, social circle, or situational context (for instance, in New York City's Greenwich Village or San Francisco's Castro Street, as well as in many academic, artistic, fashion, and theatrical circles), homosexuals and homosexuality may very well be accepted, tolerated, even encouraged—but, again, that would be "situational" in nature, not "societal."

Sociologists of deviance are much more likely to study behaviors (as well as beliefs and physical characteristics) that attract *widespread* condemnation and censure ("societal" deviance) than those that are regarded as deviant only within a specific or local context ("situational" deviance). The fact is, societal deviance has a *hierarchical* quality. What defines it is not separate and independent judgments by scattered groups and categories in the population but norms with varying degrees of strength and popular support. Societally, *the most deviant* acts, beliefs, and characteristics are those that are *strongly* and *widely* condemned.

To summarize, to the sociologist, *deviance* is a violation of a norm that is likely to result in punishment, condemnation, or social rejection. This means that, sociologically speaking, deviance is a socially constructed phenomenon. It does not refer to an objective property or characteristic but to an evaluation made by one or more actual or potential observers or *audiences*. In other words, what's deviant may vary from one audience to another. What's accepted in one group could be rejected in another. Certain norms are accepted only in particular locales, situations, or social circles; their violation can be referred to as "situational" deviance. In contrast, other norms are so widely and strongly held that a violation of them should be referred to as "societal" deviance.

THE ABCs OF DEVIANCE

There are at least three bases for social condemnation by audiences, what Adler and Adler refer to as the ABCs of deviance: A, *acts* or behavior; B, *beliefs;* and C, physical *characteristics* or traits (2000, p. 8).

Most of us accept the fact that nonnormative or unconventional *behavior* is likely to result in condemnation or social rejection. All the classic forms of deviance include behavior most of the members of the society consider wrong or unacceptable—homosexuality, murder, rape, prostitution, and so on. Even *beliefs* seem a clear-cut basis for rejecting someone. Indeed, throughout human history, millions of people have been persecuted for their religious or political views. In fact, much of human history is a chronicle of members of one group or category punishing members of another for beliefs they consider wrong. We may not accept the validity of such judgments, but such persecutions are a fundamental fact of history. As sociologists of deviance, we are forced to take note of them.

Chances are, the most difficult type of deviance for many of us to accept is likely to be *physical* deviance. It seems grossly unfair to make fun of, reject, shun, or disrespect someone who cannot walk, is blind, obese, mutilated, disfigured, extremely ugly, an albino, a dwarf, or is missing one or more limbs (Polsky, 1998, pp. 202–203). But is it unfair of the sociologist to point out that such social rejection actually *does* occur? Indeed, exactly the reverse is the case. The fact is, people with certain characteristics *are* rejected, and it would be remiss of the sociologist to pretend that such rejection does *not* take place. It is an invalid sense of tolerance to condemn the sociologist for using the term deviant to apply to persons with physical characteristics that are widely regarded as undesirable. In fact, such fake tolerance leads to more social rejection, not less. Pretending that an issue does not exist denies the possibility of change. It is our job to understand the origin and dynamics of condemnation and social rejection. Involuntarily acquired physical characteristics do make up one of the bases of condemnation and rejection. If some members of society treat dwarfs, albinos, and the disabled in a more negative fashion from the way they treat others, then people with such characteristics *are* deviants. Fair or unfair, the rejection of possessors of certain undesirable and involuntarily acquired physical characteristics is a fact of life.

It is true that the fact that certain physical characteristics are deemed "not the person's fault" may *mitigate* society's negative judgment of their possessors. Most of us do not *blame* the hunchback or the albino for his or her condition. Moreover, condemnation is greater to the extent that the condition can be ascribed to freely chosen behavior. For instance, when respondents are told that obesity is caused by a neurological or biochemical disorder, they are less ready to condemn the fat person than if they were to ascribe his or her weight to overeating (DeJong, 1980). In the early part of the twentieth century, Tourette's syndrome, a neurological condition that results in uncontrollable yelps, barks, twitches and, occasionally, uttering obscenities, was thought to be a moral failing; persons afflicted with the condition were condemned and socially ostracized. Now that we recognize its involuntary character (and now that it can be controlled by medication), this condemnation and ostracism has hugely diminished.

But a diminution of condemnation and ostracism is not the same thing as its outright elimination. The fact is, people with a wide range of involuntarily acquired undesirable characteristics *are* socially isolated, pitied, scorned, humiliated, disfavored in a number of ways, even, in some quarters, regarded as contemptible. In all societies, some subcultures *ascribe* wrongdoing to possessors of undesirable physical characteristics—a retribution from God as a result of one's moral failing, even a moral failing of one's parents. Psychologists refer to this as "belief in a just world" (Lerner, 1980), that is, the belief that good people are ultimately rewarded and bad people eventually punished; hence, if someone suffers misfortune, he or she must have *done* something bad to deserve it. In other words, involuntariness is a cultural construct, not a simple fact. As we'll see, many people still ascribe autism to bad parenting, not to an involuntarily acquired condition. Spokespersons for extremely conservative causes blame AIDS sufferers for their own condition because, in the words of North Carolina Senator Jesse Helms, they contracted the disease as a result of their own "deliberate, disgusting, revolting conduct" (Seelye, 1995). Most of us do not feel this way; moreover, Senator Helms does not feel the same way about the lung cancer contracted (as a result of freely chosen behavior) by smokers, since he is the tobacco industry's staunchest supporter. In short, negatively regarded physical characteristics cannot be ignored as a form of deviance (Goode, 1996, p. 320).

INSIDERS' AND OUTSIDERS' VIEWS OF DEVIANCE

As I suggested above, most of the early history of the sociological study of deviance—and especially crime—was devoted more or less exclusively to an examination of the "Why?" question, that is, "Why do they do it?" An exclusive focus on what *causes* deviant behavior is an *externalistic* or *outsider's* approach. "Why do some people violate society's norms and laws?" (Or, alternatively, "Why *don't* most of us violate society's norms and laws?" "Why do we *obey* the norms and the laws?") "What leads someone to break the law?" "What societal conditions are likely to produce high rates of deviance and crime?" "Why prostitution, homosexuality, illicit drug use, alcoholism, mental illness?" These questions, asked by the earliest sociologists, are the sorts of questions a conventional member of the society would ask. They are not, however, the central concerns of the people who are regarded as society's deviants. Indeed, they are the sorts of questions that someone who is distressed about nonconformity and wants to put a *stop* to it would ask.

The central concern of a person who violates behavioral norms, holds unacceptable beliefs, or possesses an undesirable trait or characteristic is dealing with stigma, censure, punishment, and social rejection. Anyone who is on the *receiving* end of conventional society's judgments about rule violations is likely to ponder what it *feels* like to be ostracized and rejected. The "Why do they do it?" question is entirely reasonable, a worthy sociological enterprise. (Though it is irrelevant for the possession of most undesirable physical characteristics, since they do not entail "doing" anything, and, in addition, what brought them into existence is rarely social in origin.) But it is not the *only* question the sociologist of deviance can ask.

The limited nature of the externalistic or "Why do they do it?" approach leads us to the heart of this book, which adopts a more *subjectivistic* approach. How do people who are seen or defined as social undesirables construct *their own* definition of deviance? How do they define their own behavior? Beliefs? Condition? How they fit into the society? How do they feel about themselves? How do they feel about society's condemnation and social rejection of them? How do they cope with that condemnation and rejection? How do they look upon the mainstream, the definers of deviance, the conventional, law-abiding members of the society? How do they live their lives on a day-to-day basis?

Today, a substantial number of sociologists of deviance are centrally concerned about the deviant's *definition of the situation*. They are interested in how deviance is socially constructed, how deviant identities are built up around this social construction, how deviants manage the stigma of deviance, what the relations between and among deviants are, how deviant acts are accomplished and managed, and how deviant "careers" are pursued—that is, entered, maintained, and, if they are, exited (Adler and Adler, 2000; Rubington and Weinberg, 1999). How is the world subjectively experienced by persons who are aware of their inferior social position? How does the stigmatized person justify his or her own behavior or beliefs? Explain or interpret his or her traits or characteristics?

Another way of capturing the flavor of this insider-versus-outsider issue is to ask, when reading an account or narrative: *Whose voice is this?* When we read a report written by scientific researchers, we have no doubt that it is the voice—and therefore the interpretation—of the researchers who wrote the report. Even if it describes the behavior of a group of people— say, the members of a delinquent gang, the monks in a monastery, or the leaders of a social movement—we know that the voice behind the words is that of the outsider, the external or detached observer, *not* the voice of the people being studied, the insiders, the members of the gang, the monks in the monastery, the leaders of the movement. Occasionally, in such a scientific report, a few carefully selected quotes from informants will be offered, but the reader is always aware that the person speaking is the scientist.

Positivism refers to the perspective that pervades traditional science: Knowledge can be obtained only though observation of the material world. In the social sciences, it is the view that sociology, political science, psychology, and economics can be "just as scientific" as physics. Positivism minimizes the importance of internal states, such as subjective experience, and maximizes the importance of observable behavior. In traditional science, it is the voice of the researcher, the expert, that is valorized or legitimated—that is, given the voice that speaks directly to the reader. The voice of the subject under observation is scientifically relevant only insofar as it can reveal patterns that only the expert can interpret and understand. In other words, the *outsider*—the scientist—knows more about the behavior of the individual or group being studied than the insider—the individual or the members of the group.

Sociology's mainstream is distinctly positivistic, as a brief perusal of its major journals, such as the *American Sociological Review* and the *American Journal of Sociology*, will reveal. But the field has always had a "minor" mode. The early Chicago sociologists, whose heyday ran from the 1920s to the 1940s, gathered and published a great many personal, firsthand accounts; Nels Anderson's *The Hobo* (1923) and Clifford Shaw's *The Jackroller* (1930) represent outstanding examples of this genre. Over time, as the field of sociology struggled to attain scientific legitimacy, the use of accounts to understand society declined in importance—until the 1960s, when a renaissance in the use of personal narratives took place. Central to that renaissance was the matter of *voice*.

Whose voice was speaking to the reader became a fundamental issue. If the externalistic scientific report valorized or legitimated the perspective of the scientist, doesn't the personal account valorize or legitimate the perspective of the narrator? And if the vast majority of scientists are male, white, and middle class, and if their views endorse those of the status quo and the powers that be, this line of reasoning went, shouldn't personal testimony from a wide range of voices—women, African Americans, the poor and powerless, the politically radical, and the unconventional—*decenter* or *pluralize* definitions of reality? That is, don't accounts release the hegemonic stranglehold or monopoly on interpretations of reality that positivistic science now enjoys? Doesn't making use of them give voice to relatively voiceless, powerless actors, subjects, informants, and observers with a multiplicity of non-approved characteristics? Doesn't the use of personal accounts *empower* the speaker or narrator? Doesn't it empower the groups or categories he or she represents? Although it is clear that these early programmatic slogans now seem a bit simplistic, they nonetheless do contain a grain of truth: The use of personal accounts offers a way out of the positivistic dominance, the narrow externalistic viewpoint of the expert; it gives a platform from which a multiplicity of voices may be heard.

These issues form the core of this book. I attempt to address them by offering accounts by people who are or would be regarded as unconventional or deviant by most members of our society. Instead of relying on an outsider's notions of what's deviant, we get closer to the heart of the matter by exploring the subjective interpretations and experiences of persons who are, or are likely to be, condemned, socially rejected, and stigmatized. It is, I believe, the very best way to begin our exploration of this complex, fascinating, and paradoxical phenomenon that sociologists call deviance.

THE MATTER OF IDENTITY

Sociologists distinguish the *social* or "public" identity (how we are viewed by others) from the "personal" or *self*-identity (how we view ourselves). Social identity answers the question, "Who is he (or she)?" And self-identity answers the question, "Who am I?" The two overlap, of course. Indeed, self-identity is formed in part by how we are viewed and treated by others. But there are many social identities, not just one, since there are many sets of "others." They include, at the very least, our family, our friends, our fellow students, our co-workers, and members of the society as a whole ("the generalized other")—each of whom may view us in a different way.

In a like fashion, self-identity may be *situated* in particular locales, so that the way we view ourselves may change as the context changes. Hence, just as there are many social identities, there are many self-identities. In the academic situation, we may see ourselves as intelligent, something of a star; among friends, we may see ourselves as a clown, something of a fool; with our boyfriend or girlfriend, we may see ourselves as romantic, loveable, affectionate; in the work situation, we may see ourselves as lazy, a goof-off; and so on. The context as much as the person determines self-identity. With deviance, we have a series of interesting paradoxical issues that center around the contrast between social and self-identity.

The first paradox is that "deviant" is an extremely rare social identity. (In fact, as we saw, the popular term usually refers to a person who is either mentally disordered or a "pervert," which is not the sociological meaning at all.) Deviance is a sociological not a popular term, a generalization or inference the expert observer makes as a result of norm violations and the way certain people are treated and reacted to. Public labels are almost never so generic as "deviant." They usually entail assigning someone to a *specific* category whose members are in fact stigmatized (such as "nut," "queer," "pervert," "slut," and "freak"). The assignation of someone as a sociological deviant, that is, as belonging to a category of humanity that is routinely condemned, is *inferential*, not direct.

A second paradox is that self-identity almost never embraces "deviant" as a generic category either. As we will see in the section on vocabularies of motive, there are many paths from deviant behavior, beliefs, or the possession of deviant traits to a particular self-identity. Many persons who engage in behavior, hold beliefs, or have characteristics that *would be* widely condemned and *would* earn them a particular stigmatizing label *do not accept that label at all*. For instance, many men who have raped women do not see what they do as rape and do not consider themselves as rapists—even though the community as well as the criminal justice system disagree with that self-assessment (Scully and Marolla, 1984). In contrast, other persons embrace the *specific* label (for instance, gay, or fat person, or atheist) but reject the legitimacy of the *generic* label (that is, they do not believe that they, or people like them, deserve to be stigmatized). They recognize that they are likely to be condemned by the general community were they to be publicly recognized as belonging to a condemned social category, but they do not embrace the identity of "deviant" because they do not believe that the condemnation is valid.

If someone has been publicly stigmatized, referred to by a pejorative name and treated as a socially inferior person, that person clearly has the social identity of a deviant. Erving Goffman (1963) argues that someone who is publicly stigmatized has a "spoiled" identity—a characterization that is likely to spill over into one's self-identity. At the same time, he also argues that there is a portion of the self that resists pejorative labels, that preserves a sense of dignity, even under the onslaught of unrelenting stigma (1961, pp. 171ff.). He also argues that many stigmatized persons band together into "self-help" organizations whose members reject society's disvaluation of them, rejecting the basis of their stigma (1963, p. 22). Hence, even for someone who has been stigmatized, "social" and "self" identity may diverge, in which case the social identity is more deeply rooted in deviance than is the self-identity.

What about the person who is not publicly recognized as a rule violator, but who nonetheless violates the rules? What about the case of "secret deviance" (Becker, 1963, pp. 20–22)—the homosexual, the atheist, the AIDS sufferer whose normative violation is not publicly known? In these cases, the person whose deviance is a secret does not have a deviant *social* identity but may identify with a category that is likely to attract public scorn *if it were publicly known.* Even if he or she does not grant the legitimacy of the negative label, it is impossible to ignore society's condemnation of labeled behavior. In other words, nearly everyone who identifies *as* a homosexual, an atheist, an AIDS-infected person knows that that status is *saturated with public scorn* (Warren and Johnson, 1972, pp. 76, 77). Again, even with someone who has not been labeled as a deviant, social and self-identity are likely to diverge. With the unlabeled person, whose identity is potentially discreditable, self-identity is more deeply rooted in deviance than is social identity.

We have to treat a deviant identity as separate and independent from identity with a specific category that happens to be publicly regarded as deviant, even though the two overlap and merge with one another in interesting and important ways. Taking on a self-identity as a gay man, for example, overlaps with but is conceptually distinct from taking on the identity of a person who is likely to be condemned *for* his sexual self-identity. Accepting an identity as a gay man leads one to say to oneself, "I am the sort of person who might possibly engage in sex with other men." Accepting a self-identity as a drug user, likewise, makes it possible for someone to come to the conclusion, "If I'm at a party and someone hands me a straw and a mirror with a line of cocaine on it, I'm open to the invitation to snort that line." In other words, embracing a certain self-identity leads to the declaration: "I am the sort of person who is likely to do the following things." While self-identities may change and the content of the activities implied by a specific self-identity varies from one person to another, embracing a given identity has major implications for further behavior (Matza, 1969, p. 112; Pfuhl and Henry, 1993, pp. 60–61).

In recent years, identity has taken on a political slant. This is especially true for categories that were once considered dishonorable or shameful. Such identities have become a basis for fighting back against the forces that previously made their members marginal, powerless, and stigmatized.

"I'm gay and I'm proud!" has become a homosexual slogan that is simultaneously an affirmation of self-identity and the expression of an ideological stance rejecting an inferior status. "I'm here, I'm queer—get used to it!" is an even more militant political rallying cry.

Rape victim is another previously dishonored category that as a self-identity becomes not only a vehicle for transforming the status of women in that specific category but also all women generally. "No longer does a woman have to stay with secrecy, guilt and self-blame," explains Plummer (1993, p. 76); instead, she can "build an identity around being either a victim or a survivor, or both," thereby asserting control over her and society's reaction to her experience, as well as any and all reactions to all other rape victims.

When a white supremacist asserts, "I'm a Christian and a racist and I'm not about to apologize to anyone for that!" (Bushart, Craig, and Barnes, 1998), the statement both affirms loyalty to a particular community and informs the listener or the reader that the possessor of such a self-identity demands to be treated in a certain way, implying that dire consequences are likely to follow.

In short, personal self-identities become transformed into a specific approach to the category and its members that have distinctly political implications. Through their use, the content of these identities enters into the subculture of like-minded persons who share them and, eventually, into the culture of the society at large. Naturally, not all deviant categories carry the same political assertiveness; indeed, assuming some discredited identities results in isolation and powerlessness, not political affirmation and ideological self-assurance. Nonetheless, many identities, once considered badges of dishonor, have become reshaped into a vehicle for political and social change.

Deviance in Everyday Life

Some sociologists have urged that the study of deviance should move away from studying the mentally ill, prostitutes, homosexuals, and society's "perverts"—the socially marginal and stigmatized members of the society. Radicals and Marxists in the 1960s and 1970s—and still cited with great frequency in the deviance literature—critiqued the sociology of deviance. They argued that deviance studies should examine the evil deeds of the rich and the powerful, society's movers and shakers, the fat cats and top dogs, the ruling elite of the society (Gouldner, 1968; Liazos, 1972; Smith, 1973). For instance, Alexander Liazos examined the content of deviance textbooks and anthologies and was distressed to find that topics such as mental illness, prostitution, homosexuality, rape, alcoholism, and drug use constituted the majority of the examples of deviant behavior. Hence, Liazos argued, the field of the sociology of deviance is "biased."

However, the argument that not enough attention is paid to "covert institutional" forms of deviance (the evil deeds of fat cats and top dogs) misses the point entirely. For the most part, the general public does *not* regard this type of behavior as an instance of deviance at all. In fact, most such acts are in the spirit of U.S. society and culture and they rarely generate condemnation. (When they do, they *are* regarded as forms of deviance by sociologists.) What the public *understands by* deviance are the "meat and potatoes" forms of deviance that sociologists have been studying all along—namely, mental illness, prostitution, homosexuality, illegal drug use, and so on. The charge that the powerful commit more *harmful* behavior than "ordinary" deviants may be true, but it is irrelevant because deviance is not centrally *about* harm. It is about behavior, beliefs, and conditions that result in condemnation. This is what deviance *means*. The classic forms of behavior the sociologist has always studied as deviance are central to the field because the *public* thinks of them as central to their notion of what's deviant.

A second reason why the "nuts and sluts" critics miss the mark feeds into one of the field's most important points: The sociological study of deviance is *not* confined to society's fringes, margins, shadows, or underworld; indeed, "Deviance Is Us" is central to the contemporary sociologist's view of nonconformity and unconventionality. The truth of the matter is that *deviance is an everyday phenomenon*. It is a process—an ongoing dynamic—in everyday life. It is part and parcel of what all of us do and are subject to, every day. Deviance and its control are essential ingredients in the give-and-take of social interaction.

This means two things. One, rule violators are all around us. They could be people we know—our relatives, friends, neighbors, teachers, fellow students, roommates, teammates, officemates, lovers, confidants, coworkers, ministers, priests, or rabbis. Indeed, they could be any one of us—including you, the reader, and me, the author of this book. And two, the attempt to monitor and control deviance is all around us, a necessary component of the lives all of us lead.

Nachman Ben-Yehuda's book, *Deviance and Moral Boundaries* (1985), expresses this sentiment well. Deviance, says Ben-Yehuda, is a central phenomenon in all societies, common to the lives of us all. It does not take place solely in any particular sector of the society, such as society's fringes, margins, or underworld. Instead, it occurs everywhere, in all social locales, contexts, and institutions. Every society, he argues, is made up of "competing centers" of definitions of right and wrong, each with its own notion of what constitutes deviance. Members of each sector attempt to legitimate their own views and neutralize contrary definitions; hence, says Ben-Yehuda, everyone experiences the application of social sanctions.

- In Renaissance Europe, witches were persecuted for "consorting with the devil" (pp. 23–73).

- In contemporary society here, there, and everywhere, millions of us dabble—or become seriously involved—in occult and paranormal phenomena (pp. 74–105).

- In scientific circles, challenges to legitimate, conventional, or normative science (such as claims of the validity of ESP, UFOs, shifting continents, or radio waves) arise and elicit rejection, denunciation, even hostility among their peers (pp. 106–167).

- Some scientists fake, fudge, or fabricate data; when their violations are discovered, they are likely to be punished, often discredited (pp. 168–207).

Exactly these same competitive processes—processes that attempt to legitimate one point of view or way of life and condemn, proscribe, or invalidate another—take place in all sectors of the society, in the lives of all of us. Central to Ben-Yehuda's book, and to this one, is the fact that deviance is not confined to the street, the underworld, the "cool" world, the fringes, the "soft white underbelly" of society. Rules and their violation are essential to everything we do, from what and how we eat to how and with whom we make love and what we do for a living. They are the threads that run through all human endeavors—all behavior, all beliefs, all social characteristics. *Deviance and conventionality are the very stuff of social life.* Deviance goes on all around us—and so does the punishment of deviance.

- Some students cheat on their exams, some do not. Teachers are on the lookout for cheating. In the academic world, cheating on exams is a form of deviance.

- Some customers steal from retail stores, most do not. Representatives of retail stores monitor their customers for shoplifting. In the world of the retail store, shoplifting is a form of deviance.

- Some motorists speed, some do not. The police patrol the highways to determine whether motorists are driving well above the speed limit; when they are, the police often pull them over and give them a ticket. In the world of the highway patrol officer, speeding is a form of deviance.

- Most spouses are sexually faithful to their partners, many are not. Husbands and wives search their partners for clues to their infidelity. Among married couples, "cheating" on one's spouse is a form of deviance.

- Some teenagers smoke marijuana, some do not. Parents try to find out if their children are puffing on the evil weed. If so, they usually step in and take action. In most parental circles, smoking marijuana is a form of deviance.

- In a retail store, stealing merchandise from the shelves or storeroom or money from the cash register is a form of deviance. Managers and proprietors keep an eye out for dishonest employees who, if caught, are usually fired. In the world of the retail store, employee theft is considered deviance.

In other words, deviance and its control are all around us. They are basic and essential components of everyday life.

Yes, rape is a form of deviance—and a crime as well—but the rapist could be the boy next door.

Alcoholism is a form of deviance—but the alcoholic could be your uncle Fred.

Drug dealing is a form of deviance and a crime, but the local cocaine dealer could be your family dentist.

The child molester, often portrayed as a monster and a psychopath, could be your father, your stepfather, your uncle, or your grandfather.

The student who cheats on the final exam you're taking could be sitting right next to you.

Do you know the piano teacher down the block? On weekends, he wears leather outfits and cruises gay neighborhoods for pickups.

Did you know that the high school coach beats his wife?

Jim, the bartender who just handed you a beer? He taps the till to the tune of $100 a night.

In short, deviance is *not* exclusively or even primarily the "covert, institutional" workings of the system or the evil, harmful actions of the corporate elite. To the extent that the man and woman on the street condemn or socially shun the person who engages in a certain act, holds a certain belief, or possesses a certain characteristic, that act, belief, or characteristic is deviant. The question is not what the public *should* condemn but rather what it *does* regard as deviant. What *really* counts in the world of deviance are the answers to the following four questions.

1. How is deviance created? Is a given form or category of behavior, belief, or physical condition considered wrong, sanctionable—*deviant*—to large numbers of the members of a given society? In other words, how is the total universe of possible behavior, beliefs, or traits conceptualized in such a way that unacceptable ones are separated out from those that are acceptable?

2. How does someone who *knows* he or she is violating a norm negotiate his or her relations with persons who accept that norm as valid? In other words, how does he or she navigate his or her way through a sea of imputed hostility (Warren and Johnson, 1972, pp. 76, 77)? How does this process of "navigation" influence his or her identity or sense of self?

3. How does a specific instance of concrete behavior, a belief, a physical trait, become *categorized* as deviant? How are real-world phenomena that are observed or heard about—an act taking place over there, a belief that was just articulated, the person standing right here—get put into the general category designated as deviant? That is, how are *judgments of norm violations* made by bystanders, onlookers, or actual or potential audiences? How are these norm violations dealt with; that is, what sorts of *sanctions* do these audiences apply to the rule violators?

4. How do rule violators *experience* these sanctions? How does the norm violator deal with the apprehension, the condemnation, the hostility? Again, how does the experience influence his or her way of looking at the world, his or her identity, his or her tendency to gravitate toward or identify with other, like-minded or similarly-labeled persons?

The processes behind the answers to these four questions are the foundation-stones of the sociology of deviance. They constitute the bone, sinew, and muscle of this book. They are the stuff of deviance: (1) how society creates the deviant category; (2) how the person who belongs to that category deals with imputed stigma; (3) how real-life designations of deviance are made; (4) and what persons who are sanctioned or designated as deviant go through, think about, and feel. They represent deviance *as it is lived*. They spell out the subject of this book: *deviance in everyday life*.

THE SPECIFIC VERSUS THE GENERAL

So far, I have argued that the "nuts and sluts" critique of the sociology of deviance suffers from two fatal flaws. The first is that the "nuts and sluts" critics confuse deviance as an absolute or inherent quality of wrongdoing (in their view, the evil deeds of the rich and powerful) with actual, real-life *conceptions held* and *negative reactions by* members of the public. The bottom line is that if wrongdoing by the rich and powerful does *not* generate widespread condemnation, we can't define it as deviant. There's no honest way of manufacturing the quality of deviance where it simply does not exist. The second flaw is that deviance is not confined to any particular locale in the society—not just the boardroom of General Motors or the War Room of the Pentagon, not just the stalls of the porno parlor or in the crack den in an abandoned building. Deviance saturates everyday life. It may be found in both the conventional and unconventional sectors of the society, between and among friends, lovers, married couples, or family members, and in relations between faculty and students, employers and employees, or parents and children. Deviance is everywhere; it is the very stuff of social life.

Which leads us to the third fatal flaw of the "nuts and sluts" argument. Deviance is not a form of behavior, it is a *process*—an *analytic* process. This means that it is generalizable to social life as a whole, not confined to specific activities, beliefs, traits, or people. Sociological researchers who study deviant behavior have been accused of focusing on trivia and minutiae—the irrelevant, far out, exotic details of the lives of persons who lead unacceptable but interesting lifestyles. In fact, this is a false characterization. Sociologists who study deviance are usually guided by theoretical and analytical concerns. They examine the same basic sociological structures and processes that motivate all social and behavioral scientists—culture, social interaction, socialization, groups, social control, and stratification. They conceptualize activities and institutions such as mental illness, prostitution, stripping, homosexuality, drug use as concrete venues or manifestations of these more analytic structures and processes. In other words, it is not the *specific behavior* that counts but what that behavior can tell us about *social life in general*.

A study of female athletes (Blinde and Taub, 1992) tells us about the process of how we deal with a stigmatizing label. A study of male street prostitutes (Calhoun and Weaver, 1996) tells us how we assess potential pleasure and pain or reward and risk in determining a course of action. A study of erotic table dancers (Ronai and Ellis, 1987) tells us about how we conduct and strategize social interaction in an attempt to maximize a social exchange with another party in a quest for what seems on the surface to be mutually exclusive goals. A study of women in motorcycle gangs (Hopper and Moore, 1990) tells us about how it is possible to maintain unconventional lifestyles and subcultures. A study of female crack dealers (Mieczkowski, 1994) tells us how, with few resources and a precarious status, we manage to navigate economic exchanges in a risky, dangerous world and avoid exploitation and violence. In other words, in the study of deviance, *the specifics are in service to the generalities*.

At the same time, in the words of Mies van de Rohe, one of the twentieth century's most influential architects, "God is in the detail." By that I mean research about a chosen scene should be much more than trimming a tree with illustrations drawn from specific contexts. The precise form or manifestation of how more general structures and processes are energized or realized is crucial to the sociological enterprise. In short, any investigation should balance the specific with the general. Some of the details of a particular scene are unique to itself; others highlight and illuminate what is distinctive about deviance; still others will provide insight into social relations in general, what *all* people do when they engage in "doing things together" (Becker, 1986).

DEVIANCE AND VOCABULARIES OF MOTIVE

Every human on earth—and that includes you and me—indulges in "vocabularies of motive." That is, we all explain ourselves *to* ourselves and to others in a way that presents us and our actions in more or less acceptable, positive terms. All of us, as functioning members of society, learn to use certain phrases to explain what we are doing and why. For the most part, these phrases make us and our actions seem reasonable. Not all vocabularies of motive are appropriate for every action, nor are they acceptable to all audiences. We learn the circumstances under which a particular explanation is acceptable, and to which audiences (Mills, 1940). Of course, we are, ourselves, one of our many audiences, and accounts are frequently directed at convincing ourselves that we are decent, worthwhile human beings.

Which actions require accounts or vocabularies of motive? We do not have to explain to ourselves or others why we tie our shoelaces in the morning. That action seems straightforward, commonsensical, obvious, and strictly utilitarian; no one is going to challenge us on it. But other actions are regarded as problematic. Scott and Lyman (1968; Lyman and Scott, 1970, p. 112) define an account as a statement that is offered for an "untoward" action. An "untoward" action is one that is regarded as unacceptable, improper, blameworthy. When others find out that we engaged in the behavior, we are likely to be challenged or questioned about it; we are likely to be called upon to provide an explanation, an account, or a justification. Hence, even in advance, we have to give some thought to why we engaged in a particular behavior.

A major type of vocabulary of motive centers around deviance, since the violation of norms is, by its very nature, problematic to the members of the society in which it takes place. People who engage in actions, hold beliefs, or possess characteristics that are widely regarded as unacceptable are frequently called upon to provide some sort of account of them. Even if we do not interact in face-to-face encounters with conventional others who challenge them, we are rarely so insulated from the norms of the society that we are unaware of what those challenges are likely to be. At the very least, we usually formulate mental responses to hypothetical objections to our deviant actions, beliefs, and characteristics.

Most deviance accounts or vocabularies of motive entail *stigma neutralization*. This is a special type of explanation used by persons who anticipate being condemned. Specifically, it reduces or obliterates the anticipated condemnation. Indeed, some versions even find positive qualities in what others find objectionable. For instance, acts that others consider wrong are seen as *not so bad*—or not as bad as others say; beliefs that others condemn are *for a higher cause*—indeed, the beliefs of the condemners are wrong; conditions that others regard as repulsive are a product of fate—or become a *badge of honor*.

Stigma neutralization has a long history in the study of deviance. It is a basic component of how discredited persons, or persons with potentially discrediting secrets about themselves, present themselves to the audiences they have met or are likely to meet.

Scott and Lyman (1968; Lyman and Scott, 1970, pp. 113–124) distinguish between *excuses* and *justifications*, and Goffman (1971, pp. 113–118) adds *apologies*. And I'd like to add a fourth: *normalization* (Goode, 1978, pp. 80–87).

An *apology* divides the apologizer into two parts: One part is guilty of the wrongdoing and the second disassociates itself from the offense, thereby demonstrating support of the rule that was violated (Goffman, 1971, pp. 113). In other words, expressions of contrition can generate a certain measure of sympathy in audiences, and they may provide a kind of partial salvation. After snapping at a colleague, if a coworker says, "I'm sorry, I'm just not myself today," she usually receives absolution because, as a result of her excuse, her colleague can clearly see that an act that is regarded as bad—snapping—can be committed by someone who is normally a good and decent person.

Excuses emphasize the involuntary nature of that which is criticized. They claim that forces are operating beyond the control of the person who anticipates or who has received condemnation. "It's not my fault," excuses declare; "It was forced on me"; "I couldn't help it"; "It was the system, not me." Excuses "are accounts in which one admits that the act in question is bad, wrong, or inappropriate but denies full responsibility" (Lyman and Scott, 1970, p. 114). Depending on the untoward behavior, the circumstances of the act, and the audience, excuses sometimes work. In any case, they salve the conscience of many actors.

A *justification* provides an explanation that makes the behavior in question seem warranted. "It was the right thing to do at the time," the justifier claims. In other words, someone offering a justification "accepts responsibility for the act in question, but denies the pejorative quality associated with it" (Lyman and Scott, 1970, p. 114). Justifications are riskier than apologies and excuses because they plant one foot in the territory of accepting the behavior as legitimate, which many conventional audiences are not willing to grant. Still, over the centuries, countless actors have satisfied themselves that, under the circumstances, they "had to do it."

Normalization moves even more radically into the territory of legitimating the act. While justification legitimates the act *under the circumstances* ("It was the right thing to do at the time"), normalization legitimates the act *in general*. It says that society's condemnation of the act is illegitimate and calls for the complete removal of stigma from the actors who engage in that entire class of behavior. In fact, in some of its variants, normalization calls for a re-evaluation of the moral order such that conventionality is seen as wrong and that which is condemned is good. Here we see the majority of homosexuals proclaiming their normalcy ("Gay is good"), marijuana smokers who believe that their indulgence is harmless and should be legal and acceptable ("Legalize pot"), and members of right-wing, white supremacist "patriot" groups ("Make no mistake about it, white racists built this country"). In the world of deviance, offering accounts is the rule rather than the exception. Indeed, it is difficult to understand deviance without an acquaintance with them.

With the use of stigma-neutralizing vocabularies of motive, embezzlers (Cressey, 1953) manage to steal money yet continue to regard themselves as basically honest. Even after they are caught, embezzlers struggle to maintain a positive self-image in the face of accusations of dishonesty. After all, these were upstanding pillars of their communities. They claim that they did not intend to steal, that they were not thieves, that they were not dishonest. "I was just borrowing," they say, "I intended to return the money eventually." At some point, they realize they were "in too deep," that they could never repay the money, and the self-justifying facade of their accounts collapses like a house of cards.

Juvenile delinquents usually offer a wide variety of explanations for their actions, including a denial of responsibility (or a "billiard ball" image of their behavior); an appeal to higher loyalties ("I couldn't let my buddies down"); an invocation of deserving victims ("I had to do it—he was dissing me"); a denial of injury ("He wasn't hurt so bad"); and a condemnation of the condemners ("The police do a lot worse things than we do"). As a result of these accounts, delinquents deflect the condemnation they know is coming their way (Sykes and Matza, 1957).

Child molesters (McCaghy, 1967, 1968) explain their actions with the use of a variety of accounts, including that they have a drinking problem and were drunk of the time of their offense ("I was drunk. I didn't realize their age"). Some even find the act so repulsive that a positive self-identity would be threatened by admitting that they engaged in it. Hence, they deny, even to themselves, that they actually committed it.

The professional fence explains his participation in selling stolen goods by emphasizing that he is not a thief. Says one fence: "I don't do nothing wrong. . . . The way I look at it, I'm a businessman. Sure, I buy hot stuff, but I never stole nothin' in my life. Some driver brings me a couple a cartons [of merchandise], though, I ain't gonna turn him away. If I don't buy it, somebody else will. So what's the difference? I might as well make money with him instead of somebody else" (Klockars, 1974, p. 139).

Convicted rapists, too, resort to vocabularies of motive in order to advance the claim that they are acceptable, self-respecting human beings. Many admit having had sex with the women they were sent to prison for having assaulted, but they "disavow" that a rape took place. It was consensual, they claim: "She wanted it," "She was willing," "She was asking for it." Others admit having raped but regard having unlimited sexual access to women as a man's prerogative: "Rape is a man's right. If a woman doesn't want to give it, the man should take it. Women have no right to say no. Women are made to have sex. It's all they are good for" (Scully, 1990; Scully and Marolla, 1984, 1985, p. 261).

Male street hustlers, who have sex with homosexuals for pay, deny that they are engaged in "real" sex. Instead, they justify the act by claiming that they engaged in it solely for the money; they did not initiate it; they remain emotionally aloof from the parties with whom they engaged in it; they received no gratification from it; and, above all, their participation in it does not indicate in any way that they are homosexuals (Calhoun, 1992; Reiss, 1964).

An extremely high proportion of college students admit they have cheated. In fact, more than half say they have done so at least once during their undergraduate careers. The majority of these cheaters use one or another of a variety of deviance neutralization techniques and choose to blame others and/or the situational context for their behavior. Many feel they aren't responsible; it's the system that's at fault: "It's the only way to keep up," "In today's competitive world you do anything to keep up," "Most of the class cheats." Others deny that there is a victim—in effect, "No one gets hurt." Some blame the fraternity and sorority system for organized cheating, putting them at an unfair disadvantage; others blame the special coddling of athlete-students. In short, most of the cheaters feel that they have very good reasons for breaking the rules (McCabe, 1992).

Nurses who steal drugs from hospital cabinets justify their behavior by saying that the drugs improve their "disposition" and, hence, make them better caregivers. Moreover, they make a sharp distinction between stealing less potent, non-narcotic drugs, such as Valium and Darvocet, and the more potent narcotics, such as morphine. Hence, their minor thefts fade into insignificance while their opposition to the theft of the major drugs seems virtuous, almost saintly (Dabney, 1995).

In short, stigma neutralization is a major component of deviance. While all of us engage in vocabularies of motive, persons who have been or are likely to be challenged, criticized, or condemned for their behavior, beliefs, or physical characteristics are especially prone to do so. Indeed, accounting for their unconventional behavior is a central task for deviants or potential deviants; the enterprise of deviance is almost inconceivable without it.

In a society such as ours, conventionals and unconventionals mingle shoulder-to-shoulder. Almost no rule violators could be unaware of the views of the majority toward their deviations or themselves *as* deviators. All are forced to conduct a kind of internal dialogue with the conventional majority which goes something like this. I am aware of the fact that you consider prostitution—or homosexuality, alcoholism, obesity, sadomasochism, dealing drugs, child molestation, or being a dwarf—as abnormal, offensive, or reprehensible. Since I belong to one of these categories, you consider me to be the sort of person who deserves to be stigmatized, shunned, and condemned. The fact is, I believe, I do not really deserve this stigma; I feel you do not have the right to direct it at me, and here are some very good reasons why. Vocabularies of motive are born out of precisely this internal dialogue of someone whose behavior, beliefs, or traits may be challenged (a real or potential "unconventional") by an audience (real or potential "conventionals"). The more influence conventionals have over unconventionals, and the more intimate they are with them, the more necessary these stigma neutralizing accounts become. In the world of deviance, they are everywhere.

Deviance vocabularies of motive often challenge the legitimacy of conventional accounts of deviance, occasionally to the point where they offer a viable and plausible cultural alternative to how behavior is explained and understood. In the accounts that follow, we should pay close attention to the vocabularies of motive of our contributors. Some of them are offering us a glimpse into our future.

Please notice that accounts and vocabularies of motive are not the *cause* of the behavior they address; stigma neutralization is not an *explanation* of deviance, as many observers mistakenly believe (Siegel, 2000, pp. 232–234). Delinquents cannot be distinguished from non-delinquents, homosexuals from heterosexuals, prostitutes from non-prostitutes, or tattooed from tattoo-free persons by virtue of the fact that the former have managed to justify a form of behavior before committing it while the latter cannot. An examination of the facts simply does not support such an explanation. The fact is, neutralization techniques are part and parcel of the deviance process, almost inevitably arising when we engage in a mental dialogue with conventional others who are likely to undermine our respectability and decency. They may be verbalized before, during, or after the questionable behavior is enacted, the controversial belief is expressed, or the discrediting trait is acquired, and they may be learned from a subculture or formulated independently. But *whenever* and *however* stigma neutralization is formulated, it cannot be thought of as a reason *why* an actor engaged in deviant behavior. I propose a very different view. All persons who face being defined as deviants face the menace of stigma, potential or real, and all likewise find neutralizing that stigma appealing.

ERVING GOFFMAN AS A SOCIOLOGIST OF DEVIANCE

It is possible that the only sociologist born in the twentieth century whose work will be read hundreds of years into the future is Erving Goffman. When he died in 1982 at the age of 60, Goffman left behind an impressive body of work. Known for his keen insight into the human condition, he wrote with wit, grace, and a generous measure of what can only be described as detached cynicism. Paradoxically, Goffman felt uncomfortable with the concept of deviance (1963, pp. 140–147), yet he also provided some of the central ideas for a study of deviance in everyday life. This book is by no means intended to systematically illustrate, explicate, or elaborate Goffman's ideas on deviance. Rather, his insights provide a *point of departure* for an understanding of the subject. Here are several of his most basic insights: *stigma*; *breaking frame*; *normalization*; *abnormalization*; *where the action is*; *the presentation of self in everyday life*; and, most importantly, *the perspective of the deviant*.

Stigma. The title of one of Goffman's most important books is the foundation-stone of deviance. The normative structure of all societies provides a system of *grading* or *evaluating* members on the basis of key characteristics or features. Goffman explores how three basic features of all humans can turn into badges of demerit. Two are relevant here.

One is the physical characteristics one might possess, mostly unchosen and unwanted, which Goffman refers to as "abominations of the body— the various deformities" (1963, p. 4). Here he includes blindness, physical disability, extreme ugliness, obesity, the possession of disfiguring mutilations, and so on. And second, there are the more or less voluntary behaviors and beliefs, or "blemishes of individual character perceived as weak will, domineering or unnatural passions, treacherous and rigid beliefs, and dishonesty, these being inferred from a known record of, for example, mental disorder, imprisonment, addiction, alcoholism, homosexuality, unemployment, suicidal attempts, and radical political behavior" (p. 4).

In short, Goffman's discussion in *Stigma* details a system of grading people according to their possession or lack of desirable traits or characteristics. To the extent that we fail to meet societal standards, we are likely to be judged unnatural and abnormal and hence, "discredited," "disqualified from full social acceptance," regarded as "not quite human." Given the consequences of such an evaluation, most people who possess discrediting characteristics try to keep them a secret; in the presence of others, they exercise "information control." When persons have become publicly discredited, they often align themselves with others who are in a similar situation, which often produces a variety of paradoxes, ambivalences, and dilemmas.

Breaking frame. Although the two concepts were formulated completely independently of one another, a great deal of deviant behavior entails what Goffman referred to as "breaking frame" (1974, pp. 345ff.). A *frame* is a definition of a situation, a conceptual and cognitive interpretation of appropriate behavior and demeanor within a given context or setting. Frames spell out the nature and degree of involvement of relevant actors, and they imply that others who are incorporated into the frame must share more or less the same definition of the situation and will act accordingly. We all agree that being sad is part of the "attending a funeral" frame; hence, laughing at a funeral breaks frame. Everyone knows that a professor is not supposed to be intoxicated while lecturing. Public speaking is not supposed to be accompanied by complete silence, incoherent babbling, uncontrollable facial tics and twitches, or violent bodily contortions. Belching or breaking wind at an elegant dinner party, likewise, violates widely-held normative expectations and thus, breaks frame.

A measure of agreement on the content of frames is necessary for smooth social relations. Hence, a "love-making" frame is accompanied by a kind of script, supposedly guiding the action of the parties involved, which include a number of behavioral and emotional particulars.

What happens when one or more parties do not share the same interpretation of appropriate behavior within a given frame? Unless a reconciliation can be reached, the result is likely to be mutual annoyance, bafflement, and antagonism. Two partners may in fact not share the same love-making frame. When one attempts to act on a given frame, the other will reject that definition of the situation. For instance, if one partner's love-making frame includes total privacy and the other attempts to make love in a crowded elevator, the first will insist that the action of the second is inappropriate, that is, it "breaks frame"; he or she is mixing a "riding in a crowded elevator" frame with a love-making frame.

Violations of frame will take place when an actor is unwilling to sustain or incapable of sustaining what is considered appropriate behavior in a particular context. Overcome by emotion, an actor may begin "flooding out" (pp. 350–359). At a dinner party, the hostess, distraught over problems with her children and her husband, breaks down and begins crying. In the middle of an operatic performance, a singer, irate at being heckled, insults the audience, and storms off to his dressing room (pp. 369–370). As a chamber music recital is about to begin, a whispered joke by one performer to another causes the second to convulse with helpless laughter (p. 351). In the middle of a discussion, a professor, angry that his students are not doing the work or learning the material, begins screaming at the class. All of these emotional outbursts break frame because they violate expectations regarding the appropriate behavior in these social contexts.

More generally, much of polite social interaction entails what Goffman refers to as "the appearance of social reserve" (p. 375). Being proper often entails being cool, that is, acting out the demands of one's role without displaying undue or inappropriate emotional involvement. Students and professors are not supposed to become emotionally involved with one another; dinner guests are not supposed to scream at on another; strangers are not supposed to embrace and kiss one another; waiters are not supposed to giggle at their customers. Frames are broken when these rules are violated. Of course, when a frame *demands* a certain measure of emotional involvement, too much reserve breaks frame. Lovers are not supposed to be emotionally cool and distant toward one another; audiences at a concert or a lecture are not supposed to act bored; students should not read a newspaper or talk to one another during a class; a well-paid prostitute should at least fake minimal interest in a client.

Frames also include norms that govern appropriate behavior for a particular type of person. Voters consider "good moral character" part and parcel of the politician frame and will react negatively when they discover that a candidate is a homosexual, a frequenter of prostitutes, or a drunkard. To these voters, homosexuality, patronizing prostitutes, and alcoholism are a violation of the politician frame. Goffman (p. 277) cites the example of Marilyn Chambers, once the model for Ivory Snow, a soap product touted for its "purity." When Chambers was discovered to have acted in pornographic films, her photographic image was removed from boxes of Ivory Snow. Procter & Gamble executives clearly regarded the pornography frame ("dirty") as incompatible with the soap frame ("clean").

Stated as broadly as possible, conventionality is a frame that is violated or broken by one or more deviant actions, beliefs, and physical characteristics. For most of us, in most settings, conventionality is expected. Adultery breaks the marriage frame, homosexuality breaks the expected heterosexuality frame, alcoholism breaks the social drinking frame, obesity breaks esthetic and health frames, all manner of mental disorders break the normalcy frame, and so on. Goffman's definition of frame is maddeningly unclear (Burns, 1992, p. 248). Still, my guess is that it is unlikely that Goffman included the full range of conventionality as falling within the scope of his understanding of "frame," or the full range of deviance as "breaking frame." I would nonetheless argue that it is fruitful to think of them as such. Perhaps the accounts in this book will document this assertion.

Normalization. All social systems strive to make their rules seem reasonable, just, and well founded. The exercise of power inevitably entails the rationalization or justification of the existing social hierarchy. Goffman chose the total institution, including the prison and the mental hospital, as a locus for the explication of this theme of normalization. In total institutions, as in society generally, agents of power exercise their power on the basis of author-ity—that is, making it clear that they possess the *right* to exercise power. The institution *strips* inmates of any and all measure of personal identity or sense of self, *regiments* inmates' lives and *degrades* inmates so that their autonomy is obliterated—all in the name of therapeutic or correctional goals.

In efforts "to control inmates and defend the institution in the name of its avowed aims," staff resorts to a kind of "all-embracing identification of the inmates" (1961, p. 85). In a mental hospital, anything and everything becomes evidence of a mental disorder; in a prison, anything and every-thing becomes evidence of wrongdoing. As soon as the inmate enters the institution, it is staff's job to convince him or her that he or she is "the kind of person the institution was set up to handle" (p. 84). Any and all efforts by the inmate to establish his or her normalcy must be countered by staff; any and all features of his or her life, however irrelevant, offer raw mate-rial for normalization. Any and all behavior or statements made by inmates become the basis of justifying institutional intervention. Only by adopting the perspective of the institution—that is to say, by abandoning their autonomy and sense of self—will inmates be judged to have made sufficient progress to be released, at which time they will be granted the autonomy and sense of self that was stripped away on admission.

Total institutions are at once unique yet paradigmatic social phenom-ena (1961, p. 5). Persons whom society deems deviants are rarely as strongly subject to the weight and intensity of societal normalization when they are *outside* the total institution as when they are *confined* to one. Still, deviants do interface with society's processes of normalization when they are at large. Teachers, psychiatrists, social workers, case workers, police officers, parole and probation officers, lawyers, and physicians are called upon to remind the miscreant, *if you stray, you pay.*

There are very good—and very rational—reasons why this should be the case, the process of normalization tells us. The expertise of the author-ity figure is called upon to provide a justification for society's reactions to the wrongdoer. The deviant cannot escape these justifications; they color the ways in which wrongdoing is conducted and how persons judged as doing wrong construct their mental and experiential worlds. The notion of normalization powerfully anticipated the thinking of Michel Foucault (Burns, 1992, p. 142), especially in his influential and widely-cited *Disci-pline and Punish* (1979). Society employs the full weight of its scientific and medical expertise to justify its judgments about deviants, their behavior, and what should be done about them. Objecting to such judgments or the legitimacy on which they rest merely emphasizes the deviant's abnormality.

Abnormalization is the mirror image of normalization. Just as society justifies and rationalizes its power over the inmate in the total institution, it also justifies and rationalizes its judgments of the norm violator at large.

Cloaked in the drapery of expertise and scientific rationality, society attempts to ensure conformity to what is defined as normality. Conventional members of society infuse details of deviants' everyday lives with the taint of the central character flaws—their deviance.

Where the action is. Goffman conducted field research in the gambling casinos of Reno and Las Vegas and published an account of that research in his essay, "Where the Action Is" (1967, pp. 149–270). *Fatefulness,* a crucial key to "action," is that the choice an actor makes determines a given outcome. Goffman defines "action" as "activities that are consequential, problematic, and undertaken for what is felt to be their own sake" (p. 185). Consequentiality refers to the fact that the outcome of an endeavor has a real-life impact (pp. 159–160). "Problematic" means that the outcome is far from certain. In fact, "action" implies that one can lose as well as win, sometimes disastrously so. In other words, what Goffman is talking about in "action" is *risk*, which the dictionary defines as exposure to the chance of injury, loss, or hazard in order to obtain something of value. As we might expect, the type of action that most embodies "action" is gambling, posing, as it does, the simultaneous risk of losing and the prospect of winning given sums of money.

In offering the actor "action," deviance would seem *almost* as prototypical a human endeavor as gambling. In many of its varieties, deviance conveys most of Goffman's basic elements, including fatefulness, consequentiality, problematicity, and risk. Deviance is often fateful. Engaging or not engaging in a specific line of action often has important consequences. Exposing or not exposing one's deviant status to others, likewise, is likely to lead one down a fateful path. Given its social unacceptability, to the extent that there is a choice in the matter, deviance almost inevitably entails risk and, quite often, the mirror possibility of gain. Even the person with a physical defect who attempts ordinary interaction risks social rejection from "normals." Examples of deviance and crime abound in Goffman's essay, including: the use of LSD and other psychoactive drugs (p. 201); homosexuality and the one night stand—or the "part-of-the-night stand" (p. 211); heterosexual seduction and the tendency for male promiscuity (p. 197); "perverse" sexual activities (p. 197); lower-class juvenile delinquency (pp. 212–214, 267); criminal occupations as a means of livelihood (pp. 173, 182); poolroom hustling (p. 185); and prostitution (p. 188).

The sociologist of deviance whose work has made the most use of Goffman's concept of "action" is Jack Katz. In *Seductions of Crime: Moral and Sensual Attractions in Doing Evil* (1988), Katz discusses a number of risky, action-oriented illegal activities that offer both the allure of excitement and the threat of danger. In fact, it is their very danger that is alluring to participants. Many crimes are much like a game (leading to what Katz calls "the ludic metaphor") or competition in which there is a clear winner and a clear loser; the loser is defiled and desecrated, the winner emerges in transcendental triumph (pp. 52–79). With every job, robbers risk their lives—and the lives of their victims—in an effort to generate a type of "action" so intense and heated that its very achievement marks one as the ultimate "badass" (pp. 80ff.). Murder, the most horrific of crimes, is often the product of rage born of humiliation—the act of killing representing the obliteration of that humiliation, a *vindication* of one's humanity in an all-encompassing explosion of righteousness (pp. 12–51, 274–309). In short, crime possesses an alluring, seductive quality that transcends simple utilitarian calculation. "What are people doing when they commit a crime?" Katz asks (p. 9). His answer is that they are engaging in a consequential action-seeking activity that offers reward and risk in the same package. Indeed, the reward is *embedded* in the risk. If Goffman had been alive when Katz's book was published and he had been asked for extreme examples of "Where the Action Is," my guess is, he would have pointed to the behaviors discussed in *Seductions of Crime*.

The presentation of self in everyday life. A central feature of Goffman's writings is a conception of society imposing rules on its members and its members acting in accordance with—or with the awareness of—those rules (Burns, 1992, p. 129). To the extent that conduct, beliefs, or appearance violate society's notion of acceptability, members will attempt to control access to discrediting information. In many contexts, the alcoholic, the homeless, or the homosexual attempt to "pass" for someone—or something—they are not by concealing signs of deviance or displaying signs of respectability. Indeed, information about their unacceptable conduct, beliefs, or appearance may be so discrediting that, even when conventional members of the society stumble upon it, they often collude with the deviant by pretending not to notice *that* they notice (Goffman, 1959, pp. 230–232).

When we enter into the presence of others, says Goffman, we commonly seek to acquire information about them or to make use of the information we already possess (Goffman, 1959, p. 1). Our information is based in part on visible signs or clues about which we draw inferences. We "decide" what people are like and what they are likely to do on the basis of what we see of them. At the same time, these clues to the other's character are partly under the control of the persons who are under our observation. Hence, they can project clues about their own character that they want us to observe so we will draw favorable inferences about them.

Likewise, they will strive to hide certain clues from our scrutinizing gaze. In short, all of us are engaged in a theatrical strategy of impression management. There is nearly always a measure of distance between the impression and the reality in what passes for naturalistic social interaction. We try to project a certain image to others that will yield maximum benefit for us and we try to hide discrediting information. Of course, not everything is under our control. Often, our images "leak" compromising information. In social life, says Goffman, we are performers, although some of us are a great deal better at it than others. Some types of social interactions are more likely than others to involve more strategies of impression management. In those situations, the image projected will be more starkly discrepant with reality. Peers, equals, and friends usually see more natural and less staged displays than strangers and unequals. For instance, Goffman would say that personnel who work in hotels and restaurants are more likely to stage their dealings with tourists and customers than is true of relations between and among friends, gang members, and relatives.

Some interacting parties perform their roles with one another in "regions." A "front region" is where the performance is held; a "back region" or "backstage" offers more cues to insiders (pp. 106, 107). In the backstage, almost by its very nature, information is revealed that contradicts the performance given in the front region. In other words, when performers can "be themselves" or "let their hair down," they reveal intimacies they don't want certain other interacting parties to know. Waiters and waitresses talk to one another revealingly and critically concerning their feelings about their customers. In the presence of their supervisors, workers appear industrious; they goof off only beyond their supervisors' gaze. Physicians talk about their patients to one another in ways that would seem offensive and a betrayal of altruistic intent to the patients themselves.

Occasionally, as a result of an inadvertent intrusion by a member of the audience into the backstage region, the frontstage performance is revealed to be a sham. Embarrassment usually follows or, less frequently, a "scene" in which the intruder tells the performer off or lets the performer "have it." Most often, however, both performer and audience are motivated to "avoid making a scene." We are more likely to cooperate by seeming to be taken in by the performance. Both performer and audience collude in the maintenance of the same definition of the situation. All social interaction requires a measure of deception, Goffman seems to be saying; too much truth is painful and disruptive. Perhaps it is more deviant, he implies, to demand the brutal, naked truth than to deceive and collude in being deceived. All of us are performers; in effect, all of us are liars. Social life can't work any other way, he argues.

The perspective of the deviant. Perhaps the main reason why Goffman's work is so directly relevant to the accounts in this book is that it avoids the externalistic gaze of the scientist and adopts the perspective of the person who is subject to society's judgments of deviance. In *Asylums*, Goffman proclaims that his view is frankly *partisan*, that it is his intention to learn about the social world of the inmate *as it is subjectively experienced by him or her*. In *Stigma*, we *feel* what it is like to be "disqualified from full social acceptance." Marcia Millman says Goffman "writes about what the world looks like to the person who is pushed around and taken advantage of" (1975, p. 273).

Another way of saying this is that Goffman's work invites *empathy* or what Max Weber referred to as *Verstehen*: the emotional capacity to see, experience, and appreciate the world from the point of view of another person. In my view, empathy is a central goal of the sociology of deviance. Getting inside someone's head and skin permits us to understand what it *means* to act in a certain way, to hold certain beliefs, to possess certain

characteristics that are disvalued, and to be stigmatized and socially discredited. It is one thing to read the results of a survey, chock full of statistics, tables, charts, and graphs. It is quite another to read the words of
someone who has gone through the experience you are trying to understand. Statistics are the product of an external or *objective* understanding.
They tell us a great deal, but they do not tell us enough. In fact, they leave
a gaping hole in our ability to comprehend the reality of deviance.

Empathy taps a very different type of understanding—a subjective,
internal, or *emotional* kind of understanding. It allows us to grasp deviance from the inside out, so to speak—to possess the actor's, believer's, or
possessor's understanding of the deviant experience. Goffman's work has
that rare quality of inviting the reader to get inside the deviant's skin and
to experience what it feels like to be born without a nose, to be the daughter of a convict, to be committed to a mental hospital, to live the daily
rounds as an inmate in a total institution. This quality characterizes far too
few sociologists of deviance.

For instance, Goffman writes that, in the face of institutional definitions (the twin processes of "normalization" and "abnormalization" mentioned above) persons designated as deviant attempt to carve out a
meaningful and dignified definition of themselves and their identities,
ones that in many ways contradict those fostered by the institutions that
confine them. While Goffman's insight into these adaptations to institutional life may not offer the image of outright revolt and rebellion that
some analysts claim characterizes the lives of the deviants to which we
ought to pay attention (Gouldner, 1968; Hebdige, 1979; Piven, 1981;
Smith, 1973), it does tell us a great deal more about institutional life as it
is actually lived. Says Goffman:

> Whenever worlds are laid on, underlives will develop. . . . When exist-
> ence is cut to the bone, we can learn what people do to flesh out their
> lives. Stashes, means of transportation, free places, territories, supplies
> for economic and social exchange—these are some of the minimal
> requirements for building up a life. Ordinarily, these arrangements are
> taken for granted as part of one's primary adjustment; seeing them
> twisted out of official existence through bargains, wit, force, and cun-
> ning, we can see their existence anew. The study of total
> institutions . . . suggests that formal organizations have standard places
> of vulnerability, such as supply rooms, sick bays, kitchens, or scenes of
> highly technical labor. These are the damp corners where secondary
> adjustments breed and start to infest the establishment. (1961, p. 305)

Prisoners accumulate items that reveal their individuality and subvert
their anonymity (1961, p. 307). Mental patients create a kind of personal
territory, much like a nest, to which they have access and over which they
exert control (pp. 243–244). Patients and inmates often "overdetermine"
certain recreational activities—that is, become intensely involved in them,
temporarily blocking out their institutional status (pp. 308–314); here,

Goffman uses the example of the infamous "Birdman of Alcatraz," Robert Stroud (p. 309). In all total institutions, practices of "ritual insubordination" develop that are rich in irony and incipient rebellion (pp. 315–318).

Although far more literary and metaphorical than empirical, the work of French sociologist Michel de Certeau (1984) parallels Goffman's insights on adopting the actor's perspective. Rather than looking at society from the top down, as is the practice of most sociologists, Certeau's point of view is focused on the view from the bottom—how the so-called "common" man and woman "inhabit" the structures in which they live. He explores in detail the human need to establish autonomy and independence in structures that are designed to obliterate our uniqueness. He argues that social institutions, such as the grammar, rules, and accepted practices of speaking a language, the way that cities are laid out, systems of transportation, beliefs about such matters as religion and death, norms surrounding cooking and eating, and the basic design and structure of the dwellings in which we live demand an operational use that follows specific principles of practice. But, Certeau asserts, everyday users or inhabitants of these institutions do not necessarily follow the dominant principles demanded by them. In fact, they adapt these institutions to their own purposes and needs. People "reappropriate" rules, regulations, and dominant practices in ways that *deflect* institutional principles and mandates. Far from being regimented—far from conforming to the rules of an "anthill society"—people "pluralize" rules and institutions, produce "mutations" of them in their everyday lives; they "borrow" them, "wander out of orbit" from them. No institution is so confining that the uniqueness and individuality of persons subject to them is ever obliterated.

In short, to Goffman and Certeau, when an institution attempts to "normalize" its judgments and its rule and "abnormalize" the behavior and character of the inhabitants subject to their control, those inhabitants will develop a way of living and operating that "conveys a moral rejection" of the dominant institutional processes. The countermeasures offer the inmate defense or sanctuary against the "social bondedness" demanded by the organization (p. 319). Our individuality, our selfhood, says Goffman, resides in the "cracks" we find in otherwise monolithic social institutions. This is true of the total institution.

"May this not be the situation," Goffman inquires rhetorically, "in free society, too?" (p. 320).

Casper and I will come out of the movie and I'll tell him, he'll go through Who Framed Roger Rabbit? and get holes and after he pushed through the glass on the TV, and the glass will disappear, and I'll go in and get Flora, Fauna, and Merriweather's magic wands, and the animals, especially Chewy and Clover, and the humans, especially me, except the Nazis, will live forever.
Danny

Danny, the Autistic Artist

I watch Danny step off the bus. Can anyone tell? I wonder. Tell at a glance I mean. Maybe. His attention is focused on all the wrong places, I decide. Still, he's a handsome lad, I say to myself with what is probably compensatory satisfaction. As he's walking toward me, he's drawing something in the air with his left index finger, his face scrunched up in concentration. Gray sweatshirt, black sweat pants, white sneakers. I approach him. "Danny, how are you?" I ask, looking closely at his hazel eyes. There are times when I see him walking along, he looks almost normal, like a regular little boy. I get choked up and tears come to my eyes thinking about what both of us are missing. What he'll never have, what I'll never have. Regular father-son activities. Baseball. Fishing. Guy talks. Proud hugs. Homework. Plans. Talks about friends, girlfriends, dates, school, sports. I feel such anguish for the little guy. And for me.

45

Despair. A sense of hopelessness, even terror. What's going to become of Little Danny?

He keeps walking toward me but begins staring at the cobblestones in the roadway. "I'm OK." He stops and begins staring at the trees. "Dad, you're here," he announces vaguely.

"Of course I'm here. You knew I was coming, didn't you?"

"When this is done, will you take me home?" he asks, his face tilted toward mine.

"We'll see, Danny. Let's learn something while you're here, OK?"

Danny nods. I greet his aide, Mrs. Scioto, and two of his teachers, Mrs. Cassese and Mrs. Lesserson. They corral first a guard, then a guide, and ask where the class is supposed to go. No one seems to know. We go to one building then another, trailing forty ten- and eleven-year-olds behind us. Finally, at the end of a cobblestone road, a building ejects a guide who tells us we are early. We are asked to wait for another class that is receiving instruction. The children sit on the grass in all-boy and all-girl clusters of two, three, and four. Danny sprawls in the dirt by himself and scrutinizes the ground for something of interest. Standing, I chat with the teachers for a few minutes, learning that Mrs. Cassese's son is a lacrosse player for Duke. She often travels with the team, she says, and occasionally brings them food. Lacrosse mom. I am jealous, acutely aware that my son may never attend college—and certainly not one as academically rigorous as Duke—or, chances are, even play an organized sport of any kind.

We have assembled at the Vanderbilt Museum and Planetarium for a class trip. My son, Danny, soon to be twelve years old, attends fifth grade at Scraggy Hill Elementary School. Although diagnosed as autistic, he has been mainstreamed only a year behind his grade level. Danny does have a full-time aide, Mrs. Scioto, but I have been asked to help keep him under control during this field trip when he'll be in unfamiliar surroundings. I try to stick fairly close to him to make sure he doesn't run off or damage something.

I squat down near the ground next to Danny and try to engage him in conversation. I pluck a dandelion and hold it in front of his face. "Danny, how many petals do you think this dandelion has?" I ask. He gives the flower a brief glance, then turns away and begins talking about the Blue Meanies. *Yellow Submarine* is his latest obsession. "A hundred?" I pull off a petal and begin counting. "One . . ." I pull off another; "two. . . ."

"Was the Chief Blue Meanie good or bad to yell at Max, 'We Meanies only take *no* for an answer!'?" He enunciates each word with a great deal of emotion, even vehemence.

"Three. . . ."

A girl sitting next to Danny has caught a tiny beetle. It is perched on her index finger. "Danny," she says, "look at the bug." He's not interested. He begins staring at the ground again.

"Danny, look at the beetle" I demand. My effort is in vain. Rebuffed, the girl looks away and chats with her friend, ignoring Danny. Finally, two guides arrive and the group is separated according to teacher. We are led around to the basement floor of the building, into a room whose windows face the Long Island Sound. The ceiling is low, the walls are white, and folding chairs are arranged in a circle. The guide asks the children to take a seat. Two girls call out, "Danny, sit here," each patting the seat between them, but he wedges himself between one of them and the occupied seat next to her. "I want to sit next to *John*," he insists. John barely glances at Danny, and the girl obliges, shifting to the seat next to her friend.

"Today, we are going to talk about the principles of biological classification," the guide begins. I groan silently, rolling my eyes to the ceiling. Next to reasoning, classification is probably the thing autistic children are worst at, I think. They have their own, idiosyncratic, classification schemes, of course, but it is hard for them to make sense of those that are based on sort of commonly accepted criteria of rationality. Kingdom, phylum, class, order, family, genus, species—how can the poor little guy sort it all out? I ask myself. I shake my head.

Danny's studying the patterns of slate on the floor. I lean down and whisper to him, "Danny, are you paying attention?" He says he is and turns to the guide. She asks the class to break up into groups of three and four, and Mrs. Lesserson, Danny's resource teacher, corrals two girls to make sure Danny is included in a group. In front of each group, the guide pours a pile of small objects onto a pasteboard chart lying flat on a table. On each chart, there are branches and circles indicating classes of phenomena. The kids are asked to arrange the objects— wooden, glass, and plastic beads of different sizes and colors, and elbow, bowtie, and corkscrew macaroni—into categories according to similarities and differences. Danny holds two tiny, red glass beads in the palm of his hand as if mesmerized by them. The two girls are busy sorting out the other objects and placing them on the chart in small piles.

"Danny, where do these glass beads go?" I ask him. "Here?" I ask, pointing to a pile of fat, red wooden beads. "Or here?" I point to a group of smaller beads. "Or by themselves?" One of the girls takes the glass beads out of Danny's hand and places them first in one, then in the other category.

"I think they belong by themselves. What do you think, Danny?" He doesn't answer. Suddenly, he looks up and screams, "A yellow jacket!"

and races to the window, swatting at the air. Mrs. Scioto jumps up and, trying to be stern, commands, "Danny, let's sit down!" He turns from the window and returns to his seat. I heave a sigh when the guide sums up her spiel on classification and tells the class to follow her to the following exhibit in the building next door.

We walk into a garage, past a 1928 Packard resting on a circular, rotating platform, and make our way one flight up to a large exhibition hall. Stuffed animals inhabit a diorama, and heads and skulls of animals line the walls. The kids are told to sit on the floor. Above our heads is a huge painting of Vanderbilt with a rifle tucked under his arm, standing in front of a dead elephant. Several African guides are smiling, standing atop the carcass of the downed beast. Our guide apologizes for the depictions and harvest of carnage and explains that wealthy men in those days did that sort of thing. Still, she says, maybe we can learn from what they bequeathed us. Danny looks around at the walls and shouts out, "Dead animals!"

I lean down, shush him, and whisper. "Danny, the guide is speaking. Try to be quiet and learn something."

"Their heads are cut off!" he announces. Once again, I try to keep him quiet. Abruptly, he lurches up and rushes to one wall and begins reading the plaques beneath each animal head. I get up and try to keep his voice down at least to a whisper. Suddenly, he grabs a mallet and strikes the Chinese gong resting on the exhibition case. Loudly. Everyone's attention turns to Danny. The children giggle. I grab the mallet away from him and admonish him.

"Danny, for goodness sake," I whisper loudly, "could you please sit down and pay attention!"

When he sits down, the sneaker of the kid next to him brushes against his leg. "Hey!" Danny shouts, "you *kicked* me!" I lean down, prepared to intervene, but the kid apologizes in a sincere tone of voice. Danny seems satisfied by the apology. Several animal parts—a giraffe jawbone, a turtle shell, the pelt of a wallaby—are passed around. Aside from wiggling the giraffe's teeth, Danny shows no interest in them. At some point, mercifully, the guide instructs us to move on to the next exhibit.

The "aquarium" is a large, long hall with stuffed fish in glass cases against the walls. The guide explains that Vanderbilt was a collector of animals and financed many expeditions. In fact, she says, he discovered a species of crab, naming it after his wife, and a species of crayfish, naming it after the Vanderbilt family. The children seem not to be impressed. They are given an assignment: Pick out a fish and draw it. Paper and pencils are distributed and the kids fan out, clipboards in hand, searching through the glass cases for a suitable model. A gigantic manta ray adorns the far wall; as far as I can tell, none of the kids decide to draw it. I see one girl drawing a poisonous sea snake; one boy has selected a giant marlin.

Danny settles on what surely must be the dullest, drabbest fish in the entire exhibit. It is a pearly, off-white color with no distinguishing features; it has the shape of a generic, all-purpose fish. But Danny draws it in three different shades of yellow, rendering it more dramatic and forceful than the fish in real life could ever have been. I am reminded of the drawing by Oliver Sacks' patient, José—"The Autist Artist"—who drew a leaping trout using an illustration as a model. "The original had lacked character," says Sacks, "had looked lifeless, two-dimensional, even stuffed. José's fish, by contrast, tilted and poised, was richly three-dimensional, far more like a real fish than the original" (1990, p. 218). Danny had achieved something even more remarkable: His drawing of a fish looked more lifelike than a real (although stuffed) fish.

We show it to the guide and to both of Danny's teachers. All praise his work. Danny is indeed an "autist artist." He looks at me. "Can I go home with you now, Dad?" he asks.

I look at Mrs. Cassese and Mrs. Lesserson. They shrug. "Why not?" they say in unison.

"Sure, Danny, we can go home now" I inform him.

Driving home, I decide to find out if Danny's learned anything. "Danny, do you remember what the teacher said about the kingdoms of living things? What are the two kingdoms, Danny?"

"I don't know," he responds.

"What kingdom does that tree belong to, Danny?"

"I don't know.

"Is it alive?"

"Yes, it's alive."

"Is it an animal or a plant?"

"A plant."

"Good, Danny, it's a plant. What makes plants different from animals?"

"I don't know."

"Plants can make their own . . ."

"Food."

"Good. And animals can't. OK, what about humans? What kingdom do we belong to?"

"I don't know."

"We belong to the animal kingdom, Danny."

"No we don't. Animals are *not* humans."

"Well, what are we? Plants? Mushrooms? Are we tiny, microscopic microbes, bacteria, germs?"

"No, but we're not animals."

"What are we, then, Danny?"

"We're just humans. We're not animals."

"OK, Danny, but the guide who showed us around the museum would disagree. She said that humans are part of the animal kingdom."

"Well, she's wrong."

Autism is typically first diagnosed in early childhood. Parents usually become aware of the condition in their child when he or she exhibits what is euphemistically referred to as a "speech delay"—an inability to verbally communicate at the appropriate age, usually by two or three. Most children whose speech is delayed are not autistic. Perhaps two out of every 1,000 children are autistic. The American Psychiatric Association's *Diagnostic and Statistical Manual of Mental Disorders* (1994) describes the condition as characterized by "the presence of markedly abnormal or impaired development in social interaction and communication and a markedly restricted repertoire of activity and interests" (p. 66).

Autism presents the sociologist of deviance with a variety of intriguing issues. It is a spectrum disorder rather than an either-or proposition, running the gamut in seriousness from near-normalcy to severe and complete incapacity and disablement. (In addition, a sizeable number of autistic persons possess one or more extraordinary skills, such as chess, calendar calculation, or graphic art.) Hence, one issue of interest to the sociologist becomes how professionals diagnose a specific child as suffering from the disorder.

How do parents accept and come to grips with the fact that their child is most decidedly not like other children and that he or she has a condition that is recognized by psychiatrists and psychologists practically the world over? Is autism an arbitrary social construction or a clear-cut phenomenon or "syndrome" in the material or so-called "real" world? How do parents accomplish the juggling act that answers to these questions demand? When Barbara and I were first making the rounds of diagnosis to determine what was wrong with Danny (the classic "speech delay") and treatment to determine what we should do about it, we had several sessions with a child psychologist who showed us a videotape that demonstrated the Lovaas method of treating autism (1977). We were stunned by the exact parallels between the behavior of the children being treated by Dr. Lovaas and that of our Danny. When the tape was over and the psychologist turned the lights back on, he was startled to see that Barbara and I had been crying. Before we saw that tape, we knew Danny's behavior was odd but we felt it could be corrected. After all, he wasn't *pathological* or anything, was he? The tape convinced us otherwise. Here were children whose condition was *seriously* abnormal, and Danny looked and acted exactly the way they did. It was an experience of profound disillusionment.

Are diagnoses such as autism a simple and unambiguous reflection of objective seriousness or are other, more social and cultural, factors at work? How does someone who manifests the disorder interact with "normals"? How are they treated by the general public—ordinary people who are unaware of that person's condition? How do laypeople characterize or categorize the odd, seemingly eccentric behavior they witness? How do they interact with the autistic person who exhibits the behavior? Do they *stigmatize* such persons? Shun, avoid, condemn, or fear them? Do they attribute the behavior to ordinary wilfulness and perversity—that is, deviance that is voluntary, freely chosen? Or do they accept such behavior as the involuntary product of an inborn condition? Do observers feel that an autistic child in the midst of a tantrum is little more than a "spoiled brat"? Do they revise their judgment upon learning of the child's condition? What are typical laypersons' explanations of the condition? How do teachers, social workers, psychiatrists, and physicians relate to the autistic clients in their charge? Do school administrators accommodate their curricula for the autistic student's special needs? Do they attempt to maximize their potential? Or do they write them off as educationally and occupationally hopeless, worthy only of being "dumped" into a supervised group home at the age of 18? Can some autistic persons be truly integrated into mainstream society?

To the parent of an autistic child, these issues are especially pressing, importunate, and anxiety provoking. Every parent of an autistic child must deal with the social fallout his or her child causes in everyday life. Whether it is throwing a tantrum in the aisle of a supermarket, hitting or threatening a teacher, insulting or yelling at a stranger, endlessly focusing on topics of conversation that no one else wants to discuss, blurting out statements that others find inappropriate or insulting, or simply behaving in a fashion deemed unconventional or bizarre, the autistic child's behavior often evokes a negative social reaction. In fact, the parent of the autistic child is often hurled into a whirlpool of troublesome behavior in more ways than one. In addition to having to pick up the pieces—both physical and social—his or her child leaves behind, the parent is typically judged deficient as a consequence of simply *having* such a child.

In *Stigma*, Goffman argues that not only are the enactors of deviant behavior, the holders of deviant beliefs, and the possessors of deviant characteristics "disqualified from full social acceptance," so are the people who associate with them. Here we have a special kind of "guilt by association." Goffman identifies "persons who are normal but whose special situation has made them intimately privy to the secret life of the stigmatized individual and sympathetic with it, and who find themselves accorded a measure of acceptance [among a particular category of stigmatized persons], a measure of courtesy membership in the clan" (1963, p. 28).

Goffman makes it clear that persons with a "courtesy stigma" will be "accorded a measure of acceptance" in the deviant group or category to which they are tied, but are unlikely to be entirely accepted as an equal by their members. But they are also not entirely accepted as outright "normals" either. Just as important, the stigma may "spread from the stigmatized individual to his [or her] close connections," providing a good reason "why such relations tend either to be avoided or to be terminated where existing" (p. 30). The "loyal spouse of the mental patient, the daughter of the ex-con, the parent of the cripple" (note how our vocabulary has changed in the forty years since Goffman wrote those words), "the friend of the blind, the family of the hangman, are all obliged to share some of the discredit of the stigmatized person to whom they are related. . . . The problems faced by stigmatized persons spread out in waves, but of diminished intensity" (p. 30).

The parents of the autistic child face a special kind of stigma: Not only do they associate with one or more members of a stigmatized category—that is, their children—some observers even regard them as *responsible* for their child's condition. It is well-nigh impossible for parents of an autistic child to shake the obsession that they have brought into this world and raised a damaged, defective offspring and that, in some way, they are responsible for his or her condition. The recognition of autism arose in the 1940s, during the heyday of Freudian psychoanalysis, a perspective which emphasized the role of abnormal childhood experiences in the origin of psychiatric and psychological disorders. In 1967, Bruno Bettelheim, now regarded as "the most notorious blamer of parents" (Cohen, 1998, p. 136), published *The Empty Fortress* (1967), which charged that the denial of a strong emotional bond by parents caused autism in their children. More specifically, Bettelheim blamed the condition on the "refrigerator mom" syndrome, the cold and emotionally rejecting mother. The cruelty of Bettelheim toward the children in his charge (he repeatedly humiliated, insulted, and slapped them) "was mild compared to his cruelty toward mothers" (Gardner, 2000, p. 14; Pollak, 1997). Bettelheim's theory, now completely discredited, was responsible for a great deal of grief and suffering among parents of autistic children. It both made them feel guilty for something they did not do but also held out false hope for a non-existent cure (Dolnick, 1998). A generation ago, Bettelheim's theory, and more generally the psychoanalytic approach to autism, blamed and stigmatized parents of autistic children. More than a "courtesy stigma," these parents were vilified, defamed, and tainted by professionals for causing their child's condition.

Three years *before* Bettelheim's book appeared, however, a report on autism, now regarded as pathbreaking, was published. Written by Bernard Rimland, it was entitled *Infantile Autism* (1964). Its argument, currently almost universally accepted as valid, was that autism is a neurological disorder that is biologically based and, in all probability, largely genetic in origin. There in fact is no consistent pattern in autism with respect to parental child-rearing practices. Rimland's book represented the first chiming of the death-knell for Bettelheim's "refrigerator mom" theory, as well as for the argument that parents are responsible for their child's autistic condition. Many informed critics now feel that most of Bettelheim's supposed "cures" were of children who either were not autistic at all or only mildly so (Gardner, 2000). The term *psychiatric fraud* comes readily to mind here.

Nonetheless, the fact that researchers and experts no longer accept the view that parental child-rearing practices cause autism has not ended the layperson's practice of blaming mom and dad for their child's condition. Nor has this fact done away with parental guilt. Added to the guilt we might feel for causing our children's condition through inappropriate parenting, we also tend to take responsibility for causing genetic defects. Did I pass on my defective genes to my child? Was it my "tainted blood" that produced my son's autism? Then there are all the sources of corruption of genes and fetus due to immoral or careless behavior the mother often assumes: Did I ingest LSD in the sixties? Did I smoke too much marijuana? Drink too much wine when I was pregnant? Did I inhale gasoline fumes? Get too close to the detergent I used to wash my clothes or dishes? Wander too near an electrical power line? Maybe it was exercise or jogging. The potential sources of blame are infinite. They can be likened to a kind of stigma—in Goffman's term, a "courtesy stigma." Parents are shamed not only by reason of "guilt by association" but take on both public and personal guilt for causing the condition in the first place. A serious— and humiliating—charge indeed.

My wife Barbara and I have a pre-adolescent autistic son. His name is Danny and this is his account. It is not from Danny's perspective, of course, it is from mine. Danny cannot conceptualize and relate social rejection in any fashion that would be meaningful to the reader or the sociologist of deviance. Danny encounters criticism and social rejection, of course, but he does not experience it in the way most of us do. And he does become embroiled in interpersonal conflict, but he is more likely to provoke it than to attract it.

Barbara and I have been shopping in stores when one of Danny's tirades takes hold of him. "Why don't you discipline your child better?" we are admonished. When we explain that Danny is autistic and, hence, often beyond our disciplinary control, we hear, "That's no excuse. He's just a *spoiled brat!*" Not long ago, I was informed by several friends that a sociologist, well-known for his theories of social constructionism, informed them that I was responsible for my son's autism. In what specific way, he was asked, is Erich responsible? "It is because he is so uncommunicative." When they responded that I do not appear to be uncommunicative *to them*, his reply was that I am only communicative *with them*, but in general, I'm not. Autism is, of course, not, strictly speaking, a communication disorder—Danny communicates what's on his mind just fine, as we can see from this account—but a *cognitive* disorder that manifests itself in a particular *manner* of communication.

The problem with such a charge is that it is non-empirical and therefore unanswerable. I managed to control my rage about the accusation (I no longer wish to strangle my smug, arrogant accuser to death). But the incident does illustrate two basic points central to Danny's account: One, even today, supposedly intelligent, well-informed observers still blame parents for their children's autistic condition; and two, in the case of autism, "courtesy stigma" spreads outward from child to parent. The fact is, the parent of a defective child *stands convicted* of bad parenting, naked before the world as guilty for having produced such a child. Imagine such a parent giving advice on childrearing. The fact is, one has no authority on the subject. On the face of it, one is, and will inevitably be, deemed an inadequate parent on the basis of the evidence before the court—that evidence being the defective child. The proof of the pudding, as they say.

One further point: Is autism a form of deviance? What is it about Danny that leads me to include his (or, more properly, my) account in this book? Danny's capacity to understand, conceptualize, and assess society's reaction to him and his behavior is limited. He knows when his parents, teachers, and other kids don't *like* what he does, and he understands that their disapproval usually causes them to react negatively. But he doesn't have a clear idea of the categorical basis for such judgments or reactions. In any case, he is rarely able to control his behavior once he is seized by the imperative of a given line of action. *"You're defying me!"* he will shout to a teacher or his mom when he demands attention and feels he isn't receiving his fair share. If the insolent behavior—that is, "defying" him—continues, it is often accompanied by slapping the offending party on the arm. (During one five-day week, Danny was sent home from school three times for hitting or yelling. Once, he was ejected from school even before he walked in the front door.) To most of us, being hit for not according someone sufficient attention is a form of deviance. In Danny's case, is this true?

As we've seen in the introduction, the fact that behavior (or conditions, or beliefs) is involuntary is no guarantee that it is not a form of deviance. In fact, involuntary deviance is every bit as prodigious a source of negative reactions—ostracism, avoidance, criticism, humiliation, stigma, disgrace—as voluntary deviance. The fact that Danny "can't help it" is only marginally relevant. Regardless of the *cause* of a form of behavior, or a belief, or a physical condition, what makes something deviant to the sociologist is the negative social reaction it tends to generate. From the perspective that deviance is *defined, constituted,* or *created* by a certain type of social and societal reaction, causality and motivation are beside the point—except insofar as they may further influence that reaction. Negative reaction defines deviance. In the words of Edwin Lemert: "deviations are not significant until they are organized subjectively and transformed into active roles and become the social criteria for assigning status" (1951, p. 75). To be assigned a disvalued role is to become a deviant; causality does not enter the picture at all, except, as we saw, if it mitigates negative reactions by audiences. But it is the negative reactions, actual or potential, that constitute deviance, regardless of their source.

What makes autism different from many other forms of deviance, however, is the fact that there is very little *bonding* of fellow autistic persons into a community based on their deviation. Lemert assumed that, whatever its basis, negative social and societal reactions would tend to created a counter-response, the creation of a community of like-minded, rejected persons. In the case of autism, this is clearly not necessarily the case.

At the age of three, after experiencing a protracted speech delay, Danny was diagnosed with a possible pervasive development disorder (an all-purpose, grab-bag category that is used when no other disorder seems to stand out). At the age of six, this was revised to a high-functioning autistic disorder. According to the American Psychiatric Association's *Diagnostic and Statistical Manual* (DSM-IV), in autism:

> The impairment in reciprocal social interaction is gross and sustained. There may be marked impairment in the use of multiple non-verbal behaviors (e.g., eye-to-eye gaze, facial expression, body postures and gestures) to regulate social interaction and communication. . . . There may be failure to develop peer relationships. . . . Younger individuals may have little or no interest in establishing friendships. Older individuals may have an interest in friendship but lack understanding of the conventions of social interaction. There may be a lack of spontaneous seeking to share enjoyment, interests, or achievements with other people. . . . Lack of social or emotional reciprocity may be present. . . . Often an individual's awareness of others is markedly impaired. Individuals with this disorder may be oblivious to other children. . . . , may have no concept of the needs of others, or may not notice another person's distress. . . . In individuals who . . . speak, there may be a marked impairment in the ability to initiate or sustain a conversation with others. . . . Individuals with Autistic Disorder have restricted, repetitive, and stereotyped patterns of behavior, interests, and activities. There may be an encompassing preoccupation with one or more stereotyped and restricted patterns of interest that is abnormal either in intensity or focus. (pp. 66, 67)

Like the children of most academic couples, Danny spent much of his early childhood in day-care centers, including two months in one (when he was two) in Brazil and six months in another (when he was five) in Israel. Between 1991 and 1993, he attended a pre-school educational and therapeutic center; there, it was recommended that he be placed in a program for children with special needs, a BOCES (Board of Cooperative Educational Services) school. Here, he received an annual psychological evaluation. The one he received at the age of nine reads as follows:

> Danny is an adorable boy with blonde hair and brown eyes [actually, his hair is light brown and his eyes hazel] who appears to be of average height and weight for his age [he is smaller than the norm on both counts]. He used his left hand to write and evidenced a normal gait, with normal coordination. Speech was usually in good phrases . . . as

well as with good articulation, but with a lack of varied tonality. Delayed echolalia [the repetition of words spoken by another person] . . . was noted intermittently. Eye contact and interpersonal relatedness were adequate but slightly deviant. Activity level was somewhat above average and attention was variable and seemed dependent on his interest in the task and the incentive used to motivate him to perform. . . . Danny displays idiosyncratic interests in [certain things, for example] making puppets of Pinocchio, [collecting] images of past US presidents, collecting coins, and writing out the words to songs. . . . He also has excellent calendar calculation skills [which is common among autistic children]. His interests . . . change, and he sometimes gets very upset if his routines are changed or if his idiosyncrasies are not addressed. For instance, at times, he becomes upset if adults use certain verbal phrases. No self injurious behaviors were noted, but when upset, he sometimes becomes mildly aggressive or verbally belligerent. Danny sleeps well. He eats fairly well but again, idiosyncratically. Specifically, he will only eat sausage pizza (after removing the sausages and cheese), chicken nuggets, with occasional hot dogs, strawberries, and corn on the cob.[1]

After four years in BOCES schools, we considered mainstreaming him into the regular curriculum in our local public school, with the assistance of a full-time aide. To that end, a psychologist from the New York Autism Network observed his BOCES classroom behavior. In this class, there were six students, one teacher, and one aide.

When the psychologist arrived, Danny was participating in a math game that involved going up to the board to solve a problem. In front of the class, Danny began untying then retying his sneakers. When he was redirected to the task at hand, he was able to answer the question. Then he took his seat. When the teacher read a story, Danny again began fiddling with his shoelaces. He began humming and looking around the classroom. The teacher redirected his focus by asking him to read from the book. Toward the end of his selection, he began writing in the air with his finger. When she asked him to stop, he said, "Don't be mean, I can write in the air." During an exercise with language workbooks, Danny sharpened his pencil several times, repeatedly asked other students for an eraser, and played with his shoelaces. However, whenever the teacher called on him, he was able to give the correct answer. While waiting for the next activity to begin, Danny took off his sneakers. When his teacher told him to put them back on, Danny announced, "You're a witch. It's a plot." The teacher allowed him to leave his sneakers on his desk and go on to the next activity, making shirts for Father's Day. He watched attentively and patiently as two other students made shirts. During this time, he did not fidget or engage in self-stimulatory behavior.[2]

Autistic persons are supposed to be incapable of empathy. Our experience demonstrates this generalization to be false—but only up to a point. Autistic children lack a sense of humor, we were told, because they can't step outside themselves and determine what is likely to be funny to someone else. Likewise, they can't lie, we've been told, because they are incapable of sufficiently putting themselves in the place of another person to understand how to conceal or distort the facts. Though he's not likely to put Eddie Murphy or Rosie O'Donnell out of business, Danny has always had a wonderful although completely idiosyncratic sense of humor—but it is true, he is a terrible liar. I hear a loud crash and run into Danny's room. "Did you break the lamp?" I ask him, broken shards lying at his feet.

"No," he says tentatively, avoiding my intense, admonishing gaze.

"Danny!" I insist, sternly, "*Did* you break the lamp? Tell me the truth."

"It was an accident." Then a sly smile creeps across his face. "It broke itself."

"Danny, are you saying that the lamp grew legs and *jumped* off the table?"

The smile has now grown into a broad grin. "Yes," he insists. "It jumped off the table." He begins giggling.

We live half a block from where Danny's school bus drops him off and it's uphill to our house. One day, after school, Danny said he was tired, he didn't want to walk back home. "But it's so close, Danny, we're almost home," he is told.

His face brightens, he looks up, raises a hand as if hailing a cab, and sings out, "Oh, *taxi!*"

Danny is rarely violent, although he is not infrequently destructive. It is not the destructiveness of a meanspirited or vicious child, rather the product of angry, frustrated outbursts or exuberant unmindfulness that is oblivious to real-world consequences. He does have frequent violent *verbal* outbursts, and he engages in what could be described as mischievous behavior—behavior that sometimes seems to border perilously on cruelty.

Some extremely puzzling things enrage him. Others would not be offended by these things or even notice them. While watching a videotape, Danny picked up on the phrase, "Why I oughta . . ." uttered by a character to threaten his companion. Danny became quite literal about it, applying it indiscriminately to sequences of words that mean something quite different. In the middle of an argument with Danny, Barbara used the phrase, "That's why I." That threw Danny into a rage. "DON'T SAY WHY I!" he shrieked and slapped his mom across the face. The argument became extremely heated with Danny demanding that she never say "why I" and she responding by saying the phrase over and over again. "I'll *cut* you!" Danny screamed. "I'll take a knife and cut your *hand* off! There will be lots of *blood!* I'll throw you to the *sharks* and there will be lots of your blood in the *water!*" Danny was distraught and it took quite a while to calm him down. The extreme nature of this exchange, I should emphasize, is unusual; Danny almost never hits his mom, and he's very rarely so blatantly and overtly verbally violent. But what marks our son off from other children is the sources of his anger. We would have to search far and wide for another child who becomes enraged by the utterance, "Why I. . . ."

It's Mother's Day, a Sunday, eight in the morning. Barbara and I are lying in bed, not quite asleep, not quite awake. A bellowing scream rouses us. "MOM! DAD! Come down here and open Snowball's cage! I want to give him a fruitstick!" Snowball is our parakeet.

"Soon, Danny," I reply, "we're not quite out of bed. We'll get up in a couple minutes."

Danny marches up the stairs to the hallway outside our bedroom and begins yelling at us, *"I thought I told you to come here this minute and open up Snowball's cage! Now you get out of bed and do what I tell you to."*

From Barbara, a groggy moan, "Soon, Danny, soon."

Danny bursts through the bedroom door and rushes over to Barbara, who's lying face down on the bed, and smacks her on the back with the palm of his hand. I become furious with him and jump up, grab his shirt, and get in his face. "Don't you *dare* hit your mother! Danny, what's *wrong* with you? You are *not* allowed to hit!"

"Hey," Danny objects, "you're *breathing* on me!"

It is Mother's Day and moms all over the country are receiving presents and flowers from their kids, and Barbara, one of the most loving moms in the world, gets struck on the back by a screaming child—*her* screaming child. She sits on the edge of the bed and begins crying.

Danny attributes intentionality to inanimate entities. If he bumps into something, he retaliates by hitting it. It could be a chair, a table, a lamp. Usually he uses his hands. Once, after bumping into a wall, he grabbed a hammer and smashed holes in it. "Danny, did the wall reach out and *hit* you?" I asked with some insistence, even vehemence in my voice.

"Yes," he answered quite firmly. "The wall was bad. It was *mean.* I had to punish it." Note, however, he never hits a *person* with a hammer. He never hits our dog or our rabbit with a hammer. Only to the misinformed observer is he out of control. His targets are specific, and his outbursts are calculated.

I'm in my study, trying to concentrate on what to say to my classes the following day. The evening air is pierced by an agonizing shriek—

"YAAAAAGGGGGHHHH!!"—followed by the sound of a child running through the house in bare feet. I look up from my desk and in a quiet, dry, low-key voice, I ask, "Danny, what's wrong?" My son comes up to my study and sticks his head into the doorway. "Daddy, don't *haunt!*" I try to sound cheerful. "Danny, what seems to be the problem?"

"*I don't want you to haunt!*" For some reason, my son seems to have associated the tone of my voice with a kind of ghostly "haunting." I try to recall, three or four years ago, when I played "ghost" with Danny and Sarah. Remarkably, I'm calm. "Danny, I am not haunting. If you think I am, I'm sorry. I'll try not to haunt. Now, why don't you tell me what's wrong."

"MY PENCIL!! *It keeps breaking!*" he screams. The boy is in agony. His face is contorted with palpable anguish. "Well, try not to press down so hard," I offer, vainly appealing to his tiny sliver of rationality.

Danny bolts from the doorway and plunges down the stairway. "WAAAAAHHHH!!! MY PENCIL! My pencil!" Five minutes later he's back, holding a pencil with a broken point. He shoves it toward my face. "Will you buy me more pencils? This one keeps breaking." I sigh. "Danny, you can sharpen this one."

"NO! NO! It keeps *breaking!*" he shouts.

I realize he is not to be reasoned with. "OK, Danny, I'll buy you some more pencils."

He smiles. He seems pleased. "Thanks, Dad," he says, and runs off. "Tomorrow," he yells over his shoulder. "At Office Max."

"OK, Danny," I say, "Tomorrow. At Office Max."

Later, I try to put him to bed. Like most kids his age, he resists. "Danny, have you brushed your teeth? Have you taken your vitamin?"

"No."

"OK, could you go into the bathroom and do these things please?"

He goes into the bathroom. Suddenly, an ear-piercing shriek. "YAAAAAAGGGGGHHHH!"

Alarmed, I run into the bathroom. "Danny, what's wrong?"

"The *towel!* Hanging *up!* I can't go in there! The towel is hanging up! It's a *disaster!* Like Miss Clavel [from the *Madeline* series] says, a disaster!"

"You mean you won't go into the bathroom because the towel is hanging up on the shower rack?"

"Yes."

"OK, Danny, I'll take it down. Now, will you go into the bathroom and brush your teeth?"

"OK."

I'm pushing my shopping cart down the dairy aisle of our local Edwards supermarket when Danny emits an ear-piercing scream. I try to shush him. "What's wrong, Danny? Why are you screaming?" I ask.

"Oh, NO!" he screams again. "Polly-O! It's HERE! We've got to get it out! Let's talk to the owners of the store and get *rid* of the Polly-O!" Polly-O is a type of string cheese product to which Danny has taken an especially intense dislike.

"Danny, we can't do that. Some people *like* Polly-O. That's the reason why they sell it here."

"NO! They DON'T like it! NOBODY likes it! It's *repulsive!*"

"Well, Danny, some people would disagree. They like it, they eat it, that's why they buy it—and that's why the store sells it."

"*How dare you defy me!* Polly-O is repulsive and *that's it!*"

I crouch down and get in Danny's face. "Now, listen, Danny, do *not* say that to me!" I say forcefully. "I'm your dad and I'm telling you some people *do* like Polly-O. If you don't like it that's fine, but people eat it. Why would they eat it? Why would they buy it if they think it's repulsive? Now that's *enough* of this silly talk!" I straighten up and begin pushing the cart.

Danny begins muttering under his breath, "You're not telling me the truth. Polly-O *is* repulsive and that's it." I do not further engage Danny in this particular debate.

A few days later, while I was waiting to put Danny on his school bus, Tony, a neighborhood kid about Danny's age, who's also waiting for the bus, asks Danny, "Hey, Danny, why don't you like Polly-O?" Apparently, Danny's dislikes are well known in his school.

Danny considers the question. "Because it's repulsive," he answers.

Annie, Tony's little sister, turns to me and asks, "What's repulsive mean?"

"Disgusting," I answer.

"Yucky," Danny answers.

"Oh," Annie responds.

"We have no idea why he thinks Polly-O is disgusting. He just does. It's one of his things." Tony decides not to pursue the matter.

Occasionally, other, seemingly innocuous subjects have surprising results. "Danny," I chirp cheerfully, "would you like to have some dinner?"

"NO!" he responds angrily, "I do *not* want dinner! This is *my* night"—the line is from a *Goosebumps* tape—"Thanksgiving is *my* night! I am *not* having dinner!" Danny begins fake sobbing. Gaining his composure, he screams, "I'm going to *hit* you!" (He does not hit me, however.) "I *hate* you, Dad! You're a *coward!* You're *dead!* You're *very dead!*" He walks over to Chewy, our dog, lying on her couch, and threatens to hit her. She looks up at him with a puzzled look on her face.

"Danny, do *not* hit the dog! We do *not* hit in this house!"

"And I'm *never* going to dinnertime!" he continues. "I give up! You're *stupid!* You're not brave! You're a *coward!* I am *not* having dinner! I am *never* having dinner!" The boy seems to be on quite a roll, I think, staring blankly at his twisted, angry face. There's more fake crying. "You're *nothing* to me, Dad," he continues after gasping for breath. "I don't like you! I don't want dinner!" More fake crying. "You're being *mean! I* am never going to have dinner! You're bad! I mean, you had a bad day!" If I weren't so involved in this bizarre drama, it might seem amusing. "You *deliberately* disobeyed me!" The crying *manque* begins again. "Dad, I am *never* going to have dinner!" He stomps off to his room and slams the door. I sigh and put six chicken nuggets in the toaster oven. A half hour later, he sits down to his usual dinner: the nuggets, strawberries, and Welch's white grape-peach juice.

"Dad, please answer me," Danny demands. I try to focus on the question. "Danny, what's the question?" I ask. "After the owners at Blockbuster hang the posters, we can get out The Beatles' *Yellow Submarine*, High Tops Video, with six Beatles, including Stuart Sutcliffe and Peter Best, and the Casper tape, with Danny playing Cat, Dr. Harvey's daughter [a character in the live-action movie, *Casper*] and the High Tops Video, *The Adventures of Puss And Boots*, and at the end of *Casper*, Casper and I will come out of the movie and I'll tell him, he'll go through *Who Framed Roger Rabbit?* and get holes [the holes that appear in the animated Beatles movie *Yellow Submarine* that permit characters to move from one dimension to another] and after he pushed through the glass on the TV, and the glass will disappear, and I'll go in and get Flora, Fauna, and Merriweather's magic wands [the three good fairies in *Sleeping Beauty*], and the animals, especially Chewy and Clover [our rabbit], and the humans, especially me, except the Nazis, will live forever."

"Oh, OK, Danny," I answer. That's one I don't even want to begin to touch. I decide to let it stay as it lays.

The previous Saturday, Danny insisted on going to Ronjo's, a store specializing in magic products and costumes. During our drive there, he explained what he was looking for. He wanted to purchase a magic set that would enable him to perform spells so that we ("the humans, especially me, except the Nazis") and animals ("especially Chewy and Clover") could live forever, although he was willing to compromise on us living until the year 3000. I tried to explain that magic was tricks, illusions, scarves, playing cards, rabbits being pulled out of hats. Magic, he insisted, patiently explaining the matter to me, was "snake guts, fly wings, bat blood, and swamp water." What he needed, he said, was "sparkles" (that is, magic wands). As I was purchasing Ronjo's standard magic starter kit, the proprietor began performing a magic trick. He showed us a can, open at both ends. Then he attached tissue paper at both ends and secured them with rubber bands. "Was the can empty?" I asked Danny. He nodded, then wandered off, looking at some of the items in the glass case. A wand poked its way through the tissue paper. "Danny," I commanded, "look, what's going to come out of the can?" He barely looked up. A multicolored scarf was pulled out of the can. "Danny, look," I exclaimed, "look at the scarf." He smiled then looked back at the glass case.

Driving back, I explained, "Danny, "that's what magic is, it's scarves, it's tricks, it's all illusion—it's not swamp water and sparkles. It's just not possible for us to live forever. There *are* no spells in magic."

He became angry and vehement, and so I decided to drop it. "OK, Danny, you and Mom can look at the magic set and see what's in it," I said, passing the buck.

Danny was disappointed at the contents of the magic set. He was most specifically disappointed at the fact that it had no snake guts, fly wings, bat blood, swamp water, or "sparkles." He found it especially galling that whatever the magic kit contained, it was not going to enable us to live forever or even to the year 3000. Through a series of imaginative leaps, he transferred his hopes to the magic wands of the three fairies in *Sleeping Beauty* (Flora, Fauna, and Merriweather), now fantasizing that it would be less problematic to make his way through the "glass" of the TV set and enter the fantasy world of the videotape than to mumble incantations over designated items of wizardry thereby achieving the desired result.

Danny is invited to PJ Mahoney's 11th birthday party. It's held at "Laser World" whose central attraction is a game of laser tag, played in a darkened room in which opponents on two sides, the Greens and the Reds, wear vests, headphones, and shoot each other with laser guns. Before the game, the kids eat pizza. I locate some napkins and Danny scrapes the cheese and tomato sauce off the pizza and eats only the triangle of dough. I've finally gotten used to his eating habits. He barely interacts with any of the other kids. Though several of them ask him questions, he replies in monosyllables, and only after I prompt him. He does not eat the chocolate ice cream sandwich. He actually likes chocolate ice cream; I suspect he's put off by the word "sandwich" as it applies to ice cream. I suit him up for the laser game but decide not to go into the darkened game room with him. Several children explain how to put on the vest, but he doesn't even look at them. He emerges ten minutes later with a wan smile playing on his lips.

"Was it fun, Danny?" I ask.

"Yes," he answers. "Now I want to go to Wood World." It's a store next door that sells jungle gyms, tree houses, swing and slide sets. He wanders desultorily through the displays, sliding down the slides, climbing the ladders, ducking into the play houses. A birthday party is being held there; an employee is performing magic tricks for three and four-year-olds. He's pulling the usual long, multicolored scarf out of his mouth.

"Danny, look," I command, "look at the scarf coming out of the man's mouth. *That's* what magic is all about, Danny, tricks and scarves and stuff like that."

"Can we go home now, Dad?" Danny pleads.

"Sure," I say, "We just have to say goodbye to PJ and his mom, OK?" We go back to Laser World and I thank them profusely for inviting Danny, and they thank me for bringing him. They sound sincere. Both seem very nice. I am happy that they have made the effort to integrate Danny into the social circle of fifth graders. I am depressed that he hasn't done anything with the opportunity. I wonder what it would be like to have a son like PJ. When I drive home, I'm still depressed.

I'm at my desk, working. Danny comes to the study door. "Dad, who sings 'Here Comes the Sun'?"

"Uh, uh," I stammer, struggling to focus, "I'm not sure, Danny. Was it Paul?"

"No. It's not Paul who sings 'Here Comes the Sun.' It's George Harrison who sings 'Here Comes the Sun.'"

"Oh, OK, I'm sorry, Danny, I made a mistake. I thought it was Paul."

"NO!" Danny shouts, now becoming quite vehement about the matter. "It *wasn't* Paul! It was George Harrison!"

He's standing in the hallway right outside my study door. His face is contorted in anguish. "Danny," I respond, "let me ask you a question. Why did you ask me who sang the song if you already know the answer?"

He points at me accusingly. "Your nose is growing, your nose is growing! You told a lie! It wasn't Paul, it was George!"

"Danny, I said I was sorry."

"Liar! Liar! You're not telling me the truth! You told me it was Paul and it was George!"

"Danny, please, are you going to start up again? Why are you getting so upset about this? I don't *know* who sings all the Beatles' songs. *You* know, so answer the question yourself."

"You are no truth teller about who sang 'Here Comes the Sun.'"

"Danny, I am not going to listen to this any longer. You just want to start an argument. If you can talk nice to me, I'll be happy to talk, but if you're just going to yell at me and call me names, I don't want to do it." I get up from my desk and close the door to the study.

"Yaaaagggghhhh!" he screams and flops onto the floor. He begins crying. "Paul McCartney did NOT sing 'Here Comes the Sun'! Waaaahhhh!"

After a moment or so, there is silence. I open the door. Danny's standing in the hallway with a blank look on his face. "Daddy, you are right. Paul did sing 'Here Comes the Sun.'"

"But I thought you said it was George."

"I did NOT say it was George!" he shouts indignantly.

"Danny, I really heard you say that George sang 'Here Comes the Sun.'"

"I changed my mind!" he snaps. "Paul McCartney *did* sing 'Here Comes the Sun.'"

"OK, Danny, let's drop it, all right? I don't know why we're arguing about who sang a song. What difference does it make?" I place my hand on his back and squat down to his level. "Danny, let's please stop yelling. We don't want to hear yelling. Do you want to go to Blockbuster this weekend?" He says he does. "OK, if you stop yelling about who sang 'Here Comes the Sun,' you can take some tapes out at Blockbuster, OK?"

He's manfully trying to hold back the tears. "All right" he says bravely.

"Good boy." I heave a sigh of relief.

Danny's sitting on the couch, watching *Yellow Submarine*, talking to himself. He's studied the entries on the Beatles in Lillian Roxon's *Rock Encyclopedia* in such detail, scrutinizing every paragraph with such rapt attention, that he's managed to tear all the pages out of the book's spine. Finally, Barbara bought a copy of *The Complete Beatles Chronicle* for Danny; so far, this volume remains intact. To protect against further damage to the Roxon volume, I gave him the Rolling Stone *Encyclopedia of Rock & Roll* and Music First *Rock Stars Encyclopedia*. In true obsessive-compulsive fashion so characteristic of autistics, Danny has become quite an expert on the Beatles.

"First John Lennon and Paul McCartney chose Colin Hanton, Len Garry, and Eric Griffiths," he says to no one in particular. "Then John Lennon and Paul McCartney got rid of Colin Hanton, Len Garry, and Eric Griffiths, and chose George Harrison, Stuart Sutcliffe, and Johnny Hutchinson. Then John Lennon, Paul McCartney, George Harrison, and Stuart Sutcliffe got rid of Johnny Hutchinson and chose Tommy Moore. Then John Lennon, Paul McCartney, George Harrison, and Stuart Sutcliffe got rid of Tommy Moore and chose Peter Best. Then John Lennon, Paul McCartney, George Harrison, and Peter Best got rid of Stuart Sutcliffe. Then John Lennon, Paul McCartney, and George Harrison got rid of Peter Best and chose Jimmy Nichol. Then John Lennon, Paul McCartney, and George Harrison got rid of Jimmy Nichol and chose Richard Starkey, commonly known as Ringo Starr." (Later, he added many more names to the roster.) This recitation is much like a prayer or an incantation for Danny. It appears to appeal to his need for order in the universe. If anyone interrupts him or challenges his chronology, or questions him about the meaning of "join" or "get rid of," he becomes irritated. If a parent is questioned about an obscure member of a pre-Beatle group and admits ignorance concerning the performer's entry or tenure in the group or his musical instrument of choice, Danny flies into a furious rage. *"Don't say you don't know!"* he screams. "It's not nice! IT'S MEAN!" he shrieks. "Don't you DARE say 'I don't know'!"

Moments after Danny's recitation, I hear screaming—*ferocious* screaming. "YAAAAGGGGGHHHH." It is coming from Danny's room. "I told you to stop being a repulsive boy!" He screams. *"Not* with another 'e.' *Without* another 'e'!" Danny is typing his Beatles chronology. He becomes enraged when he makes a typing mistake. He is quite beside himself, filling the house with an earsplitting cacophony. "HANTON," he screams, *"not* Hantin! And Garry, G-A-R-R-Y!" he shrieks. "Aaaahhhhh, YAAAAGGGGGHHHH." There's a brief pause. "It's NOT LENNIN, it's LENNON!!" I hear a slap. Occasionally, Danny slaps himself if he's made a mistake. "No-no-no-no-no-no-no-no-no-NO!!! It's like THIS!! It's 'All Together Now.' Danny," he continues, "you know better than to be violent like that! It's yucky! Now, never, *ever* make a mistake again, do you understand? John Lennon and Paul McCartney will never write another song! Together like THIS!" he screams. "With an 'e.'" He flops down on the bed. "YAAAAGGGGGHHHH!!! WAAAHHHH!!"

At this point, Danny decides to take another tack. He runs into the kitchen, where I am preparing dinner, and picks up on the theme I had hoped had been lost. "Dad, you *lied* when you said that Paul McCartney sang 'Here Comes the Sun'! It wasn't Paul McCartney, it was George Harrison! You told a lie! Wahhhh! Yahhhh!" He decides to seek another source. Frantically running upstairs, he screams, "Mom, who sang, 'Here Comes the Sun'?" Trying to concentrate on an e-mail message, Barbara answers that she isn't sure.

"Dad's *lying* about who sings 'Here Comes the Sun.'"

"Danny, what did we say about the 'L' word? Dad does not lie to you. He may have been mistaken, but he's not going to tell you a lie."

"Who sang 'Here Comes the Sun'?" Danny demanded to know, practically screeching.

"Danny, I am not going to talk to you when you are screaming like that. Talk in a normal tone of voice."

"I am not screaming!" Danny screamed. *"I am not screaming! I am talking in a normal tone of voice!"* Barbara returns to her computer screen. "Mom, you're not answering me! You *must* answer me!"

"Danny, listen to me," his mom answers, "I am not going to listen to you when you're screaming like this."

"I'm not going to listen to you!" Danny retorts. "I *am* listening to you! You're not *answering* me!"

"Danny," his mom answers calmly, "I don't want you treating me like this."

"Oh, no," he begins shrieking, "I can't believe it! Not you, not you!!" He claps his hands to his temples and runs through the hallway toward the stairs.

Barbara comes downstairs, passing Danny, and walks to the kitchen, where I am mixing up a steak marinade, attempting to avoid the tempest that shows no sign of abating. "What caused this monstrous behavior?" she asks me.

"Well," I begin, "Danny was working on the computer and something reminded him of something I said a couple days ago."

Danny pursues Barbara into the kitchen. "*Monstrous behavior? Monstrous behavior?* ME? I didn't do any monstrous behavior! YOU'RE monstrous! YOU did the monstrous behavior! I didn't do anything!"

"Danny, I just don't think I can take any more of this behavior, do you understand?" Barbara shouts.

"Yes you can! You *can* take more of this behavior!"

"Danny," Barbara says, "we're going to have to put you somewhere where we can't hear you any more, I'm becoming physically sick of your screaming. Do you want me to become sick?" She sits down on a chair in the dining room.

"You are not getting sick!" he screams, coming after her and yelling in her face. "You are *not* getting sick."

"I am, Danny, do you want to make me sick?"

Danny decides to adopt a different tack. His face is released from its agonizing contortions and, in an instant, seems almost calm. "Mom, can I have the magnifying glass with the tweezers?" He has amassed an extensive magnifying glass collection and, somehow, this particular item in his collection is lost. Exotic though it may seem to the mere dilettante, the magnifying glass with tweezers is essential to any serious collector.

I decide to burst in. "Danny, you expect us to give you something you want when you're not giving us what we want. And what is that? It's cooperation. You're not giving us any cooperation! We want you to do something for us—are you doing something for us? You want us to give you a magnifying glass? What are you giving us? Nothing! You're screaming at us!"

"I'm sorry," Danny admits, in a fake-rueful fashion.

"Well, words don't mean much," I reply, "I want action. You say something, but what I want is for you to *do* something."

"Words don't mean much?" Danny asks.

"That's right. Let me be plain, Danny. If you don't stop screaming, we won't get you the magnifying glass."

"I'll stop screaming," he promises. "I won't scream any more. Can we go to Reflex Camera tomorrow and buy the magnifying glass?"

Barbara shakes her head. "We can't promise that we'll do it tomorrow. We'll see. You have to be good for more than one day."

I put Danny's usual dinner on the table. He sits down and begins eating. As if nothing had happened, he quizzes me about whether Ivan Vaughn was a Beatle. Weakly, I answer that Vaughn was a Quarry Men, not a Beatle. "The Quarry Men were *a kind* of Beatles!" Danny counters. "The Quarry Men *became* the Silver Beetles and the Silver Beetles *became* the regular Beatles. They were *all* Beatles."

"OK, Danny," I respond weakly.

"There were 19 of them."

"OK, Danny."

It is the evening of Danny's elementary school graduation ceremony. Next year, he attends middle school—what we once referred to as junior high school. His sister refuses to attend the ceremony, and his mom is more than 4,000 miles away, on a plane that's taking off from São Paulo's Guarulhos Airport. I have to nearly drag him away from his thousandth viewing of *Yellow Submarine*. He does an excellent impersonation of Old Fred: "The Blue Meanies are coming," he says in a quavering, old man's voice.

"Danny, you have to wear dark, long pants and a dark shirt," I insist.

"No, I won't do it! It's not cold! I'm going to keep my shorts on!" he responds.

"Listen, this is a formal ceremony, Danny. You're graduating from Scraggy Hill. You have to wear nice clothes! Now please go into your room and pick out a dark pair of long pants. I have to go upstairs and change."

When I get back downstairs, Danny is nowhere to be seen. I run outside and he's sitting in my car, smiling, wearing a striped shirt and red shorts. I yank the car door open and face him. "Danny, I *told* you you had to wear long pants, now let's go into your room and pick out a pair. It's your *graduation ceremony*, you have to look good. Ms. Lesserson *told* me you had to wear long pants." We march together into his room and assemble an appropriate outfit. He's not happy about it, but he decides not to resist.

Walking through the hallway toward Ms. Lesserson's classroom, we pass hundreds of children milling about. Two of Danny's classmates smile and say hello. "Danny," I command, "can you say hello?"

"Hi, Jenna, hi, Moura," he answers. They giggle.

"Danny," I say, as we pass the pair, "that's not Jenna's sister Moura."

"I said *Maureen*, not Moura," Danny insists.

"OK, Danny." We locate Ms. Lesserson and she positions him in the hallway with the other assembled kids. I go to the auditorium and stand against a wall near what's going to be his seat. The kids file in; Ms. Lesserson walks alongside Danny, hovering near him to make sure he doesn't do anything untoward. He is in the first row at the far left, clearly placed there so that if he begins fussing, he can be hustled out with a maximum of ease. The principal begins his introductory speech. Danny jumps out of his seat, runs up to the table next to the speaker, and smells the pink roses nestled in a vase. Ms. Lesserson guides Danny back to his seat. As the principal speaks, I watch Danny from behind. He's writing something in the air with his left index finger. Ms. Lesserson leans over to him and whispers something in his ear. He puts his hand down. Now both hands are behind his head. The certificates are presented to each kid one by one. Danny receives more than his share of applause.

There's a couple standing next to me whose daughter has been extremely nice—indeed, saintly—toward Danny. They do not notice me. The dad is videotaping the ceremony and says, "There's Danny." The mom says, "He's such a cute boy." Walking back to their seats clutching their certificates, most of the girls are beaming; most of the boys express a debonair pride. Walking back to his seat, Danny seems disoriented and puzzled by the whole enterprise. The child who receives the most applause by far—very nearly *thunderous* applause—is Tammy Remington, an autistic girl with more developmental problems than Danny. I choke back a sob.

The graduation songs are "That's What Friends Are for" and "I Will Remember You." Danny knows the words to both of them, and before the music begins, Ms. Lesserson prompts Danny; he nods in recognition. But he does not sing. My heart sinks. I know that I would have been a sobbing mess if he had sung, but I suppress my tears and listen to the thin, quavering, childish voices of the other children fill the auditorium.

"I will not cry," I say, feeling sorry for myself, "I will not cry." I don't.

Three weeks later, Danny is kicked out of summer camp for screaming and hitting a counselor and another camper. After we bring him home, Barbara is lying on our bed, crying while I try to console her. Danny is in his room, screaming. It seems we made him feel bad for getting upset about his behavior. We are struck by an utter incapacity to decipher a viable course of action. I feel that putting him in a home for uncontrollable autistic boys has become an extremely appealing option. Barbara, usually adamantly opposed to the idea, seems almost ambivalent. Paralyzed by bewilderment and sorrow, we simply keep him home for the remainder of the summer.

Danny is sitting on the kitchen table, one foot planted on a chair, the other on the table, eating Cheez-Its out of a bowl. He's wearing yellow shorts, a striped t-shirt, and no socks. His casual nonchalance suggests the demeanor of near-teenage normalcy.

Later, in bed, in the dark, Barbara mentions how normal Danny seemed, eating the Cheez-Its. "Sometimes I wonder what he would have been like if he hadn't been autistic. Sometimes it seems, if only he could have been born a little different, everything would have been all right with him. There are times when I feel he wouldn't have had to be that different to be just another kid. Maybe with his own special quirks and foibles, but without all the craziness."

I become choked up. "You can drive yourself crazy that way," I respond. "There's no way of separating his autism from the rest of him. He is the way he is, and he's been the way he's been. We can't do anything about that." I turn away and face the far wall. "I don't want to think about that. That way lies madness."

We fall asleep with tears in our eyes. I know I did.

NOTES

[1] This report was prepared by Dr. Michael Eberlein, school psychologist, and is dated 7/14/97.

[2] The above paragraph is a paraphrase of the report submitted by Dr. Christopher E. Smith, New York Autism Network, dated 6/9/98.

CHAPTER 4

> *Pornography is everything. I have an enormous appetite—an absolutely insatiable appetite—for it. I need it, fresh and new every week. I need it by the carload. The Japanese make the best porn. Cartoons. Really, really bizarre shit. I love it, the more bizarre the better.*
>
> Dwight

Dwight, the Salacious Chauffeur

Nearly all norm violators have one foot in conventionality. I mean this in two senses: One, most norm violators are conformists in most areas of their lives; and two, nearly all engage in a "presentation of self in everyday life."

Consider Dwight. He is a suburbanite; a homeowner; a (more or less) doting uncle, hosting regular visits for his brother's children; a reliable employee—and proud of it; the owner of two (paid-off) vehicles, a sports car and a pick-up truck; and he was, at one time, in love with a woman and was her lover in a long-term, monogamous relationship. Intelligent and knowledgeable in a number of areas (film, for instance, and the military history of World War II), he was accepted as an undergraduate at a prestigious university. His sister and brothers are accomplished, have pursued successful, conventional careers, and hold highly respected positions.

Note too that Dwight reveals intimacies to me that he conceals from his colleagues. (As he told me, "I enjoy the respect of my colleagues and my clients. Because I never level with them the way I do with you.") More-over, he is unwilling to be forthcoming with me about some matters. He bridles at the notion that he is "to some degree a little bit different from the so-called mainstream." He makes it clear that he is not especially inter-ested in sex with children. (Although he does point out, "I like the possibil-ity of it because it's illegal.") A chauffeur, he makes sure that he is not accused of improprieties with clients by avoiding dropping off females last. He shuns local sexual contacts, confining his practices (with real-life women, at any rate) to "faraway places" where he can let go. Mexico is a "backstage region" for Dwight, as exotic vacation spots are for many tour-ists. He nurtures a public image to project to others. He is conscious of conventions and adapts his behavior and disclosures to them.

And yet, Dwight does not lead a conventional lifestyle. He does not pretend to be interested in women as companions; in fact, his views of women are extreme and frankly contemptuous. He has not had a dating relationship that has led to intercourse in six years. He openly acknowl-edges (to me, at least, knowing that he will not be identified) that his sex-ual predilections, which are focused on prostitution and pornography, are likely to be regarded as "really bizarre." His sexual practices, even with prostitutes, are ritualistic and, to most observers, likely to seem fetishistic, even more than a trace sadistic. He admits to obsessing about sex in nearly all phases of his life. (Discussing a case on whose jury he was sitting, he speculated to me: "The judge in this case, she's about 50, blonde, I wonder if she takes it up the ass.") During the interviews I conducted with him, which took place in the afternoon, he drank alcohol more or less continu-ally, and he had a marijuana pipe ready at hand for the occasional pull. Most Americans would refer to the sum total of these activities and ten-dencies as unconventional—indeed, deviant.

"If the Great DJ in the Sky calls me to the flip side of life," Dwight declares, "there aren't a lot of things I've missed out on." He apologizes for his disk jockey metaphor. Dwight spun records for two decades in clubs and at weddings, bar mitzvahs, and confirmations all over the New York City metropolitan area before CDs put him out of business. He's now in his late 40s and he works as a limousine driver for the rich, the not-so-rich, and the merely frivolous. It's a job that's clearly vastly beneath him. Dwight graduated from an elite and extremely selective New York public high school and was accepted to an Ivy League univer-sity. After attending then dropping out of a state university, he parlayed his acting skills and love of theatrics into a temporary but long-term career of supplying music and patter for dance crowds.

"Well, maybe there are places I haven't gone. India. Africa. Egypt. I guess I am cautious about certain things. I'm too worried about amoebic dysentery. Still, I have to say, I've had it all." Dwight isn't comparing himself to his three siblings—the head of a medium-sized corporation, a professor at a major university, and a sports newscaster for a television station—but with the ne'er-do-wells he left behind in his old neighborhood, as well as those he so often encounters in his current life.

He scrutinizes the label on the bottle of rum I've put on the table. "Let me say, Professor, you're no piker. Whatever they say about you, you're very generous. Actually, I've switched to vodka. Still. . . ." He pours himself a drink, a rum and cherry Coke, then holds up the bottle, cocking his eyebrows at me. "Join me? Don't make me drink alone." I ask if he has any orange juice. He does, and takes a carton out of the fridge and hands it to me. I pour myself a rum and orange juice. We settle into our chairs.

"I run into a lot of whites who think all Black people are pimps and burglars and junkies and whores. If they meet me, I'd like to hope they'd change their minds. I own this house and in a couple of years, it'll be paid off, I'll own it outright. I own a truck and a sports car. I'm reliable, I show up for work, I do my job—I'm a *professional*. I can't say the same about all the people I deal with. My last job, I was pulling out of the driveway, and these two repo dudes stopped me. 'We're here to repossess the car,' they said. 'Take it, it's not mine' is what I told 'em. What could I say? The firm went belly up. My boss didn't pay his bills. Didn't know how to take care of business. He didn't *care*. Guy I work for now is a real gentleman. From the old school. Scottish burr, everything. He runs the business, I do my job. They like me."

Dwight gets up and walks into the living room and checks on the Franklin Stove. "I'm going to turn on the heat in a couple days. Meanwhile, this little baby works just fine. Benjamin Franklin, man, now *he* was a *great* American! Scientist, inventor, diplomat, printer, publisher. The first Postmaster General. He wasn't much of a looker, but he was able to knock down Frog pussy at a rate the rest of us can only dream about."

Shifting gears, Dwight launches into some drawbacks of his trade. "I make sure if I drive kids home from a prom, I never allow myself to be alone with a girl. I never drop off a woman or a girl last. I want to make sure there will never be a ditzy dame who says"—he imitates a woman's screechy voice—"'You pinched my bottom.' Don't get me wrong, I have the greatest respect for women as *craftswomen*." I ask what he means by that. "The sexual side. What they can do for men. Sexually. I've spent a lot of time with women and I've had to listen to all that *God-forsaken drivel* that comes out of their mouths. I *rent* women—I don't devote my life to them. I wouldn't trade one lug nut on my sports car for a box of Pampers. It's like the Benny Hill joke—why burn the house down to make toast? Don't get me wrong, I love kids. My brother's kids visit, but I know after two, three, four days with them, I get to hand them back to my brother. How do men do it?" he wonders. "When those kids are here, I can't use the toilet, I can't eat when or where I want, I have to hear them whining about their dad buying *fifty* dollar sneakers instead of a *hundred and twenty* dollar sneakers. I can't see it. I don't see the appeal, I really don't."

"Well, if that's true," I ask him, "I mean, if you don't really enjoy the companionship of women and you don't want children in your life, how do you achieve emotional satisfaction? How do you receive sexual gratification?"

"I receive sexual gratification through constant masturbation. I use a *lot* of pornography."

"What about emotional satisfaction?" I ask.

"I feel emotionally gratified every morning when I shave. I look in the mirror and say to myself, 'I'm going to have a good day.' I grew up in the projects in *the Bronx*, man, my father was a *grocer*. We lived in what can only be described as a *slum*. As long as I can remember, the suburbs of Long Island struck me as having a more genteel lifestyle. I'm a city kid, but I love the country. When I go to New York City, I hear the constant cacophony of ambulances, police sirens, car horns honking. When I'm here, I can hear the caterpillars eating the leaves, a squirrel sits on a tree stump outside my door, the women who live around the corner ride their horses past my house. I've always wanted to be landed gentry."

"And do you feel that way here?" I ask.

"Fuckin' *A!*" Dwight declares, almost shouting, stabbing the air with a thin, brown index finger. "Absolutely! The neighborhood is nice and quiet, I can blast my CD player and no one will complain. I was *very* fortunate to buy in this town when I did. My house is worth six-eight times what I paid for it. Yeah, man, when I think of the neighborhood I left behind, I feel good about myself. Guys hanging out on the corner, guys in jail, guys who ended up junkies, guys who ended up dead. *That's* my emotional satisfaction, that I ended up so much better *off* than the guys I grew up with." Dwight gets up, opens the refrigerator door, pulls out then unwraps a couple of sausages, plops them into a pan and begins cooking.

"Are there any unfulfilled fantasies that you have?" I ask him.

"I have a few," he replies. "For many years I thought I'd like to be a pilot but frankly, I think I lack *the right stuff*, which is, as they say, the fire in the belly. I'd much rather be flown someplace. Pilots don't seem to get to enjoy the flying that much, I mean, in between conversations and, you know, the life-and-death situations they encounter, but frankly, I'd just rather be chauffeured around."

"That's it?" I ask him again.

"I've accomplished most of the things I wanted to do. My dream car is parked outside and it's paid off. A nice little cottage in the country. It may not be rose-covered but the dogwood are lovely this time of year. The rhododendron will be out in a few weeks. I enjoy the respect of my colleagues and my clients. Because I never level with them the way I do with you. . . . As far as I'm concerned, I am, to quote James Thurber, in the proverbial cat-bird seat."

"You mentioned that you often paid for sex," I ask him. "When's the last time you had sex with a prostitute?"

"Over the last year, not at all. The last time was 18 months ago, in Puerto Vallarta. I find Spanish women *devastatingly* attractive. I don't do this in Black communities because I don't find Black women all that attractive."

"What about ordinary dates?" I ask.

"I feel uncomfortable with that," Dwight replies. "I never know what to do. I feel awkward to be in that situation. It's *unmanly* pretending to be interested in what a woman has to say when all I'm interested in is getting her into bed." He munches a few mouthfuls before continuing. "See, the difference between me and ordinary men is that, for me, to pretend to be interested in the drivel that falls out of women's mouths when all I'm interested in is a little nookie strikes me as *undignified.* Unmanly. I'm not interested in the things that most women find interesting. Fingernails. Jewelry. Clothes. Babies. What man is? Other men pretend. I don't."

I ignore the fact that practically none of the women I know—and especially my wife—fit Dwight's description. Instead, I focus on what I see as a central issue in the interview. "When's the last time you had a relationship with a woman that led to intercourse?" I ask.

"Six years ago. Look, I have some bizarre tastes in sexual activities that lead women to head for the hills. If I ask a woman to do something, she'll say no and never want to see me again. I have to ask myself, 'What did I ask her to do?' I don't know. Whatever it was, she didn't like it. And because of it, she's not gonna like *me*. But I fantasize a lot. Every time I walk around and see a woman, I think about her in bed. You know this criminal case I'm on?" Dwight is a juror in a trial involving a man who got a little rough with his girlfriend then resisted arrest when the police arrived. In the struggle, one of the cops struck the man's head with a Mag Lite and dropped him to the floor, putting seven stitches right above his ear. "The judge in this case, she's about 50, blonde, I wonder if she takes it up the ass. If she could be a combination of a Spanish whore and a Sunday school teacher, she'd never again know the meaning of unhappiness. I'd take care of her."

"But you had dates earlier," I respond. "I mean, years ago."

"Yes, I had a girlfriend in college and afterwards for seven-eight-nine years. And she left me. I feel privileged to have known her. Here it is 20 years later, and I *still* wake up hugging the pillow. She was very good at what I wanted her to do. She was really good at *tricks*. She was *enormously* arousing. To fuck a woman who's crying—every heave, every spasm turned me on. I'd ask her, 'Could you go into hysterical sobbing while I fuck you?' And she'd *do* it. I *loved* it! I think that was my downfall—subjecting her to what she found repulsive. She lost respect for me. There's no reason why a high-class piece of ass like that should subject herself to the sort of things I wanted her to do. I drank myself through a half-dozen liquor stores trying to get over her."

Dwight sighs and seems lost in thought for a moment, contemplating his loss. "Dating, women, romance, relationships, marriage—who was it that said, 'The position is undignified, the pleasure is fleeting, the expense is damnable?' Alexander Wolcott? I can't remember. I hear from guys who have been married just a few months, they tell me, 'What could I have been thinking?'" Having finished his drink, he drinks a slug of rum directly out of the bottle then pours another one into the glass. "The loss of independence. The fact that I'd have to debate when I'll be home. Tuesday-Wednesday—whenever—*that's* when I'll be home!" More finger-stabs in the air. "What do I want for dinner? I don't want to *care* about this shit! I can't give up my independence. 'Hey,' I tell a guy who's thinking about getting married, 'you're a big boy now! Fuckin' *feed yourself!* You're going to give up your independence for a few lousy *meals?*' Not me!" As if on cue, he grabs a fork and takes another bite of the sausage.

In French, Dwight quotes Gustave Flaubert, " 'Man is nothing, work is everything.' There's going to be a time when the childbearing of women is going to be taken over by the lab. Then women are going to have to share in the *real* work of life—science, medicine, math. They won't be able to say [squealing in a high-pitched tone of voice], 'Oh, my belly, my belly!'" You don't want kids, don't fuckin' *have* kids! Hey, do something *important* for a change! Occasionally, I think I've missed out on hearth and home, but that's an extremely fleeting feeling. I'd probably end up like Jack Lemmon, you know the movie, *How to Murder Your Wife*. Press a button, make 'em disappear."

Dwight pours himself another rum and cherry Coke. "I don't find the women on Long Island all that attractive. In California, they are more aware of their bodies. More sensual, more physical. Here, most of them are fat. They let themselves be attractive only for as long as they can hook a man, then they let themselves go." He shakes his head. "I can't see marriage. It's not in the cards for me. I can't even see *dating*."

After a few sips, Dwight declares, "Pornography is everything. I have an enormous appetite—an absolutely insatiable appetite—for it. I need it, fresh and new every week. I need it by the carload. The Japanese make the best porn. Cartoons. Really, *really* bizarre shit. I love it, the more bizarre the better. She-males. Women whose bodies are distended because they're getting fucked by enormous dicks. Girls who are far too young are being done by their fathers, their uncles, their brothers. Mother-daughter incest. . . . Schoolgirls getting raped by aliens, Wonder Woman getting raped by the Joker and the Penguin. Shit like that." He reaches over, picks up the pan, stabs a sausage, and begins eating it directly out of the pan. "They're only supermarket sausages," Dwight apologizes. "Not like the ones you get in an Italian store. I know a place near here that sells sausages that are truly fabulous. Too lazy, I guess. If laziness doesn't kill me, I'll live forever."

Two weeks later, sensing I didn't have a complete description of how he felt and how he lived his life, I interviewed Dwight again.

Erich: Last time, we were talking about various things that you did that were to some degree a little bit different from the so-called mainstream.

Dwight: [A bit defensively] There you're walking a very gray area. You're going to have to tell me whatever it is that's mainstream. What's mainstream?

Erich: Well, 80 percent of the population above the age of 35 is married.

Dwight: OK, that's a good place to start.

Erich: So the *statistical norm* is to be married. And my guess is that a high proportion of the population who's married is more or less on the straight and narrow as far as sexual practices is concerned.

Dwight: Well, you have me there. I don't have a monitor in people's bedrooms. I don't know what goes on behind closed doors. I think I went into that with you before. I lost my opportunity to marry my college sweetheart. In the meantime, I have changed my attitude about relationships. At least I got it straight in my own mind that a fellow can live much better without the encumbrances of a wife and family. Guys get married for a lot of reasons. They think that people are going to wag a finger at them when they get to be 25 or 30—oh, there's something wrong with you if you're not married. They get married because they get pressure from their parents—"When am I going to see some grandchildren?" They get married because all their friends expect them to. . . .

Erich: What do you think it is that makes you different?

Dwight: It could be anything. It could be birth order. I'm the young-est in my family. It could be the years of observation—I keep my eyes and ears open as I travel through this world. Even men who earn many, many times what I do can't ask what time it is without looking over at their wives and going, is it OK? [Glances to the side, cocks his eyes and points to his watch.] Captains of industry, high ranking military men, politicians and judges, lawyers, doctors, and they get the rug *completely* pulled out from under them. It happens every day.

Erich: What is it about you that made it possible for you to presum-ably escape this net? I mean, you've got two brothers and a sister, and they're conventionally married.

Dwight: One of my brothers is divorced.

Erich: They all have kids.

Dwight: And as far as I can tell, all are excellent parents. The kids are normal—doing well in school, not doing drugs, not engaging in any of the statistically abnormal behaviors.

Erich: So what makes you different?

Dwight: Everybody's different. We're a nation of rugged individuals.

Erich: Well, we may *think* we are, but the fact is, you *are* different. I mean, three out of the four kids in your family got married and had kids. So you're different from *them*. . . . OK [realizing that this line of ques-tioning is not going to be productive], you mentioned before that you enjoyed the consumption of pornography.

Dwight: Yeah. It's a drug. I need massive amounts of it. It gives me a tickle for a little while and then I need a lot, lot more. It's very much like a drug or what it must be like when you have a gambling fever. I drink, too, but I don't drink as much as I used to. With drinking, you get to a certain point and then you either pass out or you stop. With porn, I can never get enough *pornography—not* erotica. I'm not talking about Judith Krantz or Harlequin Romances or that other kind of stuff. With the exception of some European and some Japanese stuff, it's all pretty much, you know, strip and screw.

Erich: What's the nature of the stuff that you prefer?

Dwight: Rough sex. Costumes. I don't like it when the women and the men strip down to the buff and have ordinary, missionary-type sex. It's boring. I like tricks. Kink.

Erich: What is it about costumes that you find appealing?

Dwight: Just a fetish. You know, some guys go for glasses or fishnet stockings or high heels. Stuff like that. I like military uniforms, the more severe the better. Even something you might not consider a uniform, like a regular business suit that a librarian might wear, or schoolgirl uniforms.

Erich: Glasses?

Dwight: Glasses. There used to be a really great girlie magazine, *Glasses*, a glasses magazine. It lasted for two years and then went out of business.

Erich: What is it about glasses?

Dwight: I think it's a kind of intellectuality. . . . I mean, getting a tramp to act like a tramp is intriguing enough. But to get an intelligent, nice girl to behave like that is an accomplishment. It's exciting. It's like a violation of the woman's nature. Overwhelming her, forcing her. My ultimate sexual situation is screwing a girl who's crying. Real wracking, heaving sobs, tears streaming out of her eyes and down her cheeks, snot coming out of her nose. [When this happened,] it was the greatest sexual experience of my life. Every time her body spasmed, it felt like little hands inside of her body squeezing my cock. She was crying over something else. She had overdosed on drugs. She was down on her knees, kneeling at the toilet, where it actually took place. She was a nurse, she worked for a hospital, and she had discovered the keys to the pharmaceutical cabinet, and she was crying about that. She was high, she was sick, and she was crying.

Erich: And she was actually throwing up at the same time?

Dwight: In my bathroom. With her head in the toilet. Driving the porcelain bus, so to speak. Yeah. Praying to the porcelain goddess. And I was fucking her from behind. Yeah, man, it was great. One of the greatest sexual experiences of my life. Of course, I disapproved of her helping herself to the pharmaceuticals she was entrusted to. Hospital-quality drugs, you know. This isn't like smoking a little grass or something like that, this is major league.

Erich: You mentioned it's been a while since you had a date with a woman. Why do you think that is?

Dwight: Women are smart, they're intelligent, they can sense who I am.

Erich: In the interaction, when you're talking with a woman, how do they pick up on it? What do you say, what do they say?

Dwight: I have no idea, I'm not a woman. I hardly ever flirt with a woman.

Erich: Isn't the experience of laying your hands on a woman as opposed to making use of pornography a different kind of experience?

Dwight: It certainly is. One difference of course is [that actually being with a woman is] a much more *expensive* experience.

Erich: Don't you think that if you were intelligent enough and clever enough and sophisticated enough you could manage to have a girlfriend?

Dwight: Not necessarily, because I feel that that's the kind of delusion that men have, that if I comb my hair just right or drive the right car—or *whatever*—I should be able to get women to do what I want. My point is that I don't necessarily *want* to have a girlfriend. I don't *like* the idea of women falling in love with me or *caring* about what happens to me. That *does not* appeal to me.

Erich: Why not?

Dwight: I see where it leads. A kind of domesticity. It takes all the fun out of sex. And once children show up, the guy is, like, in the *way*, interfering with something that's going on between mom and the kids. One of the cleverest comments on relationships I've ever heard came from Katharine Hepburn. She said, men and women shouldn't *live* together, they should leave *near* each other and *visit* each other once in a while. My brother is an example. He's a much less stressful and a much more caring parent now that he's not living with his wife. It can't be helpful for the kids to hear the parents fighting all the time, and now, that sort of thing hardly ever happens because he and his wife simply *don't live* with each other.

Erich: If you can't have love—or in your case, if you don't want a love relationship—then it seems to me the next best thing is to try to work out a kind of long-term, stable sexual relationship that's somewhat romantic but that's still kind of kept at a distance. I mean, you're an intelligent guy, you can be charming. . . .

Dwight: You do flatter me.

Erich: No, it's true. And I would think that if you could be a little bit cynical, a little bit manipulative, maybe a little charming, you could have the best of all possible worlds.

Dwight: I just can't seem to get my point across. In my heart of hearts. . . .

Erich: But you're an *actor*, you see, that's my whole point, you're an actor, you can put across a certain persona that makes it clear that you're somebody you're *not*. And that you can *give up* certain things so that you can *get* certain other things that are ultimately more desirable. That's what I'm asking. So, why not go for that sort of thing rather than restricting yourself to [having sex in] faraway places?

Dwight: The act is difficult. It requires effort. It's difficult to maintain over the long haul. One can get away with it for a day or two, a week or two, but then your real personality comes out and they start looking for somebody else.

Erich: I see. So you don't think you could pull it off.

Dwight: I probably could if I wanted to, subconsciously, I guess, although it's crazy to try to second-guess your own subconscious, I guess subconsciously, I just don't want to. I'd have a woman calling me up, "Where are you, when will you be home?" It's *appalling* to me—offputting.

Erich: But if you're really *successful* at this game, you would make sure that she doesn't do that sort of thing.

Dwight: It's a female paradox. You can't always be sure that other people will behave the way you want them to. People have a tendency to do what they feel like doing, that is, what they want. This way I only have one person to control, one person to feed, I don't have to wait to get into my own bathroom, I never have to argue about what's going to be on television.

Erich: Don't you ever feel lonely?

Dwight: No, not at all. I very much look forward to—although I relish your company, of course—I very much look forward to those times when I can be by myself, storm around the house. I don't even have a *cat* to kick any more. I think that's a big part of the reason why people get married and have kids, is because they're absolutely terrified about being alone in their dotage. Whereas I just don't see inflicting a child with that.

Erich: In the last few years, have you ever had experiences where you were interacting, you were talking to women and you might be, like, interested in them, but, somehow, you never really got together with them?

Dwight: I find women attractive, I just don't know how to go about asking them out for a date. I don't know how to do it. . . . It's just that I have no knack for dating, I have no aptitude, I have no facility. . . . I've had my heart broken and I'd just rather not go through that again. I'll die a bachelor. And damn the consequences. [He hoists a drink.] Cheers. [Gulps down the drink.]

Erich: Do you miss it? Dating I mean.

Dwight: What, do you mean do I miss putting my hands on girls? Yeah, I miss it like *crazy.* I'm just not willing to pay the price for it. Unless I'm actually gonna *hire* the girls and then of course you only get an *approximation* of the feeling of sexual intimacy. As Woody Allen says, sex without love is an empty sensation, but as empty sensations go, it's terrific. And it's the sort of thing where you actually *get* what you want. And, you know, there's no strings attached. Like, you know, I can *bare* my *soul* to a Mexican hooker because, I mean, the odds are very good that I'll never *see* her again. And if she has a lower opinion of me from now on, *so what?* You know, at least I got my tickle. I may have had to pay for it, but, man—I mean, a guy I drove around last year bought his wife a brand-new SUV, a Jeep Cherokee. And the deal was that he wanted to get five coughing, gagging, eye-rolling, cum-shooting-out-of-her-nose type of blow jobs, and I'll buy you a new SUV. It's something you should be getting for *free*, man, fuckin' A! You don't want to offend the dame because you have to wake up next to her every day for the next 40 or 50 years.

Erich: How do you feel about being lonely?

Dwight: When I get too depressed, I take a *long* vacation.

Erich: You mentioned that you don't usually hire women around here.
Dwight: Not usually. Not *ever*.
Erich: Why is that?
Dwight: A couple reasons. One is, as I told you, I don't usually find Long Island women all that attractive. Even their accent gives me a soft-on. . . . Maybe I'm rationalizing a little bit, but when I'm in California, even for a couple weeks, I see better-looking women working in 7-Eleven than the so-called beauties around here. The one great love of my life was from Huntington.
Erich: That's on Long Island.
Dwight: I found that Huntington, it's like an island in the wilderness. In Huntington, they raise a *superior* crop of dames. Whereas just a few miles outside of town, they start turning into Rosie O'Donnell.
Erich: But then you could go into New York City.
Dwight: It's also a question of the financial necessities. Very, very expensive. Not to mention that there, you could be knocked on the head or slipped a Mickey [a drink that renders the imbiber unconscious and helpless]. Whereas in other places, practically everywhere in the world, a certain level of prostitution is accepted as business as usual. And you get more—how shall I say it? *Bang* for the *buck*. [Chuckles.] In Mexico, for example. Puerto Vallarta. There are two gentlemen's clubs on the same street, on opposite sides of the street, and you can have whatever you want. . . . Girl supermarket. Very attractive, a lot prettier than a fellow would normally be able to get his hands on, and I found the whole thing pretty satisfying. I wish I could afford to spend more time there.
Erich: What about AIDS?
Dwight: I don't have that kind of sex with them. I don't really do the gooey, penetration-type of sex. . . . I usually just feel them up, dress them up, get blow jobs, I rub myself against them. It's pretty intimate. Maybe even being just a little bit rough. It's funny, I *fantasize* about, you know, being an ogre, but once I finally come across a woman who says, "Sure, go ahead, you know, put your hands on me, help yourself, I'm all yours for the next hour or so," once I finally come across such a creature, I can't bring myself to be mean to her.
Erich: And there are costumes, like, in the room where she works?
Dwight: I bring them with me.
Erich: Oh. Like, in a suitcase or something?
Dwight: I put them in a shopping bag or a carrying case and I bring them with me to the clubs. Or they're in my hotel room because you can bring women back to your hotel room. Yeah, I pick up the clothes in second-hand clothing stores—as cheap and as gaudy as I can find. They're disposable, really, which is the whole idea.

Erich: What about doing this sort of thing in the United States?

Dwight: I hardly ever do that in the United States. I used to, when I went to Reno or in other cities in Nevada. The Mustang Ranch. The Mustang Ranch is the only place in my life where I've been denied service, for the obvious reason that I'm Black.

Erich: Really?

Dwight: At the Mustang Ranch, a legalized bordello in Nevada—this was many years ago, I'm sure they've cleaned up their act since then. Of all the things I've seen or heard about, they never fuckin' *once* mentioned it. And it was a *Black madam* from *Brooklyn* who came up to me and said, "Hey, you're not from around here, are you?" And I go, naw, I won a couple of dollars in Carson City, I had read about the Mustang Ranch, and I thought I'd come out here and check it out. So she said, "None of the locals would do business with us if they knew we were servicing Black men." She was very up-front about it, which I appreciated, and all of a sudden, I kept thinking, gee, I'm surrounded by an awful lot of *desert* and if me and my little car was to just get *buried* in one of these *pits* out here, *who the fuck would ever know?* So the little light bulb went off, and I just went GTFOH—get the *fuck* outta *here*, man. Yeah, one can do that sort of thing in the United States. But I'm a man of limited means. And, you know, I want to spend a couple of hours getting to know the girl, the sound of her *voice*, the sound of her *laughter*, you know, the *smell* of her, the curve of her *cheek*, trying on different *costumes*, all that other kind of stuff. I want to be able to say, now, this is what I want you to say, I want you to resist a little bit here, but at the same time, I want you to give me that beautiful blow job, but I want you to stop every once in a while and go [imitates a woman's voice], "Oh, no, Daddy, please don't make me do this any more." In other words, I don't want a Stepford wife—the pussy objects, the perfect slave women, all they ever lived to do was to screw their husbands and go, "Yes dear." I don't *want* a Stepford wife. I'd like to build a Stepford wife into my *computer*. I'd like her to be one day a slim little Japanese woman and the next day a pneumatic Aryan type, and I want her to yes-sir, no-sir me to fuckin' *death*. But that's in my computer, I wouldn't want that in real life. I'd quickly lose interest in such a person.

Erich: But it sounds like you want a woman to *hire*, so to speak, to follow your instructions, which is sort of like a Stepford wife.

Dwight: Yes. But at the same time, she has to bring her own life experiences, her own *touch*, I want her to show me something. Like, do you know any tricks? Surprise me.

Erich: What would be an example of something like that?

Dwight: Oh, I don't know. When I get a really enthusiastic, coughing, gagging type of blow job. But at the same time, you know, she's *made* to do it, she's *performing,* and every once in a while, she pulls back and she says the opposite. She'll say, "This is what you want women for? You think this is all women are good for? Please don't make me *do* this any more." See, at the same time she's *doing* it, she's *performing* a German-type of blow job. *That's* a particular turn-on for me and it's very difficult to get women to do it for me, especially when they don't speak English and you're trying to explain what you want. Most of them eventually get the idea about the second hour.

Erich: So you hire them for a very extended length of time.

Dwight: If I can, two-three hours at a time. But that starts running into dough. Even in Mexico, 200-300 bucks for three hours. What I want is for the front of her dress to be all soaking wet. I'll tell her, I've been saving up for this, it's only a few minutes worth of discomfort for you, and you may find it distasteful, but that's what I'm paying for. . . . Women get their own way so often. A lot of guys go to hookers and [make use of] pornography not so much for sexual release but for revenge.

Erich: Revenge?

Dwight: Yeah, man. They want to get even. It's like, when I was your age, girls like you never gave me the time of day. Now, grab your ankles and *shut up.* If you hafta complain, stuff a handkerchief in your mouth. Do all the complaining you want. I, you know, I appreciate it.

Erich: It's actually, like, uh, uh, *brutalizing* the woman.

Dwight: There's plenty of that sort of stuff on the Internet, too. I actually prefer the animated pornography because there, you can brutalize the woman in *ultra* ways, but nobody actually gets hurt.

Erich: If the other, more violent pornography that is live action were available, would you prefer that?

Dwight: I might start to investigate it. I never have in the past, but I might start investigating it. If it's there. It's nice to know I'm not the only freak in town. There's a whole *website* devoted to rape. Animated, costumes, I don't mean friendly, consensual, rough sex or anything like that, I mean grabbing her and pulling her into the bushes. The Japanese are especially good at it.

Erich: Have you ever had any fantasies about doing this in real life?

Dwight: All the time. But I do it with women who are, you know, *paid* to take abuse. But actually, when I finally wind up saving the money and taking the time off from work and getting down to where they are, as I explained before, I'm so grateful to be around them that I can't bring myself to be more than just, you know, a *little* rude rather than my fantasy.

Erich: What would being a little rude entail?

Dwight: Spitting in their face, calling them names, you know, and what I told you before, asking them to say the opposite of what they're doing, which is, "Is this all you think women are good for, take your hands off of me, what kind of girl do you think I am, can't we be friends, oh, no, Daddy, don't do that, it's so dirty, it makes me feel so dirty."

Erich: When you see a girl—a woman—walking around in a place like that, what do you look for?

Dwight: Oh, I have my fantasy girls, the Jayne Mansfield types, the big, pneumatic blonde, with the huge tits on a slim frame, is actually my ideal.

Erich: The next time you do something like this, where would you go?

Dwight: Mexico. Puerto Vallarta. Two very well established places. The transfer time [from the clubs to the hotel] should be a little less, although the time in the back of the cab is very exiting, too, it's just that the cab driver is *right there*.

Erich: You're bringing the woman back to the hotel?

Dwight: Yeah. It'd be nice if there was a bigger car or something with partitions.

Erich: You mean you're, like, groping her in the cab?

Dwight: Oh, gosh, yeah. And her me, too, yeah. Again, the most difficult thing to do is to give you the pressing grope, to be pressing herself against you like that but at the same time, to be saying—*mouthing*—the usual platitudes, like, "What kind of *girl* do you think I am, don't *do* that," that sort of thing. That's a *big* turn-on for me, as I said before. I wanted to mention to you the next time we got into one of these conversations something that I mentioned before about *How to Murder Your Wife*. In it, there's a real glimpse of what you might call "The Bitch Book." Did I tell you this before?

Erich: Well, I remember you saying that if you got married, you said that you'd do what Jack Lemmon did, press the button and make your wife disappear.

Dwight: Oh, no, I don't suppose I'd just press the button and make my wife disappear.

Erich: I know, it's a metaphor.

Dwight: No, in it [the movie] there's a scene where, after dinner, the men are in one room talking, and the women are in the kitchen talking, and a woman speaks to Virna Lisi [the actress who plays Jack Lemmon's wife], whose English isn't very good, she goes, "Watch this," and she opens the door and she starts hassling her husband, and she says [imitating an imperious voice], "I heard that." And he goes, "You heard what?" And she says, "Never mind, you know what you said!" [And he says] "What, what, what?" [And she says] "Just wait till I get you home!" She goes back in the kitchen and she goes, "See? We're in here, they're in there, I couldn't have heard a word he said, he couldn't have heard a word I said, it's just very important to keep them [men] *off balance* like that, it makes them easier to control." So the guy goes around the rest of the night with his shoulders up, going "What did I say? Huh? Huh? What did I say?" It's what you might call "The Bitch Book." Which is not an actual *tome*, but a lesson that's passed down from mother to daughter, down through the millennia, on how to control men. It's supposedly pretty easy to do. I know I would be [easy to control]. I'd love to be a high-ranking cryptoanalyist or something like that and have the Russians send one of those sex bombs at me. Yeah, I know, the cold war's long over, but don't count the Russians out. Shit. She'd *Mata Hari* me to death. [Chuckles.] I'd tell her secrets I don't even *know*. I love the idea of being teased. Not by anyone else but professional women who are being paid to do it. Yeah, but as long as I know that, you know, I'd get a nice big payoff at the end. I'd actually pay the girl to lead me on, to give me a bad time. And after a few minutes I'd lose my temper and I'd shake her around a little bit, I'd even slap her, and she'd cry and I'd fuck her. And after, she'd say, "You wanna go again?" It's great.

Erich: You got the computer mainly for outlets for pornography?

Dwight: [Emphasizing each syllable]: *Ab-so-lute-ly!* The fact of the matter is I spend a tremendous amount of *time* as well as money flying to cities and scouring the stores to find whatever's been left over. The freaks who live there camp out outside the shops and when the Fed Ex or the UPS man delivers, they're there an hour later. The stuff you get in the magazines is, like, say, at the level of 2 or 3 and the stuff you get on the Internet is a 9 or 10. Everything you might imagine.

Erich: The scale is the degree of roughness or rawness or how extreme it is?

Dwight: It doesn't necessarily have to be violence, that's only one aspect of it. But, you know, you can have super-muscular women, 15-year-olds with huge tits, *growing* magazines [which depict] girls who take some potion and you see them growing into voluptuous women. I'm not that much into Lolitas, either, but I've seen them, 12 and 13-year-old girls, that sort of thing. Even in New York City, one of the best places in the *world* for pornography, they have to keep the best stuff under the counter. The stuff they sell openly, they have to have the girls happily smiling.

Erich: So you're saying the more extreme pornography is harder to get.

Dwight: Always has been, and much more expensive.

Erich: And there's more of it on the computer.

Dwight: Yeah. That's why I laid out my [emphasizes each word] *two thousand fuckin' dollars*. That's a lot of money for a schmuck like me.

Erich: Is there any limit, I mean age limit, in porn?

Dwight: Depending on your taste. Guys go to Cuba for 14-year-olds. But you see, that's not really my thing. I like the possibility of it because I know it's illegal, but my thing is, you know, a dame who's older and experienced and voluptuous, in her late 30s, early 40s, or 50s, something like that, *dressing up* like Heidi, dressing *up* like Little Bo Peep. People may wax poetic about the cold hands of the old pro, but there's a lot to be said for it.

Once, as a presentation for the 200 students in my deviance course, Dwight and I had a dialogue about pornography. Afterwards, we were accosted in the hallway by a young woman who was *outraged* by what he said. Her main problem, she told us, was that he projected a kind of insidious, seductive charm and hence, his message, foul in itself, seemed less odious, more normal. I said I wasn't sure that Dwight had a "message" exactly, he was just a guy who lived a life that others found objectionable. "But you *exploit* women," said the student vehemently, now turning her attention to Dwight, "and you support the pornography industry, which also exploits women." He shrugged, completely indifferent to her concern. Later, after Dwight had left, the woman explained to me that when she was a young girl, a male relative had exposed her to pornography and sexually abused her. I tried to commiserate by telling her I could appreciate her sense of outrage, but decided not to pursue the matter. Dwight would have said he wasn't abusing children, nor is he forcing anyone to watch pornography. If anyone doesn't like it, he often explained to me, they don't have to watch it.

Dwight makes use of several types of explanations or "vocabularies" to justify his use of pornography and prostitution. Yes, it's true that he hasn't had a real date or a meaningful boy-girl relationship in years, he admits. But look at what happened to me when I did, he objects. She left me! And I suffered!

More important, he would argue, is the fact that most women are not worthwhile companions for a real man such as he. In fact, he suggests, his impulses and desires are normal, commonsensical, entirely reasonable. In contrast, the motives of other men are problematic, difficult to understand, almost nonsensical. Ordinary men, he explains, "pretend to be interested in the drivel that falls out of women's mouths. . . . Other men pretend. I don't." Dwight implies that he is a better man than most men— truer to man's nature. At least he's honest. *They* deviate from their manly nature by making concessions to the unreasonable demands of females; he doesn't. Dwight even uses a hint of the "condemnation of the condemners" rhetoric that, as we saw in the introduction, juvenile delinquents and other enactors of unconventional behavior also make use of. It is a common stigma neutralization technique.

In addition, Dwight adds, consider how clever he is to avoid being ensnared in women's wily traps. They want children, they want a family, they want a *home*, they want to bring men down to earth, to the reality of confining schedules and squalling, defecating babies. And to do that, to tame a man's unruly temperament, they have to *manipulate* him, make him feel guilty, control him through a calculated formula of withholding then granting sex ("It's something you should be getting for *free,* man") and practiced cunning ("The Bitch Book"). Dwight knows from experience with his brother's children that's not his scene. "I don't see the appeal," he declares. I'm free as a bird, Dwight explains, other men aren't. They have to ask permission from their wives, he claims, even to look at their watches. Even the most powerful of men, he says, "get the rug *completely* pulled out from under them."

Besides, Dwight explains, what's the point of trying to go out with women on dates? "I have no knack for dating, I have no aptitude, I have no facility," he explains. Why attempt something you can't accomplish? "I'll die a bachelor," he tells me, "And damn the consequences." Clearly, he seems to like things the way they are.

Dwight appears to have painted himself into a corner. According to his logic, there is one and only one inescapable conclusion. He enjoys the sexual company of women but not their companionship. He doesn't want to give up his freedom in exchange for what he sees as small, carefully doled-out dollops of sex—and boring, straight, vanilla sex at that! His sexual predilections, he admits, run into the realm of the bizarre, the unconventional, the far-out, and—to most women—the distasteful. What else is there to do but make use of commercial sex? Pornography is a ready solution to all these vexations. And when he has accumulated the requisite cash and is overcome by the desire to lay his hands on a real woman, a jaunt to Mexico indulges the lust. According to Dwight's logic, the unconventional lifestyle he's worked out for himself suits him just fine. If feminists, self-righteous moralists, or henpecked husbands have a problem with the way he lives his life, he feels, they can simply look the other way. After all, he'd say, what kind of sex life do *they* have?

CHAPTER 5

Once, I called up a doctor's office. A chiropractor. I said, do you take fat patients? And he said, what do you consider fat? I said, I weigh 350 pounds, and he laughed and said, of course not! There's nothing I can do with a 350 pound person! It's like a dog pound, the animals, you know, that's the way we are treated.

Sally

I cannot understand . . . why someone would just stand and stare at some-one because they are different. I do not stare at cripples, I do not stare at somebody because maybe they have one arm, because I have compassion in my soul. . . . [When] I've been with Sally, people go out of their way, they punch each other on the arm and say, get a load of that woman, and they stare at her, they'll turn around and do triple-takes, they burst out laugh-ing, loudly, so she can hear it, they want her to know that they are looking at her, not approving. That is the thing I want to put my finger on.

Diane

Sally, the Voluptuous Venus

To repeat a question I raised earlier, are physical characteristics a type of deviance? And should we blame people for the way they look? Are all physical conditions created equal?

Sally, a manager of a small business office, is married and in her early 40s; she is emotionally estranged from her husband, and she has no children. She weighs 385 pounds and is distinctly bottom-heavy. Diane manages a retail store, is in her 30s, and is divorced with one child. She weighs about 250 pounds. Most average-sized people would use the stereotypical phrase "such a pretty face" (Millman, 1980) to describe their appearance. Sally and Diane are members of NAAFA—the National Association to Advance Fat Acceptance. For NAAFA's members, the term "fat" is descriptive, not pejorative. They reason that fat people have an abundance of fat. NAAFA, ostensibly a civil rights organization dedicated to fighting discrimination against fat people, is, for most of its members, a kind of "love boat" for fat women and their male admirers. Referred to as "fat admirers" or FAs, these men, mainly of average size, are erotically and romantically attracted to heavy women. The organization's main purpose is to facilitate liaisons between these two, symbiotically connected, social categories.

"Let me tell you about something that happened just the other night," Diane tells me. "It illustrates what I'm talking about. Sally and I were standing outside the American Legion hall during a NAAFA dance. We were taking a break, getting some fresh air, gossiping about people we know, things that had happened to us. There were several other NAAFA women there, Betsy and a couple of her friends, standing near us. And Sally and I were engaged in deep conversation. Well, a van full of kids—they weren't kids, they were men in their 20s, and one young woman—drove by and stopped at a light. They started to *howl*. They went *"Hee-hee-hee-hee-haw-haw-haw-haw!"* They laughed and pointed, and yelled things at us, as if we were *pigs*, animals without feelings, just like we were the *elephant man* standing there, a *freak* to be made fun of without restraint. I think that if they had a *squirt* gun or a *firecracker* or something to *throw*, they would have *thrown* it at us. People I've never seen before pulled up in traffic and started *screaming* at us. The other fat people who were outside on the sidewalk near us, I looked at them and thought they were all going to start *crying*. They were all, it just so happened to be, a bunch of soft, Betsy Pelligrino-type women standing out there."

Diane pauses to formulate how she should relate this experience. "So, Sally and I turned around and began *yelling* really, really *nasty* things at these young men in the van. I yelled—excuse my English—*You ugly, fucking son-of-a-bitch! Shut your ugly, ignorant, fucking mouth, you ill-mannered bastard! Look at your face, you're as ugly as shit! Shut your mouth or I'll have you arrested for being ugly! Get out of your truck, you ugly son-of-a-bitch and come on over here!* I *tore* into them! I completely went wild! But *Sally* went wild also. We were *screaming* at them. You're dumb and ugly, only a dumb, stupid son-of-a-bitch would open your mouth like that. Look at your face, you're so goddamn ugly and dumb! Your mother should have used birth control! I mean, I *really* went wild. Both of us did. Well, dead silence. The truck went dead silent. They sat there and stared at us, *stone*-faced. How *dare* we—pigs, their whipping dogs—turn around and yell something like that back at them? And it just so happened two were very ugly. How *dare* I mention that? And so I yelled, You with the big nose! You keep your goddamn mouth shut! We screamed at these people horribly, like we were screaming at a pack of dogs to run away from us, leave us alone! They just fell silent. One started giggling again. They were very uncomfortable by our aggressive reaction. They never anticipated it. Nobody would have believed that we had that in us. The people in the cars around took all this in. And it was *dead silent.* The light changed and they just left."

"All right," she admits, "I yelled something really coarse. Whether I was right or wrong, I can't say. The point is, I couldn't stand it another minute. I am a success, I am bright, I am attractive. I *will not* be yelled at and insulted like that. You yell at me, I'm going to scream at you. So help me, they're lucky I didn't blow their fuckin' brains out, that's how furious I was. I would have struck 'em if I could have gotten over the cars in between me and them. All I could see when they started this was, all these people at the NAAFA dance, they have to run and go to this secret hall, slinking around, hidden away from society, just so they can have a *dance*, just so they can relax and have a good time. So, these people at the dance, they *hurt*, they were yelled at, insulted, they were being hurt by a bunch of ignorant *shitheads!* I tell you, if I had had my gun in my hand, I would have at least blown out their tires. I will start doing push-ups again to build up my arms so I can knock the mouth off of anybody who ever does it to me again. I *refuse.* I can't stand silent any longer. Not everyone in that dance hall was strong enough to defend themselves or was willing to take the risk of defending themselves. And I'm sure that my destiny is to do it for them. But I won't take it any more. I'm mad as hell!" [Laughs.]

What makes the obese deviant?

In contemporary America, obesity is stigmatized. Fat people are considered less worthy human beings than thin people are. Goffman tells us that stigmatized persons are regarded as "not quite human" (1963, p. 5) and, quite clearly, the obese are stigmatized. Oddly enough, even though the obese offer up a nearly perfect example of a "spoiled identity," in *Stigma*, Erving Goffman mentioned obesity only twice, and both times in passing. Once, he sees obesity as the basis of one of a number of categories of stigmatized persons who form "huddle-together self-help clubs" (p. 22). In a second discussion, along with "the village idiot, the small-town drunk, and the platoon clown," he mentions the "fraternity fat boy," all of whom can serve as a "mascot for the group" (p. 142), even though "he is denied the respect accorded full-fledged members" (p. 141). Given its nearly perfect applicability to most of the central concepts discussed in *Stigma*, it is curious that in that book, obesity does not play a more central role.

Obesity is an attribute that makes people different. Goffman describes "discrediting" differentness as attracting a "tainted, discounted" identity (1963, p. 3). For the ancient Greeks, stigma attached to someone who became a "blemished person, ritually polluted, to be avoided" (p. 1). Men and women of average weight tend to feel superior to the obese, reward them less, punish them more, make fun of them; the obese may become targets of derision and harassment. What is more, thin people will feel that this treatment is just; that the obese deserve it; indeed, that it is something of a humanitarian gesture; since such humiliation will supposedly inspire them to lose weight.

The obese, in the words of one observer, "are a genuine minority, with all the attributes that a corrosive social atmosphere lends to such groups: poor self-image, heightened sensitivity, passivity, and a sense of isolation and withdrawal" (Louderback, 1970, p. v). They are subject to relentless discrimination; they are the butt of denigrating jokes; they suffer from persecution; it would not be an exaggeration to say that they attract a great deal of cruelty from the thin majority. Moreover, their friends and family rarely give them the kind of support and understanding they need to deal with this cruelty; in fact, it is often friends and family who are themselves meting out the cruel treatment. The social climate has become "so completely permeated with anti-fat prejudice that the fat themselves have been infected by it. They hate other fat people, hate themselves when they are fat, and will risk anything—even their lives—in an attempt to get thin. . . . Anti-fat bigotry . . . is a psychic net in which the overweight are entangled every moment of their lives" (pp. vi, vii).

A substantial proportion of the obese accept the denigration thin society dishes out to them because they feel, for the most part, that they deserve it. And few defend other fat people who are being criticized because they are a mirror of the very defects that are so repugnant to them. Unlike the members of most other minorities, they rarely fight back. In fact, they feel they can't fight back. Racial, ethnic, and religious minorities can isolate themselves to some degree from minority prejudices; the obese cannot. Chances are, most of the people they meet will be of average size; they live in a world designed for people of smaller bodies. The only possibilities seem to be to brace themselves—to cower under the onslaught of abuse—or to retreat and attempt to minimize the day-to-day abuse. Fighting back seems to be a rarely chosen path.

The fact is, to the thin majority, obesity is regarded as "morally reprehensible," a "social disgrace" (Cahnman, 1968, p. 283). Fat people are set apart from men and women of average size; they tend to be isolated from "normal" society (Millman, 1980). The single sin of obesity is rarely regarded as isolated. Hardly anyone who possesses one stigmatizing trait is thought to have only one. A single sin will be seen as housing a multitude of others as well, to be the "tip of the iceberg." The one stigmatizing characteristic is a master status: Everything about the individual is interpreted in light of the single trait. "Possession of one deviant trait may have a generalized symbolic value, so that people automatically assume that its bearer possesses other undesirable traits allegedly associated with it" (Becker, 1963, p. 33). Thus, we raise the question when confronting someone with a stigma: "What kind of person would break such an important rule?" Typically, the answer that is offered is: "One who is different from us, who cannot or will not act as a moral human being and therefore might break other important rules." In short, the stigmatizing characteristic "becomes the controlling one" (p. 34).

Although, strictly speaking, obesity falls into the type of stigma Goffman referred to as "abominations of the body," one of "the various deformities" (1963, p. 4), in fact, it is regarded by the average-sized majority as much a *moral* failing as a physical defect. Being fat indicates a *blemish of individual character*, more specifically, possessing a "weak will" and an "unnatural passion" (p. 4). The obese are overweight, according to the popular view, because they eat immodestly and to excess. They have succumbed to temptation and hedonistic pleasure-seeking, where other, more virtuous and less self-indulgent individuals have resisted. The stigma of obesity is, as with behavioral deviance, the outcome of a struggle between good and evil, vice and virtue. The obese must therefore pay for the sin of overindulgence by attracting well-deserved stigma (Cahnman, 1968; Maddox et al., 1968). The obese suffer from what the public sees as "self-inflicted damnation" (Allon, 1973, 1982). In one study of the public's rejection of persons with certain traits and characteristics, it was found that the stigma of obesity fell more or less squarely in between that of physical handicaps, such as blindness, and behavioral deviance, such as homosexuality (Hiller, 1981, 1982).

So powerfully stigmatized has obesity become that a *New York Times* editorial argues that it has replaced sex and death as our "contemporary pornography." Our society is made up of "modern puritans" who tell one another "how repugnant it is to be fat"; "what's really disgusting," we feel, "is not sex, but fat." We are all "so relentless, so determined to punish the overweight. . . . Not only are the overweight the most stigmatized group in the United States, but fat people are expected to participate in their own degradation by agreeing with others who taunt them."[1]

Diane explained to me how Sally reacts to the taunts she receives from average-sized persons expressing their repugnance to her size. Sally is remarkably atypical of the obese. Diane goes on to describe the full spectrum of NAAFA members, however, and many of them, it seems, have internalized the stigma directed their way over the years.

Diane: No matter where Sally goes, she is stared at. She is stared at as a freak so often that I guess, out of survival, she chooses not to notice it. Sally's attitude is—and of course, she doesn't believe it, but she uses it, 'cuz what else has she got?—she says the reason why they stare at her is because they've never seen a big woman as beautiful as she is. If you see Sally, with her filthy, greasy, orange hair and a horrible sun dress on, no stockings and no bra, and every bit of her shaking, walking along with those huge, enormous hips and those fat legs—what are you going to think? I have seen people turn around and just openly *stare* at her, and it certainly isn't because she's the most beautiful woman you have ever seen. She chooses to ignore this, but it's impossible to ignore. I've been with her so many times when people are just *staring* at her. And she blocks it out. It's a survival technique. If she doesn't do it, she will *crack*. I mean, you can't *stand* being treated like a *freak* the way she is. Every time you went some place, if you were stared at like a freak, you would *break*. So she has built walls. She completely ignores it. And if somebody is nice to her, immediately she figures it's because they think she's so beautiful and they want to sleep with her. I mean, even just common courtesy is twisted and turned by Sally. It's absolutely *heartbreaking*.

Being with Sally in public is a unique experience because I cannot get over society. You know . . . , people do not often stare at me. I mean, they may look at me and notice that I'm a fat woman, or look me up and down once or twice. But it's no big thing, there are *many* people my size. Until you go with Sally, you cannot understand the *amount* of *cruelty* and *hostility* towards her simply because of her size. I *cannot* understand, in society, why someone would just stand and *stare* at someone because they are different. I do not stare at cripples, I do not stare at somebody because maybe they have one arm, because I have compassion in my soul. If I can do this and many people I know can be that way . . . , why are there so many people—I mean, this is my own confusion—why are so many people so cruel that they just stand there and *stare* at these large women—and men, of course. But when I've been with Sally, people *go out of their way*, they punch each other on the arm and say, get a load of *that* woman, and they stare at her, they'll turn around and do triple-takes, they burst out laughing, *loudly*, so she can hear it, they *want* her to know that they are looking at her and not approving. *That* is the thing I want to put my finger on.

What is it with society that when they see somebody like a Sally that they have to make a gesture or a remark or cause an incident so that their disapproval is *recognized?* Why can't they just look at her and maybe think to themselves, "I'm glad I'm not like that," or, "Boy, that one is big"? Why does there have to be a forced *recognition* that they don't like her which causes her such *enormous pain* that the woman has become bitter, suicidal, terribly sad, and overpowering with people she is involved with? *Why* is it? Is it the need to have somebody to be better than? Is it the need to have somebody to beat down? A whipping dog? What is that *terrible need* in society to pick on fat people? It's unbelievable. And the *effect* on the person who *gets* this reaction is devastating. I just don't know what to say.

Sally had an experience recently. It was a good one. She went into a bakery to buy some bread. And the girls in the bakery laughed out loud at her and were pokin' each other and lookin' at her and being really *rude*. And so Sally walked over—waddled over—to the counter and said, "Excuse me, but which would you rather be—fat or stupid?" And the girl behind the counter says, "Stupid." And Sally says, "Congratulations, you got your wish." Those girls behind the counter were struck *silent*. They were *stunned* that *she*, a lowlife, a second-class citizen, would have had the *nerve* not to take their harassment. They just didn't know what to say. I wonder what it is in society that people have this feeling that fat people are *subhuman*. And when a fat person sticks up for themselves they are *so* stunned that they don't know how to deal with it.

This is true even of the family. You would think the family would be like a refuge, a place where you are loved and protected. But what does a fat person do when their family members are just as cruel as people on the outside? It happens to us all the time. I mean, when Sally tells the story about how her brother used to have friends over and she would be *locked* in her room, can you imagine how her self-esteem would suffer. I mean, the woman *has* no self-esteem. She feels little better than *slime*. It's so sad. There's no way in hell anybody will ever convince me that being fat deserves *that* type of treatment. There's something very wrong here. I mean, would she be locked in her room if she was six foot four? Or four feet tall? Or really ugly? Or walked with a limp? What is it about being fat that causes people to treat her that way? I just don't understand it.

This isn't just Sally. Susan, Betsy, Beverly Gray, Eve McManus, Evie Wilson [members of NAAFA]—all of them have had serious, *serious* breaks with their families, *entirely* on the basis of their fatness. Beverly

Gray's mother has, like, *disowned* her because she won't lose weight and, you know, hasn't straightened up. Beverly Gray does not deserve to be disowned. That is an absolutely stunningly *beautiful* girl. That's pure insanity. Susan's parents refuse to talk to her any more because she's so fat. They completely broke ties with her. She tried to call her father on Father's Day and he just hung up on her. He doesn't even want to bother with her any more because she's just too fat. And the reason for this break is that, previously, at Christmas, her parents were absolutely harassing her. "How can you *live* with yourself? You're so fat! *Do* something about it! You're disgusting." In front of the whole family, her parents went on and on about this to Susan. And her husband stood up for her, but her parents were so disgusted that it turned into a big family row, and they broke off with her about it. There isn't any family relationship any more.

Beverly's family broke up with her because of her weight, Susan's family refuses to talk to her, Evie Wilson's father would just torture her daily about dieting. Her mother did not want her at the same dinner table with them. She made her eat an hour earlier than the rest of the family because they were so revolted seeing her at dinner. Three Thanksgivings ago, Evie's family went to a restaurant and the father ordered the turkey dinner for the whole family, and he ordered a *broiled fish platter* for Evie. And no dessert, just the fruit cup appetizer. Since then, her family has had a complete break with her. Eve McManus comes from a family that constantly harasses her about her weight. Her brother, whom she loves dearly and was very close with, is getting married. She has two brothers and two sisters. Every single other brother and sister was asked to be in the wedding party with the single exception of Eve. They wouldn't *allow* her to be in the wedding party because she's *fat*. This is a girl who's a professional [large-size] *model*, with a professional modeling agency in the City, and she's rejected from some little *shithead's* wedding because of her *size*? It broke her heart. It's such a horrible life to lead, this being fat. I just can't understand how society can punish fat people the way it does. I especially don't understand why family members do it to their own.

Betsy Pelligrino. There are no photographs, no pictures of Betsy in her parents' home because she's *fat*. We took a bunch of pictures of her at one of the NAAFA events and some of them look *lovely*. And Sally said to Betsy, now get these developed—you know how Sally is—and get this one framed, put it in your house. And Betsy said, I can't, my parents refuse to allow pictures in the house because I'm *fat*. Not only do they reject her fatness, they are rejecting that she even *exists*. She's not even allowed to have a photograph of herself around the house. Also, her father doesn't allow her to wear a dress or shorts in front of her brothers-in-law because they would see her legs and be so *revolted* that they wouldn't come back into the house. So she's paranoid even about putting on a dress, this poor woman, because if someone sees her legs, God would strike them dead, 'cuz she's so disgusting, you know, looking at her legs is *sudden death*. [Laughs.] So I said to Betsy, well, that's ridiculous, how do your brothers-in-law feel about that? So she said, well, my one brother-in-law took me aside and said, well, your father's crazy about this fat thing, I think your legs are great, don't worry about it, you wear whatever you want around me. But her *other* brother-in-law is married to her very thin, *thin* sister and he does *not* want to look at Betsy. All he does is constantly *harass* his wife not to eat. If she picks up something, he says to her, put that down, you don't need this, you don't need that, he's made her *terrified* that she would get fat like Betsy.

Sally—her mother refuses to talk to her. Her mother introduces her to strangers as Mrs. Simon. She doesn't want anybody to know that she's related to her in any way, shape, or form because she's so fat. Sally's brother and sister are thin, they've had normal lives, normal childhoods, toys, everything. They were never hit. Sally was beaten every day of her life by her father because she was fat. He beat her, sent her to her room, locked her in her room with no toys. Then he brought home ice cream and cake and then tormented her if she didn't eat her share. It was an absolutely horrible situation. Her father was totally revolted that she got so fat.

Diane's interview with Sally illustrates many of the principles that run throughout this book.

Diane: Are you a member of NAAFA?
Sally: Yes.
Diane: How long have you been a member?
Sally: 11 years.
Diane: Do you feel more comfortable and less self-conscious at a NAAFA activity than in a similar activity that is not sponsored by NAAFA?
Sally: No.
Diane: Why not?

Sally: Because I'm very comfortable, usually, wherever I go. Very confident.

Diane: Have you been helped in any way by NAAFA?

Sally: Yeah.

Diane: In what way?

Sally: Well, I've gotten some good friendships out of NAAFA, and I feel that's a help to anybody's personality.

Diane: What is your overall attitude concerning NAAFA itself?

Sally: I think NAAFA is a very good organization. I think it's kind of like going to church. It gives you support and self-esteem. It gives you a place to let your hair down and be yourself and not have to put on airs and not have to be something that you're not. And it gives you a chance to be beautiful. Away from the maddening crowd.

Diane: What is your overall opinion or assessment of the FAs that attend NAAFA activities?

Sally: Well, I think that it's just like any place else, whether in the straight world or the gay world or whatever. It has its good and its bad. I've met some very nice FAs and I've met some jerks. But you meet those in everyday life, too.

Diane: How would you describe the way that FAs act at a NAAFA activity?

Sally: It goes to the last question. Some act like normal human beings and some are very comfortable with the situation. And some don't really know where they are or who they are. Some of them are just as bad off as some of the fat women who don't have any self-esteem. I've met men in NAAFA who have no self-esteem at all. I think some of them are worse than the women as far as self-esteem is concerned.

Diane: Can you give me an example of that?

Sally: Well, you get men that, you know, they see you and they want to take you out and they wait—I've had men call me up two weeks after a dance and say to me, gee, I met you at the dance, I'd love to take you out, well, I reply, why didn't you ask me at the dance? They say, I didn't ask you at the dance 'cuz I didn't think you'd want to bother with me.

Diane: Pitiful.

Sally: Sure it is. That's what I'm talking about, the self-esteem. There's such a lack of self-esteem in a lot of these men. I think a lot of men get hooked up in NAAFA not really because they're so enamoured with fat women but because they think that fat women are hard up and an easy mark. It's easier to get a fat woman in bed than a thin woman because there's more competition for the thin woman. I mean, I'm not saying that this is true in all cases, but I'm sure that happens, you know.

Diane: Is there anything different about the FA's conversation, compared with men who are not FAs?

Sally: Oh, yeah, well, being with an FA is more comfortable. A lot of men who are not FAs are not as *comfortable* with the fact that you're fat. They're not as comfortable saying to you, gee, you're pretty. An FA who's together finds it very easy to say to a pretty fat woman, you're very pretty. A man who's what I call a "straight" man, he finds it very *difficult* a lot of times to tell you you're pretty. Or he'll paraphrase it by saying, ah, gee, you have a pretty *face*. You know, not so much *you're* pretty. Whereas an FA looks at you and, to him, you're pretty *all over*. Whereas a straight man looks at you and says, you've got a pretty *face*. You know, that's basically the difference.

Diane: What about the activities that an FA suggests for a date, are they any different from that of a non-FA?

Sally: I don't think so. The only thing is that, with an FA, he's more aware of *seating*, you know, if you go into a restaurant, whether you can fit into a booth or a chair or go to the theater. Most FAs are more attuned to whether you can fit in a chair or he asks himself, do I want to take her there because she'd be comfortable? Whereas a straight guy, it never even *dawns* on him to think about something like that, he would never even think about it. *You* have to tell *him* that.

Diane: Do you think that FAs treat heavy women the way that most men treat women of average weight? Any differences you can think of at all?

Sally: Well, I think, the only thing I can think of is that a lot of FAs treat women very badly sometimes. And I think a lot of men treat women on the outside very badly, too. I hear stories all the time about how thin women get treated so badly by these guys, even pretty, thin women.

Diane: OK. How would the FA treat fat women badly?

Sally: Well, some FAs will gravitate toward a fat woman mostly because he figures she's hard up, she's desperate, she'll do *anything in the world* to get herself a decent guy. I mean, I've heard stories that'll curl your hair.

Diane: Like what? Give me a couple of examples.

Sally: Well, I'll give you an example. I was going to a motel with somebody one night and he said to me, am I paying for the room or are you? And I said, well, if you're *not*, we're not going. I mean, that's how simple that was. But I'm sure there are plenty of fat women out there who would say, OK, I'll pay for the room. My belief is that a woman gets treated the way she expects to get treated. If she expects to get treated poorly, that's *exactly* how she's going to be treated. The guy's going to pick up on it and treat her whatever way she expects. He's going to treat her just as badly as she expects to be treated. I mean, if you have low self-esteem and you're out in the world, men are going to treat you rotten because they can feel it, they can pick up on it that you lack confidence. If you have a lot of confidence in yourself, *everybody's* going to treat you fairly decently. At least, that's what I've found to be true. My experience has been that as long as I have confidence in myself, mostly everybody treats me fairly good.

Diane: Do you believe that FAs have a stereotype of heavy women?

Sally: Well, it goes back to the same thing, they see us as needy and grateful. Some FAs have a lot of respect for fat women, but I think a lot of them have this stereotype. You can tell the type, you can look at an FA and tell by the type of a woman that he goes with. You find an FA who picks on the women who are sloppy and unkempt, who don't take care of themselves. You find a woman who looks good and who's attractive and keeps herself nice and you find an FA who gravitates toward them, he's an FA who respects a woman.

Diane: Do you think that one aspect of the stereotype is that heavier women are *easier* sexually than women of average size?

Sally: I think that's part of it. I've heard FAs say that: "The only reason I go for fat women is because they're easier. I don't really care for fat women, but they're easier to get."

Diane: No kidding.

Sally: Yeah.

Diane: Do you believe that most men hold this stereotype?

Sally: I would say it's about 50 percent. I mean, there are the men who just happen to prefer the fat body, you know, and they're together, but there are men who have their own problems who cannot function in a straight world. So they come into what they think is a *disabled* group of people. They're more comfortable because they don't have to knock themselves out, they don't have to *try* as hard to get a woman into bed, they can just be their own raunchy self and you know, not worry about it.

Diane: Do you think that most FAs are interested in dating heavier women pretty much solely for sexual reasons?

Sally: I would say a good 80 percent, yes.

Diane: How do you feel about FAs that date heavier women solely for sexual reasons?

Sally: Most men date *thin* women solely for sexual reasons. I don't see any difference.

Diane: How do you think fat women feel about that?

Sally: I'm sure it depresses them, a lot of them. It really doesn't bother me because that's all I'm interested in also.

Diane: What is different about being in bed with an FA versus a non-FA?

Sally: When you're with an FA, he *appreciates* your body. When you're with a straight guy, he accepts it, but he's not overwhelmed. An FA's *preference*—I mean, that's like saying, well, I like a tall girl or a thin girl or a blonde girl, or I like a guy with blue eyes. Of course, if you find someone you're *particularly* interested in, you're going to enjoy it even more. It's a lot more *comfortable* to be in bed with an FA than it is with a straight guy, especially the first time. The first time going to bed with a straight guy is *really rough.* Because you don't know whether he's going to look at your body and be *repulsed* by it or turned *off* by it, or even be able to *function.* But with an FA, it's a *lot* more comfortable.

Diane: What is different generally about dating an FA versus dating a non-FA?

Sally: Well, it depends on the FA. Some FAs are very uncomfortable with fat women. They're OK in bed, but they don't want to be seen on the *street* with a fat woman. So, an FA who's confident and certain of himself, he doesn't really care about what other people or his peers think. It's very nice to be with an FA because he's proud of you. But you can't be with an FA who's just like a straight guy and doesn't want anybody to know he's dating a fat woman.

Diane: I heard a very cute joke recently. Somebody said, dating a fat girl is like riding a moped: It's fun while you're on it, but you wouldn't want your friends to see you doing it. [Both chuckle.]

Sally: Yeah. That's good.

Diane: Do you think that the quality of men who are interested in dating you would be any different if you were of average weight?

Sally: I would imagine if I weighed 120 pounds, I could go out with Prince Charming, sure.

Diane: What is the factor that is most influential in your getting dates with men?

Sally: I would say mostly my aggressiveness. Just friendliness, like in restaurants or in stores, that kind of thing.

Diane: Are there activities that you would feel reluctant to engage in or attend because of your weight?

Sally: Tennis. Horseback riding. Mountain climbing. Canoeing. Going down the rapids in a canoe. I'm not into that sort of thing. Sports.

Diane: Movies?

Sally: Well, I don't go to the movies because I don't fit in the seats. It's uncomfortable.

Diane: What about going into a clothing store?

Sally: Yeah, if the store sells mainly size nines. I feel uncomfortable about going into a *small-size* clothing store, yeah.

Diane: Outside summer activities where seating is provided?

Sally: Yeah, that can be a problem. You have these little *folding chairs* that some people have, I don't want to sit in those because they usually don't hold your weight. That happened to me. I went to a bar-b-que with some friends, and I sat down in the chair and it broke. I couldn't get *out* of it. That was the funny part, I couldn't get out. I mean, luckily, they were very nice people, I've known them for years. But I was on the ground in this collapsed folding chair. It had folded *around* me and I couldn't get out of it. It took three of them to get me up and pry the chair off my butt.

Diane: Do you feel reluctant to go to a public beach or a swimming pool in a bathing suit because of your weight?

Sally: Yeah.

Diane: If you did go onto a fairly crowded beach or a swimming pool in a bathing suit, do you think that most people's reaction would be different compared with if you were of average weight?

Sally: Oh, sure. I think they would be *amused* and I'm sure there would be plenty of heckling and making fun of me, nudging the buddy next door to take a look.

Diane: David Brenner once said, I hate going to nudist colonies, there's nothing to do but hang around the beach and try to guess which sex the fat people are.

Sally: Oh [sarcastically], yeah, he comes out with some really good stuff.

Diane: When you see a slim model in a magazine advertisement or on TV, what are your feelings and thoughts? Do you think, I wish I looked like that?

Sally: No.

Diane: Have you ever experienced a stranger making a remark on your size in public?

Sally: Oh, sure.

Diane: Can you tell us about some of these experiences?

Sally: I just had one yesterday. Two little old ladies walked out of a restaurant and they went to get on the elevator in my office building and one saw me and she nudged the other one to turn around and look at me and I ran up behind her and said I'd rather be *fat* than *old*. I've had many of those.

Diane: Have there been situations in which you felt that you were ignored or left out because of your weight?

Sally: Not so much in my adult life. As a teenager, yeah, sure. I'm sure every fat person has. Anybody who's different. You know, it's not only the fat kids. It's the *short* kids, or *super-tall* kids, or *Black* kids—or whatever. All kids, anybody who's different. If you're not normal, so to speak, mainstream, not like everyone else, you're left out of a lot of things.

Diane: Have members of your family felt ashamed because of your weight?

Sally: Yeah, all of them. My brother hasn't talked to me for 27 years because of my weight, and my stepmother still doesn't talk to me today because of my weight. When my sister was in the hospital, my father wouldn't stay in the house alone because of my weight. He didn't want to be alone with me, he might *catch the fat*, you know, he was afraid. He would *never* introduce me as his daughter. I picked up some things for my stepmother, and my dad and my husband and I drove to her apartment and I said, Daddy, let's drop these things off for her. So, when we got to the apartment, my stepmother was standing in the lobby, talking to a bunch of women. Well, when she saw me, she almost *died*. When my husband and I walked into the lobby, my stepmother introduced me and my husband to these women as Mr. and Mrs. Simon. Not as my *daughter*, but just Mr. and Mrs. Simon. And she says, go on upstairs. So we walk upstairs and my husband says, why didn't she introduce you as her daughter? I said, 'cause she doesn't want anybody to *know* that I'm her daughter.

Diane: That's horrible. Have you had any direct personal experience with size discrimination by doctors?

Sally: Sure. The ridicule. Once, I called up a doctor's office. A chiropractor. I said, do you take fat patients? And he said, what do you consider fat? I said, I weigh 350 pounds, and he laughed and said, of *course* not! There's *nothing* I can do with a 350 pound person!

Diane: You should have called up a professional association and complained.

Sally: Who you gonna call? He's a chiropractor, he is not even a medical doctor.

Diane: Yeah. They must have some kind of a professional association you can complain to. Jesus, that's terrible.

Sally: It's like a dog pound, the animals, you know, that's the way we are treated.

Diane: That's horrible. Hiring and promotion on the job? Have you ever experienced discrimination because of your weight on the job?

Sally: Not promotion. I missed out on a good job one time—as a matter of fact, two good jobs—because I couldn't pass the physical 'cause of my weight.

Diane: Just the weight?

Sally: Just the weight. I passed everything else.

Diane: Seating facilities? Discrimination there?

Sally: Oh, yeah. I find this is a *huge* problem for myself. *Theater* seats. A bunch of us girls from NAAFA went into a theater one night and bought tickets two months in advance. When we got there, we found we didn't fit in the seats. They didn't want to give us back the money. And they didn't want to do anything about giving us seats we could sit in. We made such a fuss that they had to give us back our money.

Diane: What happened that time when you went to Ohio? How did you fit into the seats in the plane? I meant to ask you that.

Sally: Yeah, well, what they did was, they put us on a flight that was not booked so that we could lift the arms and instead of having three people across in a seat, there were two of us across. They gave us an off-hour and they made accommodations. The girl who worked for the airline who made the arrangements was very nice to us, she was very accommodating.

Diane: How much more is the charge if you take up more than one seat?

Sally: Well, another half of whatever the plane fare is.

Diane: That's not fair.

Sally: It *is* unfair. It's really up to *them* to accommodate *you*. I mean, if they want your business, they should accommodate you. You see, they put in as many seats as they can get in because the more seats, the more fares they earn. And the ratio of fat people who travel is very small, I'm sure.

Diane: If you could wave a magic wand, what aspects of your life would you like to see changed?

Sally: A number of them. I'd like to be single. I'd like to be out of debt. I'd like to be about 50 pounds lighter.

Diane: Not 100?

Sally: I'd settle for 50. I'd like to have more money. A better job. That's about it.

Diane: If you had a choice, would you like to lose weight?

Sally: Yeah, sure.

Diane: About how many pounds?

Sally: Somewhere between 50 and 100.

Diane: If you could swallow a magic pill and wake up in the morning weighing 125 pounds, would you do it?

Sally: I might. I don't know, that's something I'll really have to think about. I'm not sure.

Diane: What do you think your ideal weight is?

Sally: I'd like to be about 285. Between 285 and 300. About that magic pill, I say no. But if you asked me whether I'd like to wake up weighing 160-180 pounds, yes. 125 pounds, I wouldn't *know* that body. I couldn't *relate* to it. If you start out at 125, it would be no time at all before you're 180.

Diane: If you could take a magic pill that would *keep* you down to 125, would you do it?

Sally: Oh, well, to *keep* you at 125, that's different, yeah. But if I were going to get down to 125, believe me, in three weeks time, I'd be up to 180, so it really wouldn't make any difference.

Diane: What do you think the reason is why you weigh more than average?

Sally. Psychological. I think, basically, my problem is just bad childhood. My childhood was so bad that it changed my eating patterns and as a child, I ate out of frustration, and that just stayed with me. And with the fat on, I could never get it off. The fat's *there*, it's not going to go anyplace. I think the weight's going to be there forever.

Diane: Have you tried dieting or any weight loss programs?

Sally: Yep. In Nassau Medical Center, I had the bypass surgery done and went on their 500 calorie-a-day diet. I went on the diet where you get injections of a pregnant woman's urine and you eat 500 calories a day, and that's supposed to make you lose weight.

Diane: How'd you do?

Sally: I didn't lose anything [chuckles]. I looked just like this. [They both laugh.] The bypass, I lost 150 pounds, which I put right back on. And the *pills*, which I got from a pill doctor, I lost 225 pounds, which I put back on.

Diane: What are your feelings about these weight loss programs?

Sally: I think it's worse to lose weight and gain weight and lose weight and gain weight than to stay at the same weight. I think it'd be nice to be at a particular weight and to be able to *stay* there. I mean, whether it's 350, 250, or 150, or whatever. I think it would be nice just to be able to *stay* at that weight without having to worry about gaining.

Diane: Do you feel your life would be different if you were of average weight?

Sally: Oh, sure. I think I'd probably do more things. I enjoy sports—I think I'd probably get involved in things like that. I enjoy *walking.* I don't *do* it because I get tired too fast. I'd also probably do a lot of other things I don't do now. I mean, when you're fat and you've been fat all your life, you have a set regimen that you do with your life, you don't *expect* too much, you do what's comfortable for you. You don't say, gee, I wish I could do *that*, because you don't *think* like that, 'cause you know what you *can't* do, you know your limitations. And that's the way you live your life, around those limitations.

Diane: Do you feel that you eat more than an average person?

Sally: I eat *less* than an average person.

Diane: What advantages do you see in being heavier than average?

Sally: I don't really find any advantages.

Diane: What *disadvantages* do you see in being heavier than average?

Sally: Well, I think the disadvantages are in being limited to certain things that you can do. Physical activities and social activities.

Diane: How about the social?

Sally: Well, there are certain things that you just don't want to do. I mean, like, a bicycle race or a marathon, you know, those things are just as much social activities as physical. You don't *do* them because, you know, you *can't*.

Diane: A volleyball game on the beach.

Sally: Yeah, right. You know, you want to get up, everybody's *chasing* everybody on the beach. And you don't want to do it because you can't.

Diane: Or, who wants to play hide-and-go-seek?

Sally: Yeah, right.

Diane: Well, you can play hide-and-go-seek, but *tag* is tough. [Both laugh.] We'd always be the, whatdayacall it? *It!* A lifetime of *it!* [Both laugh.] What do you think is the *worst* thing about being heavier than average?

Sally: Your physical limitations.

Diane: What do you think is the *next* worst thing about being heavier than average?

Sally: Clothing.

Diane: And what is the *best* thing about being heavier than average?

Sally: Being different. Being one of a kind. Like a gem. You know, it's one thing to be fat and pretty. It's quite another thing to be thin and just another pretty face.

Diane: Were your father or mother heavy when you were growing up?

Sally: My stepmother is heavy.

Diane: How much is she overweight?

Sally: Oh, 150 pounds.

Diane: She *is?*

Sally: Yeah.

Diane: Wait a minute, if your father wouldn't talk to you or hang around with you because you were overweight, how could he be married to a woman who's 150 pounds overweight?

Sally: He never takes her anywhere. Never takes her out in public.

Diane: Do they hate each other?

Sally: No. She worships the ground he walks on.

Diane: Are they rich?

Sally: She wasn't, he is. She was our maid. She was *gorgeous* when she got married. She put it all on after they were married.

Diane: Oh, I see, he didn't *marry* a fat girl.

Sally: Oh, no, no, no. And my mother, his first wife, was very tiny, she was like a size 5, I think.

Diane: Were you heavy as a child?

Sally: I weighed over 400 pounds when I was 14 years old.

Diane: Growing up, what was the reaction of your parents to your weight?

Sally: Bad. My father used to buy cake and ice cream every day and then make fun of me if I ate it. But I ate it anyway. I was so used to him making fun of me, it didn't make any difference. My brother always made fun of me. He wouldn't bring his friends in the house because of me. He used to tell my father to lock me in my bedroom or he wouldn't bring his friends in the house.

Diane: They didn't lock you in your bedroom.

Sally: Yes they did.

Diane: They locked you in your bedroom so your brother could have his friends in the house?

Sally: Yes, that's right.

Diane: What did you do in there?

Sally: Played, sewed, read comic books. Whatever.

Diane: Oh, my God.

Sally: I knew that was my place.

Diane: How old were you when this was going on?

Sally: Till the time I was about 16 years old. Once, I jumped off my balcony.

Diane: Did you? Good for you!

Sally: But I got the *shit* beat out of me for doing it. [Chuckles.]

Diane: What did you think—you'd go in the room, now your brother can have his friends over?

Sally: Don't come out until your brother's friends are gone.

Diane: That's one of the most horrible things I've ever heard.

Sally: Oh, that was *light* stuff. My father beat me every day of my life. From the time I was two years old till I was 17. Because I was fat.

Diane: Well, what about your brother? Did he beat your brother? What about your little sister?

Sally: No, no, no.

Diane: Growing up, what was the reaction of your friends, your playmates, your schoolmates, to your weight?

Sally: I didn't have too many friends growing up. I always had plenty of boyfriends, but I didn't have too many girlfriends.

Diane: How about teachers?

Sally: I had *one* nice teacher who really took pity on me. Because she knew the situation. Only one teacher that I can remember who was really nice to me.

Diane: Did you feel different when you were in high school, or set apart?

Sally: Sure. Just being *different* makes you different.

Diane: Have you ever *refused* to date a man because he was too heavy?

Sally: A couple of them. Maybe two.

Diane: Do you feel that, for you, there's a point at which a man becomes too heavy to be desirable?

Sally: Yes. That occurs at maybe 100 pounds over the average weight.

Diane: Can you picture yourself in a long-term relationship with a very heavy man?

Sally: No.

Diane: Can you picture yourself married to a man over 100 pounds overweight?

Sally: No.

Unlike many conditions, behaviors, and beliefs, the condition of obesity is highly visible, as Diane's opening episode makes clear. Thus, "passing" as thin in public is impossible. In Goffman's words, obesity ranks high in both "visibility" and "evidentness" as well as in "obtrusiveness" (1963, pp. 48, 49). This means it is impossible for a person of average size not to notice a fat person's condition. It is difficult for persons of regular size to *disattend* or not pay attention to the weight. In addition, for many normal-sized persons, obesity has a broad "perceived focus" (p. 49), that is, an effect in many areas of life (p. 50). The non-obese assume a wide range of incompetencies on the part of the obese: that they are medically unhealthy; cannot perform at sports and most occupations; suffer from major character flaws, including gluttonousness, laziness, and a lack of control. Most non-obese persons regard the overweight as responsible for their condition. These factors—visibility, obtrusiveness, a broad perceived focus, and personal responsibility for a condition—make for an extremely high likelihood that fat people will feel compelled to resort to accounts to minimize the stigma they are likely to attract (English, 1991).

As we saw, Sally explains her weight by psychological factors. "My childhood was so bad it changed my eating habits and as a child, I ate out of frustration, and that just stayed with me." In other words, it's not her fault. Moreover, she says, she isn't fat because she's self-indulgent; in fact, she says, she eats *less* than the average person. Her efforts to lose weight have been in vain and, considering her size, her desire to lose weight is extremely limited. When I asked Diane why she weighed more than average, she explained, "My mother fed me too much when I was a kid, and I have a borderline thyroid condition, which is inherited."

As accounts, Sally and Diane offer *excuses* for their weight; their size seems to have been fated, a product of forces beyond their control. But their causal connection with obesity is separate from their attitudes toward society's condemnation of it. Sally and Diane belong to NAAFA—the National Association to Advance Fat Acceptance. As I said, NAAFA is ostensibly a civil

rights organization dedicated to combatting discrimination against fat people—picketing stores that sell posters that demean fat people, protesting the
firing of an employee because of her weight, criticizing surgical procedures
to lose weight. All of this adds up to the vocabulary of motive I referred to
earlier as "normalization," that is, redefining society's condemnation as illegitimate, insisting that members of the condemned category have a legitimate right to be treated just like everyone else. However, as I showed, very,
very few of the overt actions of NAAFA members and participants involve
civil rights. Indeed, most of the activities of members are romantic and sexual. In fact, it is the very *fatness* of the women in NAAFA that attracts nearly
all the men to its functions. This puts a distinctive damper on the organization's civil rights thrust. Political activism or sex—what is NAAFA's emphasis
to be? There is no contest. In NAAFA's case, sex has triumphed.

Given the powerful stigma directed against the obese in this society,
the persons who are on the receiving end are forced to be especially vigi-
lant in overcoming it. Diane and Sally are rare, even among NAAFA members, in asserting "fat pride." The "party line" in NAAFA is that *fat is just as
good as thin*. In fact, some of NAAFA's members are militant, proud of their
girth, and proclaim that they would prefer to be heavy. A button often seen
at NAAFA functions states: "How DARE You Presume I'd Rather Be Thin!"
But they are in the minority. Although he did not mention the obese specifically, Goffman argued that many stigmatized persons suffer from "self-
hate and self-derogation" (Goffman, 1963, p. 7); for the obese, this takes
place especially when they stand in front of a mirror. The fact is, even in
NAAFA—dedicated, remember, to the rights of fat people—the overwhelming majority of the fat women say that they would rather be thinner, and
most in fact want to be of normal size. In other words, in spite of NAAFA's
ideology, "normalization" seems not to have taken hold. While none of
them feel that the stigma of obesity is justified—and here, they depart
from the more typical fat person (Cahnman, 1968; Louderback, 1970)—
most want to take leave of the deviant category to which they belong. In
that sense, their accounts are very different from those that issue from
homosexuals (Fisher, 1972), marijuana smokers (Goode, 1970), and right-
wing, racist "patriots" (Bushart, Craig, and Barnes, 1999).

As we saw in Danny's account, Erving Goffman indicated that people
who *associate* with deviants may be marginally accepted among deviants
but among "normals," they are tainted with a "courtesy stigma" (1963, pp.
28, 30). The repulsion of many people toward the obese is so great that
their reluctance to associate with them may be fueled by a terror of *becoming* fat if one does—witness Sally's "catch the fat" accusation of her father's
avoidance of her. Certainly the parents of a fat child are stigmatized by
association, in large part, as with autism, because the observer wonders if
they caused or are *responsible* for their child's condition.

Goffman was unlikely to be aware of their existence, but fat admirers
provide perhaps the clearest example of a category of actors who are, or

are likely to be, tainted with a "courtesy stigma." The "normal" person connected to the deviant—the brother of a convict, the sister of a homosexual—has not engaged in deviant behavior other than maintaining that connection. The same is most distinctly not true of the FA, who is seen as *actively* pursuing an unwholesome, perverted, and distinctly deviant activity. What the FA has done is to indulge in romantic and sexual liaisons with partners who are deemed by the majority of the population, male and female, to be aesthetically unpleasing, indeed, repulsive. Even more repulsive, thinks the modal thin person, is the activity in which the FA engages—sex with 300-pound-plus women. It is difficult for most average-sized persons to envision such an act without derision or obscene thoughts. Indeed, the fat admirer has overturned the entire esthetic judgment of the society, judging that which is conventionally regarded as attractive (being thin) to be ugly, unaesthetic, and sexually unappealing and that which is conventionally regarded as unattractive (being fat) to be gorgeous, appealing, and wildly sexy. It is on such alternative interpretations of reality that much of society's condemnation of deviance is based.

In spite of their seemingly counter-hegemonic esthetic and sexual impulses, however, most FAs are ruled by majority standards when it comes to being seen in public with their fat partners. Said Gladys, a 300-pound member of NAAFA, FAs look at an advertisement for a weight loss program and think the woman in the "before" picture is a lot cuter than the one in the "after" picture. "These men date fat women and they sleep with fat women. That's all well and good. But let's face it," Gladys added, "most of them are ashamed of associating with fat women." She told me about her own experience with dating a man who was fearful of being seen in public with her. "You know what he told me?" she asked me. "He said, 'I can't afford to be seen in public with you, in my position. My peers would ostracize me.' He rarely took me out. When he did, if we went to a restaurant, he'd pick the darkest corner. I had to eat quickly and slink out of there. . . . The man skulked from corner to corner, like some kind of a rat in a sewer. For many FAs, dating fat women is only for the sex. It's not supposed to be public knowledge" (Goode, 2001, p. 334).

In her speculation about why the obese are derided, Diane puts her finger on a possible motive for the entire enterprise of deviance. Why is it, she asks, that the condemnation of a large woman is so open, hostile, and wounding? Why do Sally's condemners feel compelled to make the woman feel such enormous pain? "Is it the need to have somebody to be better than? Is it the need to have somebody to beat down? What is that *terrible* need in society to pick on fat people? It's unbelievable. And the *effect* on the person who *gets* this rejection is devastating. I just don't know what to say."

NOTE

[1] These last five paragraphs were adapted from Goode, 1996.

CHAPTER 6

More and more I devoted my days to my eating disorder—my dark side. I woke up at 4:30, drank two huge glasses of water, worked out to an exercise video for an hour, took a shower, ate 40 corn flakes, drank two more glasses of water, put coffee (black, no sugar) into a 64-ounce mug, and went to school. . . . I came home, ate (not without guilt) 24 mini-pretzels dipped in mustard and then took a four-mile walk. . . . For dinner, I usually had one cup of non-fat, no sugar yogurt and a large coffee (no milk, no sugar) from 7-Eleven. Then I retired to bed, dreading waking up and doing it all over again.

Annette

Annette, the Anguished Anorexic

Anorexics and bulimics battle demons whose ferocity and tenacity the rest of us cannot even remotely comprehend or appreciate. How can a young woman who is 5'6" and weighs 85 pounds possibly believe she is fat? For "normals," anorexia is both baffling yet familiar. In a way, it is very much like alcoholism; dieting in moderation, like social drinking, is regarded as normal and conventional, yet starving oneself to the point of endangering one's health and very life, like dangerous, immoderate, out-of-control drinking, is regarded as abnormal and deviant.

Today, the ideal woman's form is extremely thin; clothes models border dangerously on the anorexic. Even within the borders of what is considered a medically healthy weight, many young American women feel fat. Readers of women's and girls's magazines are bombarded with diets that admonish them to "shed those unwanted pounds." A survey of the readership of *Glamour* magazine conducted a few years ago found that three-quarters felt that they were "too fat," even though only one-quarter were actually overweight by Metropolitan Life Insurance Company's height-weight guidelines. More surprisingly, nearly half (45 percent) who were *underweight* saw themselves as too fat. Only 6 percent were "very happy" about their bodies; only 15 percent described their bodies as "just right." Evidence suggests, however, that there are substantial ethnic differences in this respect: White girls and women are significantly more dissatisfied with their weight than African-American girls and women are (Parker et al., 1995). Still, for most American females, cultural norms prescribe an extremely *thin* ideal and call for dieting as the solution even for small departures from this ideal. Overweight bodies are widely regarded as unaesthetic, even repulsive, and people who permit themselves to become fat are seen as "lazy," "slothful," "gluttonous" (DeJong, 1980). For the majority, the result is a significant measure of anxiety about their weight.

And yet, nearly all of us recognize that anorexia entails "going too far." Anorexia, like bulimia, is referred to as an "eating disorder" (American Psychiatric Association, 1994, pp. 539–550; Davison and Neale, 1998, pp. 206–224). The 4th edition of the American Psychiatric Association's *Diagnostic and Statistical Manual* (1994) defines anorexia nervosa as a condition in which the person afflicted with it "refuses to maintain a minimally normal body weight, is intensely afraid of gaining weight, and exhibits a significant disturbance in the perception of the shape or size of his or her body" (p. 539). The vast majority of anorexics are young, white, middle-class females. In industrialized societies, its prevalence has been estimated at roughly one percent of the female population (Davison and Neale, 1998, p. 208). In adolescence and young adulthood, this condition is often accompanied by the body's inability to menstruate, since the organism is incapable of sustaining the viability of a fetus and the birth of a healthy child. The APA suggests that if an individual weighs less than 85 percent of what the Metropolitan Life Insurance tables considers normal, that person should be regarded as significantly underweight. For anorexics, weight loss "is viewed as an impressive achievement and a sign of extraordinary self-discipline, whereas weight gain is perceived as an unacceptable failure of self-control. Though some individuals with this disorder may acknowledge being thin, they typically deny the serious medical implications of their malnourished state" (p. 540). Anorexia causes crippling bone loss and osteoporosis, heart degeneration and heart disease, damage to the liver and kidneys, and dangerously low blood pressure. Hundreds of young Americans quite literally starve themselves to death each year in an effort to attain a grotesque, skeletal ideal.

Bulimia is a disorder that is related to but analytically distinct from anorexia. Bulimia is characterized by binge eating alternated with deliberate purging of food from the stomach to prevent weight gain. Bulimics, like anorexics, are obsessively and unhealthily concerned with body weight and associate eating with a lack of control. Not all bulimics are dangerously thin, however. In fact, many are of average weight and some are even above average in weight. Typically, bulimics are "ashamed of their eating problems and attempt to conceal their symptoms. Binge eating usually occurs in secrecy, or as inconspicuously as possible" (p. 546).

An eating binge, caused by a frenzied, uncontrollable hunger, is followed first by a feeling of being excessively full, then by self-criticism, extreme guilt, and anxiety, which brings about the need to expel the offending food from one's body. Inducing vomiting, often by inserting the fingers down one's throat, is the most common method of purging; for some persons who suffer from this condition, vomiting becomes an end in itself. A minority of bulimics use laxatives excessively (p. 546). Bulimia, while not as medically harmful as anorexia, also causes damage. Not only does it rob the body of necessary nutrients and vitamins, but it also depletes electrolytes, reducing the efficiency and effectiveness of the nervous system. Two other common outcomes are tears in the esophagus (as a result of the violent action of the vomiting itself) and dental decay (when the teeth come into contact with vomitus, which contains acid).

As with all the behaviors described in this book, anorexia and bulimia can be divided into two phases: *primary* and *secondary* deviation. "Primary" deviation is the simple and early enactment of the behavior before the actor is tagged or stigmatized with a deviant label and before it becomes incorporated into the actor's self-identity. "Secondary" deviation (Lemert, 1951, pp. 75–78; 1972, pp. 62ff.) occurs when someone is labeled as a deviant and begins to employ his or her deviant behavior or deviant role "as a means of defense, attack, or adjustment to the . . . problems created by the consequent social reaction to him" or her (1951, p. 76).

For the members of BANISH, Bulimics/Anorexics In Self-Help, their eating disorder gives purpose to their lives; it becomes a kind of companion, "the salient element of their self-concepts," so that they relate to "familiar people and new acquaintances [primarily] as anorexics and bulimics" (McLorg and Taub, 1987, p. 185). In a phrase, they experience "role engulfment" (Schur, 1971), with their anorexic/bulimic identity becoming a "master status," absolutely central in who they are, both to others and to themselves. Everything else about them recedes into the background.

Annette was a student in one of my courses. She was institutionalized several times in psychiatric facilities, and I asked whether Goffman's perspective on mental institutionalization remains relevant today. Goffman described a system in which mentally ill persons felt themselves to have been "betrayed" by loved ones and forced against their will into mental hospitals. When Goffman wrote *Asylums* (1961), half a million people were locked up in public psychiatric institutions in the United States, and most of them stayed for over six months. Today, there are fewer than 80,000;

they stay for an average of two weeks, receive medication, and get kicked out onto the street. I suggested that mental institutions today don't *want* patients. It's very *difficult* to institutionalize patients against their will unless they are a danger to themselves or others. Typically, the patient's problem is not being *forced* to stay in the institution, it is being *allowed* to stay.

Annette disagreed with me in the strongest possible terms on almost every point. She felt Goffman's characterization of mental institutionalization was still relevant in every respect. To begin with, she explained, *she* was institutionalized against her will, and a number of times (several times, it might be added, as a minor)—betrayed by the very people who supposedly cared about her. Secondly, she continued, upon being institutionalized, she was degraded, humiliated, dehumanized, and stripped of her dignity and identity. Aren't these the very things Goffman wrote about? she asked. Third, she continued, staff in mental hospitals present themselves as wise, all-knowing experts who are doing all they can to improve your condition. (Goffman's process of "normalization.") In reality, she argued, they are petty, ignorant, and incapable of helping the patient. They don't know how to improve the inmate's condition, and they cover that up by enforcing a lot of stupid rules and regulations. And lastly, she concluded, they do everything they can to remind the patient that she is in the hospital because she has a mental problem and is incapable of coping on her own. (Witness Goffman's process of "abnormalization.") Didn't Goffman write about these things, too? she inquired.

I told Annette she should write a paper about her own personal experiences. Perhaps readers could learn from them, I said. In fact, I added, maybe I could, too.

Annette was a bulimic in her mid-teenage years and then an anorexic until her early 20s. After college, she entered a school of social work so that she could help adolescents and young adults who were experiencing some of the same psychological difficulties she encountered in her life. Today, Annette is attractive, with straight, long, light-brown hair, above average in height, and slim but not painfully so. Her account gives us insight into both her specific condition and, more generally, into all deviant experiences.

It began one fateful Wednesday afternoon. I sat in my living room, the shades pulled down and the lights turned off. The only light in the room emanated from the television set and the Marlboro Light dangling from my lips. I paused between puffs to convey spoonfuls of ice cream from a one-gallon container to my mouth. That's when I saw it. On television, a girl draped her body over a toilet bowl, vomiting profusely. At first, I found the image so disturbing I dropped the spoon into the container of ice cream and began to drag harder on my cigarette. Something about that image intrigued me. My disgust turned into interest. I looked down at the container of half-eaten ice cream and recalled the past half-hour, during which I had devoured a major portion of it. I put out the cigarette, crushing every spark, and lifted myself from the chair. I walked slowly into the bathroom.

The floor beneath my feet felt cold, but somehow the anticipation of what I was about to do sent a hot flash from my head to my toes. I brought my right forefinger and middle finger to my mouth, inserted them, and pushed backwards until tears came to my eyes. Nothing happened. I tried harder, pushing back further, until I touched the back of my throat. Something. A cold, brown liquid emerged and fell straight into the toilet. How strange. Ice cream was the only thing in my stomach and when it came back up, it tasted the same as the first spoonful had.

I stayed in the bathroom until I had the dry heaves. Afterwards, I went into the kitchen, got the can of Lysol, and vigorously scrubbed the toilet. Suddenly, I felt ashamed. What did I do? Never before that afternoon, before watching that program, had I even thought of doing such a disgusting thing. I went back into the living room, put away the ice cream, and smoked a few more cigarettes.

Later, at night, when my father returned, while I was sitting in the same blue chair I sat in earlier, I tried to wave the smoke from in front of me. It hardly mattered. He walked into the room holding an unfiltered Camel in a death grip between his fingers. He looked at me with a dark, blank stare. I responded by getting up, walking upstairs, and going to bed.

That was about the limit of the personal contact I had with my father. Mostly, I avoided him. The fear he had instilled in me from childhood controlled the way I felt about him. Ironically, when I was little, I thought the way he treated me was normal. I actually thought that every little kid's father hit them with a leather belt, kicked them with steel-tipped work boots, and constantly berated them about how fat they were. I got along much better with my mother. At least when I talked to her, she usually responded. They had no idea about what happened on that lonely Wednesday afternoon. Not then, not even now. Nor do they know how far I've taken what happened then, how much that single event came to dictate every aspect of my life.

For a while, my binge and purge episodes were few and far between. I did some experimenting with food. I played with different types of food that I ate then puked up. In a sense, it felt empowering to be able to have my cake and eat it too. The whole idea about bingeing and purging was more or less to establish some level of control over the nearly uncontrollable situations that made up my life. Before, I had almost always binged, or at least over-eaten. Now the purging was a way of controlling the over-eating. Once, I had utopian visions of a skinny, beautiful me, with friends, boyfriends, places to go, and people to see. Slowly, those visions disappeared and I became isolated and lonely.

Without conscious effort, the frequency of my bingeing and purging escalated rapidly. All of a sudden, it became an impulse rather than a controlled response to overconsumption. Any little situation I felt I could not handle brought on the impulse to binge or at least to purge. No longer was purging a way of controlling my weight. It had become a way of controlling my emotions. Somehow, purging had a sedating effect on me. There was something extremely satiating about sticking something down my throat and hurling up the contents of my stomach.

I had become something of an expert on purging. Actual binges were reserved for special occasions, but purging was an anytime, any-place thing. I could be sitting in class after lunch at school, start flexing the muscles in my abdomen, and moments later, I excused myself to go to the bathroom for a few minutes of silent spewing. At times it wasn't quite so simple. There were times when I had to use everything from toothbrushes to hairbrush handles jammed down the back of my throat. I pushed and pressed, praying that something would come up.

After nearly three years of nearly daily purging, one day, when I had vomited 14-15 times, I was caught. I knew it was coming. I had begun to get sloppy. Babysitting was the best time for my binges. I could skim the top off of practically any food that was around. Even if anyone knew what I was doing, they weren't likely to confront me. I spent a lot of time babysitting for my little cousins. They were far too young to know what was going on, or so I thought. I tore through their kitchen cabinets, grabbing then shoving Twinkies and Devil Dogs into my mouth like there was no tomorrow. I scooped ice cream out of the container with my hand, licking my elbow before the melting liquid reached my clothes. Finally, after spending nearly an hour in the bathroom bowing to the porcelain princess, I emerged with bloodshot eyes and cheeks so swollen and red they looked as if they could be popped. Perhaps my little cousins never caught on, but my cleaning habits were not as meticulous as I had thought. Much later, I found out that my aunt came home from work and had to scrub up the mess that, in my heated fury, I had not seen well enough to clean up. It was my aunt who told my mother about what I had been doing.

Actually, my mother had been clueless about the whole thing. I knew I had a problem. After my aunt told her, she knew, too. But the thing is, she had no idea what to do. I began seeing a therapist in a nearby town whose specialty was alcoholism and drug abuse. She really didn't know her butt from her nose when it came to eating disorders. After about three sessions, she suggested that I be admitted to an inpatient treatment facility. At that point, I didn't care. I couldn't see any way out of the hole I had dug for myself, so—what the hell!—a mental hospital it is!

Going to the hospital was to be a revolving door for me. The next few years moved quickly. Perhaps as a result of an unconscious need for my own personal safety, I've forgotten or simply do not remember a lot of what happened.

My first stay was by far the easiest. Don't get me wrong, I would have given my right arm to get out of there. I hated every second I was there, from the first to the last. I hated myself for allowing it to happen. I hated my mother for not getting me out of there, I hated my father for turning me into the person I had become. Things happened to me there that I would never wish on my worst enemy. I felt persecuted and pressured into feeling and saying things that were alien to me. I felt violated and manipulated by staff. And the people who were supposed to be treating us were cold and relentless. They taunted, poked, and prodded us at every opportunity.

After four weeks, I had had it. I threatened my mother that if she applied for Medicaid and made me stay any longer, I'd *really* go crazy and she'd regret it. She reluctantly allowed me to return home. Within two days, I was back to the habits that had gotten me institutionalized in the first place. But this time around, I vowed to keep it a secret. But at school, I was labeled and stigmatized as a "puker," a bulimic, a psycho. The attention was refreshing in a way. Before, no one ever spoke to me except to call me fat. I began to feel like that girl on television. Only now, I'd have to get really sick—*physically* sick.

My goal, demented as it was, became the focus of my entire existence. This time, I needed to be careful so that no one became aware of my dark thoughts. That way, I could accomplish my goal. Over the course of the next nine months, I began starving, then bingeing. I had part-time jobs and got paid an average of about $70 a week. Every week, I set aside $30 or $40 in "binge money" to satisfy my craving. I even got a job at an ice cream store so that I had easy and complete access to my favorite binge food. That job was short-lived, however, because, one quiet afternoon, my boss caught me purging in the bathroom. She suggested that I not work there any more. My boss never told my mother about that incident, nor did I.

At the end of the nine months after my release, I passed out in my living room and was taken by ambulance to the local hospital. I had two peptic ulcers and a hiatal hernia. I spent nearly two weeks there re-hydrating and trying to figure out how I would accomplish never purging again.

I hated the life I had gotten myself into. I was just like that girl on television. I was scared and lonely. I felt helpless. I'll never get out of this mess, I thought. My effort to make myself thin and get attention had transformed my identity into "the eating disorder." In my vain efforts to fit into the puzzle of life, I had become an eating disorder. All my thoughts and actions had become reflections of my disease. I constantly played head games, counting calories, adding up grams of fat, distorting the physical properties even of non-fattening foods such as plain salad, making everything out to be much more grandiose than it actually was. I looked in the mirror and saw a fat girl. I heard the voices of my father, my classmates—taunting me, telling me how fat I was, laughing at me. I could see them laughing and giggling. At the sight of tears rolling down my chubby cheeks, their laughter became uproarious.

I wanted to become invisible. I frequently thought about death and loved feeling as though I was close to it. My days of bingeing and purging were over, but they had been replaced with days of deprivation and denial. I tried to concentrate on school, feeling that that was my only means of achieving a possible future, that is, if I decided to allow myself one. School, however, had become a nightmare. I dreaded going to school and seeing those faces, those nasty, inconsiderate people who had helped to ruin my life.

More and more I devoted my days to my eating disorder—my dark side. I woke up at 4:30, drank two huge glasses of water, worked out to an exercise video for an hour, took a shower, ate 40 corn flakes, drank two more glasses of water, put coffee (black, no sugar) into a 64-ounce mug, and went to school. At school, I sat through my classes totally unfocused, not retaining a word of what my teachers said. I had an excuse not to go to gym: My doctor felt I was underweight—as if that really mattered. During lunch, I walked around the athletic fields, alone. Occasionally, a girl I was pseudo-friends with—she just hung out with me for my tips on losing weight—talked to me. I came home, ate (not without guilt) 24 mini-pretzels dipped in mustard and then took a four-mile walk around my neighborhood. For dinner, I usually had one cup of non-fat, no-sugar yogurt and a large coffee (no milk, no sugar) from 7-Eleven. Then I retired to bed, dreading waking up and doing it all over again.

My next hospitalization came as no surprise to me. My parents had just divorced and my mother felt helpless about what to do with me. She put me in a hospital in Queens, thinking that the further away I was from the source of my despair, the better off I would be. Not necessarily so. I spent three weeks there among people with multiple personality disorder, obsessive-compulsive disorder (which was my first diagnosis), as well as myriad other mental illnesses and disorders. Now, for the first time, I began to identify myself as mentally ill. Yes, I was in a psychiatric hospital, but somehow I managed to separate myself from everyone else. I thought they were crazy, much crazier than I was. What a sickening feeling I had when I realized that I belonged here with all those other people. We were one and the same—psycho.

By now, I had grown accustomed to the structured days in a mental hospital. It was much easier to function—and to eat—when my every move was dictated by someone else. Just as my disease dictated my every move when I was not hospitalized, staff dictated my moves when I was. I had lost all sense of an identity. As far as I'm concerned, the hospital stays did not help me find one. What staff was fantastic at was opening up a can of psychic worms, then telling me that my insurance couldn't pay for my treatment any longer, so I'd have to go home and ponder my problems on my own.

Six months after my little vacation in Queens, I returned to the first institution where I had been incarcerated. This time, I threw myself on the mercy of the staff. I was so sick that I thought the hospital—this hospital—was where I belonged. I felt supported; my life there seemed stable. I recall my first day there. I sat in the waiting room with my mother. I could smell the horrendous odor of what I think was lunch and hear the calming hum of classical music emanating from the hidden speakers in the ceiling. I sat there, wrapping my arms around my chest, my mouth agape. Across the room, a mother was sobbing, clenching her daughter, patting her hair as if she were a poodle. My mother sat to the left of me, her bloodshot eyes and disheveled hair revealing the secrets of her emotions. She tried to snap out of her melancholy by reading a magazine, but she quickly put it down when tears came to her eyes.

I was too numb to cry. In the two weeks prior to that day, I had cried so much, I was relieved to be at the hospital. I wouldn't have to go through that any longer, no more starving, no more days filled with meaningless repetition, self-hatred, and thoughts of suicide. Finally I could live. I had lost all ability to function in the outside world. I had become a prisoner to my disease, isolated in my own little world, obsessed with my own private agenda. I couldn't take it any longer.

Being in the hospital had its perks. I made two very close friends there. After all, they say, misery loves company. Sometimes we had a positive influence on one another, but three 17-year-old anorexics are bound to get into trouble, and we did.

After being in the hospital for 10 days, you are eligible for a Sunday pass, if staff and your peers think you deserve it. For some reason, my two friends and I got approved for a Sunday pass, and they allowed us to go out together. It was the Sunday before Easter. Our first stop was the mall. How exciting! We walked from store to store, smiling, laughing, and being teenagers. We had a fabulous day. It was only reluctantly that we returned to the hospital.

In our rap-group session at night, we learned about and were forced to deal with the repercussions of the afternoon's events. One of the girls took it upon herself to steal a bottle of perfume. The other girl and I couldn't convince staff that we were not involved with the theft. Our friend sat in her chair sobbing in fits of relentless guilt as the other girl and I cried, frantically pleading our innocence. Well, it didn't matter. In spite of our protestations, we were considered thieves. The next Sunday, insteading of going out on pass, we were forced to remain apart from each other until further notice. Wasn't it ironic: Finally, I had close friends—and I wasn't even allowed to talk to them! The hospital also kept me from my mother; I was allowed to talk to her only three times a week. Staff said that our relationship was destructive and unhealthy. What do they know? I thought.

But mostly, I spent my time in the hospital uneventfully. During my stay there, I ate what was put in front of me. I didn't like it, but I ate it anyway. My eating disorder had gotten me angry enough to do something about it, and I was determined to be well.

I returned to high school shortly after discharge, but only for half-days. Graduation was only a few months away, and I had finished most of my requirements. I was grateful for not having to spend much time there, since I was not exactly well received upon my return. Even people I considered acquaintances were angry at me, blaming me for being so stupid as to starve myself. I didn't care. I didn't need them any more. I had my life, my recovery.

When it came to making the decision about where to go to college, I dug myself into a hole again. Initially, I had decided to go away to school, to get as far away from home as possible. But I acted out of fear and remained at home and went to the local community college for a year. I did well there, and began to feel as if I wasn't sick any longer. I tried to forget about my disease. And I did, sort of.

Somehow, weight loss crept up on me. Slowly, pound after pound, I began to get skinny again. I ignored it. So did the people around me. Frustrated by a return of my disorder, I decided to go away to school. I picked a school close enough so that I could come home when I wanted but far enough to be away from the dysfunctions of my home environment. I should have picked a school in Tibet. Being far away yet close to home was like sitting on a sharp picket fence. During my first semester away, I hit an all-time low. I stood 5 feet 6 inches tall, and my weight bottomed out at 85 pounds. After one semester, I returned home.

The most frightening thing about weighing 85 pounds was that nobody said anything. My boyfriend, who saw more of my body than anyone, made some sort of facial gestures that seemed to express disapproval of my emaciated appearance—but that was the extent of it. When I attended the winter formal in a gown that hung so loosely on my body that every vividly protruding bone was revealed, no one said a thing.

When my boyfriend and I entered at the catering hall where the dance was being held, he walked ahead of me to hold open the door. Inside, he took my coat from me and brought it to the coatroom. I spun around to look in the mirror to see how well my hair had made it in the wind. I saw a girl in the mirror who was wearing the same dress as I. My goodness, she looked so sickly! I thought—she must be anorexic. A few seconds later, my boyfriend walked up to me and put his arm around my shoulders. "My, what a dazzling couple we are!" he exclaimed as we looked at our images in the mirror. My God, I thought, that anorexic girl is me!

After returning home from school, initially, I didn't seek help. I just fell into the comfort of being in a familiar pace. In January, I began at a local community college. It was the beginning of my worst semester ever. Between the time I spent driving to school, obsessing about food, and running 10 miles every morning, I hardly found enough time to make it to class. By June, I was burnt out.

Once again, I decided it was time to seek help. I began seeing a therapist. This one specialized in eating disorders. She pointed me in the direction of someone who could help me regain my weight. I made an appointment to see the nutritionist she recommended.

The nutritionist's office smelled like incense, a stale stench of grass and spices thrown into an urn and burned. It seemed bare and sparsely furnished—her desk and chair and a huge bookshelf filled with books such as *Dying to be Thin* and *Understanding Eating Disorders*. They kind of made me feel at home. There was also a huge, white, cold-looking doctor's scale. The very sight of it made me cringe. I was not a scale person.

In college, I asked the nurse if I could weigh myself in her office. I did that every day for a week. I went at eight in the morning, just after my run, before I showered. I stepped very slowly on the scale, as if I were climbing onto a carton of eggs. Notch by notch, I moved the pointer of the scale forward until it balanced, then I passed that point, then I pushed the pointer back again. I got off and stepped back in disbelief. I couldn't imagine how I had gotten that thin. So I decided to stop weighing myself. I wanted to relish the moment of being thinner than I thought I ever could be.

In the nutritionist's office, I stepped on the scale literally shaking. I had no idea what to expect. First I stepped on backwards so I wouldn't have to look at how much I weighed. What the hell? I thought, I'm gonna know anyway. I weighed 88 pounds. I gained three pounds! What happened? I didn't eat any more than I had when I lived away from home—what the hell happened? I began to cry. The nutritionist didn't have any idea what to think. At first, she began consoling me for weighing so little, but I didn't want her consolation. I wanted to lose those three pounds!

That was how I made my way to hospitalization number four. As soon as the nutritionist realized I had no intention of gaining a pound, she made the suggestion that I go immediately to the emergency room of a hospital with an inpatient, medically-based eating disorder program. Off we went.

I spent nearly six hours in the emergency room. I was cold, angry, and damn hungry. First, I saw the nurse. She took my blood pressure; it was 60/30. My pulse was 34. According to those readings, I was nearly dead. Next, the gown. A thin, blue-and-white checkered gown with three ties in back and holes big enough to reveal everything. Then another scale. This one I liked better; it said I only weighed 84 pounds. At that point, I was so satisfied I was ready to go home. The doctors didn't agree.

After being poked, prodded, having blood sucked from my body, X-rayed, probed, then poked again, then a tube attached to my arm, I was rolled upstairs and into my room. There were two other beds in the room. It was two in the morning when I finally climbed into bed. I fell asleep to the sound of the IV pumping life back into my body.

When I woke up, a tall, super-skinny nurse was hovering over me, pressing the buttons on my IV pump. For a couple seconds, I had forgotten where I was. As soon as the nurse said, "You must be starving," I remembered. She pushed the tray on my over-bed table closer to me. On the tray sat one egg, hardboiled, a half-cup of milk, a slice of bread in a plastic wrapping, and a packet of diet jelly. Diet jelly? Was that a hint? Suddenly, I felt very upset. Tears began to roll uncontrollably from my eyes. The nurse looked at me and shrugged, "You know you have to eat." She talked to me as if I were a five-year-old.

"I DON'T HAVE TO DO ANYTHING!" I screamed back angrily.

With that, she walked out of the room without saying a word.

That wasn't a very good start, I thought. The unit I was in was made up of adolescents and children with a multitude of medical diseases and transient illnesses. For a while, I was the only eating disorder in the unit. Every morning, I got up, took a shower, dressed, and made my bed. Then I went into the dayroom, where someone watched me eat. The eating part took place seven times daily, at 8 A.M., 10 A.M., 12 noon, 2 P.M., 5 P.M., 8 P.M., and 10 P.M. Three meals and four snacks. By themselves, even the snacks were as calorically substantial as whole meals.

Parents visiting the children in the unit often questioned me about my presence there. Or they'd say, "Going home today, I see." I was hesitant to tell them why I was there. Sometimes, they said, "Yeah, I thought you looked kind of thin." Or they'd jump right to the point. "What made you do that?" My most feared comment would be, "You don't look so thin." Or, "Gee, you look fantastic! I wish I had a figure like yours!" When I heard things like that, I wanted to jump off a cliff.

After a month of hard-core eating, I had gained nearly 30 pounds. My doctor thought that it was time for me to continue my weight gain in a day-treatment program she ran outside the hospital. I was more than game for that. Anything to get away from the enclosure of that hospital. Still, I had gotten extremely close to staff. And once again, I was leaving a sense of structure and stability for the unknown.

One positive side about going home was being with my mother. When I was in the hospital, I hardly saw her. She had two jobs in addition to her own problems. In the hospital, I was left stranded 50 miles from home. Now, at home, at least I could be near her.

For the next month, I got up at 4:30 in the morning, ran seven miles, showered, dressed, and left for the day program. I had to be there at 9 A.M. A one-way commute took me about two hours. Between 9 A.M. and 5 P.M., I consumed about 3800 calories, and I was expected to consume another 500 at home. Therapy was transient, and the daily commute made me feel frustrated. So I quit. I decided it was time to get the hell out, go back to school, and attempt to mend my broken life.

The next semester wasn't bad. I was doing okay with eating. I was maintaining a semi-adequate weight. But when the semester was over, I had come to the conclusion that a change was what I needed. I decided to live with a family friend in southern California. Before I left, I got in touch with my doctor. She gave me the telephone number of an eating disorder doctor in California. She wasn't thrilled about my departure, but I didn't care. I imagined the California sunshine cleansing my spirit, washing my troubles away.

I was scheduled to leave in January. I began packing in November. The plane ride was freaky. When the plane took off, I felt my stomach sinking to my toes. I never felt it come back up. I didn't read or watch the movie or talk to my neighbor or listen to the headphones. I just sat there.

California was beautiful but I hardly noticed. I went nowhere, I did nothing. I called my mother every day and begged her to send me a plane ticket home. She refused. I think she liked her independence. In fact, I know she did. All those years when I was suffering from the eating disorder—the screaming, crying, punching, the different personalities I took on—she bore the brunt of it all. I could hear it in her voice when I called her from the hospital I was taken to, just six months after my plane landed in San Diego.

I couldn't even recall how I got to the hospital in the first place. It was just your typical hot, dry San Diego afternoon. I was doing my laundry and between loads, I sat by the pool. That's all I remember. The next thing I knew, I was lying in a hospital bed, stone-cold petrified. I couldn't remember my name, where I lived—nothing! Even if I had, I wouldn't have been able to open my mouth to speak.

After what seemed like an eternity, my roommate came in and told me what happened. "My God, you gave us quite a scare," she said to me. *I scared them!* Apparently, I had passed out and someone called an ambulance. I had been in that hospital bed for two days before I was coherent enough to speak!

I stayed there for a week and returned home a week after that. I was readmitted to the hospital I had been discharged from less than a year before. I felt humiliated riding up in an elevator, sitting in a wheelchair, everyone greeting me by my first name. The hospital had become a home, a safe haven from the rotten outside world. In the hospital, I could *be* my disorder, do what was expected of me. I didn't have to try to be anyone else—just myself.

Finally, I had identified a reason for my relapse. My disorder was the only me I had known. Throughout my entire adolescence, when other girls were dealing with puberty and boys and trying to figure out what they wanted to be when they grew up, I was jamming my fingers down my throat and counting the calories in lettuce. This deranged way of thinking and behaving was all I knew, but now after ten years of my disorder, I finally wanted something else.

After I had gained some weight, I made the decision, at the suggestion of my therapist, to admit myself to a borderline personality disorder program in a psychiatric facility. In a vain effort to find myself, the only thing I truly achieved was finding out who I *didn't* want to be.

At the clinic, I could see myself nearly falling into the role of mental patient. I followed orders, took my medications, and came running every time staff beckoned. I had become accustomed to the checks. First, every five minutes. Then every fifteen, then the standard half-hour checks. Knock-knock, just checking. I can still hear that knock when I'm lying in bed at night.

I had become used to the curtainless showers, the plastic mirrors, the rules that dictated that I ask for permission to use a nail file. It didn't even faze me when I first arrived at the clinic and staff went through my suitcases, removing my undergarments, one by one, and shaking each one out to make sure that nothing illegal was being concealed.

Perhaps because I was the most psychiatrically normal and least disordered person in the unit, I achieved my maximal goals in record time. After four days, I was unit president. Oh, what an honor that was, being the unit president of a psycho ward! Something to tell my grandkids.

Being in a position of power on that unit—so to speak—I learned a lot of things about myself. I witnessed firsthand the travesty that was going on in that hospital, in that unit. All these people—myself included—trusted in the system to make them better. We were stripped of our rights and our sense of humanity. We had become *mental patients*. Just as I had become *an* anorexic—that was the basis of my existence, that was *all* I was to staff. If you asked the patients what was the first thing they thought of when they thought of themselves, nine out of ten would have mentioned their psychiatric status. I would have said I was an anorexic. It was a system even the patients accepted.

In that unit, I made a discovery about myself; I began to realize I was not a hopeless case. I stood in the doorway of a quiet room. A single, stained mattress—stained with God knows what—was in the middle of the scratched, dirty gray linoleum floor. The padding on the walls had been ripped and little pieces of filthy cotton batting protruded. The bars on the Plexiglas window were a telltale sign that this was not a welcoming place. How easy it would be, I thought, just to hurl myself into that room, to scream, kick, and cry—let everything go. But for what? Haven't I been doing that all along? My starvation, my purging. I have been crying for love, for validation. It wasn't working. I could have let myself go but I if I had, I wouldn't have given myself a chance to get better.

It's been more than a year since that three-week admission. In some ways, I wish I had never been there, but I know that I needed to be there so that I could understand, so that I could become aware of what I know now. I have maintained my weight. I am close enough to my goal so that another hospital admission is very far from my mind. Mentally, I have never felt better. I am no longer stigmatized by the status of mental patient. The status of anorexic is a little harder to give up, however. Let's say I am an anorexic in strong recovery. Each day I come closer to getting better, each day I give up a little more of the anorexic part of my personality. I will begin graduate school in the fall. I plan to become a social worker with a speciality in adolescent disorders, especially eating disorders. I have my life and I've formed my own, true, identity. Now I have to live.

Annette describes her stigmatization, both informal and institutional, in no uncertain terms.

Informally, at school, she said, she could hear the "taunting," the "laughing and giggling" of her classmates, the insults ("I was stigmatized as a 'puker,' a bulimic, and a psycho") ringing in her ears.

On the institutional level, likewise, Goffman's characterization of staff in the mental hospital as simultaneously normalizing their often arbitrary decisions and abnormalizing any patient desires, behavior, or impulses has resonance in Annette's descriptions. She felt that "what was going on" in the hospital was a "travesty." Patients "trusted in the system to make them better," she explained. But, she said, we were "stripped of our rights and our sense of humanity. We had become *mental patients*, just as I had become *an* anorexic—that was the basis of my existence, that was *all* I was to staff." It was, she added, "a system even the patients accepted." She felt, she said, "persecuted and pressured into saying things that were alien to me. I felt," she added, "violated and manipulated by staff. . . . They taunted, poked, and prodded us at every opportunity." The half-hour checks, the "curtainless showers, the plastic mirrors," having to ask permission to use a nail file; when she was unpacking, staff shaking out her undergarments to make sure nothing was concealed in them—these and other authoritarian features of her experience may or may not have been therapeutically necessary, but they are, she said, experienced by patients, including herself, as degrading.

After reading Annette's account, I realized that Goffman's work is a lot more relevant to mental institutionalization than I had thought.

CHAPTER 7

I went in in the morning to get my clothes and there were the two of them lying in the bed. And they looked fabulous. And I'm thinking, that is exactly what I want! That's it! I want to be lying in bed with another woman! I have to find a lesbian.

Leslie

How can we continue to make our world so that we can incorporate different people's ideas and experiences? It seems too often that people who don't quite fit in get squashed. And I think the mainstream loses out, loses the contributions of these people who aren't part of the mainstream.

Helen

Leslie and Helen, Loving Lesbian Moms

The fundamentalist Christian regards homosexuality as *sin*—an abomination in the eyes of God (Falwell, Dobson, and Hindson, 1981, pp. 195–205). The old-fashioned, traditional, dyed-in-the-wool psychoanalyst regards homosexuality as *sickness*—a psychic disorder in need of a cure (Bieber et al., 1962; Socarides, 1978). To the contemporary sociologist, these two views—homosexuality as sin and homosexuality as sickness—seem hopelessly antiquated, obsolete, and most decidedly wrong.

Nearly all sociologists who research, teach, and write about the subject regard homosexuality as a normal variant of sexual behavior, expression, and preference. Most regard the view that, somehow, a particular sexual preference for men versus women is inferior, pathological, or immoral, is bizarre, biased—a manifestation of conventional morality. In fact, in recent years, a theoretical perspective called "queer theory" has arisen that regards *heterosexuality* as repressive, a distorted species of sexuality. The vast majority of sociologists, and especially sociologists of deviance, do not regard the issue of homosexuality as sin or sickness worth debating. They do, however, consider the fact that these (erroneous) views are held and acted upon by many influential actors in the society—a substantial proportion of the general public, members of religious groups and movements, and many medical and psychiatric figures. As such, the influence of these views and these actors has to be taken into account. *The very fact that many Americans regard homosexuality as sin and/or sickness demonstrates that, in some social circles, it is deviant.*

In their classic book on human sexuality (1967, 2001), John Gagnon and William Simon entitle their chapter on lesbianism "A Conformity Greater Than Deviance." In spite of the serious challenge that homosexuality offers to traditional sexual behavior and sex roles—and the even more serious challenge that lesbian motherhood offers to the traditional family—in most ways, lesbians tend to lead far more mainstream than unconventional lives. Ensconced in the more liberal communities of the country's large cities, it is often difficult to picture the furor that the issue of homosexuality generates in the more conventional parts of the country. And yet, nearly all textbooks on the sociology of deviance include a discussion of homosexuality; most devote an entire chapter to the topic. It is difficult to argue that homosexuality does not violate traditional norms or that it does not occasion negative reactions from some audiences from time to time.

Leslie and Helen are in their 40s. They have been sexual partners for nine years and they have a two-and-a-half-year-old child, Karen. Leslie is a graphic designer, Helen is an architect. Perhaps the keystone of their lives can be summed up in a statement by Leslie: "We think of ourselves as utterly conventional. Who could be more conventional than us?" She also said: "Being a mother is more of a major issue in my life than being a lesbian."

And yet, as viewed through the prism of lesbianism, one is struck by how different female sexuality is from the male version, how, for both Leslie and Helen, lesbianism is an uncompromisingly *female* orientation to sex. Both were unwilling or unable to make their compromises with the specifically and distinctly male version of sexuality that heterosexual women must make their peace with if they want to continue to have male companionship. Leslie's description of the unfulfilled ideal heterosexual relationship she yearned for in college is extremely revealing: "that's not what guys do," she explained. "That's what *girls* do." Helen, too, describes her awkward fumblings at heterosexuality, an experience that told her, *that's not for me.*

In many ways, Leslie and Helen are an interesting study in contrast. Leslie is garrulous, effusive, outgoing, and enthusiastic—an interviewer's dream. Helen is thoughtful, philosophical, introspective, and reticent, sometimes finding her words inadequate to the complexity of her thoughts. Leslie had extensive sexual contact with men prior to coming out as a lesbian; Helen had virtually none. Aside from her awkward heterosexual experiences and her consequent lesbianism, Leslie's life has been almost totally unmarked by unconventionality; her approach to life is pragmatic, no-nonsense, and here-and-now. In contrast, Helen's life has been more unconventional and has been something of a quest for spiritual fulfillment: taking LSD, dropping out of college, living for three years in a Hindu ashram, flirting with lesbian separatism, building a house in the Ontario wilderness. I commented to Helen that it is ironic that someone whose profession essentially and fundamentally deals with physical materials should be concerned with liberating herself from the material world.

I interviewed Leslie and Helen separately, Leslie first and Helen second.

Erich: I'm sure most heterosexuals don't really have a clear idea of the living arrangements of a lesbian couple. My guess is, they really don't know what it is that makes two women a *couple*. I wonder if you could construct a portrait of how you and Helen live your lives. Perhaps you could say a few things about your *couplehood*, I guess that's how we could start. For instance, how long have you known each other?

Leslie: We've known each other for years. I've known Helen because she's a friend of Jane and Roseanna [the couple who own the building Leslie and Helen currently live in], but when we first met, I was in a committed relationship. About the time I became single, Helen and I started knowing that we were interested in each other, and then we got involved. And I think our case was unusual because she was helping me renovate my apartment. I was newly renting from Jane and Roseanna and my apartment was right next to Helen's. And because her apartment was really small, we began sharing my kitchen and then, gradually, as we became even more involved, we were sort of living together all the time anyway. I think we were a fully committed couple when Helen broke down the wall separating our apartments and made a door between her apartment and mine, so that to get from her apartment to mine, we didn't have to go out into the hallway to come back in. . . . For us, what made us *really* committed was when we decided to have a child together. Once we decided to do that, we hoped and expected that we'd be together forever. But also from the time that we first got together, it

was our *intention* to stay together. I wouldn't have gotten into a relationship with someone who didn't want to have a child—that was the relationship I wanted. So, we're raising a child together. Our finances are totally mixed, we have one joint checking account. We can't file our tax
returns jointly, but if we could, we would. . . . But all the ways that finances can be mingled, ours are mingled. . . . And we make all our financial decisions together. And we certainly make our decisions about
Karen together. We don't agree all the time [sing-songy voice]. And we
sort of take on each other's families, for good or ill, whatever that entails.
I think that's also a big part of the commitment, that you take on the
other's family.

I was in a previous long-term relationship, and it was four or five
years before I came out to my family. And once I came out to them, we
went through our emotional *Sturm und Drang*. It was never about
Eloise, my previous partner. They loved her—what's not to love? She was
fabulous. And after I came out to my family and visited them with Eloise,
they treated her the way they treated my brother-in-law. So I was really
lucky. My coming out story was one of the happy ones. And my mother's
only comment was, well, how are you going to have children? So she
started sending me articles about sperm banks. . . .

My mother and I, we're a lot alike. She was fine with me being a lesbian, but felt she had to tell me that, because I'm a lesbian, I have to be
even better than everyone else. And I think it was yet another of my
mother's pitches for me to be a famous writer. But then I wrote her back
a letter saying that's ridiculous, she should get a life, then we had a fight,
and that was it, the problem was over. . . . I think my dad probably had a
harder time with it, but he would never say so. He loves his kids and he
loves to see them, and they come with who they come with. And he tries
in his own way to reach out. It's really funny. My father's a conservative,
he's seriously a Republican, both of my parents are. My dad is a corporate guy, he's made a lot of money as a corporate guy, and he thinks that
if he did, everyone else can. And he's a responsible citizen, he donates to
charity, he's on the board of a couple of charities. He's such a good person, you know what I mean? But he votes the Republican ticket. It's
enough to make you retch. So we don't talk about politics. Oh, he'll talk
to Helen about building and things like that. I guess what I'm trying to
say is he tries really hard to find things that they have in common. But in
fact they don't have anything in common. But both of my parents think
that Helen's a really nice person—anybody would. They're always really
kind to her and they accept her as part of the family and treat her like
anybody else in the family. It's just that she's different than they are—as
I am. So my family treats her really well, as do my brothers and sisters.

It's funny, when I came out, I said to my brother, you obviously know about this, what do you think of it? He said, well, I wouldn't want you to kiss Helen in front of me, but I wouldn't want to see Sally and Dick [their sister and brother-in-law] kissing, either. And Georgia, my little sister said, yeah, whatever. And Sally, my other sister, is so tender-hearted and sweet, she says to us, come to our church with us, because the minister is very progressive, he's in the forefront of the Presbyterians for Gays movement. So she leans over backwards to show how accepting she is. Nobody rejected me, or the relationship, or Helen, or anything else.

I think that's not typical, but it's not that atypical either. I think about my friends and I know most of their coming-out stories. It's not the news that any parent wants to hear, at least certainly not any parents who are in our parents' generation. It's just not their first choice. And it's not what they expected or wanted. And they have a little rocky time and, to varying degrees, they get over it. And the ones who don't are probably really assholes anyway. That's obviously my opinion, but they tend to be the kind of parents who say things to their children no parents should ever say to their kids. They clearly aren't great parents to begin with.

Erich: If it's not too indelicate to ask, how was your daughter conceived?

Leslie: Oh, no, it's not indelicate, we talk about it all the time. We have to talk about it because, when we decided to have our daughter, it's the most out [that is, the most publicly open about her lesbianism] I've ever been in my entire life. We have no choice. I have to talk about it easily and naturally because if I don't, then it makes Karen feel weird and funny about how it happened, that if we're secretive about it, it's not supposed to be talked about. Here's how it happened. Valerie was a graduate student at MIT when Helen went to grad school there. She and Helen went into business together and we shared studio space—their architecture business and my graphic design business. Valerie started seeing Dave and they ultimately got married. Well, in the course of Valerie's discussions with me about, should I marry him, should I not marry him, I really always thought I should be free, but he's a really nice guy and I want to have kids, this sort of thing, she asked me, what about you? Do you want to have kids? And I said, yeah, I'd really like to have kids. And I thought, Dave has many of the characteristics I'm looking for in a father. He's nice, he's really smart, and so on. And Valerie said, great, so we talked about it and then Valerie went home and talked to Dave about it and I talked to Helen. And he agreed to do it, under the kind of relationship that we wanted, which was to have a known father—who would be known *as* her father—but would really have more of a relationship that I think of as an uncle. I'd have him for his advice the way I would have my brother, but I wouldn't be bound by anything he said. And if I got into trouble, I'm sure he would send me money if I needed it, but I wouldn't expect it and it wouldn't be an obligation, it would just be because he wanted to. And so we wrote a little contract.

At the same time, Valerie and Dave were trying to get pregnant. So it was like, at the times that Valerie was most fertile, Dave would have to be available for her. And then I was timing it too, so, at the proper times, he would, you know, provide us with sperm. How we did it was very low-tech, actually. I had a book that told us how to do it. And we experimented with different kinds of syringes. We used TB syringes. They were the right size. We had specimen bottles. Since Dave's a doctor, he had access to all this stuff. But I suppose we could have used Tupperware and it would have been fine. And I charted myself so I knew when I would ovulate. We tried eight times. And at the right time, I got pregnant. We were all very excited. And by that time, Valerie was three months pregnant. I was really happy when she got pregnant, because before she got pregnant, Valerie and I had talked about what would happen if I got pregnant and she couldn't. In fact, it almost worked out that way—she had a really hard pregnancy and I had an easy pregnancy. And I said it would have been really cool if you couldn't get pregnant, then I could *donate an egg*, and then the two girls would be full sisters. And I'd say, thanks for the sperm and you'd say, thanks for the egg. It would have been a fair trade, you know.

We see Dave's family as much as we can. We visit them regularly. We told his parents. His mother, Bea, is hilarious. She's like everyone's stereotype of your basic New York Jewish woman. I asked her, what do you think of this [Leslie's child with Dave], Bea? Her answer is, I don't know, it's all very new to me. And I say, the relationship you want to have with Dave's child is up to you, as much or as little, I'm not going to push, you have to make your own choices. And she's, like, I'm thinking about it, just call me the minute the baby's born. And 15 minutes after Karen was born, she was on the phone, and cards and presents appeared in the mail. And she loves Karen. We see her on the Jewish holidays. It works out to maybe we see them between four and six times a year.

We had one thing that Helen thought I was overreacting to. Bea has a friend who came over while Karen was visiting, and the woman said, "Who is this little pumpkin?" And Bea said, oh, this is a friend's daughter. And I went home and got hysterical. I felt, I would have to explain to her, that's fine if you choose to do that, but you can't have your friends around when Karen is there because I won't have my daughter acknowledged that way. I won't permit that. All right, partly, Bea's an older woman and she's not going to live that long, her health is not that great. And partly, being an older woman, she doesn't know what to say to her friends. She'd rather have the conversation about who her son's child is over coffee than in front of them staring at her waiting for her to explain what her relationship is to this child. Ultimately, I never said anything to her.

Some of Karen's cousins were over on one particular occasion and Dave was there and he was saying, this is your cousin, Karen. And one cousin in particular was sort of adding it up and she's old enough to know who her parent's siblings are and how could this be, you know. And at some point, she asked, who is Leslie married to? And her mother said, oh, Leslie's not married, Leslie doesn't have a male partner. And this little girl says, "Oh, Leslie's a *lesbian!* Cool!" At that point, her mother said, "We'll talk about it in the car." And I guess they had a very interesting discussion on the way home.

And on yet another holiday, where we met another branch of this extended family, one woman comes up to me and says [forcefully], "You know, Dave never told me, I can't believe it, we would have sent baby presents, well, *mazel tov* [good luck] and welcome to the family." I mean, Dave's family is like that, and it's been really great, and I'm thrilled to death that Karen has the experience of an emotionally very different family from my family. Dave's family is a big, extended Jewish family that gets together for loud, raucous celebrations with lots of food. And we get to be a part of that, and it's great.

It may be tricky right now because Karen doesn't call him Dad— father—and it probably won't happen until she realizes that, well, do I have a father? Right now, she has a mom and a mommy. Lots of other kids she knows also have a mom and a mommy, and lots have moms and daddys, but she's two and a half years old. I think we're going to wait on telling her that Dave is the father until she asks. I asked Dave if he wants Karen to call him "Dave" or "Daddy." And he felt like it might be confusing to Clio [his daughter with his wife]. And I sort of felt, well, if Karen calls Dave daddy, Clio will get over it. But again, it's his choice. I think he sort of felt like, they [Karen and Clio] aren't really able to understand it now and so, telling them he's Karen's father is pointless. When they're four or five, it would be meaningful and we'll say to Karen, yeah, your daddy doesn't live with us, but he loves you, and he's also Clio's daddy, and she's your sister, so that'll be fun. But it's interesting because Dave will also say things like, "Clio, give your sister a kiss." And that's sort of weird because I don't know when Dave is going to sort all this out and, you know, come around on this issue. But I imagine it'll happen when it happens. And that's his choice. I'm sure there will be more to talk about and it'll work itself out.

Erich: One of the things I'm interested in is the interface between conventional society and the people who lead somewhat unconventional lives. And it sounds like so far, with your parents and with Dave's family, you've had more or less positive relations in that respect. Has this generally been your experience? Have there ever been any conventional institutions or conventional others that you've had to deal with who, let's say, reacted to your lesbianism in a different way?

Leslie: I think being in New York makes an enormous difference. It's such small things. Helen went with me to interview these doctors to find out whether we wanted them to be Karen's pediatricians. And one of them said, about Helen, "Is this Karen's grandmother?" And Helen certainly doesn't look enough older than me to be my mother. She's only six years older than me. But that was the only relationship that occurred to them. And I said, "No, she's Karen's other mother." And he's like, "Oh! Okay, that's fine." You know. And we said, for you to be our doctor, you have to be really okay with the fact that we are lesbian moms and you have to understand that you should call either or both of us on any medical decision, as one, and it's not that Helen is helping me babysit, you know what I mean? She's an equal mom here. So that incident was like a small thing that as a heterosexual, you would never have had to deal with. Nobody would ever ask the father in a heterosexual couple, are you this child's grandfather? That wouldn't be the assumption.

We're applying to nursery schools right now. As we're filling out the forms for preschool, it's very clear who's thinking and who isn't. The more open-minded, diversity-seeking type of form says "Parent or Guardian/Parent or Guardian." On a very liberal form it just says "Guardian/Guardian." It doesn't even specify that it's a parent. And we think of this in terms of an overarching social issues thing. They don't have to assume in this day and age that any child is necessarily being raised by their biological parents. There's lots of different kinds of families. Ours is only one of the unconventional kinds. One form we saw actually said, "Mother/Father." So, we had to cross out "Father" and write in "Mother." And when I find out whether or not we get accepted to that school, I'm going to call them and tell them that I think their form is really offensive. It calls into question the school's ability to deal with children with all kinds of nontraditional backgrounds. They can't even think that far ahead.

Every time we read Karen's story books, we kind of grit our teeth. Because it's almost always the mommy, the daddy, and the baby. Even the exceptions are upsetting. I don't know if you've ever read the notorious *Heather Has Two Mommies*. It's the stupidest book you've ever read in your whole life. It couldn't be more boring if it tried. No child would ever read it except under duress. It's just *stupid*. I feel like I have to write my own children's book. We have to publish it *samizdat* [self-published] for all the mommies we know because I don't want a story book about Heather has two mommies. I want a story book about Heather goes to the zoo and liberates the giraffes and has a really fabulous day and comes home and tells her moms all about it. And they call up her dad and he comes over and they all have birthday cake. I want the lesbianism completely taken for granted, not pushed in your face. What's important about the school our daughter will go to is that we want a place where her family is neither special nor singled out. Her family is normal, just like all the other families. That's what's wrong with *Heather Has Two Mommies*—Heather's family situation is singled out as different. I expect that at some point along the way, that will come up and we will be doing some agitating around that.

When I was telling my sister that I was pregnant, and I was all excited, and who the father was, and what our arrangements were going to be, she said, Leslie, there are going to be *problems*. You're acting like it's all going to be fine. And I said, compared to being Black in America? Compared to being born with a disability? Being the child of lesbian mothers is not a big problem. It's a spectrum. Karen definitely has a thing she has to deal with. It's not going to be the easiest thing in the world to deal with. But it's not the worst thing. And to the best of my ability to influence her—and I believe in my ability to influence her—she'll be taught that she doesn't have a problem. Other people may have a problem. And you have to deal sensitively with other people's problems. Still, I'll have to muster my energy for what will come.

Being a lesbian has been *situationally* major. It was major to come out. That was a very hard thing to do, although the *result* was very good. It was hard for me to decide that I was gay and find a lesbian partner. But once I did, I said to myself, oh, wow, I wish I had done *this* when I was in high school. This is a *much* better idea than being straight. Which doesn't mean that it wasn't hard. It was hard to tell my parents. Even after my father knew I was gay, he still voted Republican. I find it *completely* inconceivable that he can reconcile that with loving me. . . . But in terms of things that are really hard for me in my life, there's absolutely nothing I can possibly complain about. I really can't.

Yes, it would have been better had I gone to *Smith* [a college whose culture encourages lesbian-friendly norms]. I would have had a much better experience there instead of a little traditional college in Pennsylvania. But it could have been worse. I could have gone to Bob Jones U! [a fundamentalist Christian college that prohibits not only homosexual contact but non-marital sex of any kind].

Erich: Can you take this back a ways? Can you talk a little about your dating experiences in high school and in college? I mean, did you date boys? What kind of experiences did you have, and when did you realize that heterosexuality wasn't working out for you?

Leslie: I had dated boys in high school. I mean, I dated one boy in high school, I had a boyfriend in my senior year of high school. But I certainly *wanted* to have a boyfriend throughout all my years of high school. When I was in junior high school, I went out with one boy for a while. In high school, there were lots of boys I really had a crush on or wanted to go out with, or whatever, but I also had [non-sexual] relationships with best friend-girlfriends as well. What I really wanted was the *idea* of having a boyfriend, because you're *supposed* to have a boyfriend. That means you're popular, that means that people love you, and you're normal and pretty and, you know, I was abnormal and smart. And then I went to college and I thought, oh, I'm going to go to college, this is going to be different, and I'll have all the right clothes and I'm going to have boyfriends, and it's going to be great. And in fact, I didn't have boyfriends.

Recently, I was lamenting all this with my friend Victoria, who's straight and happily married, and I said, "Oh, I don't know, boys just never really liked me," and she said, "Leslie, you're a *lesbian*—why did you think men would like you?" I just wasn't *getting* it. I just didn't realize, hey, I don't get along with guys because—guess what?—I'm gay.

So I had no boyfriends in college. I *slept* with a lot of guys, but that was a different thing. . . . And I was drinking a lot, so that probably contributed to what was happening. I think all the freshmen on campus were drinking a lot. It was a really hard, horrible, painful time.

Erich: What was the sexual experience for you like?

Leslie: Fine. Whatever, you know. They wanted it a lot and it wasn't that big a problem for me. I mean, that's not even totally fair. I say that to be funny. There were guys I was turned on by, certainly guys I wanted to sleep with, and guys I found attractive. I always had this idea that I'd have a boyfriend and he would come over and he'd bring his books and he'd be studying and I'd be studying and then we'd drink hot chocolate and then we'd go to bed and have sex and it would be great and then we'd wake up in the morning and we'd say, "What are you thinking about first this morning, dear?" And then he'd go off to his classes and I'd go off to mine. And we'd have something to talk about when we were together again. And in fact, that's not what guys do. That's what *girls* do. Girls come over and they're cozy and they have hot chocolate and they read and have cozy sex—or wild, passionate sex, or whatever. I could fall in love with *many* different women. I could find a *huge* spectrum of women attractive. But there's a very *narrow* spectrum of guys I'd find attractive. My *odds* are better with women. . . .

For me, at this point in my life, it's almost inconceivable that I would ever sleep with a guy. In fact, after I came out, it pretty much wasn't possible any more. It just seems like a lot of work.

Erich: When you said, in college, girls liked to be cozy and have hot chocolate and talk about Proust, and so on, and guys didn't, the guys you went out with, what was their idea of a date?

Leslie: I don't know, because I never really went out with any of them. I never *got it*—dating. What it was guys wanted, what I had to do to get dates with them. I didn't get it. Yeah, I *slept* with them. I would meet them at a fraternity party and we would drink a lot, and they would say, "You're really beautiful, I want to sleep with you," and I'd say, "Well, okay." Or we would talk about something and I would think, he's really cute, he has a nice body, it would be fun to sleep with him. I have *no* idea what they were thinking. I can't separate it out any more.

I slept with a guy who subsequently married one of my very best friends. And I talked to her about my relationship with him. He totally broke my heart. I really liked him, I thought he was fabulous. I got up in the morning and he made me eggs, and I thought, this is great! But you know, he liked me *fine*. He was happy to be friends with me. But he didn't want to be in any kind of a committed relationship. He was a really cute guy and he slept around a lot. And my friend, his wife, said she talked to him about us, and she said he said, "Well, I liked her fine, but I wasn't interested in that kind of a relationship." And that was sort of the end of it. The goals of guys just seemed so different. I wouldn't say that I slept with *gazillions* of guys, but in four years of college, I probably slept with 10 or 15 guys. None of whom I was dating.

Erich: Why do you think it was that you had these encounters with guys that didn't lead to a relationship?

Leslie: I don't know. Except what my friend said—I'm gay. My feeling is, whatever the signals are that you're supposed to give off that say, "girlfriend material," I wasn't giving them off. I wasn't the ugliest girl on campus. I was fat but not that fat. I was probably 20 pounds heavier than I am now. But there were much less attractive girls than me who were having dates. At the time, I told myself, well, I'm just not very attractive and that's it. I just happen to be having sex because guys would have sex, you know, with a *dog*. Sorry. That's kind of how I thought at the time. And I was very *bitter*. I was really, really bitter and really unhappy. Because I felt like, I don't want to be treated like this. But it was also a realization that I don't know how to talk to guys. I have no idea what to say. There is a dance that men and women do that I don't know the steps to. I just don't get it. I don't get what I'm supposed to do to make them like me. You know what I mean? And the thing is, when I started seeing women, I was beating them off with a stick. I wasn't any prettier, I wasn't any better-looking than I was when I was sleeping with guys. I don't know what it was, but being with women was really easy.

I guess what it is is that I don't know how men think. I have friends who are guys, but not the way some women do. And to this day, I have no *close* friends who are guys. No, I have one—a gay man. I had one straight male friend. He was my boss at work, and married. He ultimately ended up wanting to have an affair with me, and it was a really big problem. The problem for him was that he was married, the problem for me was that I was gay. So I guess he wasn't really my friend. And we had to maintain some kind of friendship afterwards. But I don't know any other way to describe it: I'm gay, you know.

When I graduated from college, I hadn't had a sexual relationship with a woman yet. But I had started thinking about it. Because for me, a sexual relationship with a guy was *so* not working out. I was starting to feel like something was wrong. Plus, I was miserable. It had been a lousy four years. Then I moved to New York and got a job. I worked for a publisher. I ended up editing romance novels. And that was great! Because suddenly, I was around people who could use words with more than two syllables in them. I was around people who thought it was even normal to read—a *lot*—and in fact, had read everything I had read, and more, and could tell me about great things to read. And I was good at what I did and people said so. It was great. So then I was happy. But still I didn't have a boyfriend. And still I wasn't meeting any guys.

One day, my friend Sandra said, "Leslie, there's something I have to tell you. I have this friend, and she's coming to visit me. She's my lover." And then she told me, "By the way, after you graduated, all of us—a small group of women we were friends with—we all started sleeping together." This was a woman who eventually got married. And she had had a passionate relationship with a woman in college. Anyway, her lover came and so I slept on the couch and let them use the double bed that was in my room. And I went in in the morning to get my clothes and there were the two of them lying in the bed. And they looked fabulous. And I'm thinking, that is *exactly* what I want! *That's it!* I want to be lying naked in bed with another woman! I have to find a lesbian.

Erich: That's remarkable.

Leslie: It was great. It was a defining moment. So then I visited Dana, my closest friend from high school, who was living in California. She was living with her boyfriend at the time. And she said to me, "There's something I have to tell you. I feel like I'm a lesbian, and I really want to sleep with you." I was having the same kind of feelings myself but I didn't want to experiment with a friend. So I didn't take her up on her offer. So I flew back to New York. And more time went by. And then Dana came to New York to visit me. She came with some guy who was not her lover, they were just traveling together. So the three of us are wandering around the City. We stayed up all night somewhere, completely tired. So we're in the room where he's staying, lying there, trying to take a nap. Anyway, Dana and I started holding hands and kissing and I slept with her that night and it was great and I fell in love, and she said, "This has been really great, thanks, I'm going back to California." I was really bummed. It became really clear that there was no future in the relationship. So then my friend Sandra comes back to town and she said I had to meet her good friend Nora who's a lesbian. So, Nora and I got together for a while and that was it. And then I met my next girlfriend, who was Eloise, and we were together for, like, 10 years.

Erich: How did you meet the women who became your lovers—through friendship networks? In bars?

Leslie: Through friendship networks. I went to bars but to hang out, not to meet lovers. . . . And through one thing and another, we found a lesbian softball team and that was it—we lived our lives as lesbians. . . . She was the pitcher on the softball team, and so I got to go to the games and be the softball wife and cheer with the other softball wives. That's how we met Jane and Roseanna. And that's a huge network. And that network just grew and grew and grew and then it was, like, we were living our totally normal life as lesbian couples. We had couples over for dinner, and we went out with them, we were friends with them. We were just very normal, only as lesbians. And when we broke up, it was hard on everybody in the community, as any divorce would be. But it was a very close community.

Erich: When you meet somebody for the first time, is the fact that she's a lesbian something that enters your mind as one of the more important characteristics about them?

Leslie: It's always the first thing I wonder about anybody I meet. You can't always tell with women. Yeah, I always wonder. Because it means how much I have in common with them. With a straight woman, there's a level of assumption that's missing. Jokes she won't get. Like, what does a lesbian bring on the first date? A suitcase. It's the biggest cliche that lesbians don't date—they just get married. A straight woman is not going to get the joke. She's not going to have any idea what it means. Anybody who is gay would know. The first thing we would talk about, as a lesbian relationship progressed into a friendship, is being gay. When did you come out? Are you out to your parents? Even if the experiences were totally different—"Oh, I never came out to my parents," or "Oh, my mother's a fundamentalist minister," or whatever, it's a different *story* but it's the same *theme*. When did you know you were gay? This sort of thing. There are just a lot of experiences that lesbians share that straight women don't have.

Erich: When you picture your daughter 15 or 20 years into the future, do you have certain hopes or expectations that she'll have a particular kind of sexual orientation, or is that not part of your thinking?

Leslie: I hope that I don't have an expectation. And my prediction is that she'll be straight. I mean, there's a 90 percent chance she'll be straight and a 10 percent chance that she'll be gay. Just the odds, you know. At the same time, it's a new thing. There haven't been a lot of lesbians in the past who have kids. . . . I certainly don't have a *hope* that Karen will be gay. I do hope that she will be a feminist. I hope that she'll be a Democrat. I hope that she'll be not unhappy. I hope that she'll be happier than I was at her age. I hope that I'll do a better job raising her than my own mom did with me. I hope that I can do everything I can to help make her feel good about herself. The choice of her sexual orientation is in her hands. I want her to feel that she's a worthy person regardless of the reaction of whatever sex she's attracted to. I think that's the hardest thing. I think that when you're a teenager, it's so much about wanting to be loved and wanting to be wanted. She's going to want to be normal, even more than any other kid because she's already not normal—she has two moms. I really expect that that label will be tacked onto her and that's going to make her hyper-hetero. At least for a while. And then, hopefully, she'll have enough of an inner gyroscope that, even if she wobbles for a while, she'll steady out with no major damage done and make her choice, whatever choice she makes. But I just hope she gets through it with a minimum of heartbreak.

Erich: When you were growing up, when you were in high school, at what point did you think of yourself as a lesbian? Did you go out with boys? Did you have heterosexual dates? At what point did you say, this is not working out for me? Can you give me a kind of narrative of your psychosexual biography, so to speak?

Helen: Let's see. I wasn't aware of the word, "lesbian," when I was in high school. It was the '60s and there was so much other stuff going on. I was aware of the women's liberation movement starting. Some of my friends' older sisters were involved with it. But I did have a couple of good girlfriends who, in fact, in retrospect, I realize I was really attracted to but I didn't think or say that. If somebody had asked me, I think I could have pinned down my feelings as a sexual attraction, but somehow it wasn't quite part of my understanding of the world that that was really where I was headed or who I was because I had no models like that. There was nothing in my world that said that those kind of feelings between women were a viability or a reality. So I remember having those feelings but somehow, they kind of passed under the radar screen of my understanding of what those feelings meant for me. I remember at the time one of my friends telling me a story of one of her friends who was attracted to her, and she was *repulsed* by that. And I realized that *I* was attracted to her, too. And I didn't say anything to her about it. But I definitely understood that somehow I was like that other girl. But it really wasn't a big thing then.

It was during high school that I realized that it [heterosexuality] wasn't working out for me. I think that by the time I was a senior I really was kind of a loner. I just hung out with my friends and didn't pursue that [going out with boys] any more. I think that part of it was because it was the '60s and going out with boys was just so wrapped up with drugs and it just didn't make sense to me. And I think that maybe a different relationship or if a different boy had approached me in a different way, I might not have been so turned off to boys.

There was one guy I went out with. He was a nice guy. I went out with him a few times with a few other people on dates. And then another boy came on the scene kind of out of the blue. And I was definitely attracted to him. And there was some exchanging words and things like that. But he was really kind of *over the top* in a lot of ways. I think he was taking too many drugs, he was very much the rebel. It was at a party that he propositioned me. It was like, "Let's have sex!" And my reaction was, I don't even *know* you. In fact, we were actually tripping [on LSD]. I had to say no and he was very upset. The party was at a house where, I suspect, the parents didn't even know what was happening. And [later that same evening] he ended up breaking his father's arm. It was a real mess. And so I just stopped dating boys. I wasn't going to pursue it any more. That was just out of my league—the expectation that I was going to engage in sex that easily at age 15 or whatever. If he had approached me more slowly, it might have gone somewhere, because I was attracted to him. But it was just like—kaboom! You know, we were supposed to take LSD and have sex. Taking LSD, that's quite an experience in itself. So to expect me to just jump into bed like that, well, it wasn't anything that I could have had any experience of doing. So that kind of put a halt to any [heterosexual] liaisons in my senior year.

So I went to college. There, there was a straight woman I fell very much in love with. I was really very unconscious about what was happening. There was a guy who was living in the same dorm who said to me, "You know what's going on, don't you?" And I said, "Yeah, I guess you're right." Because it was so new to me. So that's really when I first became aware of what a lesbian was. That's how I felt and that's what I was. I was in love with her.

Erich: It took a heterosexual male to point that out to you?

Helen: I know, I know.

Erich: How did he know?

Helen: I'm not even sure how he knew, he just observed. It was absolutely true. I was completely head over heels in love. Probably somebody seeing me would have realized that. I was just blown over by her.

Erich: The expression on your face?

Helen: Probably, I don't know, yeah. And just that I wanted to be with her all the time. Yeah. And things like that. And I got very involved in things she said.

Erich: Did you imagine any kind of sexual contact with her at the time?

Helen: Yeah, I did. And I think also because I was just awakening in that way, my sexual thoughts were not very involved or detailed. I would imagine just touching or holding or kissing, things like that.

Erich: And did she become aware of your infatuation?

Helen: I really don't know if she became aware of it at the time. And I really didn't feel any condemnation. But then we took a trip to New York with another friend. And that's really when I realized that I wanted to do something and she didn't feel the same way.

Erich: Did you say anything to her? How did you know that she didn't feel the same way?

Helen: Actually, I didn't say anything. I think it was a physical thing. We were in her father's very small apartment and we were sharing a bed. I don't really think that she had any idea, actually, that I was attracted to her. I'm sure she knew I really liked her. She was older, by at least five years, which was a lot then—I was 17. But she may have been aware that I had a crush on her, but I don't think she knew exactly what that meant for me. It was really hard for me to be in the same bed with her, and I remember turning over toward her and her turning over the other way, away from me. So I realized how much all these feelings for her were going to be unrequited and I shelved that sort of feeling for a while. I left the next day.

Later on, during a winter trimester, I took a trip out West and to Canada, I had a lot of time to myself. I was completely alone and I did some hiking on the West Coast, that's when I really came to an awareness inside myself that I really was a lesbian. And I looked back at my past relationships and I knew that I had been really attracted and I became conscious at that point of my lesbianism. It was almost as if I became aware of someone who had an awareness of herself. So when I came back to college, that's when I was able to say who I was.

Erich: And that was before you had an actual sexual relationship?

Helen: Yeah.

Erich: Have you ever had a sexual relationship with a boy or a man?

Helen: Just kissing.

Erich: OK, what happened after that?

Helen: And then when I came back to college, I lived in the women's dorm. And I became attracted to one of the women there, and though it didn't flow real easily, that was the first person I actually had a sexual relationship with, though it didn't take place until she left college the next year and I was living on a farmhouse somewhere in northern Vermont. So it probably wasn't until I was, like, 21 that I had a sexual relationship. When I went on the trip out West, I was 18, so it was probably three years from the time when I knew I was a lesbian until I was with somebody sexually. And that relationship lasted like two months. And I think that one of the problems there too was that she wasn't so sure that she was a lesbian. I think at this point, she's gotten married.

I left college about halfway through and for a while, as I said, I lived in Vermont. I got involved in a design-construction architectural program. Architecture is so male dominated and we were trying to get women into design and construction. The other students and I made contact with various women architects who were working in Boston and New York to give lectures to us. Then I went to New York. I hadn't finished college. I was working, designing small things on my own, not houses at that point, but stairways, the inside of houses, how to utilize the whole space, things like that. So when I went to New York, it was to take courses on structural design. I happened to run into one of the women who had come up to Vermont to give a lecture. She was teaching at the university where I was taking courses and she said, do you have a place to stay? And I said, no, actually, I don't. So she invited me to stay at her house. So I did that. At that point, I had known I was a lesbian and knew that she was. She was in her 40s and I was just turning 21. And it was definitely an older woman-younger woman thing. She kind of seduced me. I was not looking for that. So we had a relationship, but that was short, really just a few weeks or a month or so. It didn't last long, and she found somebody else and I found another place to live.

What happened after that was that I went to some land my mom had gotten in Ontario and so I was going to build a house there and I decided to work on that. I was there for maybe a year or two. Up until that point, my relationships had been very short-term. And I went to school in Halifax because during the winter, there was nothing I could really do on the house. It seemed that everywhere I went I would become close with someone and fall in love with them. While I was working on my mom's house in Ontario, a woman I met in Vermont who was involved in the feminist movement joined me there. That was a two-year relationship. That broke up and then I got involved with a woman who had a farm in Vermont. There was a circle of women who were active in the lesbian-feminist movement that was happening at the time. And some of it was very separatist, definitely not in the ideological mainstream. A lot was being said at the time and I was very caught up in it. So my relationship with that person also lasted about two years.

Erich: Do you consider yourself part of the lesbian subculture or community? That is, do you think of yourself as part of a group of women who are also lesbian who share certain experiences and ideas?

Helen: To a certain degree, but much less than what I would have imagined today if I had looked at myself from 15 years ago. And the group I was with then was thoroughly involved—the writing, the movement, and the *making of lives together*. Not just in the domestic sense but in a political sense. This was in the early to late '70s. By the time the early '80s came around, in some ways, things had slowed up some politically. And I went back to school, to graduate school, then I was completely involved in that for five years. And though I had some involvements with women during that period of time, for me, the strongest thing in my life was the school experience.

By the early 1980s, there was a next wave of the feminist evolution in which everybody's writing and thinking about philosophy. It seemed that a lot of my friends began thinking about and studying philosophy so I sort of incorporated that into my work when I wrote my thesis, in terms of women building for themselves, thinking about how women build spaces. In the '70s, people were saying, it's so exciting, being a lesbian is a really different way of seeing the world, everything would be different if you see through the eyes of a lesbian. It was a whole deconstructionist movement. I think the whole gender thing is an aspect of deconstructing social reality. It calls into question established ways of doing and thinking about things, it opens up new alternatives. So back then, everybody was using the lesbian orientation as a way of going deeper into those theoretical philosophies.

But when I came back to New York, that sort of sense of a lesbian subculture dissipated. What really happened was the disappointments and people breaking up and people getting on with their lives, people making a living. You know, everybody's sort of fitting in with the culture at this point. It's hard to think that my life at this point is making a political statement, even though there are people who would look at me and disapprove of me, perhaps people I don't even know would say I am making a political statement and it's a bad political statement. Leslie and I have a lot of lesbian friends and they are probably the bulk of who we are with. But it almost doesn't *feel* like that when we're with them. And now, because of Karen, we're meeting a lot of heterosexual couples who have two- and three-year-olds. It's sort of an interesting expansion of our life.

Erich: So you're saying that the category, status, and the role demands of parenthood have become more prominent and important than those of being a lesbian.

Helen: Exactly. And becoming parents sort of upped the ante socially, so we started to spend more time with more non-lesbians. And you start to see your experience as having a lot of commonalities with non-lesbians. And I think part of it is that as you get older, that's your tendency.

Erich: So you think it's partly parenthood, partly going through the life cycle, and partly the age—the period of history.

Helen: Yeah. It's no longer '68, when you're remaking the world. In between the end of graduate school and getting together with Leslie, I joined an ashram for three years. And I think that actually took quite a bit of edge off of my political impulse. I dove into the philosophy that they were espousing, which was non-attachment to material things. And it was also based on Brahmacharia, which is celibacy, the idea that if you're not constantly in a relationship with another person, you can delve into your own psyche better. In fact, it was true. What happened there was that my relationships with many people got very deep. But it definitely was not the reality of the world. It was a microcosm of a certain world view. . . . But I have to say my experience in the ashram did take an edge off of my sexual and romantic desires. And my desires about professional accomplishment also became less in a way. I started to think I'd like to go into something else, not devote 20 years of my life to being an architect. Still, I haven't done anything to change my life around that, but that experience lessened my desires along those lines.

Erich: But you're still an architect.

Helen: Yes.

Erich: And architecture, it seems to me, is *specifically* an attachment to physical things because you're bound in by the physical world. More than almost anything you can imagine, except for maybe building a bridge or something.

Helen: [Laughs.] Yeah, I know. It's odd for me to be in a profession that's so completely materially-based and yet be so skeptical about the very basis of the job we have to do. So, anyway, over the years I've kind of shifted around. And because in a lot of ways, my experience at the ashram was about working with and being close to the men as well as the women. As an architect, I worked with a lot of the guys there. During my years at MIT and my political-lesbian-feminist involvement, I was very much questioning the role of men in the world. And then at the ashram, I kind of softened up a lot around that because I became personally involved through my work with men. Living at the ashram was such a strong experience. Only a few things in my life matched up with that. But I can't say in the nine or 10 years since then that I've sorted it all through.

Erich: Why did you leave?

Helen: Oh, student loans. And in fact, it's probably lucky because two years after I left, the guru was discovered to have been sleeping with everyone [laughs]. Even after telling everybody else to maintain their celibacy. So he got deposed. But I don't feel that I could get that involved in a guru-based spiritual practice again.

Erich: One of the things I'm interested in is the relationship that somebody who lives in an arrangement in his or her life that's different from the mainstream, like having a lesbian relationship, and the so-called conventional world. And I'm just wondering if you've had experiences along those lines. First, did you come out to your mother? Did you tell her about your sexual orientation and if so, how did she react?

Helen: I told her probably around four years after I knew it, four or five years. I think she already kind of knew it. I'm not sure if lesbianism makes a lot of sense to her. And it's the same reaction she had to us having Karen. She's really okay with it, but she's of the older order of things. So she's not completely comfortable with it. But sexual orientation isn't really on her radar screen. There are other things that are more important for her. My father, I don't think I ever really had a conversation with him about it, but it just kind of evolved. He knew who I was with and I would just talk about them with him. Actually, at the time, I wasn't very close with him, and he was living in Florida. In fact, when he came to visit with his third wife and my youngest half-sister, he spent the time in Vermont with me and a woman I was with at the time. So it was all out in the open. My family's a fairly liberal outfit. And pretty respectful of people's individual experience. They don't think it has to fit into something. They've always been a little bit involved in being on the fringe themselves. My father has been involved in the civil rights and the peace movements and things like that. We were Quakers and I think that's very much respectful of people's individuality and their own special relationship with God or whatever power they believe in.

Erich: What about any other conventional institutions or persons? I mean, do you ever get any kind of feedback or overflow from the rest of society that they feel a certain way about your sexual orientation?

Helen: Well, certainly at the ashram, it was very clear that they did not approve of homosexual relationships. And while I was there, there were a lot of people who were trying to educate this traditional Indian religion that homosexuality existed, that it was okay, that it was normal. It was an odd juxtaposition of cultures, each trying to come to terms with a different kind of fringe. Here was Indian religion, a fringe in itself for most Americans, and then there was the gay contingent, trying to influence this very strong Indian religion. And eventually the people in the ashram did become more open to our position. I didn't feel personally reviled there or anything, but still, there was definitely a pressure. We knew underneath it all that there was a certain lack of belief that homosexuality was a viable way to be in the world. . . .

Because I've always been kind of working on my own or in an alternative kind of setting, I haven't come face to face with any disapproval. And at MIT, I didn't feel disapproval there. And when I worked in a firm for a couple of years, I wasn't that open about it, and it didn't come up. And I think that for me, being different is not so much my relations with the conventional world. It's more my own comfort and discomfort with myself and my struggle with that issue. Because it hasn't been a simple, smooth, easy road to follow. The very rockiness of my early relationships and not knowing who I was was definitely a drawback for me. Although I had a very strong sense of what I wanted to do, I'm not such a secure person that I put myself across in a way that has taken me along the direction that I could have gone had I been more confident. And in some ways, that's the way that I internalize the conventions of the world. I think I have a certain lack of confidence about myself. And I think that kind of thing is rooted deep in your sense of your body and in the world of sexuality. And I don't know that had I gone in a heterosexual route— or if I could have, I don't know if I could have—would I have felt differently? But I think all that is formed by the time you're a teenager.

I remember feeling very disapproved of when I was *such* a young kid, you know, three-four years old. My grandmother saying, "Oh, she wants to be a boy," things like that. *That's* when I internalized the sense of who I am. I think I never left off that kind of feeling that there was something wrong with me. And I think all that happened at a very young age.

Erich: Do you think this feeling of being not quite who you should be is related to your being a lesbian?

Helen: In a way. I think even though I was in a Friends school that was accepting of all people, I always had a feeling of there being a mismatch, of my not really being exactly on the wavelength of most other people. And some of my feeling was a result of comments about my love of sports, I was definitely completely a tomboy and since I had three brothers, being interested in sports and being a tomboy was just my way of being in the world. I so much remember the hurt that I felt when I was laughed at about that. When I was a kid, probably seven or eight, my grandfather died. And a friend of the family took us in for a couple of days while my parents were at the funeral. She said, "I have some dolls, but I don't know if I should bring them out for you to play with." You know, things like that made me realize that I wasn't fitting into her world. Those kinds of comments—I think that's where my fit with the world didn't come together. If you had asked me as an 8-year-old how I was feeling then, or if I was going to become a lesbian, I really didn't know what was going on. But I did know that I felt different. And comments like that made me aware of the *distaste* that others had for me being so active and interested in playing boys' games. But I don't think it's happening in the same way today.

Erich: You mean the world's not as disapproving of people who are different?

Helen: Yeah, I think that's right. But you do read about peer pressure that kids put on each other. Still, I think that there's a little more movement, a little more freedom.

Erich: Do you still feel that you're not on the conventional world's wavelength at this point?

Helen: I think that my idea of what the conventional world is is that the conventions are so mutable. And I see how people say one thing and things turn out to be very different. I think that at this point, issues about being different and not being on the mainstream's wavelength don't seem to be that much of an issue. But I know things still come up for us. For instance, taking Karen to apply for preschool and the application saying "Mommy" and "Daddy." Or the application saying "Mother/Father" instead of "Guardian." And it makes you wonder, do they think there's something wrong with us? It definitely feels that way. I know that I don't fit into the conventional world exactly in its terms. Although in New York, it doesn't feel that way. I feel fairly accepted.

It does come up, though. I'm personable, I *want* people to like me. There's a guy I worked with on a job. . . . As far as I know, he thinks I'm Karen's biological mother. And that's one thing that has come up, I've referred to her as my daughter. In the beginning, I thought of explaining it to him. [Maybe I should have said to him], well, you know, I'm not actually the biological mother. But now, after two and a half years, I've grown accustomed to thinking, yeah, this is my daughter, there's not any question about it. Explaining all that didn't come completely naturally to me. Because I thought, well, I'm not the biological mother, you should know that I'm the *other* mother. Now, I just say, she's my daughter. Would he feel that I've been deceiving him?

Erich: If you were to try to picture a hypothetical reader who would be reading your account, yours and Leslie's account, is there any particular message that you would want to communicate to this person?

Helen: [Very long pause]. It almost seems to me that *normal* doesn't exist. The variations are so complex. What I want people to grapple with is that complexity. Meeting a lesbian, or anybody else's way of experiencing the world who's different, is part of a mix without it being mixed into nothing. How can we continue to make our world so that we can incorporate different people's ideas and experiences? It seems too often that people who don't quite fit in get *squashed.* And I think the mainstream loses out, loses the contributions of these people who aren't part of the mainstream.

In many ways, in the social settings in which Leslie and Helen move, it is difficult to regard lesbianism as deviant.

True, both their families were at least a bit taken aback by the news of their lesbianism. "It's not the news that any parent wants to hear," says Leslie. "It's just not their first choice. And it's not what they expected or wanted." Yet, following a "little rocky time," after greeting and assimilating the news, parents usually "get over it." Some do and some don't of course, but for most middle-aged parents, it's far from the worst news they could have heard.

And true, a majority of the United States population feels that homosexual behavior is "morally wrong"—in a 1999 Gallup poll, the figure was 59 percent. Yet, this belief varies strongly by education and the other measures of social class and socioeconomic status. In this poll, while 70 percent of respondents with no college education believed homosexual relations to be morally wrong, less than four in 10 (39 percent) of those with a postgraduate education felt this way.

And while it is true that much of the nation's heartland condemns homosexuality and socially shuns the gay people who live among them, this is vastly less likely to be true in its largest cities. A nationally representative survey of sex in the United States found self-identified homosexuals and bisexuals eight times more likely to live in the country's 12 largest cities than in rural areas; in fact, in its sample, there were no lesbians living in rural areas (Laumann et al., 1994, pp. 305–309; Michael et al., 1994, pp. 177). In this study, the tendency of female homosexuals to live largely in cities was less pronounced than it was for gay men, the authors speculate, possibly because "if lesbian couples can successfully live more closeted lives than can gay male couples, that would make the pressure to leave small towns and suburbs less pressing" (Michael et al., 1994, p.

178). However, Leslie and Helen do not live "closeted" lives. It is unlikely that in Boise, Idaho, they would have had the same acceptance they have experienced as an openly lesbian couple on the Upper West Side of Manhattan. While they might very well stand out in one of the smaller cities in the country's heartland, where they live, Leslie and Helen are not a terribly unconventional couple.

Moreover, consider the fact that they do not live in an all-gay enclave. They have continuing, ongoing relationships with their (heterosexual) families, including in-laws. They have close heterosexual friends. And more than a few of their sex partners have gotten married and had children. Their pediatrician is a straight male, they work with straight men and women, and they have made friendships and acquaintanceships with the parents of their daughter's friends. And they are the most conventional parents possible—loving, caring, and responsible. They are a reminder of the "Deviants Are Us" imagery that pervades this book.

In his book, *Gay and Lesbian Identity* (1988), Richard Troiden states that when used as a noun, "homosexual" is essentialistic, a description of an identifiably distinct type of being, a species of humanity (p. 101). The essentialistic approach to homosexuality focuses on etiology or causality and asks, "How does someone get that way? How does one *become* a homosexual?" Although usually associated with a more traditional or "conservative" approach to the subject, interestingly, a substantial (and increasing) proportion of men and women who self-identify as homosexual adopt the essentialistic perspective. That is, they feel that somewhere inside them, there is an inner core or essence that is identifiably homosexual in much the same way that everyone's DNA identifies us as homo sapiens, or a specific person. Thus, they use the phrase, "When I *discovered* I was gay," as if their quality of homosexuality could be located much as veil were removed and "the real me" was revealed.

Instead, Troiden argues—regardless of the etiology of homosexuality (and heterosexuality)—the category, "the homosexual," is a social construct, "constituted socially" and "subject to cultural and historical change" (p. 124). Lesbian and gay male sexuality are "constructed," "organized and expressed through homosexual scripts." In short, the "erotic codes or roles" that express homosexual feelings "are a product of social learning" (p. 124). Same-sex sexual behavior has existed since the dawn of humanity—or long before, since many animals engage in it—but what it *means* to be a homosexual is variable from one culture to another and one time period to another. Indeed, McIntosh argues, the very *category*, "homosexual," is an invention only of the past few hundred years (1968). Before that, she asserts, though there was "homosexual" behavior, there was no such thing as "a" homosexual.

Acquiring a homosexual identity, Troiden asserts, is both a matter of degree and an emergent process, "never fully determined in a fixed or absolute sense, but always subject to modification and further change"

(1988, p. 58). Most men and women who identify themselves as homosexual would disagree. Once they've decided that they "are" homosexual, they recognize that there is an identifiable quality or essence that is "in" them that is not likely to change. At this point, the matter is settled; Leslie and Helen consider themselves as lesbians and cannot picture themselves in a heterosexual relationship. It is entirely possible that one day the cause or etiology of homosexuality will be located—that, for instance, a "gay gene" will be discovered (LeVay, 1995). But that hypothetical discovery would still leave out of the picture what men and women experience when they come to recognize themselves as gay; what they go through when dealing with this unconventional identity; how others react to the revelation that they are homosexual; and how they lead their lives from the moment they get up in the morning to the time they go to bed at night. And for that side of the story, we need the personal accounts of the men and women who decided, one day, that they "are" homosexuals. The fact that contemporary American narratives of homosexuals are very different from those from another culture and era reminds us of the constructed nature of homosexuality (and heterosexuality), that it is as much a social role as an inner essence, that homosexuality was born, in the words of David Greenberg, "under the sign of sociology" (1988, pp. 482–499).

CHAPTER 8

Some people become bartenders. Me, I owned the bar. I rented a house. . . . I was living on student loans and I ended up $100,000 in debt. . . . It was like Rick's "Cafe American." Five nights out of the week, the place was packed with people. . . . I was like a tiny, little Hugh Hefner. . . . I had my room upstairs, I had this smoking jacket. . . . It was wonderful. . . . I would walk around constantly with a glass of bourbon in my hand, mingling and having fun. . . . At this point, I knew I was an alcoholic, but I figured I was a functioning alcoholic. And, you know, that's OK. If I ever need to, I'll just dry out.

Harry

Harry, the Debonair Drinker

From the perspective of the study of deviance, there are two things we need to know about the consumption of alcohol. The first is that, in mainstream society, *moderate* drinking is not only acceptable, it is expected. It is, in other words, conventional or *normative* behavior. The second is that *heavy* drinking is not only deviant—that is, socially unacceptable in itself—it also has accompaniments or consequences that are themselves socially unacceptable, in fact, dysfunctional. In the usual case, almost everything that is regarded as desirable in American society is undermined, threatened, or destroyed by the consumption of a too-substantial quantity of alcohol. That quantity varies from one person to another, of

153

course, but above a certain level of drinking, everyone suffers major and catastrophic consequences. One's family, career, education, economic security, indeed, one's very physical well-being, are tossed to the wind in service to a lust for a liquid elixir that promises much more than it delivers.

Alcohol promises nurturance, well-being, security, and erotic, sensuous excitation and satisfaction. It delivers all of this and more. It's the "more" that is the problem, for this includes letting loved ones down, getting into accidents one should have avoided, underachievement, failing to fulfill academic and occupational goals, being belligerent to others, getting into fights, being tempted into illicit, illegal, risky, and dangerous activities, doing many things one regrets. The list is long and its particulars are painfully obvious to any current or former heavy drinker or friend or relative of a heavy drinker. There is no mystery about why, at some level (which varies from one society to the next) heavy drinking is regarded as deviant pretty much everywhere.

How do alcoholics define their own participation in this socially unacceptable activity? What manner of vocabulary of motive do they employ? What is their perspective on their heavy drinking? And what can we learn about deviance from it?

Interestingly, alcoholics walk the fine line between self-condemnation and justification. They are fully aware of the harmfulness and the social deviance of their behavior, but they strive to *disassociate* themselves from the most extreme end of the drinking spectrum, to position themselves within the sphere of the normal, the conventional, the acceptable. Alcoholics set rules that apply to their drinking, and these rules serve a purpose above and beyond the need to control their drinking. In fact, their rules represent an effort to establish an identity. Many alcoholics believe that if they were to follow these rules, they wouldn't have a drinking problem— indeed, if they followed them, they wouldn't be alcoholics in the first place. Moreover, they have vastly more faith in these rules than an outsider does. In fact, their rules, somewhat different for each drinker, seem to a non-alcoholic almost an exercise in magical faith.

Rules alcoholics set for themselves—and almost always break—are a kind of vocabulary of motive, for they define for themselves and others who they are, and who and what they aspire to be and imagine they can become. "I'll drink this much and no more," they say. In other words, they say to themselves, I am the sort of person who can set a limit on my drinking and stick to it. And if I have that much control, I'm not really an alcoholic. I'm normal, they say, and my rules demonstrate that fact. Drinking a little more than the norm isn't really so bad—in fact, it's perfectly normal. The limits I set for myself are a bit more generous than the amount most people drink, it's true, but that's because most people are too conventional and restrictive.

These rules simultaneously *conventionalize* moderate drinking and *condemn* heavy drinking. At the same time, they criticize abstemiousness and light, extremely controlled drinking. I'm a lot better off—and more virtuous—than those alcoholics over there, they say, but I also have a lot more verve, more spirit and lust for life than the abstainers standing next to me. And if I break these rules from time to time, well, that shows I'm only human, unlike that model of moderation and self-control over there. For many alcoholics, it takes a period of abstention to become reflective about their condition and the behavior it occasioned. Of course, for the recovering alcoholic, the *drinker's* vocabulary of motives is replaced with the *abstainer's* vocabulary of motives—in a sense, exchanging one identity or persona for another— which makes alcoholism an almost uniquely fascinating form of deviance.

Harry is 39 years old, received a BA degree from a state university ("on the 12-year plan," as he explains) and took graduate courses in a variety of departments. Currently, he does not have a job; he is enrolled in a computer course. For years, Harry drank heavily and his drinking significantly contributed to his inability to achieve many of his life goals. He is also gay, a subject to which in this account he makes only occasional reference. Harry's interview is so interesting, revealing, and insightful that I decided to reproduce it more or less exactly as I transcribed it. I began by asking him to elaborate on his life of heavy drinking.

Harry: This is a pretty standard story, a typical drunkalogue. I started drinking at about [the age of] 13. And right from the start, I began drinking alcoholically. Whereas some people [I drank with] were drinking to get happy, to get loose, I was almost immediately drinking to get drunk.

Erich: I wonder if you might go over a little bit about this early period of your drinking. First of all, how does a 13-year-old get his hands on alcohol? Why don't you tell me about your early period of drinking.

Harry: At the age of 13, it was once or twice a week. Thirteen seems to be a very common year for people to start drinking and doing drugs, for some reason. We would stand outside the 7-Eleven or the liquor store and wait for somebody to buy us some. Or we would get about a quart of vodka a week [which] would mysteriously appear in my friend's hands. He was at first kind of non-committal about where he got it from. Since he was a year and a half older and he was my best friend, I didn't push him [about it].

Erich: What did he say?

Harry: There was a guy who lived down the block who we hung out with sometimes who said his uncle got it for him. He had an uncle who was 18, and at 18 at the time, you could buy alcohol. So we would get drunk once or twice a week. And right from the start, I *absolutely* loved the stuff. When you are in high school, there were more opportunities to procure. And, unfortunately or fortunately, there's more drinking in high school. Also, I was in high school in the seventies. There was a *lot* of marijuana in high school [then].

Erich: The seventies was the high point [in the recreational use of illegal drugs].

Harry: Yeah. Now [at that time, in the 1970s, in high school], we're drinking maybe *four* times a week. And it becomes important in the rituals. Especially in the mating dance, the mating rituals. One of those unspoken contract things. You know, it's acknowledged, it's there. . . . What's a football game without some beers? Especially for me because I never liked sports. I hung out a lot. Outdoors. We used to have a lot of woods in our area, and we'd hang out there. Some people would hang out at the 7-Eleven parking lot, but they were the less savory [types]— they were the gang fighters, the rough guys. I was more with the heads, which was the more numerous group. Having alcohol always made sex a little easier, because you're young and you're insecure. Guys started going out on a date [and said to themselves]—"I've got to have some alcohol, I've gotta have some vodka." *There were no consequences to getting drunk in high school!* There were *none!* Maybe you would throw up! That was it! Our parents were *remarkably* lenient in that respect. It was the seventies. It was a remarkable time to be young. OK, then there was the eighties. I went to college in the eighties [laughs] and into the nineties. I would go to college for a semester or two, [drop out,] go back to college, go to tech school, go back to college.

Erich: You stretched it out.

Harry: Oh, my God! I was on the 12-year plan! It was terrible! They kept sending me checks and I kept going [to college]. It was wonderful. I think I'm pretty well educated for somebody who's only got a BA, though. That's one good thing I have to say about it.

Erich: When did you realize you had a problem and what was the nature of this problem?

Harry: They say that alcoholics are like people whose hair is on fire, who end up drowning when they run into the sea. And you could tell right from the start, I'm sure, if there were an objective observer, that I was an alcoholic. Part of that whole alcoholism thing is that the alcoholic is the *last* person in the world who recognizes that he is an alcoholic. Often, his family, friends—everyone—will recognize that he is an alcoholic. Bill Moyers did a special [which was broadcast on public television] on addiction called "The Hijacked Brain." And I thought that was the best description I've heard so far. It really is like your brain itself has been hijacked. Sometimes I was known to have said, "My brain is *broken*. It's trying to *kill* me!

Erich: So far, it's very abstract. Hijacked brain, hair's on fire, rushing into the sea. The generalizations are important and interesting, but what

I'm interested in *in addition* is how this manifested itself on an everyday basis. In other words, what *quantities* are we talking about, what *kinds* of disruption in your life are we talking about, how did you *manage* your day-to-day affairs, how did you get through *school*—you were talking about [drinking heavily] from, what, eighth grade until fairly recently, you said—so, there's a long period of time during which you had to *cope* with the realities of everyday life [while you were drinking heavily], so maybe you can fill this out a little bit.

Harry: I never drove a car into a school bus full of nuns. But that doesn't mean that I didn't make a lot of things crash and burn.

Erich: Like what?

Harry: Relationships. I have never made a relationship, you know, the standard boyfriend-boyfriend, running-through-the-field-of-daisies-hand-in-hand kind of relationship, work for more than six weeks. I'm now 39. But it's always traceable to something I said or did, or decided to say or do while I was drunk. I can be brutally honest, still. I did everything while I was drunk. [Laughs.] I did all my eating while I was drunk, my sleeping, my watching TV. So it's difficult to separate life's mistakes from life's *drunken* mistakes. . . . [Long pause.] Why don't I couch it in general terms. I was insulting, overly honest—brutally honest—with people at times when I shouldn't have been. I've walked away from relationships or potential relationships that I shouldn't have. Or maybe walked into things I *wouldn't* have if I had been sober at the time. . . . However, realizing that you had sex with somebody you *really* wish you hadn't is worse than having to apologize for making rude suggestions to somebody that you shouldn't have the night before. Of course, you can't drive a car, or fly a plane, or work heavy machinery with the same aptitude or finesse when you're drunk, so of course, you're not going to be able to maneuver delicate situations, interpersonal conflicts, or relationships as well when you're drinking. I'm sure of it.

Erich: That makes sense.

Harry: Why don't I recall my last year or two, because every day will be full of alcoholic coping mechanisms and dysfunctions. Some people [who drink heavily] become bartenders. Me, *I owned the bar.* I rented a house as a grad student. I was living on student loans, and I ended up $100,000 in debt. And it was wonderful. As an undergraduate, they [the university] would send me loans, and once a semester, they would send me a check, once a year, I would have to fill out loan forms and do an interview. And once a semester, they kept sending me this blue slip, telling me to register for graduation. And as long as I *didn't* turn in the blue slip, they kept giving me the loans. [Laughs.] And I thought that this was the most wonderful thing in the world. They're paying me to socialize, read books, and learn stuff. And alcohol was, as they say, the organizing principle of my life, even though I didn't realize it. Everything revolved around alcohol. Some people become terribly irresponsible, they lose everything, but there's a *need* to keep your supply, your pipeline. That is the last thing that you want to lose. I'm racking up $100,000 in debts. But I'm drinking bourbon that I was budgeting for *six months* earlier. And I really, really thought that I was being responsible [laughs], that I was managing my life great. Look at that! Oh, my God, he's got a budget made up six months in advance. I didn't take many classes that started before 10 in the morning. This is one thing that you learn early. Towards the end, I simply rented a house. And I became the agent. And once again, I was being responsible. I painted this house, I did little minor repairs here and there. And I rented it out, the other rooms. My nickname was "Tigger" [after the Winnie-the-Pooh character]. I used to have long hair and a short beard and moustache and it made me look a bit leonine. I also had a certain spring to my step when I walked, so some of my friends came up with "Tigger," because "Tiggers are wonderful things. Their tops are made out of rubber and their bottoms are made out of springs." And so it [my apartment] became "Tigger's Place." It was like Rick's "Cafe American" [after the nightclub in the film, *Casablanca*]. Five nights out of the week, the place was *packed* with people. And I *liked* it. I was like a tiny, little Hugh Hefner. I swear to God. I had my room upstairs, I had this *smoking* jacket, which I wore as a bathrobe [laughs]. It was wonderful. It was either that or a cardigan. But I would walk around constantly with a glass of bourbon in my hand, mingling and having fun. Mostly the people I rented to were younger than I was. I did a quick check once, before I left campus [and before "Tigger's Place"]. I and another guy were the *oldest* people in my dorm. At this point, I had spent about five or six years in Room 106 Wagner D. [Laughs.] And I had never thought of myself as being particularly socially adept. A typical alcoholic has a very low opinion of himself. I'm an egomaniac with an inferiority complex. Never thought I was particularly socially adept. And yet, to speak to people, it seems that I really *was*. People *liked* me. People would gravitate towards my room [chuckles] when I lived on campus. Off campus, it was already an established pattern. One night a week, we would play "Risk." I would have a group of people playing "Risk." I surrounded myself with younger people, I think, largely because when you're drinking [heavily], you don't develop emotionally. You really don't grow. I had a Peter Pan Syndrome [aging, but inappropriately attempting to act like a younger person] to the point where my mother would refer to the guys that I had in the house as "The Lost Boys." Also, being gay, I liked having good-looking young men around.

[Laughs.] This is not an uncommon thing. Also, it was nice that I could jokingly—I *demanded virgin sacrifice!* [Laughs.] And I'll be damned! They [my friends] started *bringing* it! [Laughs.] What more could I ask for? [Laughs.] And the interesting thing is, if you see photos of me during this period, in *every single photo,* I have a glass of bourbon either in my hand or next to me. Which is an indicator I should have picked up on. [Laughs.] At this point, I knew I was an alcoholic, but I figured that I was a *functioning* alcoholic. And, you know, that's OK. If I ever need to, I'll just dry out. [Sighs.] So, one day a week, we would have "Risk." Either the stereo or the TV was always on in the TV room. We would have "Risk" going on in the kitchen. People would come by—first they would call, I like that. There was lots of drinking [laughs] because I liked to drink and, interestingly enough, so did the people who gravitated towards me. There was always alcohol around. I tended to take in strays. And I ended up being the cook. It's like I had one duty. [Chuckles.] And people would come. And they would [be appreciative; they'd say], "Oh, my God, have you had his basil cream sauce?" I liked when people appreciated that [my cooking]. There were drinking games. There was a whole generation who didn't know about "Think While You Drink," [a game] which I liked. You've gotta play it with beer, though. And this was all right with me, but not my favorite because I was a bourbon drinker.

Erich: Wait, what's "Think While You Drink"?

Harry: Well, the purpose of drinking games usually is to get people very drunk very quickly. "Think While You Drink" is a game where you would sit in a circle and you have to chug beer, slowly, while you thought of a name of somebody. And if you said, "Albert Einstein," the next person would have to come up with the name of a person whose *first* name started with the *last* letter of the *last* name of the person that the person *before* gave. So, Albert Einstein would lead to *Norm Abrams,* who would lead to Sally Struthers. If you got a *double,* where the first name and the last name started with the same letter, the direction of play reversed. I was pretty good at "Think While You Drink." [Laughs.] For some reason I have a large storehouse of useless information. I spent a lot of time on campus. [Laughs.] Racking up a huge debt, learning about people. So, towards the end of the last few years, I started to get *nervous* about things like getting *too* drunk and getting sloppy. . . . So what I would do is I would buy my bourbon, and instead of buying it in fifths, or half-gallons, I would buy my bourbon in *pints.* [Chuckles.] So that I would only drink *one pint a day.* Which I thought was a very good strategy. You have to worry about things like, again, not getting too drunk and sloppy. And people were *absolutely amazed* at my ability to hold on a rational conversation after downing a pint of bourbon. I only weigh

125 pounds. And I would always have a little juicer in my hand. . . . I was never a big fan of orange juice, unless it was for making vodka go down smoothly, but those little six-ounce glasses were easier to keep a firm grasp on than a big, old Scotch tumbler. Basically, as the evening wore on, drinking, you know, halfway through the night, I would be two-thirds through a bottle of bourbon, and people would comment, "Oh, my God." Because you can't see how much someone is drinking when they just re-fill that little juicer once in a while. It's because I was drinking for so long that I used to joke that, "It's because I've had my liver in training for a decade. [Laughs.] Next year off to the Olympics in Japan!" This is not an uncommon thing. I'm good at getting drunk and talking shit. I mean, *bizarre* conversations. Pros and cons on the existence of God, vis à vis particle physics versus cross-cultural comparative religions, you know, wonderful, *wonderful* conversations. That's a real example. The funny thing was, the person speaking *for* the existence of God was a particle physicist. [Laughs]. He was a born-again physics grad student. And I really miss that about not being drunk.

Erich: You mean you would have these conversations when you were drunk but you *wouldn't* have them when you *weren't* drunk?

Harry: Yeah, I think so. Because once Tigger's cookin', you know, [at] one o'clock in the morning, that's the sort of conversation [laughs] that might be goin' on.

Erich: In an average or typical evening, how many guys might be there?

Harry: I threw a lot of what were called "sausage parties." [Laughs.] Indeed, the ratio of men to women was *way* the hell off. There were mostly guys. On an average night, [there] would be, if it wasn't, like, a Friday or Saturday, 12, 15 [men there]. You know, not a *party.* Relatively small.

Erich: And then on Friday and Saturday nights?

Harry: On a night when people were actually coming over, 25. That's a big night.

Erich: If it's not too indelicate, could you tell me what a sausage party is?

Harry: A sausage party? That's when you get a lot of guys. And no women.

Erich: I see. I get the idea.

Harry: It was a lot of getting drunk and talking shit. Which is what people *like to do* when there's a lot of alcohol in the room. I was never much of a *bar* drinker. I much preferred—and this is why the campus life suited me so well—to have a group of people that I knew and not have to mingle with a bunch of strangers at a bar. Or to mingle with strangers at least at a party. Something that wasn't so bar-like. I'm one of the [few] gay people who has a genuine, very negative feeling about the bars and the bar life. For some economic-cultural reason, gay bars seem to be the absolute *hub* of gay life. And it's very shallow, and it's very predatory, and it *looks* friendly, but it's not as friendly as it looks. I think the sexual tension and the predatory aspect of it [contributes to its unfriendly aspect]. And, unless you go to a leather bar, the music is always *disco*, and the music is always too loud. . . .

Anyway, one night [at our house], we had the police come to the door. And I have no idea what's going on. I answer the door, glass of bourbon in hand, smoking jacket on. It's the police. People with a *cell phone*, driving by, called to complain. And I'm [laughs] absolutely *clueless* [about why the police were there]. But sort of impressed and worried [laughs] that people on a *cell phone*, driving by, called to complain. [Supposedly] it was a sort of *rumble*, a *gang* fight, or something like that, was going on outside of my house. No, the Lost Boys were outside, doing professional wrestling moves up against the chain link fence, across the street [laughs], on Main Street, which is a fairly busy road for a suburban area. And people on the cell phone thought it was some kind of gang fight. The police stopped by to tell us, stop that. We didn't have many neighbors, the [few] neighbors [we did have] did not complain. . . .

To give you an example—I didn't rent the house all at once, first I had to settle in. And decide that I liked the arrangement, I had the apartment downstairs, it was a studio apartment. My second day of living there, I'm moving in, my friends are coming by, helping me carry boxes. And the other guys who had moved in upstairs a week earlier, are four guys from the football team. I show up [laughs] that night, there are people sitting on the roof, and somebody is pissing into the bushes. [Laughs.] The neighbors *do not* complain. Later on, I'm walking people out, there's someone curled up on the front lawn behind the hedges that kind of separate our house from the street, *throwing up*. And, you know, I was never *at that level*. I was never *that kind* of drunk. As my first sponsor [in an alcohol self-help program] said, I drank like a lady. I didn't start to drink until five or six [o'clock in the afternoon]. After dinner was usually my rule. Of course, by three in the morning, I had downed an entire pint, maybe a beer or two. [I said to myself,] I wasn't drinking, I was just havin' a couple a' beers. Who was [it that said] that? Some comedian. But that was a good tag line. As I said, I didn't drink early in the day. However, *getting to class* could often be a problem. Well, I wouldn't schedule my classes until, the *earliest*, was 12 noon, 11:30 class. So I had time to down some ice tea, shower, clear my head, and drive to campus.

And the alcoholism impacted my ability to function, because in the last couple of years [of my drinking], I would buffalo my way into classes that I didn't really belong in, like a [graduate] sociology course with students who had taken *real* sociology. I was in a comparative primatology class with students who had amusing stories about picking fleas off of Jane Goodall [an important, well-known primatologist]. So I always felt that I was faking it and people would call me on it. To the point where, in a couple of classes, I simply did not turn in the final projects. Because I felt that I had *no business* writing a paper in this discipline. In retrospect, that was kind of wrong. But that's how you think when you're an alcoholic. And I was constantly living in fear that people were going to discover that I was a faker. And I actually didn't attend some classes toward the end. [At the time,] I didn't know what this was. I was worried that I was getting agoraphobia [fear of open spaces, fear of going outside]. I *could not* leave the house. I had a panic attack and I was just in *such fear* that I could not bring myself to leave the house and go out on campus and function. I later found out that this is a phenomenon that happens to alcoholics, called "the terrors." I had no idea. I should have read a couple of books on alcoholism [laughs], to know what I had to expect.

I thought that Korsakoff's Syndrome was the big thing I had to worry about. Korsakoff's Syndrome is where the part of the brain that sorts emotion and memory becomes damaged. And you can get Parkinson's symptoms, where you get shaking, tremors. But it also makes it more difficult for you to assimilate new information. And as the years wore on, it was true, I used to just be able to read a textbook or sit in a class, towards the end [of my period of drinking], I used to have to read and take *notes* on the reading and then read the notes again, because [it would be necessary for me to do that to have] the same memory and the same ability to retain information as I did five years earlier by putting in a minimal effort. [Pause.] I think, intuitively, I knew early on that I had a problem. It became a joke and a part of my persona for the last—I was drinking for about 20 years—I was a *heavy* drinker, in retrospect, for about 20 years. A friend of mine used to say, "You know, for a little guy, you toss your body a big man's beatin'." But you rationalize. And I rationalized. And it just became a part of my persona.

OK, so, I'm Harry, the lovable—sometimes not so lovable—*drunk*. I took on a Hugh Hefner, party-guy, with sophistication, a sophisticated—for an undergraduate crowd—drunk, with a party-guy kind of persona. Some people thought I was lovable. Especially younger people thought I was interesting. As someone said, "You know, most people, when you speak to them, you sort of *know* what they're going to say next. I *never know* what's going to come out of your mouth next!" Again, I didn't think I was all that interesting. But people did. The trauma for me was having to admit to myself that I was no longer going to be for very long a functioning alcoholic. Things fell apart.

The last six months was so. . . . I had a little "boy toy" jump ship on me. [Laughs.] He kind of deserted me. [In addition], I had someone move in who was a recovering alcoholic—a dry drunk. Who I thought might be good to have around. He dragged me to a couple of AA meetings. I wasn't ready to quit, but it sort of opened my eyes a bit. And then he started drinking. I have this effect on people. Even in my sobriety. I've only been sober for a little under two years. The other newcomers that I've latched onto. People that I affiliated with all went out [and drank]. I'm just a *rotten* influence on people. So this guy, let's call him "Butt-Wipe," he started drinking heavily. And *he* was a *serious* alcoholic. His morals went out the window, he started stealing, he lost his job, he flunked out of school, and he made no attempt to do anything aside from male prostitution. And towards the end, it was fairly obvious that he wasn't going to be able to come up with his share of the rent. He was bad. Then, Fred, the stray that I took in, bailed on me.

See, what happened was, it was kind of *my* house. So I had to maintain the standards. Such that they were. And believe it or not, I actually, I had to stomp my tiny, little foot a couple of times. Like, this guy, one of the last people to move in, there was a *hooker*, a prostitute in the neighborhood [chuckles], he started to hang out with her. I think he identified—I met his mom once for a few seconds—I'm pretty sure she was a hooker, too. And he decided he was going to be a part-time male prostitute. And I had to put my foot down. And [I said to him,] "No more! She can't come to the house!" I never had to bar anyone from the house before. "No crack whores in the house! New house rule!" I had responsibilities. Collecting the rent. All kinds of stupid upkeep. The plumbing needed work, the painting, the yard work. And more than that, I had Fred, my stray. I had to help him get his life together. I had to be sure that somebody's *car* was working. There was always something. If you give me enough time, I *will* become responsible for the sunrise. And it got to the point where I was absolutely pulling my hair out. And the house and everything was dragging me down. I bombed out of school. Which I've done before. They put you on a six-month's probationary period, you get your grades up, and you take care of incompletes, and they take you back. But something told me that it wasn't gonna happen this time.

I needed help. And my parents had been begging me for the last couple of years, "Come home, get your life together, get sober, get on with your life." So I finally took them up on it. I am very, very fortunate to have had this family, insane as they are, dysfunctional as they are, offer me that opportunity. So I came home. I severed my ties with [my former friends]. I kind of became a hermit. With the intention of getting my life together. Gave up my responsibilities [in the house I rented]. I went home. What I did was, I said, I'm fine, I've got a BA in psych under my belt, I'm four years into a master's in liberal arts—that should have taken only two years—I'll put myself on a behavioral extinction program. I'll go from a pint of bourbon a night [each day of the week] to a pint of bourbon a night six nights a week. After a couple of months, I'll go to five nights a week, to four nights a week. That was relatively easy. Then to three nights, then to two nights. And every month I would ratchet it down. I got to the point where I was drinking only one night a week. And reality struck. I could *not* get down to less than one night a week. In fact, I had difficulty, I only made a couple of weeks where I was drinking one night a week. I would find myself drinking two nights a week.

Erich: Why was that a problem for you? I mean, you would think that you had cut it down to the point where it was moderate drinking.

Harry: Well, you hear a lot of people say, "Oh, my God, I drank because everyone in my family was an alcoholic, and I was abused. Oh, I drank because I had such low self-esteem and it was the only way I could face myself and other people." *I* drank because I was an alcoholic. And I didn't realize until that point really, really, down in my heart, what being an alcoholic meant. But I found that I could *not* drink one night a week. And I put myself on a schedule. I had to be sober very soon. So, I tried and I found out that, deep in my heart that I was an alcoholic.

Erich: When you say you *couldn't* drink one night a week, in what specific way?

Harry: I've been wrestling with this since that time. I *cannot* tell you. It's so difficult to put into words. I would rationalize my drinking. I would be crawling out of my skin. And I would be *miserable*. And I would say, "All right, I'm not *ready* yet! *Next* week I'll be ready! I drank *once* last week. *This* week, I'll drink twice, *next* week I'll drink once! And the next week, *maybe*, maybe not, I would drink once. Maybe I would drink twice. And all this time, I would be overlapping into the time when I'm only supposed to be drinking every other week.

Erich: But aren't these, like, artificial rules? I mean, if you set a rule for yourself that's so stringent, then you can't follow it. But if you say, well, why have these rules, why can't you live with once a week? Or twice a week?

Harry: Because I knew that I was an alcoholic.

Erich: Maybe it's just the product of somebody brainwashing you into *thinking* that you are an alcoholic.

Harry: Right. Part of alcoholism is the denial. You're the last person to know, to *really* know [that you're an alcoholic]. In the back of my mind, as I'm drying out, I'm saying to myself, "Well, you know, I used to take that test in the back of the "Is AA For You?" pamphlet. And I would laugh because I was getting eight out of nine. [Laughs.] And the only reason I'm not *hiding* alcohol in the house [one of the AA questions asks if you hide alcohol in the house, a sign of alcoholism] is because [giggles] because it's *OK* not to hide alcohol in the house. And the other one [question to determine if you are an alcoholic] that I didn't answer "yes" to was only because there were no barnyard animals in my neighborhood.

But in the back of my mind, there is the *doubt*, well, just because I drank every day for the last 20 years doesn't mean I'm an alcoholic. But as it got to crunch time, and it became more and more difficult for me not to drink, the certainty that I *was* an alcoholic grew and grew as the realization that the depth of my problem was *deeper* [than I had originally thought]. It became like an inverse relationship: The harder it was to quit, the more and more I was convinced that I really, really had an alcohol problem. Which made it more and more important that I stick to the extinction schedule and that I *do* quit. So, it was a bit of a conundrum. And finally, I was still drinking one or two days a week, when I hit the calendar day when I was supposed to be dry—yah! OOOhhh! Panic!

But I did exactly what I was supposed to do. The Friday before I was supposed to completely quit, I enrolled myself in a professional treatment program in my local area. And that next Monday, I started going for individual counseling, group therapy, and by the end of that week, I was already finding myself [self-help meetings] in the area to attend. Drying out was harder than I thought it was going to be. Even with this extinction schedule that I was on for six or seven months. The first week was just really, really annoying. Going out of my skin, being angry, feeling sorry for myself, running the whole range of emotions, like I was 14 again. And I got through and I didn't drink. After a couple of weeks, though, I was walking around in the undersea world of Jacques Cousteau. It was like I was surrounded with a very light Jello, and like I had the flu and a head cold at the same time. There were three instances when I almost had serious car accidents. But other people swerved, other people [chuckles] got out of my way, thank God.

I found out very quickly that you're *not* supposed to listen to the people—anyone—who ever gave you advice while you were drinking. And the *last* people in the world you want to listen to are your family. They'll be well-meaning, but they are the ones, and it's true, they are the ones who know how to sabotage you most effectively. *And they will!* With the best of intentions. People say, why is it that my parents know how to push buttons I don't even know I have? And the answer is, because they *installed* them.

I made it through. Thank God for a certain self-help group that's had a lot of success with a lot of people. It's been almost two years. It's a constant struggle, but as they say—and you want to *whack* them when they do—in the first few months, "Don't drink, go to meetings, and it gets better." *It* doesn't get better—*you* get better. [Laughs.] And then if· you get better, hopefully, *it* gets better. But two of the groups that I attend, they call them "specialty" groups, that I attend are exclusively gay. Who have a much higher rate of alcoholism [than in the straight population] because of the pressure and the stress. Straight people don't realize how much pressure there is growing up gay in this culture. It's nice to see that in the last 20 years, it's lightened up a bit.

Erich: Why did you think there was a *necessity* for you to stop drinking? You mentioned that you had flunked out of school a couple of times and you had to be re-instated, and you started worrying that you might not get another chance, so, problems with school are obviously one major [problem] area, a couple of close calls as far as driving is concerned—I know that was after you quit—but what were some other areas of your life that became problematic as a result of your drinking?

Harry: I knew intellectually that I *was* an alcoholic. You rationalize some of the problems. Like being hung over. Well, when you're young, it's not so bad to be hung over. I also liked to drink alone. Because I drank every night. I was perfectly happy on those nights when the Lost Boys went out and I stayed home alone, sitting in front of the cable or the VCR.

Erich: There are some theories that argue that alcoholism is a progressive disease and that people [who are alcoholics] drink more and more until at a certain point they become self-destructive, or at least, there are certain *types* or *varieties* of alcoholics who are like that. And I notice that you kind of plateaued out at a pint [a day]. Now, that doesn't seem like an outrageous amount. What do you think accounts for the fact that you didn't escalate to, say, a *quart* a day?

Harry: Well, the thing was, I was drinking a fifth [of a gallon, or four-fifths of a quart; a quart equals two pints] a day for a while, and then I finally said, whoa, whoa, whoa! It was about five years ago, maybe. It did seem like my consumption was progressively going up. 'Cause I could drink a fifth, easily. Well, maybe not *easily*, but I could drink a fifth. [Laughs.] It had been known to happen. So, I just made a conscious intellectual decision. And I'm not saying that I *always* stuck to it.

Erich: It's interesting, because I've gone to a few [alcoholic self-help] meetings, you know, as a visitor—open meetings. And you often hear war stories. A couple staggering around after buying a pizza, dropping the pizza in the driveway, picking it up and putting it back in the box, you know, and being so woozy that they ended up *eating* it. Or somebody smashing up a car and not even remembering *driving* a car. Or getting thrown out of the army. All these war stories—*horror* stories—about what happened when they were too drunk to even *function*. Where, you know, the wife left the husband. Or creditors were coming to their house, repossessing their furniture and this sort of thing. It doesn't seem like you have had that kind of *litany* of war stories. [Compared to the people who told these stories,] it sounds like you *were* in fact able to function reasonably well.

I like to read biographies [and autobiographies], and there are a number of writers who call themselves functioning alcoholics. Or filmmakers. Sam Peckinpah, the guy who did *The Wild Bunch*, called himself a functioning alcoholic. John Huston, who did *Treasure of the Sierra Madre*, called himself a functioning alcoholic. And they put away a fifth or more a day. But somehow, they were able to do the job. They had unusual experiences [related to drinking], but they weren't necessarily *destructive* drunks. I mean, they got *diseases* and they died *early* [laughs], but, you know, they didn't crash up cars, they didn't fink out on their jobs, they made movies, they wrote books, this sort of thing. On the other hand, someone like Truman Capote drank so much that he was a falling-down drunk. Or Ernest Hemingway ended up blowing his *brains* out.

So, I'm not sure where that line is between the functioning alcoholic and the destructive alcoholic. I mean, I know what it means *behaviorally*, but in other respects, I'm not too sure.

Harry: The alcohol becomes the organizing principle. And if I had continued escalating my drinking, well, then I could not have continued to drink. Things would have fallen apart. And I think I knew that. Somewhere [in my mind], I'm pretty sure that was a fact [for me]. I mean, I did know that I couldn't keep escalating the amount [I drank]. I only weighed 125 pounds, 130 pounds. I've put on a little weight [laughs, grabs his belly] recently. But a friend of mine said, "I've never got into bar fights because they don't serve drinks in prison." [Laughs.]

Erich: You felt if you escalated the amount you drank. . . .

Harry: I know that I made a conscious decision that if I keep escalating the physical amount of alcohol that I drank, I'm gonna end up being non-functional. And I'm sure, now, in retrospect, in the back of my mind, I was thinking, "Oh, my God, then I *won't* be able to drink."

Alcoholics Anonymous is a very far cry from Goffman's total institution, but in its own way, it attempts to normalize its position on alcoholism and abnormalize or pathologize the drinker's pattern of alcohol consumption. It is AA's job to convince its members that the alcoholic has an allergy to drink, cannot drink at all, cannot drink in moderation, cannot control his or her drinking, and must abstain from alcohol altogether. At some point in his or her drinking career, to quote the AA "bible," *Alcoholics*

Anonymous, the alcoholic "has lost all control of his [or her] liquor consumption. . . . He [or she] is seldom mildly intoxicated. He [or she] is always more or less insanely drunk. . . . We alcoholics are men and women who have lost the ability to control our drinking. We know that no real alcoholic *ever* recovers control. . . . We are like men who have lost their legs; they never grow new ones. . . . Physicians . . . agree there is no such thing as making a normal drinker out of an alcoholic." In short: "Once an alcoholic, always an alcoholic."

Irrespective of whether or not this view is factually true, for many a recovering alcoholic, it serves as a *pragmatic* truth—that is, a truth to live by. For Harry, it did. Even at the apex of his alcohol consumption, Harry was a heavy drinker—not an out-of-control or falling-down drunk. And at some point, he even managed to reach a stage of moderate drinking. Could he have stabilized it there? It's not clear. Clearly, he had internalized the belief that, *for him*, any consumption of liquor was abnormal. Not satisfied to segue from heavy to moderate drinking, he found it necessary to terminate drinking altogether.

Still, in many crucial respects, Harry's drinking was dysfunctional. Harry, clearly an intelligent man, substantially delayed his educational progress, has not had any sort of an occupational career, and managed to remain in effect an adolescent into early middle age. In *Drinking: A Love Story* (1997), Caroline Knapp's own "drunkalogue," we see a confirmation of a number of Harry's observations. In many respects, she says, "you stop growing when you start drinking alcoholically. The drink stunts you, prevents you from walking through the kinds of fearful life experiences that bring you from point A to point B on the maturity scale. . . . After a while you don't know even the most basic things about yourself . . . because you've never given yourself a chance, a clear, sober chance, to find out." While the feeling of protection from life's hard knocks is "utterly false," at the same time "it feels so real, so real and necessary."

But this self-protection through drink does not last forever, concludes Knapp. At some point, "tragically," it "stops working. . . . This is inevitable. You drink long and hard enough and your life gets messy. Your relationships (with nondrinkers, with yourself) become strained. Your work suffers. You run into financial trouble, or legal trouble, or trouble with the police" (pp. 75–76). Certainly the "messiness" in Harry's life encompassed several of these spheres—for him, relations with nondrinkers (and with himself) became strained, his financial problems became almost insurmountable, and his fear of becoming ensnared in legal trouble and trouble with the police, he said, was instrumental in *not* escalating the quantity he drank, thus ensuring that he could, for a time at least, continue drinking. But at some point, he felt it was time to act, and act he did.

For Harry, Alcoholics Anonymous provided a way out of the mathematical equation that Knapp embraced then ultimately overcame: Pain + Drink = Self-Obliteration.

CHAPTER 9

We operated out of Southern California, in an area made up of very wealthy, very conservative beach communities. . . . Many of our clients were very highly respected people in their professions—doctors, lawyers, and several high-ranking military personnel. . . . We had to have discretion and keep things under a lid.

Jeff

Jeff, the Male Madam

At the time of this interview, Jeff was a 28-year-old resident of San Diego and a former male madam of a call boy agency. To me, one of the more interesting aspects of Jeff's account is the way that a seriously deviant activity—being a male madam—is linked in a variety of ways to the lives of a substantial number of extremely respectable and seemingly conventional citizens. Many of Jeff's clients were, he explains, "very highly respected people in their professions," including several "high-ranking military personnel." The disclosure that any one of them had hired a call boy would almost certainly destroy his career and contaminate or stigmatize his previously reputable character. Hence, the absolute necessity for "discretion" and keeping things "under a lid." The fact that an activity demands absolute secrecy indicates that it is likely to be deviant; secrecy is a clue that we have a case of deviance on our hands.

For any observer of deviance, it is interesting that, except for his sexual orientation and his former means of employment, Jeff is extremely conservative, and describes himself as such. Some of his criteria for the boys who were permitted to work for him were not dictated exclusively by Jeff's personal preferences but largely by the nature of his clientele. ("No nellies, no femmes, just the boy next door-type look.") But in addition, his boys were also clearly a reflection of his own preferences. For instance, Jeff's interviewer, Richard Troiden, described Jeff as a "racist," a charge revealed by this account: "We . . . didn't handle colored boys at all. . . . All of our boys were white—strictly white. . . . I myself wanted to have only white boys. That was my own personal preference. . . . This was due to my own personal philosophy and beliefs. I just wanted to have white boys." In addition, by Jeff's own admission, he did not like shaggy grooming: "I wouldn't accept anybody with long hair. Again, this is based on my own personal preferences." And it is clear that Jeff took special pride in how respectable his clientele was, again, a sign of his conservative and conventional nature.

In addition, the house out of which Jeff's call boys worked was, in his words, located in a cluster of "very wealthy, very conservative" beach communities. Much, possibly most, deviant behavior takes place not in territories of disrepute but, in effect, all around us: next door, around the block, down the street, perhaps even in our own household. *Some forms* of deviance (mainly what's referred to as "street crime," including robbery, rape, and criminal homicide) are almost certainly heavily located in stereotypically crime-ridden neighborhoods. But deviance *in general*—any and all forms of normative violations that are likely to result in censure—may be found almost literally everywhere. It is unlikely that, as a conceptual category, deviance is strongly ecologically, geographically, or spatially patterned.

Interestingly, homosexuality *is* spatially patterned. Men who regard themselves as gay and whose primary sexual outlet has been with other men are *hugely* more likely to live in large cities (Laumann et al., 1994, pp. 306–309; Michael et al., 1994, pp. 177–181) and, in those cities, very likely to be concentrated in certain communities, such as Castro in San Francisco and New York's Greenwich Village. Moreover, certain locales become known as "cruising" areas where men are on the lookout for sexual action; in some of these locales, transitory sex may be had on the spot, in the heat of the moment (Delph, 1978; Humphreys, 1970, 1975; Lee, 1978). Certain locales become well known for hot and heavy action. Just as street crime has "hot spots" where it is most likely to occur, gay "hot spots" are spatially and ecologically patterned. Given the nature of Jeff's clientele, the location of his call boy establishment in gay "hot spots" was out of the question. Indeed, the respectable location of his business was mandatory. If a highly respected person were seen in an intimate position in a locale of disrepute, that would tarnish his reputation and his career would be ruined.

Another interesting feature of Jeff's account is the fact that several of the young men who work for him and perform sexual services for clients are heterosexual. Two of them, he said, lived with their girlfriends. To the sociologist of deviance, this is hardly surprising. Jeff is confirming a generalization that many classics of the literature have verified, namely, that the world of homosexuality and the world of heterosexuality are intertwined and that, in one form or another and in a number of sectors of the society, homosexual activities are not unknown to a substantial proportion of straight men.

For instance, Laud Humphreys, a sociologist, investigated "tearoom" sex—anonymous, transient sexual encounters between men in public urinals (1970, 1975). He observed these encounters in urinals located near urban parks, then wrote down the license plates of the cars parked nearby. Later he interviewed these men under the guise of conducting a "public health" survey. One of Humphreys' major findings was that the majority of the men who engaged in tearoom sex (54 percent) were married and living with their wives (1975, p. 105). They were, as he says, "The People Next Door" (pp. 104–130).

This fact, interesting in and of itself, has several consequences and implications that feed directly into some of the basic principles I spelled out in the introduction. If in most heterosexual circles homosexuality is regarded as deviant, and men who possess a heterosexual identity engage in homosexual relations, we should expect them to engage in one or another form of stigma neutralization. And that is precisely what we do find.

Albert Reiss studied a group of young, mostly heterosexually identified, street hustlers who engaged in sex for pay with homosexuals (1964). More specifically, when they were paid for it, they permitted homosexuals to fellate them, but they did not reciprocate by fellating them in return. These young men did not regard themselves as gay because, for them, the sex was strictly means of earning money and was defined by them "as part of a versatile pattern of delinquent activity" (p. 182). Their strongly heterosexual identity was not challenged because they were able to convince themselves and others that these encounters were strictly to earn money and not for sexual gratification; if they did not sexually reciprocate, that is, if they did not perform sexual acts on their partners; if they kept their relations with their partners impersonal and emotionally neutral; if these transactions were seen as temporary rather than long-term. If their homosexual partners attempted to violate any aspect of their carefully defined relationship, they resorted to violence against them. In other words, the behavior of these young men did not threaten their heterosexual and, in their eyes, "masculine" self-image because they regarded *being* a homosexual as defined by conformity to a homosexual *role*—not by engaging in homosexual *behavior* (p. 207). Indeed, if these rules were followed, they did not even conceptualize *as* homosexual their participation in a sexual act that was performed on them by a man. In short, and once again, the worlds of homosexuality and heterosexuality intersect and mingle in crucial and fascinating ways.

Calhoun and Weaver (2001) interviewed 18 male prostitutes who "hustled" homosexuals and found that 17 regarded themselves as either straight or bisexual. How did they maintain such a self-image in the face of engaging in behavior everyone else would regard as homosexual—behavior, one might expect, that would *challenge* or *undermine* that self-image? After all, nearly all of these young men grew up regarding homosexuality as a stigmatized or "discredited" status (p. 214). Like the Reiss informants, the Calhoun and Weaver street hustlers "attempt to avoid the stigma associated with homosexuality by rationalizing their behavior as nonsexual and by evoking negative images of their clients' sexuality" (pp. 213–214). Says one of their informants: "I ain't gay. I just let them suck me and that's for the money. I think of myself as a woman lover and not a man lover." Says another: "If I was a faggot I wouldn't have gotten my old lady pregnant" (p. 215). The fact that almost everyone of these young men restricted their activities to receiving oral sex but not giving it, acting as the inserter but not the insertee in anal sex, indicates that they wanted to reinforce their straight identity to themselves. "I'm a straight man," said one. "It means I wouldn't get fucked by nobody and suck nobody's dick. I'd fuck them and let 'em suck my dick" (p. 219). And, since both being a male prostitute and engaging in homosexual behavior are stigmatizing, these men keep their street activities a secret. Said one of the researcher's informants: "You don't want nobody to find out" (p. 220). Say Calhoun and Weaver, "Discovery can have devastating effects" (p. 220).

Jeff does not have a straight identity, but several of the "boys" who worked for him do. And so do most of his clients. And, like the male hustlers in the literature, Jeff kept the nature of his business a secret from conventional society. At the same time, his enterprise is nestled into conventional society much like the local supermarket, the pediatrician down the block, the town lawyer, the accountant on Main Street. In a very real sense, patronizing the call boy enterprise is like a "back region" in the clients' lives, much the way the kitchen is a back region for the staff in a restaurant. Symbiotically integrated into the lives of their customers, the restaurant employees retreat from their customers' gaze into the kitchen where they can "let their hair down," be themselves, and engage in behavior their customers would find offensive. Like the restaurant staff, the men who patronize Jeff's establishment—respectable members of the community all—retreat from the public gaze into a back region where they can be themselves, express their true feelings, their true nature. The fact that they felt comfortable enough to disclose their prestigious professions to the boys they had sex with, or to bring these boys to their residences, indicates the division of their worlds into "front" and "back" regions. Like Goffman's restaurant staff, the "discovery" of their untoward, socially unacceptable behavior would "have devastating effects." Likewise, any disclosure of the nature of Jeff's professional activities was likely to be devastating.

In fact, the inadvertent discovery of Jeff's business *did* have such effects: A few months before this interview was conducted, the operation was raided by the police and Jeff was arrested. (Ironically, the original police investigation had nothing to do with Jeff's call boy business, but entailed drug dealing by one of the boys.) Because of a legal technicality, Jeff was not prosecuted for his illegal business, and he's currently retired from the call boy enterprise.

The following interview was conducted by Richard Troiden. Shortly before his death, he made it available to me and urged me to publish it. Below, "Q" indicates Troiden's questions and "A" indicates Jeff's answers.

Q: How and why did you become a male madam?

A: I was approached on the idea through a friend I had met in Southern California soon after I arrived here. The reason, I suppose, was the novelty of it, and the money. I had heard that there was money in it.

Q: What was the arrangement as far as payment was concerned?

A: I received a percentage of each assignment. Of course, this varied from week to week. I'd say it was a steady income for me.

Q: About what percentage of the total amount of money made by each call boy did you receive?

A: About 35 or 40 cents out of every dollar. About a third.

Q: What was expected of the boy on a call?

A: They were expected to do anything the client wished them to do. That was one of the prerequisites. When they came into our employ, they had to agree [to be], as we call it, "versatile." The client, whatever his preference, expected our boys to go along with it. We didn't expect them to get into heavy S&M sex or weirdo sex, real far-out, strange people with weird sexual hang-ups. [But] normally, the boy had to go along with [what the client wanted].

Q: For instance, then, just to clarify this point, if a client wanted to be beaten, the boy was given the option of following through or turning him down?

A: Yes, he is given the option. Also, in light of this, several of the people who worked for me did go along with the S&M route. Usually, a customer would indicate that this was what he wanted, so that we could line him up with somebody whose preference was the same as his.

Q: How did a client go about picking the boy that he wanted? Or, did you just send someone? In short, how did a client get a [particular] call boy?

A: There were usually two ways. If the client was new, he would call us and describe over the phone what he wanted. We'd try to send him approximately what he wanted. If he wasn't satisfied, we'd send him someone else or, in most instances, he came over to the apartment we had. We had people around he could choose and we also had pictures of boys we could get him in contract with.

Q: Were these pictures kept in an album?

A: Right. In an album, like a family album. You could just leaf through it and pick out your choice.

Q: When these pictures were taken, was the boy clothed or was he nude?

A: It was all strictly nudes.

Q: Was he in a state of sexual arousal?

A: Yes. It pays to advertise, especially to "size queens."

Q: How did you go about taking these pictures? More specifically, who took the pictures of the boys?

A: I took some and another person who worked with me took the others. When a kid came to us wanting work, he had to agree to have nude pictures taken for our album, which was like a catalogue, an advertising catalogue. It was very difficult for some of the boys to become sexually aroused and maintain their erection long enough to have their picture taken. The problem was solved by having the boy engage in sexual relations to the point at which he was just about to reach an orgasm, at which time the boy would rush into the camera room and have his picture taken.

Q: How did a client get in touch with you? How did you recruit clients?

A: We operated out of Southern California, in an area made up of very wealthy, very conservative beach communities. One person would refer another person to us. We did no advertising. We knew desk clerks in several of the [local] motels. We actually took nobody that was not referred to us from somebody that we already knew.

Q: In other words, in order for a client to receive services, he had to be vouched for by a proven client or someone you knew?

A: Right. Many of our clients were very highly respected people in their professions—doctors, lawyers, and several high-ranking military person-nel. . . . We had to have discretion and keep things under a lid.

Q: How did you learn the occupations of the clients?

A: In some cases, they told us. In some cases, we found out from the kids who went to their residences. . . . It is very surprising, very few clients tried to hide what they did, although they wanted discretion on our part.

Q: I've been told that some female prostitutes or female madams will keep a book containing information regarding their clients.

A: Oh, yeah.

Q: What they like sexually, what they do for a living, and so on. Did you have any such arrangement?

A: Yes. We had a complete book. Actually, we had two books. One book consisted of all transactions—monetary transactions. The other book contained the names of all regular clients, their sexual preference, and what they liked as far as boys that worked for me. These books were all written in a code that only I knew. Anybody else looking at it wouldn't know how to decipher it.

Q: How could you tell that the person who claimed to be a client was indeed a client and not a member of the vice or morals squad? Is this why you had clients referred through other clients and reliable sources?

A: Yes, that is right.

Q: Did you pay the police for protection?

A: No. Of course, I must say that we came under a certain organization that handled prostitution and other things in Southern California, who themselves, I believe, had an agreement with the police. So, in a sense, we had blanket protection.

Q: Did you manage this call boy service in the sense that you had to answer to someone—this "certain organization" you mentioned? Or were you completely your own boss?

A: We didn't directly answer to anybody above us. In a sense we indirectly did. We had to send our two best boys up to Los Angeles once a month to work for someone. What the boys earned went into this person's pocket. In a sense, then, I suppose this was our pay-off.

Q: When someone called your service, what did they ask you? How did they indicate that their call was a request for a call boy?

A: Usually when someone called for the first time, he would use the name of his reference, for instance, John Smith told me to call you in regards to [so-and-so], and then he'd indicate that he wanted a model or companion or some other such terminology.

Q: Did you publicly advertise, in the newspaper, for instance?

A: No. Our only means of advertising was the use of cards on which were printed the name of the agency and our phone number. We left these cards at certain motels and hotels with the desk clerks. Several of our kids served as sources of referral since they worked in hotels, worked in restaurants, or worked where they made contact with large numbers of people.

Q: How long were you a male madam?

A: For approximately five months.

Q: Could you describe the physical layout of the area where you worked? What was the place like?

A: We had a very unique arrangement. We had two apartments, one above the other. We were located in a family complex which was very nice. These apartment buildings were like duplexes—large, house-like structures. Each major unit was separated from the other by shrubbery, a driveway, and a balcony. Our unit had a top and a bottom floor, each floor consisting of two, two-bedroom apartments. The bottom apartment was used as a workshop, a living room, and a dining area. We also had a bar area and two bedrooms down there for those customers who preferred to use the apartment instead of their own home. In addition, any of the kids who needed a place to stay stayed there. The upstairs apartment was mine. We also used one of the bedrooms for picture-taking and for any of the kids who needed a place to say. So, we actually used two units.

Q: You mentioned that you could provide rooms for a client if he decided to come to your apartment. You also mentioned that you'd also, on occasion, send a guy on call to the client's residence. Did you ever rent rooms in certain motels or hotels which could be used as meeting places?

A: No. Never, at any time. Some of our clientele stayed in hotels or motels in the area, but we never rented a room for that purpose. If anything, we preferred them back at the apartment.

Q: Why were you reluctant to rent rooms for this purpose?

A: Well, for one thing, it would be a needless expense when we had rooms already available at the apartment. And secondly, it was easier for the kid who was working. Instead of wasting his time chasing all over the county trying to make contact with clients, he could just move them into and out of our apartment faster, which helped him make more money.

Q: How old were you when you operated this service and why did you discontinue it?

A: I was 27 at the time. We discontinued our service thanks to the police. This brings me back to an earlier question about police protection. We were not busted because we were a call boy agency. Unfortunately, one of the kids who worked for us—and we didn't know it at the time—was pushing drugs on the beach and was under police surveillance. The squad found out where he lived and made a raid on our place. In the process, they found enough [evidence] to convince them that more was going on than a bunch of guys simply living together. The police managed to find pictures and my code books, which they could not decipher. Luckily, when they broke into our apartment, they did not have a search warrant. So, although we did spend several days in jail, all charges were eventually dropped or dismissed due to the lack of a search warrant. They took both apartments apart, however, and our phones were tapped. At this time, I decided to get out of the business while the getting out was still good.

Q: Back to the clients. Roughly how many clients would you estimate you had?

A: That is hard to say. I had 12 boys working for me. We didn't want any less than 10 and no more than 12. Twelve, especially during the summer, when business was busy. On an average night I'd say that one-half of our boys were gone all night and the others would probably pull in two or three clients.

Q: Roughly how old would you estimate the average age of your clients to be?

A: This might be surprising, but we had clients in their late 20s and early 30s. [They were also in their] 40s, 50s, 60s, and [there was even] one who we all guessed to be between 70 and 80.

Q: You'd say, then, that the age of your clients spanned a wide age spectrum?

A: Yes.

Q: What was the most frequently occurring age group of your clients?

A: I'd say that it fell between the late 30s to 50. All were fairly well-to-do, fairly wealthy, mostly professional or military men, and very well educated. In fact, we strived for only this kind of trade. They could meet our prices and we had the kind of service that they wanted.

Q: You previously mentioned your code book. Did you happen to have any information regarding the incomes of your clients?

A: No, but some things are fairly obvious. The type of home they lived in, in some cases, the type of car they drove. They took several of our boys on trips to Hawaii, Las Vegas, New York. So I'd say they were fairly well-to-do.

Q: Why did you want no less than 10 but no more than 12 call boys?

A: That was just an arbitrary number we set, depending on how much business we wanted to handle per night. Besides the money factor, we could handle this much business per night, and we had enough business to warrant employing this many boys.

Q: Did you yourself ever go out on call when business was heavy?

A: Sometimes. However, this was very rare. It happened several times that someone decided to take a liking to me. I only went with a client if the person himself was very attractive and appealed to me and if I had nothing else to do. I shouldn't put it like that. If I wasn't busy, I would go. There were a couple of nights when we were short and I went out. However, I preferred not to, I preferred to keep my eye on the business. I made one exception, however, with one individual who came down from San Francisco once a week on business. I was very, very attracted to him. I made a point of being with him every Thursday night, all night.

Q: How did you go about recruiting or obtaining the boys who worked for you?

A: This might surprise some people, but I'd say approximately half of our boys were straight—if you can use the word, perhaps bisexual. I found them on the beach. Several were students. Two were from nearby state universities and came to California for the summer to make enough money to go back to school in the fall and attend school all year without having to work. I was also referred to several through the gay bars. And of course the kids themselves referred some boys to me if they knew anybody who would fit what I was looking for.

Q: You mentioned that some of the boys were straight or bisexual.

A: Right. They considered themselves to be straight or bisexual even though they worked as call boys. Two of them set up housekeeping, lock, stock, and barrel, with their girlfriends in a two-bedroom apartment approximately a block from me. They were straight. They attended the University of Arizona. They made enough money during the summer—this was their summer work—so that they didn't have to work during the year. This was the second or third time they came to California to hustle for the summer.

Q: Regarding the guys who were living with their girlfriends, did their girlfriends know that their boyfriends were hustlers? That they worked in a call boy agency?

A: Oh, yes.

Q: You mentioned that somebody could conceivably have five clients a day. Would the boy come on these occasions or did he purposely refrain from coming, making it easier for him to become aroused when he went on his next call?

A: Oh, this is very hard to answer, and of course, it depends upon the individual himself. You must realize that in several cases, the client did not want sex at all but companionship. Someone with whom to go to a ball game or to go out boating, to the movies, or out to dinner. This was especially true of older clients. Sex was not important—or was not as important—to them as it was to the younger clients. But going back to the specific individual, clients are often more interested in getting their own rocks off than they are in the boys reaching an orgasm. Of course, you must also consider the fact that several of the kids had remarkable stamina, they just kept going.

Q: Did you ever talk to the boys about why they decided to become call boys?

A: No, never. The universal thing, I suppose, was money. It was a good way of picking up money and gifts. No, you didn't discuss it. It was just something we didn't touch on unless someone wanted to talk about it himself. It was mostly the money.

Q: What would you say the ages of the call boys were? Their rough age span?

A: One thing I was pretty much insistent upon was that they be [at least] 21 years old, because many of our clients liked to take them out for dinner or for drinks, and of course the boy had to be 21 years old. There is also the legal aspect too, of not having a minor [be involved with sexual activities with an adult]. We tried to find guys who looked younger than that—say, 17, 18, 19. If we have a request for a younger guy, we could find one. Generally, I'd say our most common requests were for an 18, 19-year-old. I therefore tried to get most of our kids to look young, to pass for that age. The client didn't know [that they were over 21], or if he did know, he wouldn't mind. And many clients liked the idea that the boys were of legal age.

Q: One of the questions we kind of drifted into at the very beginning of the interview was the question as to the kinds of sex acts a boy was expected to perform when he went out on call. You mentioned that you left it up to him as to whether he'd get involved in heavy S&M sex or weirdo sex. Were the boys expected to "rim" someone [perform analinctus] or "bring someone off" [swallow his semen during an act of fellatio]? Or was this optional?

A: The people who worked for me were supposed to be versatile. That was the very first question I asked them, are you versatile? Would you do anything? If they wanted the job, they had to say yes. They were expected to do it [pretty much what the customer requested]. If we had any complaints from the customers, we got rid of the boy. He was supposed to be completely versatile.

Q: If someone said, no, I am not versatile, did you immediately cool him out or did you ever hire a boy and then teach him how to perform specific sexual acts?

A: No, they had to have, let's call it, "natural talent." No. I didn't want anybody who had recently come out. I wanted someone who was experienced, or [if they were gay] who had been gay a while. There was no teaching or anything else. If they said no, I am not versatile, I just told them I couldn't use them.

Q: In other words, someone who was sexually inexperienced or just recently out as gay was disqualified?

A: Yes. I couldn't use them.

Q: Did a boy have to prove his versatility by having sex with either yourself or anyone else?

A: Yes. With myself or someone else who appealed to him. If it was someone else, his competence was then reported to me. If he had any hangups, he was let go. He had to do passably well with whatever act he was called upon to perform.

Q: Did you ask a boy when he first came to you if he had any qualms about the types of people with whom he went to bed?

A: Oh, yes. I stressed the fact that he'd have to go to bed with all types of people. I must add that our clientele was all white. This is the way we wanted it. As far as physical characteristics, I stressed that he'd have to be prepared to go to bed with anyone.

Q: Would he have been disqualified if he had refused?

A: Yes. Definitely yes.

Q: You mentioned that your clients were all white. What kinds of physical attributes did your clients prefer in a call boy?

A: I'd say they wished him to look like the kid next door, the All-American Boy. Not necessarily a super-he-man, but a person who looks just like the average, good-looking kid next door. Maybe a college kid, who might play football or be on the swimming team. No Nellies, no femmes, just the boy next door-type look.

Q: Was there a demand for Blacks or other minority members as call boys?

A: We had a few demands but we didn't handle colored boys at all.

Q: So, in other words, none of your call boys were minority group members?

A: Right. All of our boys were white—strictly white.

Q: Why was this?

A: For one reason—the clientele. They were very wealthy and conservative and they preferred white boys. Also, I myself wanted to have only white boys. That was my own personal preference.

Q: Why?

A: This is due to my own personal philosophy and beliefs. I just wanted to have all white boys.

Q: Did you refrain from employing someone if he had previously been arrested on a morals charge?

A: We never even questioned that. [However], I did not want to hire any obvious junkies or people on drugs.

Q: Did you allow the boys who themselves were gay to have sexual relations with each other?

A: No, especially if they lived in one of our apartments. There would be just too much hassle, too much jealousy, too much grief. There was a "strictly save it for the customers" rule.

Q: Would you say then that you discouraged emotional involvements between the boys?

A: Yes, absolutely.

Q: Mainly to avoid the impairment of job performance?

A: Basically, yes, though I won't say that once in a while somebody didn't fall into bed with someone else, which is all right. But it was one of the house rules, you just don't do it. But of course, as I said, there were times when it happened, but as a regular practice, such behavior was discouraged.

Q: Did you discourage the boys themselves from becoming emotionally involved with a client?

A: No, I didn't. It was good for business. I encouraged it. Several of the boys had one person who preferred them. It brought money into the house and made more money for the boy.

Q: That is interesting because I have been led to believe that it might have been bad for business in the sense that the guy might up and quit and go off with the client, leaving you with one less call boy.

A: I've never had that happen. If anything, it brought the client back every night, which meant money, more money. It never happened.

Q: How long would you say the boys tended to work for you?

A: At the end of five months, the original boys I started out with were still with me. They were making good money and they had pretty easy living. I must say that some of our money, our percentage of the boy's earnings, went toward the upkeep of the two apartments, plus liquor and food, since they mostly ate their evening meal at the apartment. Every now and then, for our customers who had spent a lot of money with us, we had what we called appreciation night [which was] a small party at the apartment where each client had his choice of a boy for the entire night, free.

Q: In other words, part of the percentage you received from the boys went toward paying their room and board?

A: Well, in part. Those who lived in one of the two apartments all of the time were charged a nominal sum beyond our percentage of his profits to help defray expenses.

Q: Did you ever fire anyone who worked for you?

A: No. I didn't fire one person.

Q: Did the call boys adopt pseudonyms or nicknames rather than using their real names?

A: I don't believe one of them actually used their real name. I didn't even use my real name.

Q: Why is this?

A: I suppose due to the police. Also, the guys who were straight didn't want to use their real names. This was an impersonal situation. A monetary transaction.

Q: If you were to give a conservative estimate, what would you say the minimum number of calls made by a boy per day would amount to?

A: Well, it depends on whether the boy's client wants him all night or if he wants him just for an hour. You must realize that we operated day and night, not just in the evening, although most of our business was in the evening. Our boys, if they wanted to, could have two to four or possibly even five calls a day.

Q: Would you say a person tended to have more one-hour calls than all-night calls?

A: In the beginning, I'd say yes. A new client calling up in all probability would just take a boy for an hour. And afterwards, if he liked a boy or found another boy he really liked, then he'd probably take him for an entire night. There are two things that I should probably clarify. First, this was during the summer months, when the normal population of the area where we were was swelled by tourists and other people, which in part accounted for our heavy business. Also, as far as money goes, we were located in a very wealthy area. People could afford our prices. That is why we opened in that area.

Q: Well, in other words, then, chances were that a boy would tend, over time, to have more all-night engagements?

A: Yes. They would develop a trade, their own following who came back and asked for them. This was especially true when we had a lot of businessmen who could come into town one or two days a week and they would often ask for a certain boy all the time.

Q: Well, did you ever have to deal with the problem of one boy trying to "poach" on another call boy's regular customer?

A: No, it was one of the unwritten house rules, you don't "claim jump." If a client had already made his selection or preference known, you don't try to change his mind.

Q: What other house rules do you have?

A: Not that many. The basic ones were, no drugs, keeping out of one another's beds, no bitch fights. The guys could drink but I didn't want any heavy drinking or drugs laying around. I tried to keep it on a fraternity house level as far as these kinds of things go.

Q: How did a boy prepare himself physically for a call? Did he dress up? Was there any special kind of preparation that he had to engage in?

A: No. The main thing was to use common sense. We expected a kid to be clean-cut looking, cleanly shaved and showered. As far as dress goes, since we were right on the beach, and most of our clients preferred it, we wore outfits we referred to as "casual beach": blue jeans and a white T-shirt. No special preparation was demanded other than the clean-cut look.

Q: Did you allow long hair?

A: No. I wouldn't accept anybody with long hair. Again, this is based on my own personal preferences and the personal preferences of our clients as well.

Q: Some people have indicated that in some instances a call boy might shave off body hair on his legs or buttocks as well as give himself an anal douche before he would go out on call. Was anything along these lines mandatory?

A: No, it wasn't mandatory. We just expected common sense. If they wanted to, they could stay in front of the mirror for two hours and primp. This was left up to the individual.

Q: You mentioned several times that you didn't want to hire anyone who was into drugs. Do you mean drugs categorically? Or were there some drugs which you allowed? For instance, you mentioned earlier that you allowed occasional drinking. Did you allow people to smoke grass?

A: When I say drugs, I mean by this absolutely no hard drugs were tolerated, along with speed. Of course, all the guys smoked pot once in a while. I've smoked pot myself. I don't allow it on the premises or its use among the clients on the premises. You'd be surprised how many liked to turn on and just sit with a joint. That is fine with me as long as it's not done on my premises.

Q: Was this mainly because of the legal aspect?

A: I didn't want any drugs in the apartment or anybody on hard drugs. No speed freaks, juice freaks, or anything along that line.

Q: About how many years would you estimate a man could last as a desired and sought-after call boy? I mean, is there an age span which you would see as the prime call years?

A: It's a very demanding job, both physically and emotionally, especially if you have to deal with people who are not desirable to you sexually. I'd say—just my own estimation—that a kid with good looks and a good body can maybe push it for two years, and I think that is about it. Perhaps not even that long. Two or possibly three summers might be a better estimate. It depends upon what the person looks like. In any case, I think they reach a point, physically and emotionally, when they go downhill.

Q: In what way emotionally?

A: Like I said, you are dealing with people, a great percentage of whom don't appeal to you physically, and yet you have to get yourself psyched up to achieve a response on your part so that you can satisfy them. Also, I think it's the nature of the work. It is prostitution, and this is degrading to people in the long run.

Q: Would I be accurate in assuming that you see one of the reasons for leaving the call service results from becoming turned off to the sexual attitudes involved in the nature of call work? As you mentioned, its degrading aspects and the impersonality.

A: Yes, I'd say so.

Q: What about the physical costs? Did people really show the wear and tear? I mean, did the physical strain [get to them]?

A: Yes, in a sense. Take the kid who has been working every night, turning three or four tricks a night. At the end of the week, he is going to look pretty fagged out. It takes its toll. One of them remarked to me that after working three months as a hustler, he felt as if he had worked three years.

Q: You mentioned before that you basically liked to hire people who were 21 years old but looked 18 or 19. Would you say, then, that a guy is finished by the time he is 23?

A: Yes, in my opinion. They last about two years. I am not talking about the cheap street hustler. We considered ourselves a very select agency, dealing with very select people. We wanted the best to offer them. . . . And that is why I wouldn't want anybody who's been on the streets for a number of years.

CHAPTER 10

I was going through the airport with a heavy cock ring and it came up on the security device. . . . and I said, "It's my cock ring, would you care to see?" And her reaction was, "No sir, you can go on through." For all she knew, it could have been a pistol.

Lenny

Lenny, the Laissez-Faire Leatherman

"Leather" or "leather sex" refers to sado-masochistic sexual practices, whether homosexual or heterosexual. (Just as leather sex is a fairly rare practice in the heterosexual world, it is a minority activity in the gay world as well.) S&M refers to sadism and masochism (or, with the meaning of the initials reversed, to "slave and master"). In this sexual practice, the "top" is the dominant partner, usually the penile inserter, and the "bottom" is the submissive partner, typically the insertee. "Fisting" is the practice of inserting one's entire fist into one's partner's anus.

The first and most fundamental principle to keep in mind when considering deviance as a sociological phenomenon is "things are not always what they seem" (Berger, 1963). In other words, the popular and official understanding of deviance may be spectacularly inaccurate in capturing its reality. (Let's also keep aware of the fact that myth may *become* a kind of reality in its own right if it is acted upon *as if it were* real.) In very few other areas of deviance do we notice such a wide and yawning chasm between myth and reality as with S&M.

185

What is the public understanding of S&M? It is that one partner (the sadist), the "active" partner, obtains sexual pleasure from inflicting pain on the passive or semi-unwilling partner (the masochist), who nonetheless obtains pleasure from receiving pain. It is widely understood that the practice is a "perversion," a psychological disorder, that the sadist and the masochist are mentally ill. In addition, it is assumed that the sadist often includes unwilling partners within his sexual practices, often forcing them to submit to his twisted lust. S&M is widely regarded as a form of cruelty and, by some feminists, as a model, paradigm, or slight exaggeration of conventional male-female relations, which contain a generous measure of coercion, domination, cruelty, and violence (Linden et al., 1982, p. 78). Pornography, likewise, represents the essence of male domination, and, whether in diluted or pure form, is based on sadism (Dworkin, 1981; Lederer, 1982).

These views (all of which are not necessarily held by the same ideological or intellectual circles) are mistaken, and for at least six reasons.

First, pain is not the central or guiding principle of S&M. Indeed, it is not even essential to sadomasochistic activities (Baumeister, 1988, p. 37; Weinberg, 1995b, p. 291). In fact, it is the *illusion* of pain that is crucial; it is *symbolic* of dominance and control (Moser, 1988, p. 50). S&M is about dominance and submission, controlling and being controlled (Weinberg and Kamel, 1995, p. 19). Pain is far from unknown in S&M, but the pain is secondary.

The second point is that the masochistic partner is far from passive. S&M is a *social* and *interactional* activity. The masochistic (or "bottom") partner emits cues to the sadistic (or "top") partner as to what he or she wants to do, and vice versa. Both partners "are actively involved in the development of the scenario" (Califia, 1994; Weinberg, 1995b, p. 294). Collaboration, not force, is the foundation stone of S&M. Sadists who force their partners to engage in activities against their will "are avoided and quickly find themselves without partners" (Weinberg and Kamel, 1995, p. 19). Weinberg describes a scene in which a man was hoisted up onto a wall by a hook. At a certain point, the two women who were engaged in the action whispered into the man's ear to ask whether he was uncomfortable. He nodded to assure them that he was okay (Weinberg, 1995b, p. 295).

The third point is an outgrowth of the second: It is *scripted* behavior—it is more or less planned out in advance (Gebhard, 1969, p. 78). This does not mean that there are no departures from the script. Limits are negotiable, scripts may be tossed aside—but the partners involved map out the dynamics of the action before it takes place.

Another way of saying S&M is reciprocal and that it is scripted is that partners agree, in Goffman's terminology, on a particular S&M *frame*. S&M is theater, a world of make-believe, a shared fantasy that becomes a mutual creation. Frames inform participants "what is and is not proper, acceptable, and possible within their world. They define and categorize for their members situations, settings, scenes, identities, roles, and relationships" (Weinberg, 1995a, p. 134).

Just as frames can be constructed, they can also be violated. In the world of S&M, breaking frame is communicated in much the same way as in more conventional worlds. Brodsky (1995, p. 213) describes a scene during an especially crowded weekend at the Mineshaft, an S&M bar, in which frame was broken. A man yelled out very loudly, "I said STOP THAT!" and struck another man. "The crowd was stunned, and in Goffman's terminology, the frame was obviously broken—no one knew what to do. All sound but the disco tapes ceased. People all around stopped what they were doing and stood frozen as if in a tableau." The assailant was removed from the scene, several people were distressed by what they had witnessed, left, several others moved in, "and the frame was reestablished within a few minutes" (p. 213).

Fourth, the two positions, sadist ("top") and masochist ("bottom"), are not fixed; there is a substantial amount of movement from one position to the other. In fact, far from being mutually exclusive or contradictory, being a "top" trains the participant into being a good "bottom," and vice versa. In one study, only 16 percent of the sample said that they were exclusively dominant or submissive; the remainder—the vast majority of the sample—was made up of "switchables" (Moser and Levitt, 1987).

Fifth, no evidence from any study based on a reasonable cross-section of S&M participants has demonstrated them to be any more mentally disordered than the population at large. Studies based on non-clinical samples have found that they are essentially normal (Moser and Levitt, 1987; Thompson, 1994, pp. 88–116; Weinberg, 1995b). The fourth edition of the American Psychiatric Association's *Diagnostic and Statistical Manual of Mental Disorders* (1994, pp. 529–530) is careful to distinguish between being sexually aroused by "real" as opposed to "simulated" beating, humiliation, and suffering. While men (and women) exist who are excited by real (and unscripted) pain and humiliation, for the most part, they are not devotees of S&M, and they are not part of the mainstream S&M subculture. If they were to attempt to participate in that subculture, chances are they would be avoided and stigmatized. There are, after all, proper rules of behavior, even in a deviant context, and a violation of rules constitutes deviance in any context.

Sixth, the extrapolation from S&M to ordinary male-female relations, as some feminists have done (Linden et al., 1982), is misleading and inaccurate. The question of whether or not violence, coercion, dominance and submission, and/or humiliation are characteristic or typical of male-female relations in this or any society is not related to how S&M is conducted. As we saw, S&M behavior is mutually arrived at, reciprocal, scripted, fantasy-oriented, theatrical, carefully choreographed, socially constructed, and subculturally framed.

An obvious point, though one worth stressing, is made by Lenny in this interview: Not all participants in S&M are into the same activities. No deviant scene is an either-or, all-or-nothing proposition. There is no less variation in deviant than in conventional behavior. Lenny tolerates but does not participate in some of the more extreme S&M conduct, just as he recognizes that not everyone who is interested in S&M partakes of some of his activities. Much deviant behavior is stereotyped by the majority, and most stereotypes "flatten" the people or their behavior into a misleadingly homogeneous consistency. S&M is far from consistent. Differences and distinctions within a particular unconventional scene and the roles they play among their members are some of the more interesting aspects of deviance.

This account is composed of several interviews conducted by "Jerry" (a former student of mine who prefers to remain anonymous) with "Lenny," a 37-year-old salesperson working in a retail store that sells sexual paraphernalia in Greenwich Village. (I have edited these interviews slightly, mainly for continuity, clarity, and focus.)

Lenny: In Europe, they use a double mold system for making dildos and it leaves a seam that some find irritating. [Our dildos don't have that seam.] We're one of the largest [manufacturers of dildos] in the world. . . . We're known all over the world. We've even had people come from the airport straight here. We make 90 percent of what we sell. . . .

Jerry: Is alcohol a good disinfectant?

Lenny: It's good as a basic cleaner for a dildo or something like that. Bleach can be used depending on what it is that you're cleaning. The item can dry out, so alcohol may not be the best thing but neither is bleach, but it is one of the better things. As a general cleaner it's decent.

Jerry: What would you use as a disinfectant for leather goods?

Lenny: Well, generally, you don't have to disinfect leather. . . . If you're working with a butt plug, most butt plugs are rubber, so with something like that I happen to like bleach. I use one part bleach to a sink full of water. . . . This is after I've washed it. The thing that I found out, and you find these things out through trial and tribulation, is that Dawn, the dishwashing liquid, does everything it says it does. It lifts grease, so I wash it first then I'll fill the sink again with one part bleach to the rest water. . . .

Jerry: Hey, do these things really work? [Referring to penis pumps.]

Lenny: Yeah, they do. I have to tell you that, yes, they really work, yes, they will enlarge the size of your cock. But for everything in life there is a payment and the payment is . . . what happens is that they [the men who use the penis pump] lose the ability to retain a hard-on. They're still able to come, and they're still able to function somewhat sexually, but if it comes down to anything where penetration is necessary, you might have difficulty.

Jerry: What are the most esoteric items here?

Lenny: I live a leather lifestyle and part of living in the leather life-style is that it tends to open your eyes. I also work in a situation where I have to be non-judgmental. Not everything may be for me. Probably anything that's inserted inside the penis is quite esoteric, although that's having [a] resurgence in interest. Things like catheters. . . . Sex toys seem real popular. I think as popular or more popular than they've ever been 'cause they can be a good form of safe sex. If you've been married for a long time, and I consider any two people who have been together for a long time as married, a part of that is keeping an open mind to sexual experimentation, and I would think that people would find the larger dildos and ass beads esoterics, [but] they're real popular and we sell a lot of them. People think that they're a form of violence [but] they're not because there should be no pain involved. But people think that there is 'cause they're big. . . .

Jerry: You have a lot of penis restraints here. Tell me about the Seven Gates of Hell.

Lenny: There are so many rumors about that item it's ridiculous. Now, they actually come in two, three, five, and seven [ring models] and what this is is a severe cock bondage device. The largest ring acts as a cock ring, the rest goes along the shaft. When you're wearing it, it should initially be snug when you're soft, so that when you get hard it's gonna really be very tight. So the bottom ring goes around the penis and the testicles, right, and the rest goes along the shaft. That's supposed to be really restrictive but if you're into cock bondage, it will hurt. Hurt is an esoteric word; I'd use the word uncomfortable. I'm not into cock bondage but what you or I might find uncomfortable someone else, well. . . . The idea is that this will be-come more uncomfortable as I get hard, but that's the attraction.

Jerry: How do you keep it on?

Lenny: Well, you've got to realize that all of that kind of stuff has to do with how excited you are. And generally if you bought an item like that it's because it appeals to you. And if something like that appeals to you, the idea is that initially it should be tight. And also it stays on any-way because the first ring is a cock ring and that's already around every-thing and even if it's a loose cock ring . . . , the rest of the rings will do the job because you're excited by the fact that you've got this on, [and so] the likelihood is that it won't fall off.

Jerry: Before, you told me a cock ring story. Could you repeat it?

Lenny: I was going through the airport with a heavy cock ring and it came up on the security device. . . . There is very little I'm embarrassed about. Plus the fact that part of my turn-on—and this is not to do with exposing myself in the subway to 8-year-old little boys because 8-year-old little boys don't appeal to me in the least, in fact, I like men my age or older, but in the right situation, I can be a voyeur or an exhibitionist. Also, when asked even by the wrong person, [I'll say,] "Oh, gee, I want to look at that." And what happened at the airport was this woman was waving it [the security device] and I said, "It's my cock ring, would you care to see [it]?" And her reaction was, "No sir, you can go on through." For all she knew, it could have been a pistol. Which I thought was really rather funny. Actually, it wouldn't have affected me one way or the other, 'cause I just would have probably shown her my cock ring and just had gone [moved] on. But it wouldn't have bothered me, and I think my comfortableness with it seemed [to make her] feel [that] I don't look like [I'm] a bomb threat or something [like that]. . . . And I guess there aren't that many people that ballsy that would say, "This is a cock ring, do you want to look [at it]?"

Jerry: Has anyone ever gotten a metal cock ring on and been unable to get it off?

Lenny: Only in legend. . . . What I'm going to tell you now goes along with the headlines of, if you believe that there are alligators living [in the sewers] under New York City, you believe that the emergency room is filled with guys who had cock rings cut off. But I never knew someone [who went through that]. It's kind of like the old [saying], "If your head goes in . . . , you can get it out, 'cause however you got it in, you can reverse the process." It's even more so with a dick. A lot of people panic before orgasm because they are perceiving the cock ring, the tension, as pain. No, I'm not saying that people don't know what pain is, but sometimes a different sensation or a specific type of tightness will be perceived as discomfort. [But] it relates to that if you make it to orgasm your cock's going to go down . . . and you will have gotten past that discomfort area, that's where [some] people panic 'cause they have gotten to the feeling [where it] is unfamiliar and so therefore they don't get past that and then they begin to panic. The only things that I've heard is guys who say, "I put my cock into a sink of cold water until everything deflated." If they had gotten to the point of orgasm, they at least would have had a better time of it.

Jerry: Is it good to come while the passage [of the penis] is restricted? I've heard conflicting stories. Some people say it is not good to have an orgasm while your penis is restricted. Other people say it is fine, we do it all the time. What have you heard on this?

Lenny: The only thing I can say is that the only time the question comes up is if you want to be a father. Children are a consideration. You see a lot of times [when] you restrict certain vessels and certain vessels are kind of delicate, and if you restrict them for long amounts of time, you won't necessarily do yourself permanent damage, although if you have been doing that particular whatever for a long, long time, you might do yourself some small amount of vascular damage. I never consider those things because I never want to have children. To me, [it is] enough when I go visit my nieces and nephews. I'm glad, I don't want to raise them so I don't think about it.

Jerry: So you *can* do some damage?

Lenny: You know, probably small amounts of temporary damage.

Jerry: So you heard this one before?

Lenny: No, I just know that I do not know about anyone that has had physical damage that has been anything that has restricted him [in a sexual way]. . . . I am speculating that if there is a possibility of doing yourself some vascular damage with some veins and stuff like that. . . , somebody might be more delicate [and] . . . as far as fertility is concerned [it is because] . . . somehow these veins or capillaries have collapsed . . . and whether it's directly related I don't know. If you have some straight guy whose sex life has been very benevolent and it's happened, that means it's happened on its own. . . . Some people have circulatory problems and that [the penis] is part of the circulatory system.

Jerry: [Tell me about the] penis cage [pointing to one of several in a glass case].

Lenny: That's actually a male chastity device. . . . This is what can be referred to as a functional device. Now, what I mean by functional is that it will be uncomfortable if you get hard. It would make insertion impossible or at least very, very difficult. . . . And you can pee with it on, that's what I mean by functional. . . .

Jerry: What are some common misuses or misconceptions about the use of the stuff here [that you sell]?

Lenny: For instance, the gates of hell, people will ask me, "How do you fuck with that?" And my opinion is that you'd need a galvanized asshole for that. You know, it's not impossible. . . . I mean, I guess it's possible but I don't want to see the butt hole it actually goes into. . . . Anybody who isn't into heavy ass play thinks that using a large dildo is either ripping their intestines apart, loosening up rather than learning to relax, or generally don't have any more bowel function. . . .

Jerry: Not everybody's into everything.

Lenny: This is another one [misconception]. They [people who are not familiar with leather sex] think that everybody who is into S&M is into everything. The community is stated as [everyone who is into an] S&M leather fetish. There are people who are into the wearing of leather who would never raise a hand to slap a butt in their entire lives. There are people into fetish who never put on a piece of leather. There are people who are into a fetish but never go beyond to anything else. There are people who might try a little of everything. I might fall into that category, but not all things are good for everybody. Generally, you get into that high plain of sexual experimentation, the people tend to be extremely bright and intelligent and to suggest that everybody's into everything would mean that they're not selective and, therefore, I think that only people who are not selective are not intelligent because it means you haven't thought about it. If that makes sense. And one of the other things, we get a lot of tourists who wander in here, and say some husband and wife from Long Island or Iowa . . . , somehow have this . . . attitude, like, "No one knows me here so I can act like an asshole." So you'll have some wife who picks up a paddle or something and says something like, "It's my turn to hurt you." It [S&M] has nothing to do with that kind of pain. . . . It has to do with the fact that . . . , if they've either been with their lover or their wife and they're having a very passionate lovemaking and she slaps her hands against his hips or he slaps his hands against his lover's hips and the guy gets a real rush from that. . . . It's a lot different from somebody hurting somebody [else] for the sake of hurting [them]. It's like, "Oh, yeah, I'll hurt you." It's like I don't want to be hurt, thank you very much. I don't want anybody to hurt me, but have I ever had somebody slap my ass until I've gotten a bruise? Yeah, but it's not more esoteric than a hickey mark when you're 16. And that's a mark, and out of context that would hurt.

Jerry: About misconceptions, what's the difference between loosening someone up and learning to relax?

Lenny: What I was saying is the misconception that when people talk about the difference between wanting to relax or loosen somebody up and loosening muscular abilities, let's say. The difference is night and day. People think that people who play in a large way, meaning that people who play with larger dildos and stuff like that, the misconception is that they believe that they're able to accept these things, people who have the ability to do that have these big, stretched-out assholes. The truth is that the people who have the ability to do that have the mental and physical powers to know how to relax or how to have the right partner to give them the ability to loosen up. Did I explain that well?

Jerry: Yeah. What are some other general misconceptions that you've encountered?

Lenny: It fits into a lot of things. Well, there are people [who come] in here who think that being kinky and S&M-ish is putting on a cock ring, and they don't know how to do that and they just find out at the age of 21 or 31 or 41 or 51 or whatever that you put everything [your genitals] through [the rings]. And that the function of the cock ring is that . . .

it's gonna make the orgasm so incredible that you're not gonna wanna have sex any other way. No, it's just different. But everything is a matter of degrees. . . . What we're talking about is individual views. You know, everyone has different outlooks. Believe it or not, a lot of the construction of the items [we sell in this store, that is, sex toys] came from the Dark Ages and from the Victorian era. . . . [That is where] a lot of what is used today in . . . fetish wear [comes from], particularly for women who are kinky or fetishy. Corsets all come from the Victorian era and in fact, one woman's corset that we have is called a discipline corset. And it was called a discipline corset during the height of the Victorian era and the idea was that it would bring the waist down five inches from the natural waist. . . . It's something you have to train yourself for and it's a very particular type of fetish. . . .

Jerry: Have you heard any stories about people getting into a bondage belt and getting stuck [in it]?

Lenny: We warn people all the time when they buy handcuffs. I always say to people, "You know, there should always be two keys." I always say to people, "Keep one where you know it's accessible." Well, my finish to that line is, "Yes, I make house calls at four in the morning, but never to let you out." Most people laugh a lot [at that]. I have yet to get a house call at four in the morning, 'cause I wouldn't let them out. I might play with them for a while, but I wouldn't let them out. Some people are into—believe it or not—some extreme forms of self-bondage, and the one common story that I've heard from a couple of people, which I only became aware of about a year or so ago, [was] that there are people who get pleasure out of figuring out ways of tying themselves up and then trying to figure out how to get out. And one guy said he was lucky that his downstairs neighbor was friendly, and that he had to call him either by throwing things on the floor . . . because he once or twice had gotten himself in an embarrassing situation where he was all tied up and couldn't get out. The guy [his downstairs neighbor] was at least understanding. . . . To me that's a little bit frightening but only because there's no one in my building that I would want to have seen me tied up. Plus the fact that I can't imagine what it would be like to have to face anybody like that.

Jerry: Some of this stuff does sound pretty extreme and potentially dangerous. What makes you uncomfortable as far as going too far [is concerned]?

Lenny: Sometimes people will go to great lengths to study anatomy to see how far they can push the edges with themselves on very extreme levels. And part of the [S&M] community is stretching levels but some of it goes further than I am comfortable with. Like, there are certain people that are into breath control . . . , [who are into] restricting it with a rope or something. It's really dangerous and it's really out there on the edge and it's something that I really don't know anything, or enough, about. I think that I would have to know more about it than a doctor would [in order for me to participate in it]. But I also had those same people say to me that when they orgasmed that way, that it was incredible. I'm just hoping that it's not their last [orgasm]. They say it's supposed to be the most supreme orgasm you'll have. . . . I have pretty incredible orgasms now. I think I'll stick with those.

Jerry: In my travels, I have noticed *Grey's Anatomy* and other [such] reference books on S&Mers' shelves. I see you sell anal pleasure and health. I've been told that some knowledge of anatomy is important, especially if you're into assplay. What neat points of anatomy have you picked up?

Lenny: You don't have to be into S&M to be into fisting. In fact, there are a lot of people who would, by the standards of the [straight world] be considered vanilla. Vanilla is a street term for [conventional and] run-of-the-mill. . . . Taking a major amount of drugs . . . is really not the way to do it. You have to learn a little bit about anatomy because you learn what certain things are. For instance, if someone has a teeny tear [in the rectum], they can have what seems like a surprising amount of blood. But [that's] . . . because of where it is. There's a difference between that and the need to get to the hospital, which is hopefully rare.

Jerry: How can you tell the difference between a tear in the lining [of the rectum] and a puncture that might cause peritonitis?

Lenny: You would have great amounts of what you would perceive as severe abdominal cramping and pain. And also, the blood flow continues. You're not going to die immediately. But these situations, I'm telling you, are seemingly rare, but it's good to know about them . . . to take care of yourself as the bottom or to take care of yourself because you care about the bottom.

Jerry: You told me before when you had your nipples pierced that it was a spiritual experience. What did you mean?

Lenny: I understand the need for rites of passage. When I got my nipples pierced, it came out of a deep fear, that one of the reasons that I wanted to do it was because it frightened me so much. . . . I had some major mouth surgery and I made it through that and that to me was like, it had to be done and there was no question [about it being done]. There was no one saying you have the option [to have it or not have it]. . . . If I can survive that, and if some of the worst pain you can sustain is in your mouth, I could certainly take a needle in my nipple. When they do it they do it with a surgical needle, which is not like a sewing needle, it's like a razor. And when they do it, it's so fast, it's faster than a human breath. . . . And when I did it I had a great spiritual sense of myself. I'm not religious in the traditional sense 'cause I don't go to church, but I do believe in a higher power.

Jerry: So this was a transcendental experience?

Lenny: I'm very aware of the focus of light. In the Indian philosophies, [they] have the center of light that comes from here [points to his forehead], so they put a dot here. I've always seen that. I can see in my focus, it's like I look at life almost through a tunnel and the tunnel is usually so full of light it's incredible, but when the needle went through my nipple, that light went [holds his hands out in front of him to indicate a widening then contracting circle] this way and then came down to normal size again and, oh, I giggled, I laughed, one leg kicked out, and all this stuff.

Jerry: Since I've started this research, I've seen guys with extremely large nipples. I mean eraser-sized. Can you expand male nipples?

Lenny: Yes, there are several ways. One is to use a snake bite kit. . . . In these . . . kits they have little cylindrical rubber things . . . that come with a tourniquet, a little vial of iodine, and these two suction cups, because the idea is that you're supposed to suck out the poison. But they're big enough to fit over nipples and they really work. But you have to do it fairly consistently. Some people use them in their foreplay 'cause they feel good too. Well, if you do use them like once a month, you're not going to get larger nipples. If you do them pretty regularly, whether you play with yours or another partner's, then you get results.

Jerry: Do they stay that way?

Lenny: Eventually they enlarge permanently. Another way is having your nipples pierced, that permanently enlarges the nipples. Yeah, because you pierce into the areola and that becomes nipple. And even if I got rid of my rings tomorrow, my nipples would always remain bigger. And lastly is the pump. Because it's an extreme version of the snakebite kit, it creates an extremely high vacuum and although it will exaggerate them, eventually they will always go back to something bigger than what you had before.

Jerry: What are the major differences between the leather community and the gay community at large?

Lenny: There is a difference [between the gay community and the straight community] and it seems that is why some people are attracted to the gay community initially. . . . I can talk about this personally and directly. When I was 21—and the attraction of youth has prevailed since man has walked the earth—my attraction [to] the gay icon initially [was to] the leathery type . . . called [the] clone. It was a man in a pair of Levis, leather jacket, pair of black boots, moustache, maybe a beard and short haircut. The man who usually fit this image [and] who got it together [was] . . . at least 30 [years] or over. And a lot of these people [aren't able to grow a full beard until they are a little older]. . . . You can't grow that great moustache until later in life and . . . your skin gets clearer and you're over that anxiousness and that *Angst* and usually [you] get to a point that . . . to the world you are showing at least outwardly to the world [some] self-confidence. Self-confidence can be really attractive. And then comes the physical part of the attraction. . . .What seems to prevail in certain parts of the community is men who like heavier men, who are called "bears." The fashion right now is men are shaving themselves but there is still that whole faction of men who want hair all over their bodies because they feel it's the ultimate of masculinity. . . . [In addition, there is a segment of the gay community] . . . who like older men. And it's something because those who prize youth still grow older and still have [a sex life]. When I was in my 20s and early 30s [I was told that] you'll like younger men as you get older [but] those things will change. The only thing that has happened is that now I'm in the age group I like. I think I'm hotter now at 37 than I was at 21. I do realize how youth has its beauty and I can admire beautiful youth and I can understand [that men who are fashion models] . . . are beautiful, and we get model-like men who use this [their youth and beauty] as a lifestyle . . . because they go to clubs [and they are considered attractive by the men in the clubs] . . . but they are almost like one-dimensional in my eyes. And that kind of feeling seems to be more accepted within the gay S&M fetish [scene]. . . . [Some men in the gay community] like heavy men [but] you don't find that generally. [In general, this is] . . . a very youth-oriented community. You should be thin and pretty.

Jerry: Is there a correlation between youth and age and tops and bottoms?

Lenny: Sometimes in the classic sense, yeah, because a top can be an older man. . . . [But] it can also be non-chronological . . . I'm in a situation where I'm younger [although] I'm the more dominant [partner] in my personal relationship. . . . People who look at us who do not know how to read the symbols will see a youngish [man with] . . . a very good-looking [older] man, but you can notice an age difference. . . . People that can't read the signs think that he is the dominant [partner]. And he will proudly brandish to anyone who might be listening that he is a card-carrying bottom. . . .

Jerry: In the past, were there restrictive subcultural rules about what tops and bottoms were supposed to do? Did you have an apprenticeship as a bottom?

Lenny: Yeah, that's what I did. . . . For the first half of my relationship with my first lover . . . , I was a great bottom. I wouldn't mind trying that again. I also learned what I needed. He also was someone who was even more of a bottom than I am emotionally but he was very smart because he told me—he showed me through physical pleasure—what he wanted for himself. . . . I love the male ass. I adore the male ass and he had a great one. It was really hot-looking, hot to play with, it was just hot. And I would turn around and his thing was he would play; as I've said, I like the male ass, I like others and, as much as I like others, I like my own, and physically and emotionally, he would dominate me, and as a kind of reward, he would submit to me playing with his. And he admitted he would like to get me to the point of making me come in the other situations where I would throw this furious, passionate fuck in his direction. 'Cause our relationship was more of a mental dominance rather than a physical one. . . . He might hold my hands down, but there wasn't any heavy physical bondage. And what I mean by mental [is that] nothing was torturous as far as, there was never a line that was crossed where it was like, no, I don't want to do that, it was all, you know, verbal and stuff like that. But it was considered on both sides to be very exciting. . . .

Jerry: [Where I live], we had a handkerchief code that's going out of style, light blue for bottoms, dark blue for tops, black for leather. I hear that in the leather community, there are signs that break what people are down even further.

Lenny: Yeah. The codes. That's either called coding or flagging. . . . Generally, anything worn on the right is passive or bottom, anything worn on the left is active or top. Now, when I say anything, that doesn't mean that bottoms have to suddenly start wearing their wrist watches on the right hand. No one cares about wrist watches. It can be such things as keys. It can be a lot of things.

Jerry: Do people still follow it in the general gay community?

Lenny: No. It's fallen out of favor. It kind of went by the wayside. I think it's really kind of a real cool way of identifying each other. It's still very strong in the leather community. As for right or left nipple, some people [in the leather community] will do things like that because they want the symbol. [It refers to the fact that] they are strictly top, they are strictly bottom. Some people just do it, they want the thing on the right or the left nipple because it's a fashion preference. . . . I myself got both nipples done because it was the balance. I'd walk funny [with just one nipple pierced]. When it comes to a nipple some people will use that as a symbol. [But] for other people it isn't a symbol. It might work out that they got the right one done and they might be a bottom, but they didn't think it through. . . . They did it and said, well, do this nipple, that's the one I want [to have pierced] because people are right-handed or this is their favorite nipple, therefore they want to gift it with a piercing. It could be for many reasons. [But still] the flagging or what is the showing of colors or stuff like that is still strong in the leather community.

Jerry: Is there any leather item that conveys top or bottom from a glance?

Lenny: A whip or a paddle. You can carry a whip or a paddle on the right or the left. If you're wearing it on the right, it means I want you to use my paddle on me. If you're wearing it on the left, I want to spank you or whip you. [In the past] it would have been thought, there were times when I would hear from people, and I think it had to do with people who didn't know any better, that bottoms wore chaps. Because one of the showpieces is a pair of chaps that reveal the crotch and the ass, and it really emphasizes the butt. But I'm here to tell you that if there were people who believed that, it went by the wayside. . . . There are also people who feel that full body harnesses should mainly be worn, depending on the style, by the bottom. Particularly if it has a center strap. Because the center strap goes up the crack of the ass, and some people are so into the machismo of top they don't want anything up their ass, even a piece of leather. . . . The only thing that I can think of in leather that's strictly a bottom thing is a collar. You don't wear a collar if you're a top. . . . A lot of the stuff, whether it's top or bottom, would be how the individual portrays it. . . . I find rules really having to do with how one perceives oneself and what they project when they're wearing it. If someone puts an item on and says, oh, I think that only a dominant man can wear this, then he can't wear it [if he's not a dominant]. Because if he doesn't see himself as a dominant man who could wear that, it becomes the old adage about clothing. You have to wear the clothing, it can't wear you. It's like the woman in a fabulous evening gown. If she doesn't have confidence to wear that fabulous evening gown, she can't wear it because she'll look like the dress is wearing her. It's the same thing in leather. It has to do with how you wear it, how you feel when you wear it. If you feel like the most fabulous top . . . or the most wonderful bottom in it, then that's what you'll project. . . .

Jerry: Tell me about the mating ritual in bars.

Lenny: Well, I look for those flags and the signs. I have some very specific interests. I'm into fisting, so I sometimes look for a red hankie. If I'm not looking for anything in particular, they have to at least have a light blue hankie. Or any other flags if it doesn't have to lead to ass play specifically to see if they're of interest. Hopefully, they're wearing things on the right [indicating that they are a bottom]. It's nice if we can make eye contact. I kind of like to talk to somebody. Part of the leather community is in the fact that those people who function really well, they put stuff right on the table because likes and dislikes and wants are very specific and a lot of people feel really angry if you waste [their] time and if you end up going home with someone who says something and they're not into it and they can't function in the sphere, it can be really frustrating. And hopefully if that happens, you get somebody who is at least understanding that you might be dealing with a novice. This way, if you're into teaching somebody, you can get off on that, but if you're not into it, at least you're not wasting an entire night. . . . I'm in a relationship but it's open and . . . I'm right up front in my conversation. [I say] well, I have a lover and he's first. And generally I'm not usually going home with people. . . . But I also don't wanna get you home and hear you're not up for ass play and I just thought you would go home with me because you thought I was hot looking. That's crap, and I don't need any games like that. You know, or we can't go to my house because I'm out cheating on my lover and I don't want him to know. If I'm out at night and I am in a situation where I'm going to find some-body, we can go some place and play. I'm not keen to know your entire life's history. I mean, I'm gonna know a little bit about you. I'm also gonna showcase you around the bar a little. Let everyone in the world see you be-cause I don't want to be going home with a maniac, either. You know, but in general I'd like to acquire some kind of eye contact because a lot of times, eye contact will be the first thing that gives you an indication that you can approach. Being more dominant, I don't leave this stuff to other people to try [to determine the nature of the action]. A lot of people are frightened in a social setting [to reveal themselves sexually]. I think this is the same, straight or gay, and it's unfortunate that straight men are not al-lowed to be more submissive socially, 'cause I think there are some women who would [take the initiative and] go up to somebody. But in general, it's top and bottom. I don't need to have the bottom come up to me. It creates an interesting scene if he does, you know, it's kind of nice if he comes up to me and says, "Sir, I'd like to serve you," or something like that, whatever he might say. That's hot, you know, especially if he's really cute. . . . But for me, it starts with eye contact. But I look for very basic stuff. His body, does he have a nice butt? It's rare that I'm in a bottom situation, [so] it's not al-ways important to me how big his dick is. It's nice if it is. 'Cause it's nice to look at if I am dominating him in some fashion. Because it's [more] fun to watch a large phallus respond than a small one, but I don't particularly care. It's an odd thing to say in the gay community. I might care, but it's been a rare instance where it's minute or tiny. Most people are average.

Jerry: Tell me more on the mating ritual. Tell me more about hook-ing up in a bar.

Lenny: Rituality starts with eye contact. It can be with a gesture. It can be sometimes the raise of an eyebrow. It's almost the same thing as the flirtation can be for a man and a woman. It can be a bumping into somebody. If you're cruising somebody in a bar, it depends on what [sig-nals or cues] you pick up. . . . You get sexual vibes from a person and the person maintains something in their stance that says I'm open to this. It's almost like the dance of a certain species of birds. You just know that this other bird is ready for your dance and you can saunter up [to him]. Sometimes as aggressive [a move] in a leather situation as, you can literally brush up against them or grab their butt, or whatever. Usually it's not that invasive though. But it's enough so that after you have gotten the raised eyebrow or the look, I can only show you that I can look at you, and then if you're not interested, you can do one of these [looks off in the other direction], like, oh, I'm really not interested in you, don't come near me. For whatever reason, whatever the thing is about me that doesn't appeal to him. But if you get it and they kind of look and, you kind of do an up and down and maybe give a smile or a smirk, you know, and that might say, yeah, I'm open to the possibility of this. And you walk up and you generally say something as mundane as hello, how are you? You then go through the niceties, you know, nice day. I'm an inveterate flirt. . . . I can say, nice day . . . , and if I look up and look down and I look you square in the eye, [I'm flirting]. Also, I'm not afraid to do little things that are considered kind of effeminate. I wink. That flips people out. I like to kind of catch 'em off guard a little bit. . . . It's kind of like, yeah, I know what you want, you don't have to tell me. And it's also, it provides a little bit of a giggle, it provides a little bit of humiliation, and that can be kind of cute and fun in a sexual excitement kind of way. You're dealing with just basic sexual things rather than [specifically] S&M things. . . . After you've passed [talking about the subject of] the weather, and you've passed what his name is, [let's say it's] Tom, and you hope you remember that [his name] in the conversation. You've passed, gee, you're really kinda cute. [Then you go on to ask] what do you like, Tom? If it's [a] typical conversation, he'll say, well, I like a lot of things. And you kind of try in a nice way to kind of zero down just a little bit. And say, well, I'm into bondage. Oh, are you into heavy bondage or light bondage? And I like to be spanked. Do you like to be spanked or do you want to be flogged? There's a difference. And, ah, do you want some of your limits tested? Can I do that for you? But most of it is the same . . . thing that has prevailed since man has walked on the earth and has been attracted to someone else. It's just faster in the gay community [than in the straight community]. It's faster if you're vanilla [that is, if you do not have unusual sexual preferences]. It's just faster. Men react faster. Men have no problem with the sexual. That's not true, men do have problems with the sexual but they have no problems approaching the sexual. It's the relationship later that might be a problem. But that's a whole 'nother story.

CHAPTER 11

I have no money, no job, no scholarship, and I'm depressed. . . . Because I can't understand how God would let me get into a situation where there are people who are insensitive, you know, to Him. Because I think that God was really inspiring me to do this. . . . I thought, maybe . . . God has abandoned me. As result, I figured, well, maybe . . . I shouldn't . . . trust God any more. . . . So I hung around here. And at that time . . . , there was a strong communistic-socialistic-revolutionary type movement here. I was hostile and angry, so I got involved. . . . But I could never be fully committed to that because they didn't believe in God, you know, and I couldn't completely get rid of God.

Sam

Sam, Defender of the Downtrodden[1]

Sam is a large man, well over 200 pounds. He wears a gray sweatshirt and gray sweatpants. Dreadlocks sprout from his head, and one strand of his gray beard falls to his chest. Although when I interviewed him, he was just a few months short of his 60th birthday, he exuded an aura of impishness that belied his age. He often chuckled or laughed out loud at statements that summed up the many years of foibles, absurdities, and injustices he felt he had been forced to endure. When Sam speaks, the listener senses he is extending an invitation of camaraderie. In our interview, he was never coy, evasive, or reticent with me and he answered my ques-

201

tions readily, at length, seemingly without reserve or inhibition. If Sam chose to conceal something, he was open and up-front about it.

"One of my goals is to fight against poverty," Sam asserts. "I connect with the soup kitchens for that reason. I have a friend, a mentor, a millionaire at Brown University named Feinstein, who's going to contribute a million dollars of his own money to help the soup kitchens." Sam can't recall Feinstein's first name.

Sam is asked where he slept last night. "I was hiding," he answers in his deep yet soft baritone. "I'm not going to tell you." A sly smile plays on his lips. "It's a secret. If I told you, it wouldn't be a secret any more." When asked about his usual sleeping arrangements, Sam becomes voluble. He is explicit and detailed about his options. Sometimes, undergraduates he's made friends with allow him to sleep in a vacant dorm room. Or he'll bed down on a couch in the lounge of a dormitory. Occasionally, Sam says, he'll "find a nice classroom and scribble on the board. Then I'll turn out the lights and sleep there. On the floor." He uses the library from time to time, but if the campus police discover him there, they kick him out. "Sometimes I've slept on top of a building. They told us we couldn't sleep *in* the building, so. . . ." Sam chuckles about his liberal interpretation of the rules. "There used to be tunnels underneath Central Hall and we used to sometimes hang out there."

"Who's *we?*" he is asked.

"Some of the people I hang out with. Haitians, Jamaicans. I'd rather not get any more specific than that," he answers.

Since they figure so prominently in his stories, one senses Sam has a problem with the campus police. He describes an encounter he had with the police more than two decades ago. It set the tone for his relations with security over the years. It seems he was looking for a student. "I walked into the wrong room. I walked into the room of a girl who was into witchcraft. God woke me up and sent me to the room of someone who was into witchcraft. And security came in and kicked me out. They accused me of stealing. It's really insane, because I wasn't trying to steal. I just wanted to get an education. I don't have to steal—God gives me everything." His shaky relations with campus police began, he says, when he "went into that room by mistake."

Sam elaborates. "When I started using my staff ID, Greg Waddle [spokesperson for the campus police] started showing up and told me that I couldn't use it. I took it as a personal vendetta against me by Waddle."

Later, I called Officer Waddle, who denies the charge. "He's speaking a lot of fantasy when he says that. First of all, he's not a staff member and so, he's not entitled to use a staff card. If he has staff status, he's welcome to use a staff card. But as far as I know, at no time when he's used a staff ID has he been a staff member. Second," Officer Waddle continues, "I have never shown up when he's tried to use a staff card." When asked why the campus police should bother with Sam in the first place, Waddle is specific. "There were concerns expressed to us by some members of the campus community. Some people have called us and asked, 'Who is this man? What is he doing here?' Some people work in labs at one in the morning. . . . People have seen him in places they feel he shouldn't be. They have concerns. We have to respond to their concerns."

Waddle pauses to contemplate Sam's presence on the university campus. "I do not know why he is attracted to the university. I've been here 22 years and Sam preceded me on this campus. At times, Sam has been a student and most of the time he hasn't. It appears that he has made the campus his home. His sleeping in lounges causes our office concerns, as it does other members of the campus community. We're trying to advance the concept of team policing, which is to get the whole community involved."

I decide to play the devil's advocate. "Let's say for the purpose of argument," I begin, "and I'm not trying to take sides, I'm just trying to get a sense of who Sam is and how he fits into the university community, let's say at some point, the police, when they are told about Sam's presence, they say, oh, that's just Sam doing his thing."

"Well," Officer Waddle begins, "we do get calls from people who are concerned, who question his presence here. We would not be doing our job if we did not respond to their concerns. May I also say that there have been times when we've also responded to Sam's complaints. For instance, if someone has thrown out his papers, we've tried to do something about that. But frankly," Officer Waddle says, trying to slam the door on Sam's presence on the university campus, "I don't know why he's here. I know why I'm here, I know why you're here, but I don't know why Sam is here."

Once again, to elicit a response, I take Sam's position. "He says he's trying to live simply and humbly to work for progressive causes."

"Well, he has been allowed to stay," responds Officer Waddle. "There are people who help him. We only respond to requests from people who are concerned about his presence on the campus. As far as my showing up when he's tried to use a bogus staff ID, that's fantasy." I sense the interview is over and I thank Officer Waddle for his time.

Sitting in a second-floor TV lounge in the Student Union, Sam describes how he came to end up living on the State University campus. He was born and grew up in New Orleans. He lived in a neighborhood that boasted a half-dozen churches and a bar. These institutions were significant in his life, he explains. "We had the struggle between good and evil in our neighborhood. You either went to church or you went to the bar. My family chose to be Christian. I grew up not drinking, fornicating, dancing, or gambling. It was the Southern Baptist way." His laugh is deep, rumbling, rich.

Sam attended Dillard, Xavier, and Loyola universities in New Orleans, but dropped out before he graduated, then did a three-year stint in the Air Force. After his discharge, he worked at a variety of jobs, including off-shore navigation. In 1972, he won a scholarship to go to a monastery in France. "They help young people make a commitment to God," he explains. "The brothers there listened to young people and found out that they were concerned with the world's problems." During the fellowship, Sam tells me, "I had a dream about these gigantic gates, and the name 'LOYOLA' ran across the top of the gates." During that summer, while on a sojourn to Rome, Sam says, he "made a commitment to God." The following fall, he returned to college, at Southern University and, after graduating in June, 1973, Sam entered a Jesuit seminary. Less than a year later, as a novice, he began teaching high school students. "I was doing things that were disturbing to the community I was in. You know, they weren't ready for it."

"What would be an example of something you did that the community didn't like?" Sam is asked.

"Well, I was teaching the Scriptures and I had designed a course called 'Facing the Problems of Racism.' I asked the question, can you be a Christian and a racist [at the same time]? When my students started looking at the issue—I didn't tell them what to think—I gave them examples from the Scriptures to give them an idea as to how to look at this [issue]. And many of them came to the conclusion that they couldn't [be both at the same time]. And some of them started dating one another, you know, a young [white] lady had dated Africans because her father had been in the petroleum industry in Nigeria, and she had been dating African men, and she dated this [Black] guy and they actually went out into this Southern town and [laughs] even though it was supposed to be integrated, it never did [laughs]. In the public high school where I worked, they still had [racially] separate clubs, and the school was supposed to be integrated. So the priests called me in. They wanted to know what was I doing, what was I teaching. And so I showed them the Bible [laughs heartily] and they said, well, we can't have this happening. In this town, these people aren't ready for this. And so, the next thing I know, some bullets were flying by my head. And I called the sheriff and he says, 'Well, they weren't trying to kill you, they were just trying to warn you. People in this area, they're good shots. They don't miss.' [We both laugh.] Thank you, sheriff, I needed that." [Laughs.]

The warning had its intended effect: Sam left the seminary and abandoned his aspiration of becoming a priest. He claims his superiors told him he was "too recent a convert" to become a successful candidate for ordination.

Sam continued to work in off-shore navigation and, during shore leaves, he returned to New Orleans and hung out with the students at Xavier University. There, he met a faculty member and a graduate student from the sociology department at State University, which was intent on recruiting African-American graduate students. "They invited me to go to State. They said all those nice things [laughs] and I said I would consider it. I gave them my work number, and one day, somebody from the university called me. And the boss starts freaking out, he figured maybe I was going to quit and go to school. [Laughs.] Which he didn't like very much. And he sent me out on the boat with this guy who was a crazy ex-Marine. [Laughs.] This guy would go into bars and start fights. Anywhere in the world! [Laughs.] And we're on this boat and we hit some 12-foot waves, and we're going over the waves [laughs] and I'm seasick, I had never been on anything like that before. And one of my so-called friends told this guy how much money I was making. I have a college degree and he has a high school diploma. And so I'm making more money than he's making. And he's my trainer, which was not good. I should never have said anything to my friend. He asked me about my salary and I was foolish enough to tell him. So he went and told this guy, the Marine. So he goes into a rage and decides that he has to kill me. And he said it! He said it twice! [Laughs.] And I heard him! So I went and confronted him right then while we were on the boat. And he said, 'Is that all you have to say?' And he walks away. So I called our supervisor and I said 'I do not want to work with this guy, I think he has a mental problem.' And so I left the station. That guy was serious. And so my boss fired me. [Laughs.] Yeah, he fired me."

"Was the guy who threatened you a big guy?" I ask.

"Naw, he wasn't that big. That's what one of the other guys I worked with said, you coulda killed him. Just kill him and throw him out to the sharks. [I laugh.] Yeah, that's what he told me. You know. Which coulda happened. When we were out on the boat, we went swimming. Beautiful water. We were in an area where there were sharks, and so one of us would always keep an eye out [for the sharks] while the other one was swimming. Well, if you don't like your partner, some day you may see a shark, you just turn your back. [Laughs.] You know, I figured, if I could do it to him, he could do it to me. So I decided I didn't want to work with him. You want to work with somebody you trust."

"So you got fired."

"I got fired." [Laughs.]

Sam entered State University in the Fall of 1974. He lived in a lay Catholic community in New Jersey, conducted a survey for them, and attended graduate school on a two-day-a-week basis. He said that, after the survey, he was going to "build a Christian community in that neighborhood. They have an organization that developed after that called Brothers and Sisters in Christ. Well, I was going to do that for that parish, which would include Protestants, Catholics, everybody—Brothers and Sisters in Christ. It would be a community of love." Sam claimed that when he showed his parish priest what he was doing, the priest "got jealous and said 'I can't have you do both. Either you do the parish work or you go to school.'" So, Sam says, he chose to concentrate on graduate school. He began working with a faculty member who received a "better offer" from the University of Chicago. "I think Bishop Cody did that," he opines. Elaborating, he explains that Bishop Cody "was responsible for my getting a scholarship to Rome and I think he wanted me to come to Chicago and work, and so he brought my teacher onto a project he wanted me to work at the University of Chicago. I should have followed but I didn't." Sam didn't explain why he didn't and I didn't ask him. Not long after, he was defunded and he ran out of money. A semester later, he stopped taking courses.

At that point, he explains, "I got spaced out. I just couldn't work any more because I had received too many disappointments. The priest kicks me out of the rectory, I ran out of money, my professor leaves. And he gives me a bad evaluation."

"Really?" I ask. "Why?"

"When I was TAing for [this particular professor], there were about 300 students in the class, and I taught them how to read. I took a speed-reading course at Loyola. Evelyn Woods. I read between 1100 and 10,000 words a minute. At the seminary, I taught them the techniques of speed-reading. It really motivated my students to read. The next class, they were told by the students and their parents that the previous class's students had never read so much. They wanted me to come back for that reason. But I decided [to do] other things. I tried the same thing here. So [the professor] gave me the opportunity to have them read the books on a list. I broke them up into groups. Showed them how to read the books, how to share the material. Once they shared the materials I put together, they went back and read it again and discussed it, then made a presentation before the class. And it worked. But [this professor] marked me down. . . . He found out the students had learned so much that he changed the whole test. And he gave them a test only on his notes. He gave me a key to mark it. I did exactly what he told me. And then he changed everything. And then he marked me down. He told me I was a hard worker but I was not too bright." [Laughs heartily.]

Sam feels his evaluation was unjustified. He says he sued the sociology department. "The Justice Department told me to negotiate," he explains, "so I went back and negotiated. They held a meeting and told me that they were going to get rid of me. One prof in particular prejudiced the other ones in the department so that they decided that they weren't going to work with me or put money into me. I'm not saying it was for racist reasons, but it hurt me. It hurt my pride and my self-esteem."

Sam contemplates his loss. "I had lived for a time off-campus, but I wanted to live on the campus with the students. Which was more like it would have been if I had become a Jesuit, because at Loyola, most of the priests live right on the campus. They're a part of the campus community, and they're always available to the students. They give retreats, the younger guys play sports with the students, they go on trips, they take a group of students and go to Europe. They really get involved in their lives. And I wanted to have that kind of community, so I wanted to live on the campus. But it never really worked out like that. . . . There were some other forces guiding me. I believe God was guiding my seminary experience a lot more than I've experienced here on this campus."

"So, you were a student in the sociology department for about a year and a half," I begin, formulating a question, "and at that point, you weren't a student and you didn't have any means of support. So what happened then?"

"I had no means of support. . . . Somehow, my rent money vanished and I couldn't pay the bill. I had the receipts on my desk and a letter from my grandfather, and one day, I was coming from class and I saw these two guys locking my door. And I confronted them and one of them said he was going to become my roommate. I said I never heard anything like that, I have a single room. I went to the quad office and the guy there said he didn't know anything about it. By then, these guys had vanished. That Friday the people from the housing office asked me for my housing money. I said, what do you mean my housing money? I paid you. And they said, no, I hadn't. And so I look for the receipts, and there's no receipts. Plus, the letter from my grandfather, that's gone. My grandfather wanted me to research the mortgage premiums. For the insurance. I was supposed to get it back. So they wanted me to pay them again. I said no, no, no, I'm not going to pay you any more. So I wrote to Mr. Berke. Mr. Berke was one of the engineers for the Superdome. When we surrounded the government, when we had the student strike, I was standing right next to the government, and I asked Mr. Berke to come to the university to take a look at what was going on there so that he could remember the promises that they had made to the university."

I'm having a hard time following Sam's train of thought, but I nod anyway and say "yeah" from time to time.

"And in the meantime," Sam continues, "I said, we need something in New Orleans, you know, like they have in Dallas, the Astrodome [which is actually in Houston], we need something like an Astrodome in New Orleans. When I was growing up, we had Pelican Stadium, which was about 10 blocks from my house. And they tore the stadium down and got rid of the Pelicans. They did that basically because they didn't want to integrate. And they tore the stadium down [laughs]. It just destroyed me. You know, they tore it down and they built some kind of a hotel. I mean, it hurt a *lot* of people. . . . So I asked the governor during the time that we were demonstrating, and he put a commission together and they got the Superdome [in New Orleans]. And Mr. Berke was one of the people that worked on the Superdome, he designed it."

I'm wondering where this is going and what its connection is with Sam's rent money. "So Mr. Berke helped me with the rent," Sam finally says. "And I showed the people at the housing office the cancelled check to try to prove I had paid the bill. When I brought the cancelled check to them, I said, look, I paid you. They said, well, that check doesn't prove anything. All it proves is that you cashed a check. Because they wanted to take the whole check and send it to Albany and then I'd have to wait for the money to come back. And I said, no way, I'm not going to do that. You know, so I cashed the check and gave them the money. But when it got back to Mr. Berke, they decided that I couldn't have any control over what I do with the money, so they cut it off."

"So what happened then?" Sam is asked.

"So I was losing my teaching assistantship. I ran out of money. Actually, I was having some problems with [one professor in particular] when I came here. The first eight days. But I'm not sure it was him. It might have been some people in the department who were, you know, after me. But [a graduate student] comes to me and tells they had a meeting on me and they said that I shouldn't remain in sociology, that the school of social welfare was more appropriate for me. In the meantime, I'm hooked on this project with Father Fichter, I'm going to do the thing on institutional racism, and I wanted to do social psychology. I was going to study what's called institutional stress. So, what happened was that I have no money from Mr. Berke, I have no money from the university, and I have no housing from the university or from the parish. And now everything is gone."

"So what happened then?" I ask.

"I got very disillusioned. Because [prior to this, all my life], I've thought that God is leading me toward a goal. You know, I went to Rome, I met Bishop Sheen, I meet him in Rome and he prays over me, next thing I know, I get a scholarship, and I was also offered a scholarship at Boston University. I went there through Father Cohen's charismatic leadership thing. I went to Boston University to a charismatic prayer meeting. Actually, Father Cohen gave enough money to go across America to decide what I wanted to do. He gave me a vacation so I could travel. I bought a bus ticket and travelled for 30 days. I went to Boston University, talked with the chaplain, and he offered me a full scholarship, a job, and an opportunity to be ordained in two years. I could have gone to Boston University for one year, studied philosophy, worked as a chaplain and then I would have gone to Catholic University for one year to study theology. And the end of the year of theology, I would have been ordained a priest. And then I came and checked the State University out. I prayed and talked to Sister Mary Mathias. And I realized that the thing God wants me to do is to be at State."

I wonder why but don't ask. Never question God's wisdom, I remind myself.

"I had met the governor of the state of Washington. I met him at a governor's conference in New Orleans. I went to the conference because of my trip to Rome. I was in a little team and we made commitments to do something for God. One of the guys there was an organizer for the governor's conference and he invited me to attend and so there, I met Jimmy Carter [former President of the United States], George Wallace [former Governor of Alabama, now deceased, once a staunch segregationist, later an advocate of integration], and a whole bunch of people, and that's how I got to go to Boston University and be offered a scholarship there. I met Governor Evans at the governor's conference, and he invited me to come to Seattle, Washington, he told me I could get a car and a place to live. [Laughs.] And I had a chance to go to school there."

"But you came here," I state, still wondering why.

"Yeah, so I came here." [Laughs.]

"And so what happened after that? OK, you don't have a TA, your money runs out. . . ."

"I have no money, no job, no scholarship [laughs] and I'm depressed. And I can't get into working. I can't get into working on any of my projects. Because I can't understand how God would let me get into a situation where there are people who are insensitive [laughs], you know, to Him. [Laughs.] Because I think that God was really inspiring me to do this [the particular path he had chosen]. And it was really something, because when I was praying to determine what I was going to do with my life, I went to Louisville, Kentucky, and I stayed at Father Merton's hermitage. Which I had had a vision of before I got there, about six months before I got there. I got taught something about the tree of life. Father Merton had worked in Harlem. And all these things were saying that I ought to be working here. All kinds of things happened that were leading me to Harlem. But I wouldn't take it. Because I got here and it didn't work out, and I thought, maybe I missed God or God has abandoned me. [Laughs.] As a result, I figured, well, maybe I shouldn't do anything, I shouldn't trust God any more." [Laughs.]

"And so?" he is asked.

"So I hung around here. And at that time [the mid-1970s], the atmosphere was like, there was a strong communistic-socialistic-revolutionary type movement here. I was hostile and angry, so I got involved."

"Was that the Red Balloon?" [a small radical-anarchist group that was active on the State University campus between the late 1960s and the 1990s].

"Yeah, the Red Balloon. You know, Mitch Cohen and his group. But I could never be fully committed to that because they didn't believe in God [laughs], you know, and I couldn't completely get rid of God. Yeah, I was angry, but I couldn't get rid of God because I've had too many experiences. I was supposed to die the day I was born, in 1940. I was supposed to die the same day. Babies in the same hospital having the same procedure done were killed, and I lived. You know. And my mother says I lived because three women prayed for me and got in touch with God and God answered them and healed me. So, I just can't abandon God. Then when I went into the seminary, I had religious experiences. And even though I had the negative experiences happen, I still have religious experiences that would not allow me to give up on God. You know, but when I was in high school, the things that I wrote, I believe God was telling them to me. You know, President [John F.] Kennedy answered the article I wrote in high school. He answered it by saying in his inaugural address that a torch has been passed to a new generation of Americans. He said that the work of God must become the work of men. That was the answer that I was looking for. And then I really got hung up on him. . . . He challenged that entrenched power base, so they got rid of him."

I decide not to challenge his conspiracy theory, although the use of the impersonal "they" always makes me feel uncomfortable.

"At that same time, I went to my master sergeant and I told him, 'They're going to kill the President, I think they're going to kill him in New Orleans.' The President was passing right down the same street where I went to school. And I thought they were going to kill him. They didn't kill him when he went to New Orleans, but I got put on KP [kitchen patrol, such as peeling potatoes or washing dishes]. I got punished for even saying that [the President was about to be killed]. Next thing, the President's dead. Then, I understood what his inaugural address said. I felt a part of it. Then, he's dead. And then, I feel I'm supposed to do something religious. Then, I start doing it and then, all of a sudden, shoosh! The rug is pulled completely from under my feet."

Except for brief trips elsewhere, Sam has resided, without a fixed address, for 25 years on the State University campus. How has he managed to live during that period of time? I ask him.

"I'll tell you how I've lived. I have done research. You see that right there?" Sam explains, pointing to a shopping cart parked in the corner of the room, filled with boxes. "Those are all books that I've collected. I used to have a lot of papers in there but now, I don't get the papers as much as I used to, I used to get different papers every day, the *Wall Street Journal*, *The New York Times*, *The Post*, *Newsday*, *The Daily News*, I used to get all those papers, I used to research them, I'd get articles out of them, deal with things like drugs, you know, racism, police brutality. I used to go through all those things and get articles on them. I'd find books that are related to these problems."

"Yeah," I offer.

"Plus, starting in 1976, I got into the Black Congressional Caucus. I'd go for a week or two there, I'd do research there. And I've made contact with the congresspeople. I actually won a $30,000 Jeep in one of their raffles. I've met Jesse Jackson, the President, the Buffalo Soldiers, the Tuskeegee Airmen, the tank battalion that pushed the Germans into the Rhine—they have the longest consistent time in battle. I've met a lot of people through the Caucus. I've gotten involved in several projects. I've tried to get people at the State University involved in some of the projects. I stay here because I can get involved in things which kept me alive, basically."

"I see" I interject agreeably.

"Like, last week, I came here [the Student Union] Sunday night, went through a training, got up at 5 o'clock Monday morning, took a shower, got on a bus at 5:30, we went to Albany, we lobbied, we went to see the legislators and the senators, and we lobbied for cutting tuition. And I've gotten involved in religious retreats. I've gone to all of the Christian fellowships and prayed with the people in the fellowships. I've given some retreats. I became a facilitator. I helped other people reach their goals. I talk to students and teach them things I've learned. I helped organize Tent City that helped get higher pay for TA lines. . . . I'm the chaplain for the veteran's students' organization. At Adelphi [University], they asked me to do a presentation on belief and healing. I started love therapy. There are different meanings of the word 'love' in Greek. I've gotten into these different research projects."

"What else do you get out of staying on the State campus?" I ask.

"I go to all the lectures. I go to the parties after the lectures and the concerts, where they serve drinks and have a table full of hors d'oeuvres. I'd eat the food there and interact with the people who were involved. I got my picture taken so often that security would see my picture in *Statesman* and complain that I wasn't paying my activity fees. [Chuckles.] I go to the lectures at the Humanities Institute. I learn about comparative literature from the Humanities Institute. I started having a problem with Jewish people, so I joined Hillel to find out that they weren't monsters."

"When was that?"

"When I first came here." I decide not to touch that one.

"At 9 tonight, I'm going to talk to a student. I'm going to counsel him. He's having problems and I'm going to help him. After that, I'm going to talk on the campus radio station."

"What about the financial side of it? How do you raise enough money to survive from day to day?" Sam is asked.

"I have survived by collecting cans. One time I collected over 23,000 cans. I actually paid tuition with it."

"You collect cans from around the campus?"

"Yeah."

"And then where do you take them?"

"I used to take them to 7-Eleven. But, you know, security kept going over there and going over there, so now 7-Eleven has changed their policy completely. . . . I used to do $60 a week at least. I used to do $12 a day. I started at 3 o'clock [in the morning] and I'd go across the campus and collect cans until I got 10 cases. I'd use a shopping cart. On a weekend, I'd get $100 or more. And the students would tell me when they had a party and I would go [and collect the cans]. They used to close the Student Union at 3 o'clock. So I would stay there and sleep there maybe from 12 'til 3. Then they would kick me out at 3. So I would go to the parties because then, the parties would be ending. And I'd collect the cans from the parties. They used to have a party in almost every building. And I'd go and collect the cans. So I would get $100-125 on a weekend. I even attempted to pay taxes on it. [Laughs.] But most of the time I wouldn't be getting enough to pay taxes on it. I did it anyway, I would mail in the thing [file his tax return] anyway, because just in case, in the future, they [the government] would try anything [on me]."

"Really?" I ask.

"Yeah. One time, one summer, they had so many conferences here, they had an Oktoberfest and then they would have one conference after the other, I collected enough cans to fill up half of this room. And I was taking them over to 7-Eleven. I would take 20-30 cases at a time. And security kept going over there, going over there, and they finally convinced 7-Eleven to take only 10 cases [at a time]. So I have to go there, try these other places, to go all the way down to Edwards [a supermarket]. It was taking up too much time. They [the campus police] kept saying something to the boss over there [7-Eleven] so that they would now only let me take the cases from 9 o'clock to 5 or 6. Which is prime time. That's when they have classes and conferences. So I couldn't do that. So, instead of spending so much time collecting cans, I started going to the soup kitchens. I'd collect just enough cans to use the bus. When I don't get enough money to ride the bus, I have to walk to the soup kitchens." [They are located several miles apart from one another.]

"There are different soup kitchens on different nights?" Sam is asked.

"Yeah, there's one every night [at different churches]. I also get contributions from Christians I've worked with in the past. I've done temp work. I worked as a dishwasher for a while. I've received food stamps, but I stopped doing that—I didn't like the way I was treated. I thought the people who dealt with me were very disrespectful. I've worked as a line server in soup kitchens. For a while, I was trained to make pizza."

We are at St. Bartholomew's, a local Catholic church. The pantry has just served its evening meal and Sam and I are seated in its auditorium with dozens of homeless and poor people. He stabs at his baked ziti with a white plastic fork and begins describing some of his business and creative enterprises. The roster becomes detailed extremely quickly. "My background is in electronics," he states. "I designed a solar satellite, fiber-optic, long-distance learning project. I tried to do this at State, and the application got stolen." Before the implications of that theft sinks in, another is offered. "I did a project on critical thinking and that application got stolen, too. I anticipated voice-activated computers and solar-driven satellites. I designed a new classroom." At this point, a request for specifics seems futile. Sam seethes with resentment over past injustices. They are as importunate as if they happened yesterday. "I helped a woman do her master's thesis by explaining triangulation to her," he says. "It's sending a signal from a mobile station to find minerals in the ocean." Sam claims that, after returning from a visit to Marquette University, he "brought back two books that formed the foundation for the walk service on this campus. I was the person who started that service." One senses that Sam feels he is denied the recognition he deserves. "Dr. Max Dresden asked me, 'How would you like to win a Nobel Prize?' He went to Stanford and he won it in areas we worked on here. But we didn't have the equipment here. If I had left with him, I'd have a Nobel Prize." Even triumphs are turned into adversity. "You know that $30,000 Jeep I won?" he asks me. "It took me three years to pay off the $3,000 in taxes. It's like a conspiracy to stop my progress. I was chosen one out of 300 men to be trained by Bill Gates. If I had invested that $3,000 in stock in Microsoft, I'd be a millionaire."

Sam sums up his experience here. "I could have left. I was offered scholarships to Marquette, to Oswego, to Liberty University, and to Hawaii. I've lost a lot staying at State. I used to read 10,000 words a minute. I have lost the ability to read as much. They're trying to distract me from doing what I'm trying to do."

"Who's 'they'?" I ask him.

" 'They' is anyone who tries to stop me from reaching my goals."

"And yet you stay," I add, indirectly asking him why.

"Because I've made contacts with good people."

Sam recalls an outrage against him that stretches back several years. He used to use the lounge and refrigerator in the political science department, but was forced to stop. Of the members of that department, he says, "some of the same people who used to say racist things to me—they're still at State." His chuckle no longer seems so mirthful.

"Really?" he is asked.

"Yeah. But I don't get upset about that. God will deal with them." Sam becomes no more specific than that.

Abby Beth Dell, staff associate in the human resources department and director of the Good Fellowship Pantry, is asked about Sam's charge of racism. She says, as far as she knows, no such thing ever happened. "For a while," Dell explains, "he was sleeping in the student lounge, which is locked but somehow he got ahold of a key. He was lying there on the floor at eight in the morning when a young woman came in. His pants weren't completely on, and she got scared and called me." Dell sums up Sam's situation. "He really has to get on with his life," she asserts. "He gets off on all these little adventures, he starts these various businesses and they don't go anywhere. I tried to help him secure some kind of job," she says, "but lately, all he's done is to connect with the Black Congressional Caucus, which holds its meetings in Washington."

Skeptical as she is of Sam's version of things, Dell is also critical of the efforts of the police to oust him from the campus. "Sam is getting the short end of the stick," she says. "There have been public occasions, open events, where he was told to leave. He has a right to be there. Recently, he was allowed to stay for a time in a house with someone he befriended, but he had a hygiene problem and he was asked to leave. He is a great guy. He takes students under his wing. He has a very good heart."

Dell is asked what she thinks will become of Sam 10 years down the road. "He's been in the system so long that there's no hope of him getting out of it. I did have hope for him 10 years ago, but he's basically become dysfunctional." Dell pauses to contemplate her answer. "He's become a kind of folk hero to the students because he's so unusual. He'll make friends with students and continue to live pretty much the way he lives now."

Sam has been avoiding the Good Fellowship Pantry since Dell admonished him about the graduate student lounge incident.

Sam shows me a children's book he purchased at a church thrift sale, *Old MacDonald Had a Farm*. "I was in educational experiments," he explains, "I can use this to start a program at the daycare center." He slowly turns the pages of the book. Closing it, he pulls out a pamphlet and shows its title page to me. "I have to read this pamphlet on 'Instrument Data Aquisition.' I have a background in electronics." He shows me several envelopes; the letters they contain are responses to inquiries Sam has made to parties connected to the electronics industry. "I can teach electronics to kids. I can do this through the Challenge program in different churches. I met the astronauts—the minority astronauts."

"You know," he says, beginning on a new topic, "the university has people who attempt to criminalize other people. I overcome them through prayer." Rebutting Dell's claim of a dysfunctional future, Sam asserts slowly, with strong conviction, "I started researching real estate. I have a real estate licence. I'm going to buy property. And I started a market research firm. I'm putting together a grant application with the small business administration."

Sam asks me to drive him from the church to a friend's house where he had stored some of his material. We take leave of one another at the walkway to the house. "Good luck with your article," he says to me, referring with feeling to my journalism paper. I watch him walk toward the front door and wonder what is to become of this complex, troubled man. When his friend appears, I drive off, my mind aswarm with Sam's multitudinous contradictions.

Although he is a homeless man living on the tolerance and largesse of a university community, Sam is extremely conventional in many ways. He invokes the names of authorities and prestigious figures who, he says, he met or who helped him or his causes at one time or another. He values the conventional achievement represented by these figures, and invokes their names and their achievements as a means of drawing himself close to them. Sam is not so alienated from conventional society that he rejects its success symbols. Far from it; he displays them like glittering talismans, recites them like prayers, trots them out for any interested party to contemplate—and assess him correspondingly. It is clear that Sam yearns for the interlocutor's respect, and his means of attempting to gain it is covering himself in the mantel of reflected or borrowed conventional achievement.

But it is only a mantel, of course, not the real thing. And hence, Sam needs to bridge the gap between the prestige of his supposed mentors and the fact that he collects cans, stands in soup kitchen lines, and sleeps on borrowed couches. That bridge is a vocabulary of motives. To borrow a Brooklyn phrase, Sam's technique of neutralization is, "I wuz robbed." He would be wealthy and covered in glory if he had not been deprived of his due. He says he "designed a solar satellite, fiber-optic, long-distance learning project," but "the application got stolen." He did "a project on critical thinking" but that idea, likewise, got stolen. He "helped a woman do her master's thesis by explaining triangulation to her"; again, recognition was not forthcoming. The housing office kicked him out of his dorm room because he hadn't paid his bill when he actually had, leading to his downward spiral to homelessness. At other times, he says, he made a wrong decision by not following up on offers that would have made him famous, rich, and showered with prestige. If he had gone to Stanford with Max Dresden, he says, he would have won the Nobel Prize. He claims to have been offered fellowships and scholarships at a half-dozen colleges and universities, but he turned them down. Bishop Cody wanted him to go to Chicago to accompany his graduate professor but somehow he didn't go. Sam's choice of deviance neutralization technique reaffirms that he has at least one foot planted in conventionality.

Unlike Fred, a convict and the contributor of our next account, Sam does not reject God or religion. In spite of his anger over the way he feels he was treated by the parties who short-changed him, Sam was unable to become totally involved in Red Balloon, the campus radical-anarchist group—and an appropriate vehicle in those days for expressing such anger—because it rejected God and religion. Sam says he couldn't "get rid of God." Religion is simply too major an element in his life for him to scuttle it. His "commitment to God" is too strong, too abiding to give up. Rejected as a candidate for the priesthood, he maintains his faith. Faced with racism in the church, Sam points to the Scriptures as the font of the true religion. Kicked out of the rectory in which he lived, he nonetheless maintains a longing for the true spiritual community he was denied. As Sam said, in the New Orleans community in which he grew up, the choice was sin or the church. Sam has never wavered very far from his choice of the church.

Sam's evildoers are mainly specific persons who have engaged in specific acts against *him*. In fact, unlike Liazos' evil top dogs and fat cats, some of Sam's wise and benevolent benefactors (and supposed benefactors) *are* top dogs and fat cats—as we saw, the very prestigious figures he invokes to elicit our respect. In other words, Sam's analysis of good and evil is not structural in nature, but personal. When discussing his struggles, he specifies the parties who are making his life difficult by identifying them as "they." In his words: "'They' is anyone who's trying to stop me from reaching my goals." As for racists who treat him badly or discriminate against him, "God will deal with them," he tells us. With respect to people who "attempt to criminalize other people," that is, make it difficult to live and operate on the campus, "I overcome them through prayer," he says.

At one time, it seems, his vision was much broader. Recall that in the early 1970s, as a novice in the Catholic Church, Sam designed and taught a course to high school students entitled "Facing the Problems of Racism," in which he raised the question of whether one can be a racist and a Christian at the same time. In that case, the wrongdoing he isolated was abstract and general, not immediately relevant to his personal problems. And Sam is involved in local political issues, such as protesting the plight of graduate teaching assistants in the state capital. But that involvement is as much a product of the campus circles Sam moves in as his own ideological commitments. It seems the struggles he has experienced over the past quarter century or more have consumed his ideological fervor to the point where "them" and "us" has been replaced with "them" and "me." Sam believes that the deviant deeds of the present system can be overcome through vigilance, love, and progressive social movement activity.

One of the more interesting features of Sam's current life relates, in an oblique fashion, to social disorganization theory. We may recall that this perspective, born in the 1920s at the University of Chicago, waned in influence during the late 1940s and began making a comeback in the late 1980s. Social disorganization theory argues that poor, central city neighborhoods tend to attract residents who are mobile and unstable, who fail to sink roots in the community and hence do not monitor or sanction the untoward behavior of their neighbors. Therefore, they experience high rates of deviance, delinquency, and crime. In the words of one sociologist, these communities "give licence to nonconforming behavior" (Suchar, 1978, p. 74). The university campus is not poor or disorganized. What then is the relevance of social disorganization theory for the "nonconforming" behavior that may take place there?

The fact is, the denizens of a university tolerate and accept a much wider variety of "nonconforming" behaviors than would be accepted in other situations. Behavior that is so unacceptable it is prohibited in one place will find a niche or haven in another. For instance, artists' colonies, bohemian neighborhoods, and homosexual enclaves are well known for their acceptance of behavior that is frowned upon or punished elsewhere. All manner of odd and eccentric characters may enter and congregate in settings that are accessible to the general public—sidewalks, parks, bus and train stations—yet they will be excluded from spaces that fall under private auspices, such as factories and commercial offices. Indeed, even employees, that is, the people who are authorized to enter these privately administered spaces, are subject to more detailed and stringent rules and regulations than is true in public spaces. (Try showing up at work in a bathing suit and flip-flops!) Flirtatious and seductive behavior is more acceptable in bars than in places of worship. As we saw in Dwight's case, tourists often use their vacations to faraway locales as excuses for indulging in behavior they would not contemplate at home. Cities accept more unconventionality in their midst than small towns, and some cities do so more than others. "The Culture of Civility"—tolerating a wide range of non-harmful deviant behavior—is the watchword of the city of San Francisco (Becker and Horowitz, 1970). The fact is, in an expanded version of social disorganization theory—one not contemplated by its original framers—there is a *geography* of deviance and conventionality.

Secular universities are precisely the sort of enclaves that harbor odd and eccentric behavior. Access to most universities is fairly open, of course. But there is more to the matter than that. Professors themselves are granted a measure of unconventionality that would be unacceptable in the traditional business world or the professions. (An exception: the brand-new and most decidedly unconventional dot-com businesses.) Undergraduates are allowed a measure of wildness with respect to sexual behavior and the consumption of drugs and alcohol that did not prevail when they were in high school, and will not prevail once they graduate from college. Ideas that are considered radical, utopian, impractical, idealistic, subversive, or even crackpot are discussed openly. ("Is *that* what they teach you in college?" students are often asked by their disapproving parents.) True, completely unfettered, unbridled academic freedom does not prevail on any campus in the world. But at the university, compared with almost any other social institution, the open discussion of thoughts that are widely considered deviant is perhaps unparalleled. More to the point because of academic tolerance and open-mindedness, many campuses attract their share of unusual characters who are allowed to mingle more or less freely with the campus community.

- A man in his 40s who, for years hung around the entrance to the main library of a major university wearing orange sneakers, talking to himself, sometimes gesturing, is seen at night in an empty classroom in the Math Tower, wildly writing formulas on the blackboard. He is thought to be a "math genius gone mad." (As it turns out, he later wins a Nobel Prize.)

- A man in his 60s, standing on the sidewalk on a wooden box across the street from a major American university, clutching an American flag, makes speeches about the moralistic, utopian community he wants to institute. It would consist of himself and dozens of young virgins living on a Pacific island. He distributes leaflets detailing his plan to anyone passing by.

- A man in his 30s arrives at a university library early in the morning, sits down at a desk, and begins opening books and scribbling on a yellow legal pad. He takes occasional breaks and at night, collects his books and legal pads and leaves. This continues for many months. During one of his breaks, a graduate student wanders over to the man's desk and looks down at his legal pad. Each page on the pad, page after page, consists of a series of dozens of jagged lines. There are thousands of them on the pad. A few weeks after that, the man disappears and is never again seen in that library.

And of course, Sam makes his rounds at State University.

The acceptance of unconventionality is the flip side of rejection, and both acceptance and rejection are socially patterned (Bogdan and Taylor, 1987). It is to the academic community that we must look as a kind of model for understanding the dynamics of how unconventional behavior comes to be tolerated. In that understanding, we acquire a deeper, fuller grasp of the many sides of deviant behavior.

NOTE

[1] I interviewed Sam for a paper I wrote in a journalism course on feature writing. The assignment was a personal profile paper. This chapter is an expanded version of that paper. I would like to thank Paul Schreiber for comments on the earlier version of this chapter.

CHAPTER 12

I knew Jimmy had two guns in the car—he showed them to me the night before. So when he pulled into the parking lot of a Safeway, parked, and pulled out the guns, I wasn't surprised. The idea of robbing the store wasn't no big deal to me. Shit, I'm sure we talked about robbing and stuff. . . . But remember, I was just a kid who stole cars and wrote checks I had taken from places I had burglarized. There wasn't a mean bone in my body. On my own, I don't think I would ever have thought of robbing some place with a gun. . . . But Jimmy started talking about all the money Safeway had on Monday mornings before the armored truck came to take it away. So it didn't take much for him to talk me into robbing the store with him.

Fred

Sum, ergo cogito.

Fred

Fred, the Philosophical Felon

The author of this account is 47. Since his teenage years, he has spent nearly 22 years as an inmate in one or another correctional facility, mostly in Texas. His two brothers are also convicts in the same correctional system. We came into contact because he wrote to me requesting a copy of a book I wrote. Since he and I share a number of interests—including rational and critical thinking, what attracts people to paranormal beliefs, drug legalization, the criminal justice system, and matters such as liberty, rights, and justice—we began a correspondence. When I asked him to supply me with a personal account of his life, he agreed.

This account is stitched together from more than a dozen letters Fred wrote to me over a period of a year or so. His words are edited slightly for continuity, referents, and spelling. I have not eliminated the rough, raw language that is characteristic of prison talk and writing. In prison, Fred earned a high school equivalency diploma and has taken some college courses. He believes that he is a very different person from the "smartass kid" who entered the prison system as a teenager and feels he deserves a chance to live in what he refers to as "the free world."

Let me tell you about a real Texas prison spread. First, there has to be some big event. A lifer being released, a god's birthday, a new year, a special old con's birthday—or just three or four guys with a few extra dollars who want to eat something special. For a real king's spread, you must have the following: roast beef, bar-b-que beef, chili, refried beans, some sloppy Joe, Squeeze Cheese, Fritos, potato chips, flour tortillas, and hot peppers. And sodas on ice. We lay everything out on the table—a bunk with the mattress folded back—then stand in line, each of us makes two tacos, we put 'em in our bowl along with the potato chips, and get the fuck outta the way for the next guy.

We gather around just like people in the free world. From start to finish, the banter is no different from what it is anywhere else when friends gather. You'll hear remarks from "My mother's fine" to "Fuck you, punk." It's a subculture thing. We smile, we eat, we laugh for an hour or so. And for that hour we're no more in prison than people on the outside. The joy radiates from our eyes as we bite into our rich food, smiling as sauce oozes out our mouth and dribbles down our chin. And there will be a lot of sexual banter. In prison, making sexual remarks without anyone taking umbrage is the strongest sign of acceptance by our peers. You'll hear remarks like, "If you got a dick, you bought it in the commissary." "Suck my dick, bitch." "Hot damn, baby girl, you can really do wonders with some meat, can't you?" "You're going to make someone a good housewife one day." After we've eaten, one of the guys who didn't cook will clean off the table, another will wash up.

We break into groups of two and three, and talk turns back to prison. One guy who's served 15 years of straight time will be released in a week. He talks about sending the guys letters and cards with pictures of naked women. He'll stay in touch, he says, and for a few months, he will. But before long, most of us will become fleeting silhouettes in his mind's light. Talk of release reminds us that our ephemeral escape is over. Each of us returns to his bunk for a nap. Our thoughts return to loved ones, to freedom, to the world outside. After they are released, most of these guys will never return to prison.

Over the years, we've helped each other change. There's a sense of closeness you on the outside probably can't understand.

Most of my adult life has been spent in the Texas prison system. When I'm released, I'll have to provide for myself. More than likely, that'll mean working outdoors in the hot sun. My office and management skills are salable, but those jobs go to good ol' boys. At 47, I'll be in grand shape. Of the two choices open to me after release—working and taking care of myself, or returning to prison—I am determined to remain out of prison for the rest of my life, so I choose work, no matter what kind. Twenty-two years is more than enough.

It's 8 o'clock in the morning, Christmas day of the year 2000. I'm staring out of the window of my prison cell. The murmur of "Silent Night" or the scrape of reindeer hooves on the roof does not fill my head. I think about my mother, who hasn't written since the parole board turned down my request for release. Which means I'll remain a convict for another two years, at which time they'll reconsider releasing me. The members of the board never talk to me in person. All they have in front of them is my file—marks on pieces of paper. They never see the caring, responsible, thinking human being I have turned into. If they did, they would be able to look into my eyes and hear my voice and know that I have become a person who deeply regrets the pain and misery I have caused my victims, the innocent sufferers of my crimes. And my mother, I have caused her pain as well. She too has been an innocent sufferer. Only after contemplating the suffering of my victims and my mother do I allow a few moments of regret for myself. On paper, the parole board never gets to see the compassionate side of me.

I do not feel resentment. I am a 47-year-old who now understands the severity of his actions, undertaken when I was an immature, naive teenager in the body of an adult. I look back, knowing how wrong it was of me to use fear to take someone's property. And fraud, too, fraud perpetrated against the elderly who fear that their life savings will be taken, that there won't be enough money to sustain their lives or even to bury them when they are gone—I now see how wrong this is as well. If I had this awareness 25 years ago, I never would have robbed or defrauded anyone. The thought of the harm I inflicted on innocent victims still haunts me. Still, I can't help but wonder about the difference between the length of time I've drawn for my crimes and the time the corporate and white-collar criminals of the world get for their theft of billions of dollars. What kind of time do they serve? Certainly nowhere near the more than 20 years I've been incarcerated.

Outside my prison window, there's a fine, cold, drizzly rain. Ten years for the theft of a truck valued at $20,000. That's how much I'll have served until I come up before my parole board again for review. I picture the corporate billionaires, sitting at their 50-foot walnut dining tables, cutting into their succulent lamb chops on fine China plates with their polished silver forks and knives while the poor eat with plastic forks off paper plates. I can see their smug, sanctimonious smiles as the favorable economic news soothes their troubled brows. For a moment, a note of empathy creeps in. "What about the poor? What are they eating?" the rich are asked. "What a silly question," they respond. "Let them eat cake!"

This weekend didn't turn out like I thought it would. We were on lockdown status from Tuesday morning until lunch time on Friday. Nothing serious, just a general search for nuisance contraband. Could even call it a yearly rat-pack cleaning. Some of these guys don't throw anything away. Nuisance contraband is any item not in its original purchased state, like jars that are used after their contents have been consumed, or any item that is altered in any way. For instance, if a wire comes loose on a headphone or if the frame of eyeglasses breaks and it is taped together, they are contraband items, subject to confiscation at any time. Also, not having a property slip for a nonconsumable item will result in confiscation. Any item given to or borrowed by another inmate, like a girlie magazine, is contraband.

Did you ever watch *Schindler's List*? If you've watched any movie on German concentration camps, you've seen how a camp search is conducted. Here's how it is with us. Without warning, early one morning, officers march into the assigned area. They prevent anyone from discarding or returning contraband items. They issue an order for all prisoners to strip down to the skin. The only items in our possession must be state-issued clothing—pants, shirt, socks, underwear, and boots; any other items must be accompanied by a property slip, left on your bunk. Ten at a time, we are marched out of the dorm area into the hallway. At this point, we resemble the inmates in the concentration camp, naked, clutching our meager possessions, waiting for officers to point to us, left or right—left to the gas chamber and a swift death, right to a slow death of backbreaking labor and a near-starvation diet. In our case, it was just some discomfort and having each article of clothing searched before we dropped it at our bare feet. We are told, raise your hands, open your mouth, raise your scrotum (most of the guards can't pronounce "scrotum," so they just say "nut sack"), turn around, raise your feet, and then—the most humiliating part—bend over and spread your cheeks, let's see what's in there!

Once you are checked over, you move on to a holding enclosure where we sit or stand until all of us have been moved from the dormitory area. Then two officers escort us to a large recreational area where we wait until our cubicle is searched. This generally takes about three or four hours. During a search like this, every item—every envelope, book, nook, and cranny of your cubicle area is looked into. Here's what it's like. Pack all the stuff on top of your desk into a box, tape it closed, then shake it for 10 minutes. When you open the box, you'll see what the belongings you have in your cell or cubicle look like after a contraband search is conducted. When the search has been completed, we're called back 20 at a time. Again, we strip naked, stand in front of an officer, and are subjected to yet another strip-search. Our ID card is returned to us, then we dress and walk through a gauntlet of guards back to our living area.

You walk into your cell, take a deep breath, and sort through what's left of your life. Sadness, frustration, and anger all seem to settle in on you. Rarely is anything that's taken ever returned. During this search, I lost a watch, two electric coils for boiling water, two bags of coffee, a bag of powdered milk, all my drinking glasses, and an assortment of miscellaneous items, all declared contraband. I lost the coffee because it was inside a peanut butter jar, I lost my watch because I didn't have a property slip for it—a friend left it to me. (They sell them at the commissary for $6.95. I think I'll break down and buy me one.) I lost my drinking glasses because they are not sold in the commissary.

Mind you, I lost all these items because I am a devalued human being. I'm not even allowed to read the file the state of Texas has on me. Hell, some people gasp when they hear this sort of thing happens to Russian prisoners. It's happening right here, in the United States! Now, if I were a sex offender, by now, I would have been released into the free world, because the Texas Parole Board decided to parole all sex offenders—they say they can supervise them for a longer time. Don't fuckin' ask me why they did it—I don't understand it either. It's hard for me to grasp why I should stay locked up while child molesters and rapists go free.

This search took three and a half days. During that time we weren't allowed out of our cells or cubicles for any reason. Officers bring meals in a sack three times a day. Pancakes and a box of cereal for breakfast, a couple of sandwiches for lunch and supper. A few trusted inmates are allowed out after each meal to clean up the mess. Imagine 1200 discarded meal sacks tossed into the run in front of the cells, along with any other items an inmate decided he doesn't want in his cell. Since I was one of the privileged inmates, I was allowed to get out of my cubicle for a couple of hours each day to clean up. We got to shower at the end of each day, but everyone else didn't get to shower until the third day of lock-down. There are some guys in here who hate any activity that could be called work, but I enjoy working. Any opportunity to get out of my cell.

When we lived in Mississippi, my mother ran off to Little Rock to give birth to me. I think the guy who knocked her up wanted her to abort. Her mother and stepdad might have agreed. She married Norman H. Jones when I was a year and a half old. He was my dad for 18 years. Norman's people lived in Beaumont, Texas. Back and forth we went for the first 13 years of my life. It wasn't until I was 12 that I learned who my sperm father was. I was quick in school—at least that's what my mother told me. But all that moving didn't allow me enough time in one school to learn much.

I had a buddy named John. He was the son of my dad's cousin and he was close to my age. His parents drank beer any time they weren't working. On occasion, they would drive around and let us sit in the back seat and drink a few beers. John was an only child, spoiled rotten. When his parents wouldn't give us money, he'd throw a fit. So we'd skip school and break into homes for spending money. We'd saunter up to the front door and knock hard four or five times. If no one answered, we'd go to the back door. Usually it wasn't locked. If it was, hell, we'd just break a window out. Once we were inside, we ransacked it for money, gold, watches, stuff that would fit in our pockets, stuff we could quickly sell.

Once, we walked into a house through an unlocked back door. Inside, we stopped in the kitchen for a snack. Hey, kids who skip school get hungry too. I made a sandwich and, sandwich in hand, I checked out the other rooms. When I opened the bedroom door, there stood a half-dressed woman, bent over pulling up a pair of slacks. At that age, I hadn't seen too many bras or panties. John had caught up with me and was standing right behind me. The woman straightened up and stared at us. Shit, for a few seconds no one moved or said a word. "What the hell do you want?" she asked. It was like releasing the rabbit at the dog races—we were out of there, lickety-split. For the next week or so, that was good for a laugh.

For the next year or so, John and I broke into a lot of homes—and I do mean a lot. Sometimes several in the same day. When I finally got into trouble for skipping school, burglarizing, and stealing, mom sent me off to Texas to stay with her brother for several months.

When I was 14, we lived in Greenville, Mississippi. I had a girlfriend named Dixie. I tattooed her name on my ankle. It's still there. I was going out with her when my parents sent me to Beaumont. I cursed them all the way there. Well, not all the way—a few slaps put an end to that. A few months later, I stole a car and four of us were on our way to Mississippi, back to my first true love. Gosh, even today, I'd still like to see Dixie. Not too many days passed before I was arrested for several thefts and break-ins. As a result, the state of Mississippi introduced me to one of the most notorious juvenile correctional facilities in the South.

Knowing the brother of a guy in my dorm prevented me from getting raped at the ripe age of 14. I may have been able to plan a break-in, but I wasn't quick-witted enough to have prevented being raped myself. It must have been a truly frightening event for me at the time because the memory of it still sticks with me. Those guys arguing over who would decide if I got fucked is something I'll always remember.

For several months, we planned our escape from the reformatory. Once a week or so, several of the other boys got together and ran off during daylight hours. When they were caught, we'd all have to hear the same damn old story about how you couldn't escape. Then they'd be taken into the coach's office in the gym. The sound of a paddle smacking their butts and the back of their legs is hard to forget. Their screams were painful to listen to. The rest of us weren't even allowed to stop playing during the beatings. No one cared, so what's the big deal about their screaming?

Our dorms were built like the top of two giant Ts butted together. Down each long hallway, rooms were set off; there were six boys in each room. Most of the windows faced the compound outside; a chain-link fence covered each window. The window in my room faced inside.

One of us stole wire-cutters from our auto repair class. Three of us from my room and three from the room across the hall got together. We cut the wire covering the window. It was scary. We were tense because each time the nips cut through a strand of wire, it made a loud sound like a "snap" of metal on metal. The dorm mother, who weighed almost 300 pounds, positioned her oversized chair in the doorway leading out of the dorm area. We were sure she'd hear the sound. She didn't. The six of us escaped out the window and into the surrounding woods.

When we made it to a railroad bridge just outside of town, we stopped. I may not have been all that quick-witted, but I had learned enough to know that an escapee has a lot better odds evading capture alone than in a group. So while my buddies sat around talking about what they should do, making all kinds of noise, I slipped away from them, climbed up an embankment, and took off on my own. In a clearing in the woods, I came upon an old-style country church built two feet off the ground and set on cement bocks. I crawled underneath it and went to sleep. I stayed there through the next day until it got dark. Then I crawled out, went back to the railroad tracks, and walked to Jackson. Along the way, I noticed footprints along the tracks. Maybe one of the other guys had made it this far, I figured.

At one point, the railroad tracks ran so close to a road that anyone driving on the road could see me, so I lit out through the woods. Finally, I saw a little country store where two roads came together. Since I had $5 in my pocket, I dragged my sorry ass inside to buy something to eat and drink. Boy, talk about being nervous! I walked out of there, returned to the railroad tracks, and began running. I ran and ran until my young ass couldn't run any more, all the time thinking, in the store, they must have known I was running away, they'll be after me right quick.

I reached Jackson that night. I asked people on the street where the bus station was and found it. Along the way, I passed one of my fellow escapees. All we did was wave to one another. At the bus station, I hung out and smiled at the queers. See, at the bus station back home, my friends and I would use queers for fast cash. You stood in a stall, he sucked your dick, and you had ten dollars to party with. It didn't take long for one to find me. Two of them refused my price—a bus ticket back to Beaumont. But the third one went along with it, though I had to agree to stay at his house for two days. Shit, what's a dumb kid to do?

A couple days later, I walked into my house in Beaumont. Everyone was very, very surprised. I didn't return to Mississippi until after my 18th birthday. I joined up with a guy to do drugs and some small-time break-ins. Mostly, I broke into places that had checks and an imprint machine. Stores cashed these checks faster than a regular check. We burglarized a catfish house, a hardware store, and stole a couple of cars. Eventually, we got caught. Before the court heard our case, one night, somehow, we convinced each other to join the Army. The recruiter said we could see the world on the buddy plan. We took the GED test and we were in. We signed the papers drunk as skunks.

After basic training, I went AWOL to be with a 14-year-old girl who lived in Walls, Mississippi. It was just what you might call young sex stuff. (Oh, hell, her mother would suck and fuck me, too.) I don't even remember her name. I went back to stealing what I could and of course, I was caught again. The judge gave me a choice of prison in Mississippi or be sent back to military service on condition that if I were ever arrested in Mississippi again, it was straight to prison for me. I wound up in the Fort Hood stockade. The army gave me an undesirable discharge.

I hitchhiked to Lake Dallas, where my mother lived, then I took off for Mississippi to see my girlfriend. It didn't take the state of Texas very long to come after me for the catfish house, the checks I stole from there and the hardware store, and the car theft. I received a two-year proba-tion for all those charges. Couple months later, I violated probation and was sent to the Texas prison system for the first time. I was 19 years old.

If I thought being in jail was a frightening and horrifying experi-ence, it was nothing compared to the prison system. Inmates were liter-ally bought and sold like slaves, mostly young, white boys were the prop-erty of Black prisoners. Sex, drugs, fighting, and poker filled the days of the prisoners who were in charge. You had three choices: You fought, paid for protection, or had sex with a "daddy." You could also get pro-tection by knowing someone in the power circle. Because I was so young, pretty, and naive, they assigned me to a protection dormitory. Here, the prison tenders, the prisoners who were in charge, watched over us. Still, sex, drugs, fighting, and gambling ruled the day. No cards were allowed, so we played dominos. The tenders escorted us everywhere we went, so those of us who were in the protection unit were shielded from most of the worst brutality the inmates inflicted on each other. No one protected us from the backbreaking work, though. All of us worked hard, long days. Rain, sleet, even hailstones had no effect on our workday—picking cotton, hoeing fields, or chopping weeds that grew three feet high.

After five months, I was paroled. Since the bus didn't stop in Lake Dallas, I was left off by the side of the highway and I had to walk to town. When I got to my mother's house, no one was home, so I crawled inside through a window. Like the teenager I was, I celebrated my free-dom by raiding the refrigerator and watching television.

When my stepfather arrived home, he told me that my mother had left him and was living in Louisiana with my first stepfather, Norman H. Jones, the guy who had raised me. Hell, in spite of the abuse he had dished out, I sincerely loved and cared for the guy. I even called him dad. Well, I told my stepdad, let's go get her and bring her back home. What did I know about life or happiness? Well, we went to Louisiana, got my mom, brought her back to Lake Dallas. My mom and my stepdad drank a lot and fought, and we kids had to fit our lives in as best we could. Still, we were something like a happy little family for a while.

At the time, I had three siblings—Terry, who was 14, Robert, who was 12, and Becky, who was only eight. Terry was away at one of the nu-merous juvenile reformatories he got sent to. My mother and her hus-band were out drinking. I decided to take Robert and Becky to a drive-in movie. I had one picked out and was all set. I hadn't planned on Jimmy. Jimmy was the brother of a local part-time policeman who worked in the Lake Dallas department. Hell, the whole damn department consisted of one full-time and three or four part-time officers. Jimmy had done some time in a prison up North somewhere. He had pulled a robbery of a small motel, which netted him hardly any money—and eight years in prison. He settled in Lake Dallas, doing his parole while he lived in his brother's house. Now that I think back on it I can't even remember speaking to him before that day, but he drove up our driveway in a jalopy you wouldn't even think would crank.

It didn't take much for Jimmy to convince me to desert my brother and sister and my movie plans to go out drinking and drugging with an older guy who was cool. We drove around drinking beer and taking pills I had stolen and what other drugs he had from who knows where. I never even went back to check up on my brother and sister. The first night, we slept in the car. The next day, we started up drinking again and taking the pills we had left over from the night before. I knew Jimmy had two guns in the car—he showed them to me the night before. So when he pulled into the parking lot of a Safeway, parked, and pulled out the guns, I wasn't surprised. The idea of robbing the store wasn't no big deal to me. Shit, I'm sure we talked about robbing and stuff the night before. But remember, I was just a kid who stole cars and wrote checks I had taken from places I had burglarized. There wasn't a mean bone in my body. On my own, I don't think I would ever have thought of robbing someone or anyplace with a gun. But Jimmy started talking about all the money Safeway had on Monday mornings before the armored truck came to take it away. So it didn't take much for him to talk me into robbing the store with him.

My part in the robbery was to stand by the magazine rack to watch for anyone approaching the check cashing booth while Jimmy was inside holding up the manager. All of a sudden, Jimmy's in the booth, pointing his pistol at a guy wearing a white shirt. Then the guy bends down to open the safe. A woman walks in and approaches the window of the booth to cash a check. Hell, I didn't know what to do. In my best Jesse James voice and manner, I walk up to her and said, "This is a robbery, don't move." She looked real scared. That's something that has stuck with me over the years—that frightened look on her face.

When Jimmy got the money from the safe, we ran to our getaway car. He had parked the car one street over, in the parking lot of a nearby apartment building. We got in and Jimmy started up the car, but then the engine went dead. He started it up again, backed up a short distance, and it went dead again. By this time, people were all around the car, but keeping a safe distance away. Jimmy kept trying to start the car. I jumped out, scared shitless. A man pointed a gun at me. To this day, I still wonder why he didn't fire. I jumped back into the car and screamed to Jimmy to start up the damn car. It cranked up, backed up a little more, and then went dead again. Finally, I jumped out again and ran to one of the nearby apartment buildings. Then I remembered I had left my wallet in the glove compartment of the car, so I ran back to the parking lot. Jimmy was still trying to start up the car, hollering his damn fool head off. When I got in, he began glaring at me. I grabbed my wallet. Scared, crying, I left Jimmy behind in the nightmare he had created for himself, ran back to the apartments, ran through one of the buildings, and through an open field to some apartments nearby. Just then, I heard a shot and ran around the corner of a building, and ran right into Jimmy. Damn, I thought, I wish I had never met this guy! Later, I found out that when he jumped out of the car, Jimmy had dropped the bag money we stole from the Safeway. It contained about $800. At the time, we were too scared to worry about the money, so we didn't get a dime from the robbery.

We walked to his brother's apartment. We changed into work clothes and hard hats, trying to look like a couple of working guys. Jimmy and his brother cussed each other out. Mainly, I was just plain scared. Then we got into his brother's car and he drove us to Lake Charles, Louisiana, where he dropped us off on the street, almost dead broke and on the run. We spent the last few dollars we had on beer in a bar nearby. Jimmy suggested that we follow a guy out of the bar, rob him, take his car, and drive north. For some reason, this plan never materialized. Jimmy was stuck on robbing someone and taking their car. He walked over to a woman in a car, but when he returned, he gave me some reason why he didn't carry through with his plan. The more he talked about robbing someone and maybe hurting them, the more frightened I became.

We wandered around aimlessly for hours before we wound up in the bus station. On a bench, we discussed me calling my mother. He didn't want me to call, but somehow I worked up enough courage to convince him to let me phone home. I talked to my mom for more than an hour, maybe two. She made me think about what I was doing and helped me make a decision about what I ought to do. Without her help, I don't think I would have made the best decision. Chances are, I might have gone off with Jimmy, and there's no way of telling what might have happened if I had gone with him. My mother told me to stay put, she was wiring me money to go to my dad's home in Illinois.

I never saw Jimmy again, at least not on the outside. Four years later, when they brought me back to Dallas County to testify against him, I wouldn't do it. They put me on the stand and tried to force me to say things about what I had done with Jimmy. But by this time, I was living by the convict's code—or so I thought—and there was no way I was going to cooperate.

A childhood friend of my dad's owned several tugboats that moved barges around on the Illinois River, so he put me to work on the tugboats at night. When a barge had to be moved, it was my job to radio the pilot. To do my job, I had to jump from barge to barge. If the ropes weren't tight enough, there was a gap between the boats. Waves would cause the boats to bang together, so if you fell into the gap, you'd be crushed like an egg. On top of everything else, it was dark and windy. It was a scary experience.

About a month after I got to my dad's place, my 14-year-old brother Terry came to visit us. He rode a motorcycle alone from Dallas to Peoria just to be with us. We worked, we drank, we worked, we drank. We drank at a small bar a few blocks from our trailer. One night, an older girl and I began playing pool. Terry and I began having an argument over this damn slut. Before my dad could break up the fight, I had punched Terry and broke out one of his front teeth. I still regret that. But life went on—me with a swollen hand and Terry with a tooth missing. We continued working and drinking.

A fat girl lived next door to us. She was married, but Terry and I both fucked her during the same period of time. One day, when her husband was at work, we loaded up her clothes, along with anything of his we could sell, and the three of us left for New Orleans. She had most of his last pay-check, so that helped with expenses. A few weeks after settling into New Orleans, Terry and I got into a fight with a next door neighbor, over what I can't recall. They called the police and so we hid out in the woods until the cops left. Then we got into the car and drove to our cousins' house. But before we got there, the police tried to pull us over, but I refused to stop the car until I had reached their house. I got out of the car, but an officer grabbed me, slammed me to the ground, stuck the barrel of his gun in my neck, yelled at me to stay still, and slapped handcuffs around my wrists. Terry hid in a ditch and escaped apprehension. I got taken off to jail.

Meanwhile, the state of Texas was still looking for me. It didn't take long for the Texas authorities to come and get me. My dad sent me money to hire a lawyer, who told me to write out what had happened. During that detention, I was housed in the infirmary. See, two weeks before, in the midst of an argument with Terry, I slammed my hand into the rearview mirror of a car, so I was wearing a cast on my wrist and hand. That's why I was put in the infirmary.

By the time the lawyer got back to me, I had been moved into a regular jail tank. Back then, as you were being walked into the tank, the guys in the cells yelled out, "fresh meat!" [first-time arrivals in the tank, also called FM]. Eventually, you had to be put into a cell with the other inmates. As soon as you were admitted, the prisoner in charge told you to stand against the wall for inspection. I'm sure you've seen movies in which there's a slave auction. It was just like that.

The ruling cons, in order of rank, picked out the prettiest and young-est guys. Cell assignments were determined by who picked you. Or if you knew someone inside who could protect you. Or how well you fought. Within an hour of being admitted, you'd either have to fight or fuck. One of those, or if someone spoke up for you. It happened that one of the prisoners in charge knew me from the bars in Dallas where my dad used to drink while we boys sat on the floor or played pool. Having someone speak up for me meant I could go into a cell with seven other guys who weren't punks or coffee pots. "Coffee pot" is prison slang for a convict who isn't a sexual punk but was a kind of punk who did menial chores for the other convicts, like making coffee or washing their underwear.

Eventually I had to fight, but it was mostly for show. Bored and tired of gambling, the head prisoners set up boxing matches. Humans can be very ingenious when they use other humans for entertainment. Some blood, some choo-choos [cookies or other sweet commissary items] change hands, and then it's suppertime. These boxing matches were only one of many forms of distraction. The more experienced cons seemed to enjoy testing fresh meat. Fear. Fear is the tool of choice, just as it has been since humans began to band together millions of years ago. How else can a person look inside another quickly for strength of character except to see what he does under conditions of fear?

Without fail, on the third day of observing new arrivals, one of them would be singled out as having more weaknesses than the others. The ugliest, largest, meanest-looking lower-ranking con would serve as the foamer-flipper. (You'll find out who he is in a minute.) Breakfast time— a scary time indeed. Tempers are short. Everyone is disoriented. More fights start at this time than any other. Fresh meat don't know what the fuck to do but stand and wait, trying to prevent the roiling fear inside from bubbling up to the surface for someone to see.

The foamer-flipper comes out late. Feeders have left. The food chute is closed and locked with a loud, resounding clang by the hateful guard. Fresh meat are relieved to have a tray of food. They are told what table to eat at. Suddenly a guy starts hollering, "*Who the fuck has my tray?*" No one but the fresh meat will pay him much attention or even look around. Old cons know they have their tray and won't fall for this trick. They may even have two, three trays—in prison, cons often buy and sell their food trays—and the fresh meat sees this and figures, the missing tray has gotta be one of those extra trays, heck, I'm OK.

By this time, as planned, the foamer is angry about being ignored on top of some scumbag motherfucker having taken his food. By now, all his hollering has awakened some of the monster-looking guys who start pay-ing attention and hollering, too. Now you have five-six guys hollering. For the next 10-20 minutes, tension in the dayroom grows thick. Some of the guys in the room have even put their hands on makeshift clubs and other weapons. Finally, the head con tells everybody to shut the fuck up. With all eyes on him, he gives the guy who took the tray one last chance to confess up. The designated finger-pointer says, "Look, Joe Bob"—or whatever the fuck his name is—"I bought that guy's tray," pointing at one of the fresh meat, "so how can you sell your tray and still have one? Tell me."

Shit, the poor guy can't say anything that will change the hell he is about to suffer for the next hour or so. Only one action can save him now. He must attack his accuser. Make him retract what he said. If he won't, he has to get on his ass. Anything else he might do only leads to more misery. The foamer is trying to get to the poor bastard, but the others are holding him back. Everybody's watching the reactions of the fresh meat to all of this. Any—and let me stress this here, *any*—sign of weakness will inevitably result in sexual advances. It'll come, no doubt about it. If the guy draws the line at fucking or sucking dick, he will never be more than a coffee pot. The question is, how far will a guy go to prevent being harmed.

By this time, the foamer has faked an epileptic fit. He falls to the floor and spits out foam. (It's just toothpaste or some other similar shit, but the fresh meat don't know that.) All this has happened because *you* took his tray! Once he's stopped rolling and flipping around on the floor, he's helped up. Then the cons let him get to the fresh meat. Then he'll do whatever it takes to make the fresh meat fight. If he won't fight, he'll be beaten on, kicked around, made to do all kinds of humiliating things till the guys get tired of him. At some point, the call will come for him to show his ass—literally. If he shows his ass, there's no turning back. He must become someone's sexual punk and allow that guy to fuck him up the ass or suffer beatings until he passes out. In some cases, he will be allowed to buy protection—but he's going to have to have a lot of money to do that.

Jail life consists mostly of eating, poker, TV, sex, and walking back and forth. And drugs. Drugs come into jails the same way they do everywhere else. One time, we convinced a woman to help us smuggle some drugs into the jail. At this time, Dallas County Jail was right smack in the middle of downtown. Late one night, we dropped a line of string to the street 11 floors below, where she tied some pills, a sharp point, and some sipping straws onto the string. We used a needle point (smuggled in earlier), a Bic pen casing, and a pencil eraser to inject the pills into our veins. A couple of us just swallowed the pills.

While on these drugs, I got called on a down-and-out, which means I went to the courthouse, made an appearance, and got returned to jail.

(If you get a "hat-on-tight," that means you get out of jail.) The lawyer my dad paid to represent me was in the courthouse. I was told to plead guilty. For my minor role in the robbery, I was offered a plea-bargained sentence of 16 years. Don't ask me what I was thinking or even if I was thinking. Looking back, I say it was a combination of peer pressure and the desire to be a real gangster like the ones in the tank who told me, "Man, they can't convict you, you gotta make 'em crank it up!" [In other words, reject the plea-bargain and go to trial.] So I refused the offer. Whatever my attitude was, part of it had to do with my dislike of the assistant DA, who never offered me any other plea arrangement. So, the next time I went on a down-and-out, I talked to my lawyer about getting my trial started.

Fuck, nobody in my family knew what was going on. The trial lasted for four days. My mother and her new husband were there. Most of the time I was on downers—Nembutal—and I just went through the motions, doing what the lawyer told me to do. On the second day, the bailiff took me to an adjoining courtroom and had me stand in the jury box. There were five or six people sitting in the visitor's area. I didn't think about it then, but years later, I realized that these were the same people who took the stand to ID me during the trial. Aside from their ID, there was absolutely no evidence to tie me to the robbery. Each of these eye-witnesses pointed to me as the perpetrator. (Actually, I was too out of it on Nembutal to remember much of what happened. Later, I read a transcript of the trial, so I know they fingered me.) During the sentencing, the bailiff came to the holding tank to tell me that the jury had sent a note to the judge asking what's the difference between life and 99 years. DUH! Whatever the judge told them, they decided on 99 years. At the sentencing, my mother was crying. My state-appointed lawyer told my mother not to worry, I'd be home in about two years. He said that's how long it would take to straighten it all out.

Back in the tank, I became one of the main gangsters to contend with. I was a lifer—nothing to lose. Big guy on the walkway. So I began to settle in with the thought of spending the rest of my life in prison. Eating, poker, TV, and sex filled my days and nights.

Sex. I often wonder how men can rationalize male-on-male sex. The guy doing the fucking remains a man while the receiver or sucker becomes a queer bitch. During my year or so in Dallas County Jail, I had a little Mexican who sucked my dick or let me fuck him up the ass three or four times a week. Get this now: The vast majority of convicts [who aren't punks] had a kid like this. Try for a moment to understand what I'm saying here: These are tried-and-true homophobics. Yet in their minds, their homosexual acts do not brand them as homosexuals. I know

I thought that way then. Don't ask me how the fuck to explain it, but we did it.

Letting a guy suck my dick wasn't all that new to me. Back in Mississippi, there was a small homosexual who would let us ride his motorcycle in exchange for us letting him suck us off. He would do one of us for the bike and one for gas money. But I never fucked a guy up the ass until my stay at Dallas County Jail. For some reason, this queer in Mississippi never asked any of us to fuck him. Sometime later, when I was in prison, I thought back on this sex thing. I recalled the time an older cousin forced me to masturbate him. I was 7 or 8, he was 17 or 18. I was lying in bed and he took my hand and placed it on his dick. It scared me more than anything else. I closed my eyes tight the way kids do when they're scared by the boogeyman and did what he said. He kept insisting I squeeze it harder. It was so big I couldn't get my hands around it. After a while, he made me lie down so I could put both hands on it and I moved up and down, up and down, for what seemed like hours. After he came all over my hands, he made me continue. This scared the shit outta me. Hell, I didn't know what was going on. I thought maybe he had pissed on me. About five years later, when I was 12 or 13, a babysitter came to our house. She was 18 or 19. Once, she took my little dick out of my pants to play with it. She had me rubbing her pussy while she played with my dick. I was scared. This reminded me of what happened with my cousin, when he made me masturbate him. Even though I was aroused, when someone came to the door and the babysitter answered it, I was so scared, I ran outside and hid. Kids do the damndest things, don't they? Shit, a year or so later, we were fucking our female cousin, four or five of us at a time, like there was no tomorrow. She got many a quarter from us guys.

In November 1975, after I had been in jail for over a year, I was sent to prison—the Clemens Unit down in south Texas. My little stint in the army, in reformatories, and in jails were all behind me now. I was going to prison as a big-timer, a real gangster. A convict. In reality, I was just a punk kid who spent most of his days in diagnostic status, locked up because of smartass shit. Clemens had been racially integrated for just a few years. At the time, it was one of the designated Black farms in the Texas prison system. They moved some whites and Mexicans into the unit, but we still didn't live together. Whites and Mexicans lived in one tank, Blacks in another. Work squads were also separate. We ate, went to the gym, and showered in separate groups of whites and Mexicans in one group and Blacks in another. In reality, back then, there was very little integration.

Arrival at the gate of Clemens Unit was the beginning of a 10-year stay. It took me from one extreme to the other. Ass-whipping began at the back gate and continued on into the building. These areas were controlled by Black turnkeys [inmates who were granted some measure of authority over other prisoners]. It wasn't until you reached the security office that you ran into a white boy who was running something. Until you reached the security office, you were at the mercy of large, monster-looking Black guys. Blacks were definitely running the show. Throughout your first few hours there, they spanked your ass, though it wasn't anything serious. Unless a white boy got to winning a fight with a Black. Couldn't have that. Then four or five turnkeys would beat that white boy's ass real good. My guess is, to them it was fun. That and to prove a point early on: "You will not win against us."

Back then, security office convicts did all the paperwork. A prisoner's paperwork was delivered to one of the bookkeepers who prepared it and got you ready for an assignment. The security office cons knew everything about you that was on record—snitch reports, catch-outs, rape reports. And you would be judged and assigned accordingly. The bookkeepers were usually more intelligent than the average convict, and usually smaller in stature as well. Considering they were prisoners, they had a lot of power. They worked for and reported directly to the building majors and wardens—what we used to refer to as God and Jesus. They were called that because they quite literally had the power of life and death. They could save your ass and, I've heard, even make you disappear. Now, it's possible that the disappearances are folklore, I can't say. I don't have personal knowledge of this happening, but there's stories of convicts going to watering holes, never to return. It's like I was saying before: Fear. Fear even of some imaginary horror is enough to keep the meanest men alive in line. And take it from me, there were some of the meanest men alive there on Clemens Unit. But they did exactly what the Major and the Warden told them what to do—no matter what that might have been.

Orders from one of these men were carried out just as a slave carried out an order from a plantation owner or an overseer. There was an incident back in the 1920s that tells you what I'm talking about. There were 11 transients who were convicted of vagrancy and leased out to local farmers. One farmer thought the FBI was going to send him to prison for violating the anti-slave labor law, so he told the Black overseer to kill the transients so they couldn't testify against him. These 11 human beings were chained together, thrown into a river, and shot. At the trial, the overseer said, "I killed them men because Mr. John said to. I don't know anything to do except what Mr. John says to do." This is the mind-set I'm talking about here.

In 1975, orientation consisted of a convict handing you a move slip. This had all the information you needed: row and cell location and job assignment. Turnkeys and building tenders provided you with any other instructions. If curiosity got the better of you or if you were stupid enough to ask a question during those first few days, a quick gruff rebuff would follow. If you came across as a smartass, another ass-whipping awaited you.

I didn't have the mental training to survive by being part of the power structure. So, I went to work, ate, showered. Became as unfriendly as a rabid dog. I took a couple of good ass-beatings. Four months after my arrival at Clemens, I went to the dayroom to watch a little TV. Another guy and I watched a movie and talked for about an hour when one of the building tenders walked up to the end of the bench. He asked the guy I was with how he was doing. Before he could answer, the tender hit him in the face. For what seemed like hours, this guy fought four tenders. There was a lot of blood on his face. At some point, one of the tenders asked me, "You want some of this?" and he smacked me in the face. I had already proven I would fight before I'd fuck, but two of the tenders gave me a real good ass-whipping. I woke up with black shoe polish marks on my sides, my ribs aching, and blood all over my face. I hurt like hell. Later, I learned the tenders had decided to teach me a lesson: "Don't talk to snitches." Hell, I didn't know the guy was a snitch.

The best medical advice came from inmate prison doctors—if you could pay, that is. Otherwise, you just got cleaned up and sent to the security office. A real, freeworld doctor looks at you only if you've got guts hanging out or you're already dead. Evidently, the guy I was with who got beaten snitched about what had happened. My turn came to talk. Tired, my ribs and face hurting, able to see out of only one eye, my lips still bleeding, I went into a small room and faced four men, one of them the warden. I refused to answer their questions. To them, I was being a hardass, a "Cool Hand Luke" kind of guy. The warden had to restrain one of the captains from getting on my ass for my minor insolence. The warden finally asked me a direct question: "You're just not going to tell us anything, are you?" My answer was "That's about the fucking size of it!" Over the next four years, I was to pay the price for that statement. But it was worth it. Word traveled fast that I hadn't talked. I got a lot of respect for that.

That was the end of my trouble with the other convicts. Oh, I got a few ass-whippings, but nothing serious. I did come real close once to causing the Mexicans to give me a severe beating. I was in the field and we were hoeing, and a Mexican striker [the field equivalent of a turnkey] began giving me shit, so I smacked his ass with my aggie [hoe], and he took off running, that weakass motherfucker. The boss pulled his pistol on me and told me to drop the aggie. "No way, buster," I told him, "not until the captain gets here." I had enough sense to know the captain was the only one who could save me from another severe beating. There were some pretty mean guys in the field with me, but none of them wanted to be the first to get chopped with my aggie. Remember, I was sentenced to 99 years and had nothing to lose, so most guys figured I should be left alone.

The captain arrived, acted mad as hell, and handcuffed me. Later, he told me it was about time somebody busted that sorry-ass Mexican's cover. He had a reputation of sneaking up behind everyone he fought. I got sent to prison jail. Court back then was a couple ranking officers cussing out your ass before sending you to solitary or shelling peanuts. Shelling peanuts—what an ingenious form of punishment. Minor infractions got you one to three gallons of peanuts. More serious infractions got you 10. Peanuts were shelled in what we called the sweatbox, a hot, stuffy place where we were packed in together, sitting leg-to-leg with other prisoners, a gallon can and peanuts between your legs, which were spread out V-shaped on the floor. The peanuts came out of our own fields. We picked them and sacked them in burlap bags. What a deal. Those of you who eat roasted peanuts: Try shelling a gallon of raw peanuts, you'll see what I mean. Remember, we had to sit in that sweatbox shelling peanuts till we filled up our quota. You worked all day in the box and if someone tried to steal your peanuts, you fought in the box. Fighting cost you another gallon or two.

For using a weapon—the hoe—I drew a 15-day stay in solitary. One full meal every three days. At the other meal times, you got a spoonful of vegetables—greens, beans, stuff like that. Believe me, this is a guaranteed weight loss program. I did my 15 days without incident. When I returned to my cell, the leader of the Mexicans paid me a visit. Came to my cell door talking shit. My cell partner was only in for a five-year hitch, he was scared shitless. I suppose I was too, but I didn't show it. I finally told him get the door open and let's get it on or take his sorry ass on back upstairs, because he wasn't helping me do my 99 years by just talking. Well, my threat worked because he left. Only later I learned that the white leaders weren't going to let him and the other Mexicans beat my ass for my disrespect. All of us lived together, but we stood the race line when a member of another race tried to discipline one of our own. It wasn't allowed.

Think of the hardest work you've ever done, then increase the pain threefold, and you have some idea of how hard we worked in the fields back then. From the time we left our row to the time we returned there was no such thing as a walk. We ran every place we went. There was no talking in the chow hall. We had to knock on the table to be excused.

Fuck, who had the strength to talk anyway? Pisses me off today when these guys knock on the table. These pussies talk, laugh, and cut up in the chow hall—they haven't earned the right to knock the way we did.

Once a year I wrote the head warden a request. I'd go into his office and he'd ask me the same question, "What do you want, Keaton?" And I'd reply the same thing every time, "A job." His answer was always the same, as if it was a recording, "What did I tell you last year?" And I'd reply, "See ya next year." He'd just look up from his doodling and ask, "Anything else?" I'd reply, "No sir," turn, and leave. He usually drew me with a hangman's noose around my neck or depicted as a devil, something like that. This went on for four or five years. The second time we had this exchange, he said, as I walked toward the door, "Keaton, you might try putting a little more diplomacy in your approach."

I couldn't get anyone else to help me. Each time I asked a boss or ranking officer who liked me, he'd tell me, sorry, but the head warden has his thumb on you, Fred. Finally, one Saturday morning, a few days after I wrote my yearly requisition, I was summoned into the security office. This time, the warden asked me if I could type. Hey, I couldn't type a lick, but I told him, sure I can. You're going to work in the office at night as a bookkeeper, he told me. Fuck, talk about surprised! This was one of the most coveted jobs on the farm—not to mention one of the most powerful. And if he found out I couldn't type, what the fuck was he going to do—put me back in the field? Hell, I had proven I could outwork any bastard out there and I could outfight just about anybody my size. I had what we called "heart"—lots of it. Once I got started, I didn't like to stop fighting. Once or twice, I even hurt some guys more than was necessary. Anyway, I got the night bookkeeping job in the security office.

I ran the night shift for the next four years. Then I got moved to the dayshift, where I stayed off and on for the next three years. After I served 10 years in Clemens, I got paroled. During that time, I did all the things powerful cons do. For most of that time, I had a personal punk, a youngster who had been turned out. I probably saved each one of them from a worse fate at the hands of one of those sadistic cons. Remember the mind-set here. The pitcher (that's me) is a real man while the catcher (the kid) is a punk, a queer—a homosexual. Come on, I lived it, I can't explain it. I'll tell you this: It's still like that today. The guys who have a punk still call themselves straight, even though they do the fucking and get sucked off. Hell, you figure it out. I can't.

It was a long ten years. I studied hard, received my high school equivalency, and attended some college courses. I read any time I wasn't in the craft shop. So when I was paroled in 1985, I adjusted quickly. My mother got me a job managing a small park for recreational vehicles that was attached to a large mobile home park, where my mother was a supervisor and manager. I was paid over a thousand a month plus my bills. My office was in the mobile home, provided along with the job. For a year, I stayed clean of all drugs except alcohol. I went to night school in Washington, D.C., and received certification as an apartment manager. I worked, went to school, lived with a couple of different women, had straight sex just like a regular guy. Enjoyed it, too. This was the real me.

I bought a spanking brand-new Camaro Z-28. Brenda moved into the trailer park in June, and we started fucking about a month after that. She was a former prostitute, stripper, nude dancer, and drug addict. She loved to fuck as much as I did—my kind of girl. When my dad was dying of cancer, he told me Brenda wasn't the kind of female one man could hang onto. Shit, what did he know? He couldn't tell me jack-shit—I was in love. We got married. We went to Cozumel, in Mexico, for a honeymoon of drugs, sex, and sun. I gave her an ass-spanking for coming on to some guy down there.

Within a year, I was managing the main park. I hired my sister to run the RV section. I went over the paperwork each month to make sure she was posting correctly. I showed her how we could skim up to $4,000 a month in cash. My alcohol and drug consumption had increased to the point where I couldn't do my job. Finally, late in '86, I was fired. Brenda and I drifted around from one place to another. We were separated a few times, got back together, and then we settled in Greenville, Texas. I worked at a job my mother got for me. The fact is, my mother gave up her job so I could have one. She's probably the only true, loving friend I've ever had. Always there for me no matter what.

For a while, Brenda and I did OK in Greenville. We made pretty good money on top of my paycheck by skimming from the company, stealing credit cards, stuff like that. We did speed and various other pills. Brenda was an expert at talking doctors out of scripts [prescriptions]. Hell, we stole a lot of scripts, too. Meth, pills, sex, stealing with credit cards—till about June 1988. We used her mother's credit card to buy a brand-new Chrysler New Yorker from a dealership right in Greenville. By this time, everything had gotten out of hand. The pills we were popping were taking their toll. We were like zombies. We were fucking not only each other but everyone else who came into contact with us. We decided to skip town, move to Florida. We packed up and down the road we went.

While I was driving, we got pulled over. The cop found an old pistol, packed away in a box, that wouldn't even fire. Charges of felon in possession of a weapon, securing execution of a document by deception, and aggravated assault with a deadly weapon were filed against me. My mother paid $2,000 to have me released on bond.

I learned that the owner of the dealership we had bought the car from had claimed that I pointed an Uzi submachine pistol at him and threatened to shoot him. I had very little reason to lie about the incident—it never happened. Fuck, except for what I saw on TV, I didn't even know what an Uzi looked like. That's what the assault charge was all about. The "securing execution of a document by deception" was based on the fact that I had reactivated some of my wife's mother's credit cards without her knowledge. Hell, she had triple-A credit from her dead husband. We even bought two cars on her credit cards, and the sales manager was quite impressed with them. If I hadn't been so fucked up in the head on dope, the entire purchase might have worked without her ever knowing about it. I fouled up by not contacting Citi Corp Credit before they mailed out the payment books. All I had to do to make it work was file a change of address—and of course make the payments.

While I was out on bond, I got a call from a detective who requested I come to the Greenville police station the next day. The Chrysler dealership owner came into the station wanting to press charges on the supposed Uzi assault. What had actually happened was this. At the time, I was in a drugged-up state and I talked some shit to a mechanic and a salesman at the dealership. I said something like, you know what an asshole the owner is and he better watch out. Well, the owner called my wife and told her to tell me he'd better not hear of me even saying his name again or he'd see to it I'd get more than just prison. Some shit like that must have happened. That's what I got busted for.

My mother paid a lawyer $2,500 to represent me. He got the prosecutor to agree to have me plead guilty to all three charges in return for 15 years on each one, to run concurrently. It didn't do any good to say I didn't do the Uzi thing—it was a package deal. I was allowed to plead out to all three or to none. I took the 15 years. I arrived back in the Texas prison system at the end of 1988.

I served three years on these charges. I was assigned to the Goree Unit until 1991 and I was paroled that year. A couple prison buddies who were on parole wanted me to join them in Cedar Creek Lake doing a little plumbing and other odd jobs, so that's what I did. Things went OK for a few months. Brenda divorced me, but we still fucked a few times. I saw a female prison guard for a while, she had some money and was a quick fuck, but she wasn't what I was looking for, so I stopped seeing her. My brother was stealing some stuff and selling it. He kept after me to go out with him, so one night I did. On the night I decide to go with him, we get pulled over by the police. Shit, what gods had smiled down on me! Mother again bonded me and my brother out. A $500 lawyer and a guilty plea got me 15 years for theft of a truck worth $20,000.

For two weeks awaiting my trial date, I fucked Sandra, my buddy's wife. She had left him a few weeks before. She was trying to make her way back to her mother's house in Mississippi or Arkansas, some place like that. Sandra drove me to the courthouse on my trial date. In the car, she gave me one last blow job and drove away. I stood on the steps watching her wave. I walked into that court room thinking, this is it, never again. I'm going to straighten up. Whatever it takes. The judge sentenced me to 15 years to run concurrently with any other charge or time I may have had. At the most, I figured I'd be home in 18-28 months.

Well, here it is, almost 10 years later. My file is up for review in the year 2002. Check back with me then and I'll let you know how things have turned out. I've managed to teach myself how to think instead of what to think. I had to discard a lot of childhood fantasies and take responsibility for my life away from the gods. Teaching myself to think critically has been the turning point in my life. I love and live my life the way most people only dream about. I'm the kind, caring, considerate person who was trapped in a shell by fake religion and the culture that imprisons most of us. Once I'm released on parole this time, I'll never again return to prison. I don't desire the things that brought me here so many times before, and I use logic and reason, tempered by critical thinking, to make decisions in my life.

To the constructionist, one of the more fascinating features of Fred's account is the distinction convicts make when they consider sex between men in prison. The inserter, the "pitcher" in anal sex, or the one who has oral sex performed on his penis by another man is regarded as supremely masculine. The fact that he engages in a homosexual act does not undermine or threaten his masculinity. Indeed, he is regarded as *even more* masculine for having convinced or forced another man to serve as his "bitch." In fact, such a man is not regarded as having engaged in homosexual sex at all. He was the man; hence, what he *did* was not homosexual in nature. In contrast, the insertee, the "catcher," is regarded as effeminate, less than a man. In prison, he is most decidedly deviant, someone worthy of contempt. He was the one who engaged in the homosexual act, even though he was the receiver not the initiator (Gagnon and Simon, 2001, 1967, pp. 247–250).

In many ways, prison sex involving an aggressive, stereotypically masculine inserter and a smaller, weaker, more passive insertee is even more about power and subordination than it is about sex. Some psychiatric observers have even gone so far as to concur with this judgment, regarding the behavior engaged in by the inserter as not "real" homosexuality (Lindner, 1948). Fred wonders about this division, questioning "how men can rationalize men-on-men sex. The guy doing the fucking remains a man while the receiver or sucker becomes a queer bitch. . . . Don't ask me how the fuck to explain it," he exclaims, "but we did it." To the constructionist, far from being a rationalization, the fact that this particular delineation of the world of sexuality is promulgated and believed means that it corresponds to a legitimate definition of reality. Such a delineation points not to self-deception but to the imaginative powers of the human mind to construct meaningful definitions of the material and social world.

At first glance, Fred represents the very antithesis of this book's "Deviants Are Us" approach. While this initial observation contains at least a grain of truth, it is wise to keep in mind the fact that deviance is a matter of degree that stretches from near-conventionality to extreme and almost unimaginable reaches of criminal depravity. (Consider the character Hannibal "The Cannibal" Lechter, a truly spine-tingling fictional monster.) Hence, someone who committed burglary, armed robbery, and auto theft represents one point along that continuum. Correspondingly, then, Fred's degree of difference from the conventional world is instructive at the very least for a comparison with other, less strongly condemned, forms of deviant behavior.

Initially, Fred seems to correspond very closely to Gottfredson and Hirschi's improperly or inadequately socialized deviant. Recall from the introduction of this book that Michael Gottfredson and Travis Hirschi hypothesized that deviant and criminal behavior is the product of low self-control—which Fred seems to have exhibited in abundance throughout most of his life—that, in turn, is the product of poor, inconsistent, and/or inadequate parenting (1990). Fred tells us he was conceived out of wedlock, raised by his mother and stepfather, and didn't learn who his "sperm father" was until the age of 12. His family moved frequently; he was often slapped by his parents (although Fred acknowledges that he often deserved it), and his mother and stepfather often fought; he describes numerous times when his parents were absent from the house; he and a male relative his age were often allowed to drink in a car with the boy's father— his father's cousin—and mother; and on at least one occasion, after being released from a juvenile facility, he and his second stepfather drove to Louisiana to retrieve his mother, who was living with his first stepfather. The fact that both of Fred's brothers also ended up in the Texas penitentiary system argues in support of the theory that inadequate upbringing creates a deviant with low self-control.

Gottfredson and Hirschi would point to Fred's background and say it all adds up to extremely poor parenting, one highly likely to produce someone who grows up to exhibit very low self-control. Indeed, that is precisely how Fred turned out. His entire criminal career seems a study in caprice, impulse, and recklessness. The sheer volume of his criminal behavior, his inability to conceal his identity, and his tendency to get apprehended with great regularity ("Shit," he moans, describing one arrest, "what gods had smiled down on me!") bear eloquent testimony to a risk-taking, impetuous, and unthinking pattern of behavior. Low self-control is the very watchword of Fred's career in crime. Indeed, even the non-criminal features of his life manifest a high level of impulsiveness. Consider Fred's sexual promiscuity, which included sex with: a female cousin for quarters; the wife of a close friend; when he was an army enlistee, a 14-year-old girl as well as her mother; and "queers" and "punks" both in and outside of prison. Moreover, as he admits, his drug use exacerbated the risks he took and the consequences he suffered as a result.

Fred's lack of self-control seems to verify Travis Hirschi's theoretical shift from a *social* control theory of crime, delinquency, and deviance to his current *self*-control theory. In 1969, Hirschi published a book which argues that deviants and delinquents are characterized by weak or absent bonds to conventional society. They lack the kinds of social, emotional, and financial investments that would reign in their impulsive, selfish, risky, and destructive behavior—a job, an education, a family, a house, or a close relationship with parents, a spouse, an employer, a teacher, a priest, minister, or rabbi. Emotionally, Fred's mother seems a beacon in an otherwise turmoil-filled life. Indeed, he mentions her as his "only true, loving friend" who was "always there for me no matter what." In a personal letter to me, Fred is poignant and detailed about the feelings that overcome him when contemplating the inevitable death of his mother. He mentions a "stabbing pain," a "crushing sadness," knowing that, at some point in his life, he will never again be able to touch or embrace her.

Clearly, however, this relationship was not sufficient to insulate him from a life of crime. Nor was the job he obtained, through the intervention of his mother, after he was released from prison in 1985. Indeed, managing the trailer park was for Fred simply an invitation to rip off his employer. Social control theory argues that a decent job and a mother's love should have exercised at least a modicum of *social* control in Fred's life—he had emotional and material investments in people and activities that, one would imagine, would have operated to keep him on the straight and narrow. What he lacked, however, was *self*-control. It is likely that Gottfredson and Hirschi would have argued that Fred's criminal behavior is a clear vindication of their "general theory of crime."

Yet, there are some decidedly conventional features of Fred's life. He managed to complete a high school equivalency diploma and some college courses in prison. After working on the prison farm for several years at back-breaking agricultural labor, Fred managed to obtain a highly coveted bookkeeping job, a feat which required persistence (given the disfavor he earned with his warden). Once he started working at that job, he gained a certain measure of competence. Today, Fred is a veracious reader; he has aspirations to write essays, articles, perhaps a book (this account is evidence of that fact), and he regards himself a reformed man. He does not display the self-righteous fury that characterized another prison writer,

Jack Henry Abbott, whose rage produced essays that attracted the attention of influential authors and others (1981), who exerted their influence to get him released. Soon after his release, Abbott exploded into violence against an innocent victim over a "misunderstanding." In stark contrast, while Abbott blames everyone except himself for the misfortunes of his life, Fred admits to foolishness and a distinct lack of good judgment. Unlike Abbott, for whom prison *is* "the belly of the beast," Fred's complaints about the prison system are few and far between. In fact, when I asked him directly to describe his current prison life, he declined to do so, as much out of loyalty to his guards and employer as from fear of retaliation. His description of a prison search is extremely mild compared to what many prisoners have to say about their incarceration.

Going back to our vocabularies of motive or deviance neutralization techniques, it is interesting that Fred offers a diminished capacity, "billiard ball," or "sad story" account only rarely. This type of account says, "I couldn't help it, I didn't have any choice, the circumstances forced me to do it, if you were in my shoes, you would have done the same thing." Fred offers this line of reasoning when he was on the run from a Mississippi reform school and decided to stay at a homosexual's house and permit the man to fellate him in exchange for a bus ticket back home: "Shit, what's a dumb kid to do?" He also blames Jimmy more than he does himself for becoming involved in his one armed robbery. Fred also often blames diminished capacity on his drug abuse, which frequently led to poor judgment about the crimes in which he engaged and the plea bargains he accepted. Likewise, he attributes the violence in which he engaged in prison at least as much to the provocation of others as to his own hotheadedness. The diminished capacity line of reasoning *excuses* or *mitigates* the wrongfulness of an action; it argues that what the actor did shouldn't be judged as harshly as would be the case in the absence of the excuse. Nonetheless, Fred doesn't expend a great deal of energy on excusing his actions.

The vocabulary of motive that emerges most strongly from Fred's account is the *apology*. The key to the apology as a neutralization technique is that the actor alienates, estranges, or separates portions of himself or herself relative to his or her actions. The apology, like the excuse, affirms the validity of the social norm that condemns the act in question, but the apology basically offers no excuse for the act. It splits the actor into a "blameworthy" part and a part that "stands back and sympathizes with the blame giving." Hence, by implication, the apologist will be deemed "worthy of being brought back into the fold" of acceptable, right-thinking people—in effect, no longer stigmatized (Goffman, 1971, p. 113).

The apology doesn't always work, of course, and it works better with some audiences than with others. For certain actions and certain types of apology, it is often effective. And the fact is, for the actor, the mere utterance of an apology is frequently effective—that is, apologies are often sincerely believed in by apologists. Fred says right off the top that he "deeply regrets the pain and misery" he caused "the innocent sufferers" of his crimes. "The thought of the harm I inflicted on innocent victims still haunts me," he adds. One searches in vain throughout Jack Henry Abbot's *In the Belly of the Beast* for anything even remotely like an apology of this sort.

Fred also makes use of another deviance neutralization technique that is very similar to the apology: splitting his *contemporary* self off from his *past* self. He looks back on his actions as the work of "an immature, naive teenager in the body of an adult." (Even though, let's recall, his most recent incarceration was for criminal activity enacted when he was in his mid-30s.) He vows never again to return to prison. More importantly, he claims he doesn't desire the things that led to actions that, in turn, led to his incarceration. He attributes the change to reading and contemplating, to the development of a critical, rational, logical mode of thinking, to learning "how to think instead of what to think," to wresting responsibility for his life "away from the gods."

Whether sincere or not, accounts display a certain allegiance to conventional norms. At the very least, they indicate that the account giver is capable of being sufficiently empathetic to conventional others that he or she renders accounts that seek to be plausible to them. And plausibility is independent of their truth. A "good" account is one that is believed by an audience and succeeds in reducing the actor's blameworthiness; a "bad" account is one that is either implausible or does not succeed in reducing the actor's fault. Says Goffman: "True accounts are often good, but false accounts are sometimes better"—that is, if they are more effective in convincing an audience not to blame the account giver (p. 112). Are you, the reader, convinced of the sincerity of Fred's account? My intuition tells me he sincerely believes in its validity. The fact that he couples remorse with a criticism of unjust disparities in criminal sentencing lends a certain credence to this view. True, prisoners often try to "con" parole boards and sympathetic outsiders. But how to distinguish the con jobs from the sincere apologies? It's not always easy. Fred invites the reader to "check back" with him in 2002 to find out if the parole board grants his next request for release. Even better, perhaps the reader can "check back" with Fred in 2012 or 2022 to find out how he has lived his life as a free man.

CHAPTER 13

The Use of Accounts in the Study of Deviance

Three decades ago, overwhelmingly, personal accounts were examined by researchers and scholars more or less exclusively with respect to their factual accuracy. The issue that guided such investigations was whether accounts could be used to determine "what happened" in the literal, concrete sense. "Good" accounts were empirically accurate; "bad" accounts were those that were factually false or distorted. But in the 1970s, an Italian historian, Alessandro Portelli, noticed that the oral histories of the people whom he interviewed contained systematic omissions, distortions, and imaginary embellishments of events that had taken place 20 or more years before. He decided that the construction of the stories told by his informants was *itself* a historical datum worth investigating. Instead of simply being factually accurate or inaccurate, accounts are also social and historical creations in their own right. They represent testimonies that are organized according to principles that convey cultural, social, and personal truths. This recent stress on "subjectivity" does not mean that the issue of empirical or concrete facticity must be abandoned altogether. But it does mean the value of an account does not lie in its factual accuracy alone.

All contemporary observers who study the subject of personal accounts agree on at least one basic assumption: Narratives are *not* a simple *reflection of* or a *window on* material reality, that is, the events that are narrated. All students of narrative argue that "Just the facts, ma'am" is quite

249

literally an impossibility—in effect, a fiction. Events and experiences do not simply imprint themselves on our brains and come out in the telling—intact and identical for all narrators. The meaning of events and experiences is unstable, liable to interpretations that vary from one teller to another. Stories get told in particular ways, both with respect to a particular cultural and social setting and with respect to individual predilection.

Why do we tell stories in a particular way? Why do we include *these* events in our narrative and leave *those* events out? Which events get recalled? Which ones are forgotten? Everyone who studies narrative assumes that a great deal of variation prevails from one teller to another in the stories that are told. Even the same set of events will be narrated in radically different ways. For instance, if we were to ask Alan and Sarah, a divorced couple, about their marriage and why it broke up, we would receive two very different accounts of supposedly more or less identical events. Yet, those two accounts are not necessarily contradictory. Both may be literally and factually true; if we had videotaped the events each describes, chances are, we would have seen more or less exactly what Alan said and more or less exactly what Sarah said. But Alan's account left out much of what Sarah's account included, and vice versa. Again, their accounts are factually true—but highly selective, a particular spin or interpretation on the events that took place.

Consider the following story. It is the narration of a literally true event. (I was not a witness to the event but heard the story from a friend who was a participant.) The setting is the funeral of a well-known feminist leader. Prior to the ceremony, several dozen women are talking to one another informally about the experiences they had with the deceased. In this informal, one-on-one conversation, the consensus is that she was difficult, demanding, imperious, dictatorial, self-centered, and even, at times, cruel. The talk exchanged between and among these women is a kind of narrative, an account of events to which they were a witness or a party or of experiences they had. During the ceremony, however, when the public eulogies are delivered to the entire assembly, almost entirely positive words about the deceased are spoken. The eulogies are unstinting in their praise of the tireless, fearless leader, who fought for truth, justice, and human decency. These eulogies, like the informal talk, are narratives—personal accounts describing and evaluating the life and character of the deceased. Any potentially critical comment is cast into the context of establishing a multidimensional character. Pointing out minor flaws in the eulogy, said one participant, is "humanizing, you don't want her to be an icon. . . . You knew her, she was a real person." The minor flaws are included in the eulogies only to give her character shading and nuance; they add the human dimension.

Which of these two sets of accounts is true; which one is false? One might be tempted to say that the accounts spoken in private were *truer* than those spoken in public, but this is not entirely true. Both accounts represented *a kind* of truth, *aspects* of the truth—a *slant on* or a *version of* reality. To the mourners assembled at that funeral, the deceased *was* tireless and fearless, a fighter for justice and decency. That narrative is not false—but it represents only a partial truth. Indeed, the words spoken informally before the ceremony are *also* partial truths. When those statements were uttered, it was *assumed* that their leader fought for justice. Otherwise why did so many of her followers, admirers, and colleagues come to her funeral? That self-evident truth did not have to be stated; in that setting, personal (and private) gripes were aired. But if a journalist had overheard the informal talk and reported it in the form of a newspaper or a magazine article, these feminists would have been outraged at the invasion of their privacy, the reckless and malicious disclosure of intimate secrets revealed, and might very well have denied the reported negative characterization.

Again, I'm not talking about the issue of factual truth or falsity here but interpretation and selectivity. In the two sets of narratives, what counted in *private* was the personal complaints of these women against the deceased; what counted in *public* was praise for the deceased in recognition of her contributions to the feminist movement. In fact, both narratives were selective accounts of events—events that in both cases actually and literally took place—as well as subjective evaluations or interpretations of those events. Yet both narratives, contradictory as they sound, were literally and concretely *true.* The participant who described these events to me concluded: "Like Robespierre [a leader of the French Revolution, known for his ruthlessness], she was a terrible person, but she changed the world."

Hence, my second point: The narrative-producing *context* shapes the content of the account. This means that someone is more likely to produce one kind of story among friends, another among relatives, yet a different account among employers, and so on. As we saw, entirely different accounts were produced in two different social contexts—the informal talk among friends *before* funeral orations, and the funeral orations themselves. We have to ask ourselves: What *end* is the account or narrative designed to serve? Entertainment? Career advancement? Gossip? Idle chitchat? Dinner conversation? Convincing a potential partner of one's romantic prospects? Exonerating oneself in a trial? Winning an argument with a driver whose car you've just crashed into? Each of these social contexts will bring forth *distinctive* and *identifiably different* stories or accounts. Each will be selective, each will be partial. *What one says* in each context is likely to be particular to that context. Moreover, the *form* of the narration will influence its *content*. For instance, written tales differ from oral tales; accounts offered when filling out an application are likely to differ from stories told in sign language.

In short, a given narrative account of a particular life represents one of an infinite number of "partial truths." Narratives are constructs, as one anthropologist said of ethnography (Clifford, 1986), they are *fictions* in the sense of "something made or fashioned." In the sense that all truths are partial truths, narratives are "true fictions," not only made but *made up*—that is, conjured up, or called forth and fashioned, out of the raw material of a life. This does not mean that they are, in the conventional sense of the words, false or a lie, only that they represent a selection from the details of a life and are therefore "inherently partial—committed and incomplete." Moreover, not only are the facts (or supposed facts) selected, all facts are subject to interpretation; a "spin" is placed on the facts. A narrative issues from a particular *voice*, that is to say, a narrator, and that voice casts a certain light on the events described. Affirmations of their truth are offered, documentation is trotted out, narrative structure draws the listener or reader into the talk, metaphors, "tropes, figures, and allegories . . . select and impose meaning as they translate it" (Clifford, 1986, pp. 6, 7).

In short, all statements—autobiographical narratives included—are *made*, that is, uttered or written down *by* a particular person *in* a particular sociocultural and situational context *for* a particular reason. Writing or speaking—making or fashioning or stringing together—a set of sentences is not the same thing as picking an apple off a tree or a rock up off the ground. In short, narrative is *constructed* or *fashioned* from the rough clay of life. No two authors, even if they witnessed the same set of events, will produce identical accounts of those events. We all have our own take or slant on the world, we all interpret and experience events in different ways. These assumptions are shared by just about everyone who investigates this interesting yet controversial area of study.

WHAT ARE ACCOUNTS TRYING TO ACHIEVE?

In 1983, *I, Rigoberta Menchu*, a book made up of the testimony of a Guatemalan peasant woman of Mayan ancestry, was published. It detailed the oppression of her people and the savage brutality of her country's military regime. So moving, powerful, and evocative was Menchu's book that in 1992 she was awarded the Nobel Peace Prize. Anthropologist David Stoll investigated Menchu's claims and found some to be factually untrue (1999). Contrary to her book's claims, Stoll says, Menchu was not an unschooled, monolingual peasant who learned Spanish shortly before narrating her autobiography. She was not only literate and had years of education in four different schools, she also received years of Spanish language instruction and was completely fluent in that language. Moreover, says Stoll, Menchu's account was propaganda for the leftist guerrilla forces she supported as well as international revolutionary Marxism. In fact, her book was the product of edited transcriptions of interviews with Elisabeth Burgos-Debray, a Venezuelan anthropologist living in France, formerly married to the well-known revolutionary Regis Debray. Further, Stoll says, Menchu was many miles distant from some of the events she claimed to have witnessed. Moreover, he argues, a few of the events she describes never happened at all. For instance, she recalls a younger brother Nicolas who starved to death. In actual fact, she did not have a younger brother; her brother, Nicolas, is a decade older than she, and none of her siblings starved to death. Much of the local violence she describes was between her father and a rival Mayan peasant family (in fact, her father's in-laws) and not, as she claims, inflicted on her family by a greedy European-descended elite "who wanted to take our land."

There are several entirely different issues here.

Even if some of Menchu's *specific* claims are false, the Guatemalan military regime, supported openly and generously by the U.S. government in its fight against communism, *did* commit uncountable acts of oppression and brutality. Peasants who opposed the regime *were* slaughtered in the thousands. These are historical facts. Hence, however inaccurate some of her details, critics of Stoll's book argued, Menchu's claims should be evaluated as a cry for attention to injustice in a land that had been previously ignored by persons of conscience in Europe and North America. Was the presentation of Menchu as a simple peasant woman the most effective means of getting her message across? Did the false claim that she had personally witnessed all the atrocities she described better dramatize the plight of Guatemalan peasants? What was the most effective means of putting an end to the slaughter? Did Stoll's revelations endanger the cause of justice and reform? And was that *his* intention in writing his book? Was he implicitly endorsing the brutal military regime in Guatemala and opposing the democratic movements that sought to put an end to it? These are important questions that underscore the slippery border between literal factual truth of an assertion and the content of that assertion.

It's also interesting to examine how *I, Rigoberta Menchu* was constructed. Menchu regarded her book not as *her* autobiography but as a testimonial, her account, a story told, through her, "of all Guatemalans." The book was not about her, she would have argued, but about the Guatemalan people. Arguing that she did not personally witness or experience a given event is irrelevant, a distraction, she would have said. Each and every factual claim she made about what happened did not have to take place specifically in *her* life as long as it took place *somewhere*, to *some* Guatemalans. Consider, too, the input of her interlocutors, translators, and intellectual inspirations. Since the book was as much a product of the encouragement and enterprise of the circle of French and Latin American Marxists with whom Menchu was friendly as it was of Menchu's life and experience, we might wonder about the input of her radical, non-Guatemalan peers into the book.

Did their notions about the nature of Third World oppression by imperialist powers shape the presentation of Menchu as a hapless, innocent witness to acts of savagery by a brutal puppet regime propped up by the U.S. Central Intelligence Agency? And shouldn't these intellectuals and revolutionaries have been aware of the fact that, given the contentious nature of politics, a thorough investigation could very well have dug up discrediting information about Menchu's claims, thereby undermining the very progressive cause they supported? Wasn't it their responsibility to have been as scrupulous as possible in factually verifying their claims so that they could have made the most plausible case possible? Another question: Were issues of factual scrupulousness as relevant in 1983, before the collapse of the Marxist-inspired Eastern European regimes, as they are today? The fact is, both exaggeration and literal facticity are rhetorical devices whose role has to be understood when accounts are rendered and their implications are debated. Issues such as these must be considered when thinking about how autobiographies are put together.

Once again, narratives of lives are *not* a simple window on the past. They are constructed out of protean or changeable raw material, capable of being shaped into a variety of forms. As a result, they are as much a social and cultural product as the very behavior they claim to describe.

What about the accounts in this book? To reiterate, let's be clear about this: These accounts were solicited by me for the purpose of this book (or, in two cases, by colleagues for their purposes and "borrowed" by me). Moreover, my theoretical approach and intellectual concerns shaped my selection of the cases as well as the slant presented on the lives they describe. Consequently, the features of the lives of these informants that appear in the pages of this book reflect this particular contextual constraint. It was specifically the contributors' unconventionality in which I was interested; hence, their unconventionality is at the core of their accounts. Moreover, it is important to emphasize that, unlike autobiographical accounts that are rendered by the author in a continuous stream, without constraint or directive probing, all but one of the statements in these accounts (Annette's) were elicited as a result of the researcher's direct questions. In other words, the subject of topics discussed is likely to be very different when authors versus researchers control the flow of the narrative. My control of the questions means that the answers tend to focus on my interests.

In addition, let's keep in mind another issue: The physical and contextual rendering of these accounts took place in a private, one-to-one encounter. People will say things in face-to-face interaction that seem shockingly raw, intimate, and brutally frank when read on the page. In fact, I suspect, when reading them, a majority of the contributors of these accounts will feel alienated from them. It is one thing to sit down and say something in private to an interviewer, especially if you have developed a comfortable, close relationship with him or her. It is quite another to encounter the innermost secrets of one's unconventional life spread out in black and white, knowing that thousands of undergraduates will read it and wonder what kind of person lived this life.

VERISIMILITUDE AND NEGOTIABILITY

These contextual issues should steer us away from the naive notion that these accounts simply reflect events in the lives of our contributors in a straightforward fashion. *How* lives are rendered influences *what* is rendered. Hence, we should think about what these accounts tell us beyond the narrowly factual dimension. *At the same time*, we have to balance these contextual factors with issues of content. After all, when reading these accounts, every one of us makes certain assumptions about a factual core contained in all of them that is grounded in events that take place in the material world. In other words, readers assume that contributors of these accounts didn't "just make it all up."

In the words of Jerome Bruner (1993, p. 46), all autobiographical accounts possess "both verisimilitude and negotiability." As for "verisimilitude," there are the "bare bones" of the events themselves, not subject to interpretation. Did these events take place or didn't they? *For certain purposes*, the verisimilitude of these "bare bones" matter. As with history, explains Bruner, there are "matters of consensual public record to be taken into account" (p. 46). Certain versions of a life are constrained by the events that take place in the material world. Just as ignoring matters of record makes bad history, subverting the factual record makes bad autobiography. Setting aside or falsifying the "bare bones" of a life lends an aura of unbelievability to autobiographical accounts.

Thus, Harry's alcoholism account would make no sense whatsoever if he had been drinking grape juice all those years rather than bourbon; Lenny's S&M account would have been utter nonsense as autobiography if he were a happily married heterosexual who only engaged in "missionary" sex with his wife. And if Sally were really a svelte 120 pounds rather than an obese woman, would her account make any sense to us whatsoever as a rendition of lived experiences? (Actually, if it *were* true that Harry had been a teetotaler, Lenny a conventional heterosexual, and Sally of average weight, the observer would have to wonder how the contributors of these accounts had been able to narrate the supposed events of their lives without actually having lived them. And if this were the case, their accounts would have been very interesting, but in *very different ways* from the ways that make them interesting as descriptions of lived experiences.) We would be forced to say, as Bruner does when the autobiographer's account is alienated from the "bare bones" of his or her life: "It just doesn't make sense" (p. 47).

Notice that what is at issue here is not the sheer facticity or material existence of the conditions or the literal occurrence of the events under description—what Bruner calls *verisimilitude*. Many of the assertions contained in autobiographical accounts can be checked against the documentary record: photographs; hospital records; employment records; school records; college transcripts; physicians', psychiatrists', and psychologists' diagnoses; arrest records; DNA tests; blood and urine tests, and so on. In addition, we are free to consult co-participants in the events being described to seek independent confirmation. Many autobiographical claims are unmasked as false after the historical record is checked. And for many autobiographical accounts, the question of whether the narrated events actually took place *is* important and interesting. After all, if some people *really were* abducted by extraterrestrials (Mack, 1995), the world would be a very different place from the way it is had those stories been imagined or invented. But for *most* narratives, literal facticity is *not* the most interesting issue. Once again, the reader *assumes* a core of verisimilitude.

Bruner reminds us that, just as there must be a foundation of verisimilitude in a valid autobiographical account, there is *negotiability* as well. What are some crucial dimensions of negotiability? In short, what explains the "same events, different accounts" phenomenon? Here, slant, emphasis, and focus loom large. Three mutually interactive sources come readily to mind: individual variation, cultural variation, and the interpretive dimension.

Individual variation refers to how and why different people narrate different stories about the same set of events, the personal, idiosyncratic reasons all of us select certain events to tell and filter out others.

Cultural variation refers to how and why norms about life stories that are appropriate (and inappropriate) to tell are disseminated throughout a society and influence the content of what is narrated.

And the *interpretive dimension* refers to how people *experience* events, what they *make* of them both cognitively and emotionally, how these events filter through their special way of looking at and feeling about what's happening in their lives. The interpretive dimension focuses not so much on how and why certain events are narrated as the special *meaning* that is attached to them. Two narrators may report the same set of events but impart a very different emotional *spin* on these events. For instance, a man and a woman may narrate exactly the same set of events in their sexual encounter but feel completely differently about the experience.

Interpretations are, of course, configured by the social characteristics and memberships of an account's narrator—most notably age, sex, race, and social class. With respect to the content and substance of this book, these characteristics and memberships turn most centrally on unconventionality: How do we *define* and *experience* unconventionality? What is the experience of being stigmatized? How do conventionals regard, think about, and act toward persons whom they define as socially unacceptable? And how do such experiences shape the content of the accounts that these persons contribute?

INDIVIDUAL VARIATION

Goffman reminds us that "presentation of self" is central to how we act in public. In a like fashion, Bruner (p. 47) asks, what about the "presentation of self" in autobiography? What kind of impression is the author or contributor of an account trying to achieve? What self-image is he or she trying to portray? What sort of identity do these accounts affirm for their contributors? What stance or posture are they striking with respect to the reader or the listener?

Along these lines, then, we are forced to ask questions, as Bruner does, about the "negotiability" of these accounts. We have to think about how their contributors position themselves, what self-conception or identity is expressed by their narratives. Why did they present themselves in the way they did? What sort of persona or image of themselves would they have projected if their account had been elicited by a different vehicle, venue, or context?

Did Diane seek to elicit sympathy for fat people by telling us about her confrontation with the hecklers? In describing that episode, why was she so brutal and direct in discussing the crudeness of her language? Did she want us to know how heroic she was when she stood up for her dignity and self-respect? Or perhaps how unheroic most fat people are? Was Lenny trying to shock Jerry by describing the uses to which the S&M paraphernalia he sold were put? Why did he tell Jerry the "cock ring" story? What was Annette's intention in telling us that at one time she weighed only 85 pounds? Why did I offer up the example of my autistic son as a deviant? Am I positioning myself as a long-suffering parent to whom considerable sympathy is owed? Do I experience a special feeling of injustice around the issue of "courtesy stigma"? Does Dwight delight in narrating the details of activities and predilections many readers are likely to regard as shameless degeneracy? Does he take special satisfaction in tweaking the nose of conventional society? Is he trying to shock me, a conventionally married man, by being so brutally honest? Do Leslie and Helen's accounts serve a political or ideological purpose?

What about the opposite side of the coin: What are these narrators *not* being forthcoming about? What are they hiding, forgetting, filtering out, being evasive about? Surely there are relevant events in their lives that they do not want to talk about. What are they? And what about the people who live unconventional lives who *refused* to be interviewed, or whom I decided not to interview? Three drug dealers refused for practical reasons: They were afraid their revelations would result in arrest. A lesbian couple refused because their teenage daughter did not want their relationship to be publicized—anonymity or no anonymity. I decided not to approach three teenagers who led troubled lives because my relationship with their parents was too close for me to feel comfortable about revealing the details of their lives to readers who might know them.

The lesson should be clear: In spite of the fact that the accounts contained in this book were narrated by people, one or more features of whose lives are nonnormative, in all likelihood the narrators filtered *out* some of the more unsavory (or—who knows?—altogether too wholesome) aspects of their lives to project a self-image with which they felt comfortable. In addition, these accounts, even if in slightly self-edited form, were contributed by people who were *willing* to reveal some of themselves to me. This makes us wonder about the nature of the distinctly unconventional lives of people who, as a result of their choice or mine, remain unvoiced and in the shadows with respect to the nature of those lives.

CULTURAL CONSTRUCTION

Along with these personal issues, there are larger cultural and structural matters to consider in thinking about how personal accounts are constructed. Bruner refers to "canonical forms" of autobiography, located within normative conventions that determine what should and shouldn't be said, what should be emphasized and what should be left out (p. 49). Autobiographies that fall outside these canonical forms are not regarded as acceptable, not accorded recognition. Stretching the point a bit, they are treated as "deviant" autobiographies. Hence, when considering writing one, the prospective autobiographer knows to adhere to the proper format. Certain subjects and styles are unacceptable they are told, while others are normative, acceptable, and welcome among the relevant autobiography-reading audiences. Ken Plummer (1995) examines how autobiographical sexual accounts—contemporary "sexual story telling"—fall into a small number of identifiable genres or literary styles. For instance, says Plummer, there are genres of tale-telling of coming out (narrated by homosexuals), resistance and survival (about rape), and recovery (sexual abuse). Each genre has its own canonical rules that determine whether its relevant audiences will be receptive to a particular tale. If these rules are adhered to, the tale and its teller will receive attention and be valorized; if violated, both tale and teller will be ignored or denounced.

Canonical forms change over time. What used to be private, says Plummer, has become public. Today, personal accounts concerning homosexuality, rape, and sexual abuse victimization are talked about and written about at length and in detail; years ago, they were not told because these were not considered acceptable autobiographical subjects. Moreover, what has become public is communicated to and among members of a social community—fellow homosexuals and rape and sexual abuse victims—whose members exert influence back on the community concerning appropriate, acceptable, or approved accounts about these phenomena. Over time, a consensus is reached about the style and content of an appropriate account in each of these genres or styles. Stories or accounts become embedded in a social world, and an "intimate citizenship" is formed that becomes, in a sense, a political constituency, a kind of social movement pressing for representations of sexual experiences along the appropriate lines. Telling sexual stories is culturally channeled into specific styles or genres. And, by expressing sexual experiences in a certain way, someone who lived them joins a moral community, a political constituency whose members make demands on the society concerning how they and their experiences are to be treated and thought about.

Following Plummer, we might designate several deviant account genres or literary styles. For the most part, they parallel the deviance vocabularies of motive we looked at in the introduction.

For example, many alcoholics offer the *salvation* genre: I was an alcoholic; I drank abusively and destructively; I found Alcoholics Anonymous (or God, or the ideal partner, or the perfect therapy); I gave up drinking and pulled myself together, saved my life, put my life on track, and became a more worthy human being. Interestingly enough, Harry does not offer a perfect example of this literary genre, since his reminiscences of his alcoholic days are very much tinged with nostalgia and longing for a lifestyle whose demise fills him with a certain measure of regret. Still, he gave up drinking because he was convinced he had to grow up, accept adult responsibility, and get on with his life, so there's a large measure of the salvation rhetoric in Harry's account. Annette comes a bit closer to the salvation genre in that she expresses fewer positive sentiments about her experiences as an anorexic, which caused her far more pain than pleasure. Now it's time to live a life of fulfillment.

In contrast, another type of deviance account is the *normalization* genre: "I am what I am, and if you don't like it, you're a narrow-minded bigot!" Certainly Dwight (our patron of prostitutes and purchaser of pornography) comes as close to this literary style as it's possible to imagine. Dwight doesn't want to be judged (although he has plenty to say about lifestyles he disapproves of!) and he doesn't want to change, either. "You don't like it?" he challenges. "That's OK—just look away!" He likes the way he lives just fine, and if the mainstream sees "warts," well, that's their problem. He considers the way he lives every bit as acceptable as the conventional Dagwood Bumstead lifestyle; in fact, he feels superior to it. Lenny (the devotee of S&M) and Jeff (the former male madam) are not nearly so militant about the matter as Dwight, but they, too, express the view that what they do should not be condemned by the social mainstream. Dwight manifests an "in your face" style while Lenny and Jeff do not—in fact, their approach is much more matter-of-fact. And Leslie and Helen not only assert the "normality" of lesbianism—their lives *affirm* it. They are sufficiently conventional that rarely do they have to put forth the effort to normalize the lives they lead.

Third, there is the "fighting back" genre. Certainly Diane's confrontation with her young anti-fat hecklers represents that tradition; Sally, while not nearly so militant as Diane, does lob assertive responses back to her harassers from time to time. The organization to which they belong, the National Association to Advance Fat Acceptance (NAAFA), has the ostensible purpose of fighting for the rights of fat people. Sam's account is filled with expressions of fighting against society's neglect of homelessness and the stigma that often accompanies living on the street.

We can imagine any number of literary styles of deviance accounts. The literature is fairly bursting with "vocabularies of motive" in the world of unconventionality. Not all of them are examples of "everyday" deviance—and that's exactly the point: If even the most notorious and serious of deviants employs stigma neutralization techniques, this indicates the (at least partial) hold that conventional society has on nearly all rule violators.

I corresponded very briefly with a convict who argued that he was improperly convicted—hence, the "I'm not guilty, I didn't do it, I was unjustly condemned!" genre. (He discontinued our correspondence when I informed him that I was powerless to engineer his release.) Outright denial is relatively rare in the world of deviance, but it is far from unknown. Scully and Marolla show that denial is common among convicted rapists (1984), and McCaghy found denial to be frequent among convicted child molesters (1967, 1968). Then there is the "I have a condition, I can't help myself; I deserve pity, not scorn" literary style. At one time, the handicapped were more likely to express their condition in this genre; today, it has faded from the landscape (Charlton, 1999; Linton, 1997). "I had to do it, you would have done the same thing in my shoes" is yet another rhetorical device into which people who render an account of their lives cast their narrative. Many delinquents engage in it (Sykes and Matza, 1957), as do many murderers (Katz, 1988, pp. 12–51), student cheaters (McCabe, 1992), and white-collar criminals (Benson, 1985). Then there is the "deviance is bad, but what I did isn't really deviant—or at least, it's not *seriously* deviant" genre. As we saw in chapter 2, this is engaged in by nurses who steal hospital drugs (Dabney, 1995), male street hustlers (Calhoun, 1992), and the professional fence (Klockars, 1974). Knowing what's been written about the vocabularies of motive that explain deviance to their actors, believers, and possessors makes us aware of the specific genres that are likely to be applied to autobiographical accounts such as the ones in this book.

The point is, as functioning members of society, most of us are aware of the cultural conventions that dictate how an autobiographical account should look and sound. Those conventions are readily available and are applied when deemed appropriate; they lend structure and direction to the details of one's life, they *shape* the sort of tale that is told and is heard or read by audiences. Once again, it is naive to imagine that by reading an autobiography or a narrative we open a panoramic window on someone's life. The contextual factors that constrain the rendering of such accounts determine the nature of the lives we are permitted to see.

THE INTERPRETIVE DIMENSION

The third source of "same events, different accounts" is the *interpretive* dimension: What do the narrated events *mean* to the narrator? How are they experienced, interpreted? How do narrators feel about themselves, their lives, their relations with others, their place in society? And what do these events mean to audiences? For instance, how do you, the reader, react to the stories in this book? How would the modal or typical person in the society react? What do these accounts reveal about how mainstream society constructs its conception of deviance and treats persons designated as deviants? Do these accounts have a lesson to teach us about the structure and dynamics of deviance? How is the content of the narratives socially constructed in the minds and emotions of all the relevant parties in the drama of conventionality and unconventionality?

The answer to these questions may be found in the pages of this book, both in the accounts themselves and in my comments on those accounts and in your own responses.

Diane is *outraged* by the injustice visited upon fat people, and that anger simmers in the words she uses to describe the events that took place in her life. At the same time, she wishes fat people had more gumption and strength to stand up to the taunts they face from a cruel and censorious thin world. She does it, she reasons, why can't the others? In contrast, Sally works herself up to a state of anger only occasionally and only when she is personally confronted.

Lenny maintains a cool, detached, laissez-faire attitude toward the straight world. "Hey, *whatever*" seems to be his guiding principle.

Jeff tried to juggle the demands of two distinctly different worlds that overlapped in ways that resulted in his forced retirement from a distinctly unconventional profession. In many ways, he is the most conventional of our narrators; he displays many of the prejudiced, elitist, and snobbish attitudes that those segments of the mainstream who are most likely to condemn him also display. He tried to fit into the mainstream, but couldn't accomplish the juggling act. What does his account tell us about how he feels concerning the events he narrates?

Sam yearns to reform the ills of a most imperfect society, inflating his role in that struggle. His heart is good, his will is unfocused, and he holds a Christian, almost apocalyptic vision of forthcoming developments. Sam survives from day to day by virtue of the largesse of an institution—the university—that tolerates unconventionality. His emotion veers from impassioned outrage to an ironic, Olympian detachment that comes from the secure knowledge that God will eventually punish the wicked.

Dwight wishes to be left alone to do his own special thing. He expresses contempt toward the men who are controlled, manipulated, and dominated by the women in their lives. He lives and works among these men—and women—but he neither respects the way they live nor does he express that lack of respect openly. In fact, in his profession, the accent is on servility.

Annette wishes nothing more than to put her past behind her and live a normal life free of the "hunger artist" demon that once infected her soul. She is consumed by the mission to do what she can to help girls who are now living the tortured life she used to live.

Who is the contributor of Danny's narrative—him or me? What's my emotional stance toward my son's autism? Can the reader tell from this account? With respect to Danny, when his outbursts dissipate, he responds with a bogus "*I'm* sorry!" Sometimes expressing his rage calms him down for the rest of the day, but all too often, within a few minutes, he works himself up into yet another tirade. What's to become of this tormented yet talented and often charming, sweet, and intelligent boy? How does he feel about his life? Perhaps a more astute, knowledgeable observer than I is capable of plumbing the depths of Danny's inner life. He is simply too unreflective for me to assess his emotional state in terms I can understand or convey to any reader.

After a quarter-century of heavy drinking and resultant spotty educational and occupational careers, Harry has managed to put his life on track. He looks back on his earlier life with a mixture of relief and wistfulness. It was fun while it lasted, he seems to be saying. Have I got some stories for you! ("It was wonderful!" Harry says at several points during the interview, describing his earlier life.) But, hey, you can't live that way forever. Time to stop acting like a Peter Pan, put my life in order, and do what I have to do. Harry's emotions are a mixture of nostalgia, relief, and anticipation for the future.

Fred positions himself as a reformed ex-felon, impatiently awaiting his release and the chance to demonstrate that he can be a law-abiding citizen in the "free world."

Leslie and Helen successfully convince us that they are as conventional as two people with unconventional sex partners can be. Even most religious and sexual conservatives are likely to think long and hard about condemning their way of life.

A FEW LAST WORDS

Recall a point I made early in this afterword: Accounts should not be looked at solely for their factual accuracy. There is a great deal more to a life story than that. We are curious about just how account givers structure their stories, what they include and exclude, how they organize and shape the raw material of their lives. (My hand in shaping these accounts is yet another interesting issue as well.) In scrutinizing accounts of deviance, we are in an especially fortunate position in that what is most interesting to us is *specifically* how the account giver experiences the events being narrated. Again, we have to assume that the bulk of the stories are more or less factually accurate. (And if they were wildly inaccurate, that itself would be a fascinating topic for investigation.) What is of central concern for us here is how stigmatized persons feel about and manage that stigma, what they go through when they interact with persons who regard them as an inferior species of being. More than the biographical events they narrate, it is their words, a crystallization of those feelings, that are of central concern here.

Does it make sense to regard the people who contributed the accounts in this book as "deviants"? Is their unconventionality the most interesting feature of their lives? Are their lives, and those of people who lead similar lives, interesting enough to detail at length? In contrast, is flattening out their lives into tables, charts, and graphs the *only* productive way of presenting who they are and what they do and believe? Are there better ways of understanding the phenomenon of unconventionality? Can gathering and presenting autobiographical accounts help us understand their lives in ways that more quantitative, more statistical research methods cannot? Do we understand behavior better if we can get inside the skin of our narrators, stand in their shoes, and see the world through their eyes, their point of view, experience what they go through, feel what they feel? Are these worthwhile sociological objectives?

I sincerely hope that reading these accounts has been something of a voyage of discovery for the reader. I know that I have learned a great deal from gathering and putting them together. Everything in this book has been devoted to two interlocking goals: understanding how the social world works and developing a meaningful appreciation of our place in it. Only the reader can determine whether these goals have been accomplished.

References

Abbott, Jack Henry. 1981. *In the Belly of the Beast.* New York: Random House.

Adams, Timothy Dow. 1990. *Telling Lies in Modern Autobiography.* Chapel Hill: University of North Carolina Press.

Adler, Patricia A., and Peter Adler (eds.). 2000. *Constructions of Deviance: Social Power, Context, and Interaction* (3rd ed.). Belmont, CA: Wadsworth.

Aho, James A. 1994. *This Thing of Darkness: A Sociology of the Enemy.* Seattle: University of Washington Press.

Allon, Natalie. 1973. "The Stigma of Overweight in Everyday Life." In G. A. Bray (ed.), *Obesity in Perspective.* Washington: U. S. Government Printing Office, pp. 83–102.

Allon, Natalie. 1982. "The Stigma of Overweight in Everyday Life." In Benjamin B. Wolman (ed.), *Psychological Aspects of Obesity: A Handbook.* New York: Van Nostrand Reinhold, pp. 130–174.

American Psychiatric Association. 1994. *DSM-IV: Diagnostic and Statistical Manual of Mental Disorders* (4th ed.). Washington: American Psychiatric Association.

Baumeister, R. F. 1988. "Masochism as Escape from Self." *Journal of Sex Research,* 25 (1): 25–29.

Becker, Howard S. 1963. *Outsiders: Studies in the Sociology of Deviance.* New York: Free Press.

Becker, Howard S. 1986. *Doing Things Together: Selected Papers.* Evanston, IL: Northwestern University Press.

Becker, Howard S., and Irving Louis Horowitz. 1970. "The Culture of Civility." *Trans-action,* 7 (April): 12–19.

Benson, Michael L. 1985. "Denying the Guilty Mind: Accounting for Involvement in a White Collar Crime." *Criminology,* 23 (November): 589–599.

Ben-Yehuda, Nachman. 1985. *Deviance and Moral Boundaries: Witchcraft, the Occult, Deviance Sciences and Scientists.* Chicago: University of Chicago Press.

Berger, Peter L. 1963. *Invitation to Sociology.* Garden City, NY: Doubleday-Anchor.

Bettelheim, Bruno. 1967. *The Empty Fortress*. New York: Free Press.

Bieber, Irving, et al. 1962. *Homosexuality: A Psychoanalytic Study of Male Homosexuals*. New York: Vintage Books.

Blinde, Elaine M., and Diane E. Taub. 1992. "Women Athletes as Falsely Accused Deviants." *Sociological Quarterly*, 33 (4): 521–533.

Bogdan, Robert, and Steven J. Taylor. 1987. "Toward a Sociology of Acceptance: The Other Side of the Study of Deviance." *Social Policy*, 18 (Fall): 34–39.

Brodsky, Joel I. 1995. "The Mineshaft: A Retrospective Ethnography." In Thomas S. Weinberg 9th ed.), *S&M: Studies in Dominance and Submission*. Buffalo, NY: Prometheus Books, pp. 195–218.

Bruner, Jerome. 1993. "The Autobiographical Process." In Robert Folkenflik (ed.), *The Culture of Autobiography: Constructions of Self-Representation*. Stanford, CA: Stanford University Press, pp. 38–56, 242–245.

Burns, Tom. 1992. *Erving Goffman*. London & New York: Routledge.

Bursik, Robert J., and Harold G. Grasmick. 1993. *Neighborhoods and Crime: The Dimensions of Effective Community Control*. New York: Lexington Books.

Bushart, Howard L., John R. Craig, and Myra Barnes. 1999. *Soldiers of God: White Supremacists and Their Holy War for America*. New York: Pinnacle Books.

Cahnman, Werner J. 1968. "The Stigma of Obesity." *Sociological Quarterly*, 9 (Summer): 283–299.

Calhoun, Thomas C. 1992. "Male Street Hustling: Introduction Processes and Stigma Containment." *Sociological Spectrum*, 12 (1): 35–52.

Calhoun, Thomas C., and Greg S. Weaver. 1996. "Rational Decision-Making among Male Street Prostitutes." *Deviant Behavior*, 17 (2): 209–226.

Calhoun, Thomas C., and Greg S. Weaver. 2001. "Male Prostitution." In Dennis L. Peck and Norman A. Dolch (eds.). *Extraordinary Behavior: A Case Study Approach to Studying Social Problems*. Westport, CN: Praeger, pp. 212–226.

Califia, Pat. 1994. *Public Sex: The Culture of Radical Sex*. Pittsburgh, PA: Cleis Press.

Callaway, Helen. 1992. "Ethnography and Experience: Gender Implications in Fieldwork and Texts." In Judith Okely and Helen Callaway (eds.), *Anthropology and Autobiography*. London & New York: Routledge, pp. 29–49.

Certeau, Michel de. 1984. *The Practice of Everyday Life* (trans. Steven Rendell). Berkeley: University of California Press.

Charlton, James I. 1999. *Nothing about Us without Us: Disability, Oppression, and Empowerment*. Berkeley: University of California Press.

Clifford, James. 1986. "Introduction: Partial Truths." In James Clifford and George E. Marcus (eds.), *Writing Culture: The Poetics and Politics of Ethnography*. Berkeley: University of California Press, pp. 1–26.

Cohen, Shirley. 1998. *Targeting Autism*. Berkeley: University of California Press.

Cressey, Donald R. 1953. *Other People's Money*. New York: Free Press.

Dabney, Dean. 1995. "Neutralization and Deviance in the Workplace: Theft of Supplies and Medicines by Hospital Nurses." *Deviant Behavior*, 16 (3): 313–331.

Davison, Gerald C., and John M. Neale. 1998. *Abnormal Psychology* (7th ed.). New York: John Wiley & Sons.

DeJong, William. 1980. "The Stigma of Obesity: The Consequences of Naive Assumptions Concerning the Causes of Physical Deviance." *Journal of Health and Social Behavior*, 21 (1): 75–87.

Delph, Edward William. 1978. *The Silent Community: Public Homosexual Encounters*. Beverly Hills, CA: Sage.

Dolnick, Edward. 1998. *Madness on the Couch: Blaming the Victim in the Heyday of Psychoanalysis*. New York: Simon & Schuster.

Dworkin, Andrea. 1981. *Pornography: Men Possessing Women*. New York: Perigee.

English, Cliff. 1991. "Food Is My Best Friend: Self-Justifications and Weight Loss Efforts." *Research in the Sociology of Health Care*, 9: 335–345.

Falwell, Jerry, with Ed Dobson and Ed Hinson. 1981. *The Fundamentalist Phenomenon: The Resurgence of Conservative Christianity*. Garden City, NY: A Doubleday-Gallilee Original.

Fisher, Peter. 1972. *The Gay Mystique*. New York: Stein & Day.

Foucault, Michel. 1979. *Discipline and Punish* (trans. Alan Sheridan). New York: Vintage Books.

Gagnon, John H., and William Simon. 1967, 2001. *Sexual Conduct: The Social Sources of Human Sexuality* (1st, 2nd ed.). Chicago, New York: Aldine, Aldine de Gruyter.

Gardner, Martin. 2000. "The Brutality of Dr. Bettelheim." *Skeptical Inquirer*, 24 (November/December): 12–14.

Gebhard, Paul H. 1969. "Fetishism and Sadomasochism." In Jules H. Masserman (ed.), *Dynamics of Deviant Sexuality*. New York: Gruen & Stratton, pp. 71–80.

Glassner, Barry, and Rosanna Hertz (eds.). 1999. *Qualitative Sociology as Everyday Life*. Thousand Oaks, CA: Sage.

Goffman, Erving. 1959. *The Presentation of Self in Everyday Life*. Garden City, NY: Doubleday-Anchor.

Goffman, Erving. 1961. *Asylums: Essays on the Social Situation of Mental Patients and Other Inmates*. Garden City, NY: Doubleday-Anchor.

Goffman, Erving. 1963. *Stigma: Notes on the Management of Spoiled Identity*. Englewood Cliffs, NJ: Prentice Hall/Spectrum.

Goffman, Erving. 1967. *Interaction Ritual: Essays on Face-to-Face Interaction*. Garden City, NY: Doubleday-Anchor.

Goffman, Erving. 1974. *Frame Analysis: An Essay on the Organization of Experience*. New York: Harper & Row.

Goffman, Erving. 1971. *Relations in Public: Microstudies of the Public Order*. New York: Basic Books.

Goffman, Erving. 1983. "The Interaction Order." *American Sociological Review*, 48 (February): 1–17.

Goode, Erich. 1970. *The Marijuana Smokers*. New York: Basic Books.

Goode, Erich. 1972. *Drugs in American Society* (1st ed.). New York: Alfred Knopf.

Goode, Erich (ed.). 1996. *Social Deviance*. Boston: Allyn & Bacon.

Goode, Erich. 1996. "The Stigma of Obesity." In Goode (ed.), *Social Deviance*. Boston: Allyn & Bacon, pp. 332–340.

Goode, Erich. 1999. *Drugs in American Society* (5th ed.). New York: McGraw-Hill.

Goode, Erich. 2001. *Deviant Behavior* (6th ed.). Upper Saddle River, NJ: Prentice Hall.

Gottfredson, Michael R., and Travis Hirschi. 1990. *A General Theory of Crime*. Stanford, CA: Stanford University Press.

Gouldner, Alvin W. 1968. "The Sociologist as Partisan: Sociology and the Welfare State." *The American Sociologist*, 3 (May): 103–116.

Greenberg, David F. 1988. *The Construction of Homosexuality*. Chicago: University of Chicago Press.

Hebdige, Dick. 1979. *Subculture: The Meaning of Style*. London: Methuen.

Hiller, Dana V. 1981. "The Salience of Overweight in Personality Characterization." *Journal of Psychology*, 108: 233–240.

Hiller, Dana V. 1982. "Overweight as a Master Status: A Replication." *Journal of Psychology*, 110: 107–113.

Hirschi, Travis. 1969. *The Causes of Delinquency*. Berkeley: University of California Press.

Hirschi, Travis. 1973. "Procedural Rules and the Study of Deviance." *Social Problems*, 21 (Fall): 159–173.

Hopper, Columbus B., and Johnny Moore. 1990. "Women in Outlaw Motorcycle Gangs." *Journal of Contemporary Ethnography*, 18 (4): 363–387.

Humphreys, Laud. 1970. *Tearoom Trade: Impersonal Sex in Public Places*. Chicago: Aldine.

Humphreys, Laud. 1975. *Tearoom Trade: Impersonal Sex in Public Places* (enlarged ed.). New York: Aldine.

Katz, Jack. 1988. *Seductions of Crime: Moral and Sensual Attractions in Doing Evil*. New York: Basic Books.

Klockars, Carl B. 1974. *The Professional Fence*. New York: Free Press.

Knapp, Caroline. 1997. *Drinking: A Love Story*. New York: Delta Press.

Kotre, John. 1995. *White Gloves: How We Create Ourselves Through Memory*. New York: Free Press.

Laumann, Edward O., John H. Gagnon, Robert T. Michael, and Stuart Michaels. 1994. *The Social Organization of Human Sexuality: Sexual Practices in the United States*. Chicago: University of Chicago Press.

Lederer, Laura (ed.). 1982. *Take Back the Night: Women on Pornography*. New York: Bantam Books.

Lee, John Alan. 1978. *Getting Sex*. Don Mills, Ontario: Musson.

Lemert, Edwin M. 1951. *Social Pathology: A Systematic Approach to the Theory of Sociopathic Behavior*. New York: McGraw-Hill.

Lemert, Edwin M. 1972. *Human Deviance, Social Problems, and Social Control* (2nd ed.). Englewood Cliffs, NJ: Prentice Hall.

Lerner, Melvin J. 1980. *Belief in a Just World: A Fundamental Delusion*. New York: Plenum Press.

LeVay, Simon. 1995. *The Sexual Brain*. Cambridge, MA: MIT Press/Branford.

Liazos, Alexander. 1972. "The Poverty of the Sociology of Deviance: Nuts, Sluts, and Preverts." *Social Problems*, 20 (Summer): 103–120.

Lieblich, Amia, Rivka Tuval-Mashiach, and Tamar Zilber. 1998. *Narrative Research: Reading, Analysis, and Interpretation*. Thousand Oaks, CA: Sage.

Linden, R. R., et al. 1982. *Against Sado-Masochism: A Radical Feminist Analysis*. San Francisco: Frog in the Wall Press.

Lindner, Robert. 1948. "Sexual Behavior in Penal Institutions." In Albert Deutsch (ed.), *Sex Habits of American Men*. Engelwood Cliffs, NJ: Prentice Hall, pp. 201–215.

Linton, Simi. 1997. *Claiming Disability: Knowledge and Identity*. New York: New York University Press.

Louderback, Llwellyn. 1970. *Fat Power: Whatever You Weigh Is Right*. New York: Hawthorne Books.

Lovaas, O. Ivar. 1977. *The Autistic Child: Language Development Through Behavior Modification*. New York: Irvington.

Lyman, Stanford M., and Marvin B. Scott. 1970. *A Sociology of the Absurd*. New York: Appleton-Century-Crofts.

Mack, John. 1995. *Abductions: Human Encounters with Aliens* (rev. ed.). New York: Bantam Books.

Maddox, George K., Kurt W. Back, and Veronica Liederman. 1968. "Overweight as Social Deviance and Disability." *Journal of Health and Social Behavior,* 9 (December): 287–298.

Matza, David. 1969. *Becoming Deviant.* Englewood Cliffs, NJ: Prentice Hall.

McCabe, Donald L. 1992. "The Influence of Situational Ethics on Cheating Among College Students." *Sociological Inquiry,* 63 (3): 362–374.

McCaghy, Charles H. 1967. "Child Molesters: A Study of Their Careers as Deviants." In Marshall B. Clinard and Richard Quinney (eds.), *Criminal Behavior Systems: A Typology.* New York: Holt, Rinehart & Winston, pp. 75–88.

McCaghy, Charles H. 1968. "Drinking and Disavowal: The Case of Child Molesters." *Social Problems,* 16 (Summer): 43–49.

McIntosh, Mary. 1968. "The Homosexual Role." *Social Problems,* 16 (Fall): 182–192.

McLorg, Penelope A., and Diane E. Taub. 1987. "Anorexia Nervosa and Bulimia: The Development of Deviant Identities." *Deviant Behavior,* 8 (2): 177–189.

Menchu, Rigoberta. 1983. *I, Rigoberta Menchu.* New York: Verso.

Merton, Robert K. 1938. "Social Structure and Anomie." *American Sociological Review,* 3 (October): 672–682.

Merton, Robert K. 1957. *Social Theory and Social Structure* (rev. & exp. ed.). New York: Free Press.

Messner, Steven F., and Richard Rosenfeld. 1997. *Crime and the American Dream* (2nd ed.). Belmont, CA: Wadsworth.

Michael, Robert T. John H. Gagnon, Edward O. Laumann, and Gina Kolata. 1994. *Sex in America: A Definitive Survey.* Boston: Little, Brown.

Mieczkowski, Tom. 1994. "The Experiences of Women Who Sell Crack: Some Descriptive Data From the Detroit Crack Ethnography Project." *Journal of Drug Issues,* 24 (2): 227–248.

Miller, Walter B. 1958. "Lower Class Culture as a Generating Milieu of Gang Delinquency." *Journal of Social Issues,* 14 (3): 5–19.

Millman, Marcia. 1975. "She Did it All for love: A Feminist View of the Sociology of Deviance." In Marcia Millman and Rosabeth Moss Kanter (eds.). *Another Voice: Feminist Perspectives on Social Life and Social Science.* Garden City, NY: Doubleday-Anchor, pp. 251–279.

Millman, Marcia. 1980. *Such a Pretty Face: Being Fat in America.* New York: W. W. Norton.

Mills, C. Wright. 1940. "Situated Actions and Vocabularies of Motive." *American Journal of Sociology,* 5 (December): 904–913.

Moser, Charles. 1988. "Sadomasochism." *Journal of Social Work and Human Sexuality,* 7 (1): 43–56.

Moser, Charles, and Eugene E. Levitt. 1987. "An Exploratory-Descriptive Study of a Sadomasochistically-Oriented Sample." *Journal of Sex Research,* 23: 322–337.

Nettler, Gwynn. 1974. "On Telling Who's Crazy." *American Sociological Review,* 39 (December): 893–894.

Parker, Sheila, et al. 1995. "Body Image and Weight Concerns among African-American and White Adolescent Females: Differences Make a Difference." *Human Organization,* 54 (Summer): 103–114.

Peck, Dennis L., and Norman A. Dolch (eds.). 2001. *Extraordinary Behavior: A Case Study Approach to Understanding Social Problems.* Westport, CN: Praeger.

Pfohl, Stephen J. 1994. *Images of Deviance and Social Control: A Sociological History* (2nd ed.). New York: McGraw-Hill.

Pfuhl, Erdwin H., and Stuart Henry. 1993. *The Deviance Process* (3rd ed.). New York: Aldine de Gruyter.

Piven, Frances Fox. 1981. "Deviant Behavior and the Remaking of the World." *Social Problems*, 28 (June): 489–508.

Plummer, Ken. 1979. "Misunderstanding Labelling Perspectives." In David Downes and Paul Rock (eds.). *Deviant Interpretations*. London: Routledge & Kegan Paul, pp. 85–121.

Plummer, Ken. 1995. *Telling Sexual Stories: Power, Change, and Social Worlds*. London & New York: Routledge.

Pollak, Richard. 1997. *The Creation of Dr. B: A Biography of Bruno Bettelheim*. New York: Simon & Schuster.

Polsky, Ned. 1998. *Hustlers, Beats, and Others* (expanded ed.). New York: Lyons Press.

Reiss, Albert J., Jr. 1964. "The Social Integration of Queers and Peers." In Howard S. Becker (ed.), *The Other Side: Perspectives on Deviance*. New York: Free Press, pp. 181–210.

Richardson, James T., Joel Best, and David G. Bromley (eds.). 1991. *The Satanic Scare*. New York: Aldine de Gruyter.

Rimland, Bernard. 1964. *Infantile Autism*. New York: Appleton-Century-Crofts.

Rivera, Joseph de, and Theodore R. Sarbin (eds.). 1998. *Believed-In Imaginings: The Narrative Construciton of Reality*. Washington, DC: American Psychological Association.

Ronai, Carol Rambo, and Carolyn Ellis. 1987. "Turn-Ons for Money: Interactional Strategies of the Table Dancer." *Journal of Contemporary Ethnography*, 18 (October): 271–298.

Rubington, Earl, and Weinberg, Martin S. (eds.). 1999. *Deviance: The Interactionist Approach*. Boston: Allyn & Bacon.

Sacks, Oliver. 1990. *The Man Who Mistook His Wife for a Hat*. New York: HarperPerennial.

Sacks, Oliver. 1995. *An Anthropologist on Mars*. New York: Vintage Books.

Schur, Edwin M. 1971. *Labeling Deviant Behavior: Its Sociological Implications*. New York: Harper & Row.

Scott, Marvin B., and Stanford M. Lyman. 1968. "Accounts." *American Sociological Review*, 33 (February): 46–62.

Scully, Diana. 1990. *Understanding Sexual Violence: A Study of Convicted Rapists*. Boston: Unwin Hyman.

Scully, Diana and Joseph Marolla. 1984. "Convicted Rapists' Vocabulary of Motive: Excusing and Justification." *Social Problems*, 31 (June): 530–544.

Scully, Diana, and Joseph Marolla. 1985. "Riding the Bull at Gilley's: Convicted Rapists Describe the Rewards of Rape." *Social Problems*, 32 (February): 251–263.

Seelye, Katherine Q. 1995. "Helms Puts the Brakes to Bill Financing AIDS Treatment." *The New York Times*, July 5, p.A12.

Siegel, Larry. 2000. *Criminology* (7th ed.). Belmont, CA: Wadsworth.

Skogan, Wesley G. 1990. *Disorder and Decline: Crime and the Spiral of Decay in American Neighborhoods*. New York: Free Press.

Smith, Duskey Lee. 1973. "Symbolic Interactionism: Definitions of the Situation From Becker to Lofland." *Catalyst*, (Winter): 62–75.

Snyder, C. R., Raymond L. Higgins, and Rita J. Stucky. 1983. *Excuses: Masquerades in Search of Grace*. New York: John Wiley & Sons.

Socarides, Charles W. 1978. *Homosexuality*. New York: Jason Aronson.

Stark, Rodney. 1987. "Deviant Places: A Theory of the Ecology of Crime." *Criminology*, 25 (4): 893–909.

Stille, Alexander. 2001. "Prospecting For Truth In the Ore of History." *The New York Times*. March 10, pp.A15, A17.

Stoll, David. 1999. *I, Rigoberta Menchu and the Story of All Poor Guatemalans*. Boulder, CO: Westview Press.

Suchar, Charles S. 1978. *Social Deviance: Perspectives and Prospects*. New York: Holt, Rinehart & Winston.

Sumner, Colin. 1994. *The Sociology of Deviance: An Obituary*. London: Open University Press.

Sutherland, Edwin. H. 1949. *White Collar Crime*. New York: Dryden.

Sykes, Gresham M., and David Matza. 1957. "Techniques of Neutralization: A Theory of Delinquency." *American Sociological Review*, 22 (December): 664–670.

Thompson, Bill. 1994. *Sadomasochism*. London & New York: Cassell.

Tonkin, Elizabeth. 1992. *Narrating Our Past: The Social Construction of Oral History*. Cambridge, UK: Cambridge University Press.

Troiden, Richard R. 1988. *Gay and Lesbian Identity: A Sociological Analysis*. Dix Hills, NY: General Hall.

Victor, Jeffrey S. 1993. *Satanic Panic: The Creation of a Contemporary Legend*. Chicago: Open Court.

Warren, Carol A. B., and John M. Johnson. 1972. "A Critique of Labeling Theory from the Phenomenological Perspective." In Robert A. Scott and Jack D. Douglas (eds.), *Theoretical Perspectives in Deviance*. New York: Basic Books, pp. 69–92.

Weinberg, Thomas S. (ed.). 1995a. *S&M: Studies in Dominance and Submission* (2nd ed.). Buffalo, NY: Prometheus Books.

Weinberg, Thomas S. 1995b. "Sociological and Psychological Issues in the Study of Sadomasochism." In Thomas S. Weinberg (ed.), *S&M: Studies in Dominance and Submission* (2nd ed.). Buffalo, NY: Prometheus Books, pp. 289–303.

Weinberg, Thomas S., and G. W. Levi Kamel. 1995. "S&M: An Introduction to the Study of Sadomasochism." In Thomas S. Weinberg (ed.), *S&M: Studies in Dominance and Submission* (2nd ed.). Buffalo, NY: Prometheus Books, pp. 15–24.